COMMON INTEREST THEORY

- DENNIS CHI

Contents

Chapter I Introduction ········· 001
  Section I Topic Source ········· 001
  Section II Basic Research Ideas ········· 003
  Section III Main Contents ········· 004
  Section IV Innovations and Deficiencies ········· 008

Chapter II Theoretical Basis of Common Interests ········· 010
  Section I The Essence and Composition of Interests ········· 010
  Section II The Meaning and Characteristics of Common Interests ········· 019
  Section III Theoretical Origin of Common Interests ········· 023

Chapter III Theory of Common Interests: Literature Review ········· 030
  Section I Bibliometric Analysis of Research Literature on Theory of Common Interests ········· 030
  Section II Marxists' Discussion on Interests ········· 037
  Section III Discussion on Common Interests in Marxist Classics ········· 058
  Section IV Chinese Communists' Thoughts on Common Interests ········· 063
  Section V Literature Review on Common Interests in International Economic Relations ········· 103

Chapter IV Analysis of Common Interests in International Trade ········· 152
  Section I Interest Analysis in International Trade Theories ········· 152
  Section II National Interests in International Trade ········· 159

	Section III	Common Interests of China and Developed Countries in Trade ………………………………………… 172
Chapter V	Analysis of Common Interests in International Capital Flow ………… 190
	Section I	Interest Analysis in Theory of International Capital Flow ……………………………………………………… 190
	Section II	Analysis of Common Interests in Outward Direct Investment ……………………………………………… 204
	Section III	National Interests and Common Interests of Countries amid Financial Crisis ……………………………… 213
	Section IV	International Capital Flow and Common Interests of Mankind ………………………………………………… 228
Chapter VI	Analysis of Common Interests in International Technology Transfer ……………………………………………………………………… 236
	Section I	Analysis of Common Interests of International Technology Transfer ……………………………… 236
	Section II	Analysis on Benefits of FDI Technology Transfer ……………………………………………………………… 243
	Section III	Analysis of the Interests of Developing Countries in Participating in International Technology Transfer …………………………………………………………… 252
	Section IV	Realization of Common Interests in Technology Transfer between China and Developed Countries …… 261
Chapter VII	Analysis of Common Interests in International Human Capital Flow ………………………………………………………………………… 281
	Section I	Analysis of Interests with Theory of International Human Capital Flow ……………………………… 281
	Section II	Analysis of Common Interests in Practice of International Human Capital Flow ……………………………… 290

	Section Ⅲ	Realization of Common Interests of China and Developed Countries in Human Capital Flow ·············· 306
Chapter Ⅷ	**Analysis of the Common Interests of International Community** ········ 319	
	Section Ⅰ	Common Interests and State Interests in International Community ················· 319
	Section Ⅱ	International Common Interests and International Cooperation ·············· 334
	Section Ⅲ	Common Interests of Mankind and China's Peaceful Development ·············· 344
Chapter Ⅸ	**Countermeasures and Suggestions for Realizing Common Interests** ······ 363	
	Section Ⅰ	Principle of Common Interests in International Trade Policy ················· 363
	Section Ⅱ	Common Interests in Economic Globalization and Countermeasures ················ 367
	Section Ⅲ	International Economic Order and the Realizing of Common Interests ·············· 386
	Section Ⅳ	Actively Participating in Global Governance to Realize Common Interests ············· 400
	Section Ⅴ	Actively Promoting Belt and Road Initiative to Realize Common Interests ············· 408

References ················· 424

Chapter I

Introduction

Section I Topic Source

Interest is the fundamental driver and ultimate goal of human activities. As such, research of interests exists as a key path for analyzing social phenomena, especially economic phenomena, and exploring the internal laws of social and economic development. Economics refers to a discipline that studies the interests in the process of production, exchange, distribution, and consumption, with economic interest as the core content. Interests refer to the sum of material and spiritual wealth that can meet people's own needs and other needs. Interests mostly refer to economic interest, namely interests in the process of production, circulation, distribution, and consumption. Karl Marx noted that "everything for which man struggles is a matter of his interest,"[①] and Sima Qian, the first great Chinese historian said that "the world is bustling with people who come and go for interests." They both revealed that pursuing interests is human's fundamental motivation. Despite changes of time, interest is the eternal theme. Since the second half of the 1980s, amid foreign direct investment spree of multinationals, economic globalization has become the most prominent feature

---

[①] Karl Marx and Frederick Engels, *Marx & Engels Collected Works Vol. 01: Marx: 1835-1843*, London: Lawrence & Wishart, 1975, Electric Book, 2010, p. 171.

of economic development in the world today: market, information, talents, rules and other factors have transcended the boundaries of individual countries and regions; worldwide, countries and regions have participated in economic globalization in different ways at varying degrees; and whether a state's national interest will grow, the pace and path of growth are both related to the globalized economy. At this point, since the interests of countries are closely intertwined, countries not only compete with each other for interests in each field but also engage in extensive cooperation for common interests. As a developing country, China is facing a relationship of internal and external interests that reflects the interest relations between developing countries and developed ones, or one between developing ones. Considering that today's world order is dominated by developed countries, this book mainly studies the common interests between China and developed countries and the relevant changes. Take the China-U.S. economic and political relations as an example, since both are large countries, on one hand, China cannot develop without the U.S.; on the other hand, China is increasingly indispensable for the U.S. in terms of economic and social stability and major foreign policies such as counter-terrorism. Because of this connection, cooperation is increasingly becoming a consensus between leaders of the two countries. Amid economic globalization, China-U.S. cooperation is not an empty slogan. As the most prominent issue in the China-U.S. relationship in recent years, the economic issue is in essence a "win-win game." Against the backdrop of economic globalization, the essence of China-U.S. economic relationship is the interdependence generated in the structure of global division of labor. Because the two countries' industrial and trade structures complement each other, both have benefited hugely from business exchange. For all the above reasons, this book will discuss common interests from five perspectives: common interests in international trade, common interests in international capital flow, common interests in international human capital flow, common interests in international technology transfer, and common interests in international politics.

Section Ⅱ Basic Research Ideas

The basic research train of thoughts are as follows: first comes the introduction, second the theoretical basis of common interests, third a literature review of common interests, fourth an expounding on common interests in terms of international trade, international capital flow, international technology transfer, international human capital flow and international community, and fifth the measures and suggestions for realizing common interests. See Figure 1-1.

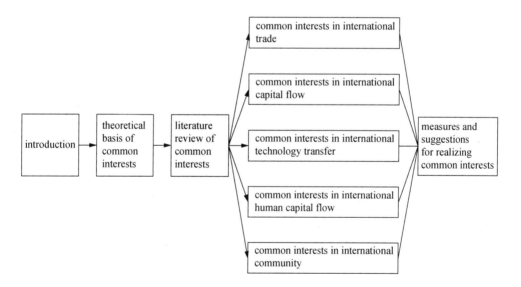

Figure 1-1　The Research Train of Thoughts

Section III Main Contents

This book contains nine chapters.

Chapter I is the introduction, consisting of four sections which respectively introducing the topic source of this book, basic research ideas, main contents, and innovations and deficiencies.

Chapter II features the theoretical basis of common interests, consisting of three sections. Section I expounds on the essence and composition of interests. The author of this book believes that interests are the sum of material and spiritual wealth that meets people's own needs and other needs; then the author will analyze the composition of interests from perspectives of the subject, the object and the intermediary of interests. Section II expounds on the meaning and characteristics of common interests. The author believes that common interests are the interests shared by at least two people or by the majority among a group or society. Common interests are universal, shared, heterogeneous, independent, and historical. Rather than isolated, these characteristics are interconnected with and influenced by each other. Moreover, with the development of times, they show rich connotation and contents of the era. Section III deals with the theoretical origin of common interests. This section explores the theoretical origin and social attributes of common interests from the perspective of Marxist philosophy and economics.

Chapter III focuses on the literature review of common interests, consisting of four sections. Section I is about Marxists' discussion on interests. It features the elaboration of Marx, Engels, Lenin, Stalin, and Chinese Communists on interests. Section II is about Marxists' discussions on common interests. It mainly features the expounding of Marx, Engels, and Lenin on common interests. Section III includes what Chinese Communists expound on common prosperity. Since common prosperity represents the common interests of people of all ethnic groups in China, this section mainly introduces the thoughts of Mao Zedong, Deng Xiaoping and the third generation of collective leadership on common prosperity. Section Ⅳ is a review of study on common interests in international economic relations. This section summarizes researches in the changes of common interests caused by international trade, international capital flow, international technology diffusion, and international human capital flow.

Chapter Ⅳ analyzes common interests in international trade, consisting of three sections. Section Ⅰ features interest analysis with international trade theories, analyzing changes of interests with David Ricardo's theory of comparative advantage and Marx's theory of international value. Section Ⅱ deals with national interests in international trade. It stresses that a state is a "shadow body" in international trade, with independent interest objectives. Friedrich List's theory of national economy is also used to analyze common interests in international trade. Section Ⅲ expounds on the common interests of China and developed countries in trade. With developed countries, especially the U.S., as examples, this section analyzes the development status quo of China-U.S. business relations. The author believes that despite the China-U.S. conflicts, there are reciprocal demands that call for cooperation given the extensive common interests between the two countries in terms of economy, politics, culture, and other fields.

Chapter Ⅴ analyzes common interests in international capital flow, consisting of four sections. Section Ⅰ analyzes interests with the theory of international capital flow. Dividing the period from the end of the Second World War through the 1970-80s into three stages, this section analyzes viewpoints on the interests in international capital flow and their distribution during the three stages. Section Ⅱ analyzes common interests in foreign direct investment. First, it studies common interests from the relationship between international direct investment and interest distribution. Then it analyzes the common interests in China's outbound direct investment. Section Ⅲ deals with national interests and common interests among countries amid financial crisis.

With the threat of global financial crisis, countries should be encouraged to properly handle the relationship between monetary policy coordination and state interests, shoulder risks collectively, and stabilize international financial order so as to realize their common interests. Section Ⅳ expounds on international capital flow and human's common interests. This section first expounds on the principle of human's common interests and then analyzes and assesses two important international investment agreements from the principle of human's common interests.

Chapter Ⅵ analyzes common interests in international technology transfer, consisting of four sections. Section Ⅰ analyzes interests with the theory of international technology transfer. The theory of international technology transfer is used to analyze changes of common interests. Section Ⅱ analyzes interests in technology transfer of foreign direct investment (FDI). This section mainly analyzes how technology transfer of FDI affects the interests of host countries. Section Ⅲ analyzes interests of developing countries in participating in international technology transfer. After briefing on the development trend of international technology transfer in open economy, this section analyzes how international technology transfer affects the interests of developing countries. Section Ⅳ expounds on how China and developed countries realize common interests in technology transfer. First, it analyzes the status quo of China's technology transfer; then, taking the U.S. as an example, it expounds on common interests in the China-U.S. technology trade.

Chapter Ⅶ analyzes common interests in international human capital flow, consisting of three sections. Section Ⅰ analyzes interests with the theory of international human capital flow. It explores changes in common interests caused by international human capital flow from the perspective of trade in services. Section Ⅱ analyzes interests with the practice of international human capital flow. It analyzes how specific international human capital flow affects common interests. Section Ⅲ expounds on how China and developed countries realize common interests in human capital flow. First, it analyzes new features of the Chinese worldwide human capital flow; then, it expounds on how those new features will affect the interests of China's innovation system; finally, it proposes a mechanism design that leads China's human capital flow.

Chapter Ⅷ analyzes common interests in international community, consisting of three sections. Section Ⅰ deals with common interests and state interests in international community. The author believes that common interests are the spillover of national interests, and the latter are still the most important leading forces in international community. Although there are conflicts between common interests and national interests, common interests still hold the international community together. Section Ⅱ deals with international common interests and international cooperation. After the Cold War ended, major countries have made important policy adjustments in their diplomatic practices and engaged in close international cooperation, realizing their own national interests as their fundamental goal. The same process also comes with common interests. Section Ⅲ deals with human's common interests and China's peaceful development. In today's world where mankind is facing challenges in pursuing common interests, it is imperative for China to realize peaceful development for the common interests of mankind.

Chapter Ⅸ offers measures and suggestions for realizing common interests, consisting of three sections. As the last chapter of this book, Chapter Ⅸ summarizes contents of the previous chapters and offers suggestions. Section Ⅰ features the principle of common interests in international trade policy and explores the common interests safeguarded by international trade policy and the mechanism for realizing the principle of common interests. Section Ⅱ deals with common interests in economic globalization and measures for their realization. First, Section Ⅱ explains benefit distribution from the perspective of institutionalism; then considering the trend of economic globalization and international relations, some strategies are proposed for China to participate in economic globalization, cope with the transnational flow of global talents, and engage in international technology transfer. Section Ⅲ deals with the international economic order and the realization of common interests. Currently, a growing number of countries are urging for the reform of current international agencies and rules and the establishment of a new international political and economic order that is fair and rational, so as to make economic globalization conducive to the world's economic and social development and the realization of common interests worldwide.

Section IV Innovations and Deficiencies

I. Innovations of the Book

First, from the perspective of internal and external interests, this book analyzes systematically and deeply the common interests between China and developed countries and their changes. It is a pioneering exploration in this academic field.

Second, though the concept "common interests" already existed in the academic community, this book defines the meaning and level of the "common interests" between China and developed countries for the first time and pointed out that the "common interests" in today's political and economic circumstances are in essence the interest relations of a positive-sum game between developed countries and developing ones.

Third, while discussing the interest relations of a positive-sum game between China and developed countries, this book introduces the responses of developed countries to China's game strategies and stresses that China's game benefit is determined not only by its own game strategy but also by the strategic responses of developed countries, thus making up for the deficiency of a research by China's own perspective. Furthermore, this book notes that when one cannot get desirable benefits from a game played originally for the maximization of one's own interests, it is better for the two sides to cooperate with each other for common interests.

Fourth, this book approaches China's external relations of interests from the perspective of common interests between China and developed countries. This will contribute to the realization of China's external interests, the world's prosperity and stability, and a long-term win-win relationship.

II. Shortcomings and Deficiencies

Objectively, it is a totally new project to study common interests from the perspective of international economy. Since such an exploration is only the first step, the depth and width of the research are limited. Therefore, many problems are still to be resolved: the expounding of the theory of common interests is not enough; there should be further expounding of the quantitative analysis of common interests and institutional arrangement, as well as further analysis and assessment of the practices of common interests in international economy. As such, I should keep studying and thinking and thus further enrich and refine the theory of common interests.

Chapter II

Theoretical Basis of Common Interests

Section I The Essence and Composition of Interests

I. Essence of Interests

"Interest" is a most frequently used word in our daily life. As for the meaning of "interest," various explanations can be found in the theoretical field, making it difficult to find a unified answer. Those explanations can be summed up as follows.

(1) Seeing interests as benefits. Such a viewpoint clearly defines interests as "benefits." *Cihai*, a large-scale dictionary and encyclopedia of standard Chinese, defines the word "interest" as benefit, such as collective benefits and individual benefits. Verifying from the perspective of etymology and ancient Chinese culture, we find that the character "li" ("liyi" means interests in Chinese) means using farm tools in agricultural production, collecting fruits in the nature, or harvesting mature crops. Afterwards, "li" gradually evolved into "jili" (auspicious) in sacrifice and divination, meaning that certain activities can achieve desired goals and expected effects. Later, its meaning extended to "benefit," contrary to "hai" (harm). For instance, as recorded in *The Commentary of Zuo*, in the 27th Year of Duke Xiang's reign of Lu State, Song State once again asked Jin State and Chu State to stop the war and arranged them to meet in Song State for the matter. However, Chu people took armor

and weapons stealthily, trying to replace Jin State as the leader of the alliance. Bo Zhouli noted that this was "dishonesty" and asked Chu people to take off armor. Zi Mu refused and said, "It has been a long time since Jin and Chu showed dishonesty, and they do things only for their own 'li.' If they achieve their ambition, will they still honor credibility?" Here, the word "li" refers to the "benefit" of Chu State in fighting for the position of alliance leader, and "li" means "benefit," contrary to "harm." Another example can be found in the chapter of "Biography of Guo Tai" in the *Book of the Later Han*. It says, "Since the crockery is broken, what 'yi' would it do to see it?" Here the word "yi" also means "benefit." Such an explanation is only a general description of the manifestations of interests: interests equal to benefits, and benefits equal to interests. Such a loop cannot touch upon the deeper essence of interests, and cannot explain the meaning of "interest" clearly.

(2) Seeing interests as "needs." Different from the viewpoint of seeing interests as "benefits," many scholars and thinkers have explored the essence of interests from the perspective of need, and believe that the essence of interests is people's needs, which constitute the prerequisite and foundation of interests. As long as we figure out the essence of needs, we can see through the essence of interests. Therefore, we have to study needs before studying interests. As Marx noted in the introduction to his *A Contribution to the Critique of Hegel's Philosophy of Right*, "In Germany, on the contrary, where practical life is as spiritless as spiritual life is unpractical, no class in civil society has any need or capacity for general emancipation until it is forced by its immediate condition, by material necessity, by its very chains."[1] Marx wrote the book when analyzing Germany's situations back then and proposed the concept of "material necessity." In his *Economic and Philosophic Manuscripts of 1844*, Marx expounded further on needs and proposed a series of concepts like social needs,

---

[1] Karl Marx and Frederick Engels, *Marx & Engels Collected Works Vol. 03: Marx and Engels: 1843 – 1844*, London: Lawrence & Wishart, 1975, Electric Book, 2010, p. 186.

physical needs, workers' needs, civilized needs, rough needs, people's needs, self-interested needs, the need for interaction, and natural needs. In his *Foundations of the Critique of Political Economy*, Marx proposed the concept of "necessary needs," linked necessary needs with necessary labor, and explained the basic meaning of social needs. He pointed out that in a society of commodity production, people do not produce products for his own direct needs, but for the needs of other people. The three important viewpoints of the Marxist needs theory are as follows: people's needs are the essence of human beings; people's needs are social needs, which generate social relations; production determines needs, and needs propel production.① Ota Sik also believed that interest is a concentrated and long-lasting purpose for people to meet certain objectively generated needs; or this kind of satisfaction is not sufficient, and people keep deliberating on how to meet their needs; or this kind of satisfaction (because of the triggered emotions and feelings) attracts people's special attention and repeated and sometimes more intense needs.②

(3) Seeing interests as "social relations." In *Encyclopedia of China: Philosophy Volume*, interests are defined as different needs expressed by people through social relations.③ Here, interests can only be realized through social relations. In *The Complete Book of Marxist Philosophy*, interests are defined as socialized needs and needs expressed by people through certain social relations.④ In essence, interests belong to the category of social relations. For social subjects to survive and develop, they have to possess and enjoy social labor products. Such a unity of opposites between social subjects and social labor products is interest. Such a Marxist viewpoint reveals the essence that interests belong to the category of social relations. The biggest difference between human

---

① Wang Weiguang, *On Interests*, Beijing: People's Publishing House, 2001.
② Ota Šik, *Economy-Interests-Politics*, Beijing: Encyclopedia of China Publishing House, 1987, p. 263.
③ *Encyclopedia of China: Philosophy Volume*, Beijing: Encyclopedia of China Publishing House, 1982, p. 483.
④ *The Complete Book of Marxist Philosophy*, Beijing: China Renmin University Press, 1996, p. 376.

and animal lies in the social nature of human needs. Of course, there is something common between the needs of human beings and animals, namely natural attributes, such as breathing the air of nature, bathing in the sunshine, and taking in all kinds of resources that exist in nature to sustain life. Yet, we can see that as the society develops, the natural attributes of needs take up an increasingly smaller proportion in total needs while the proportion of social attributes is increasing. Needs with natural attributes are needs for "natural" goods (natural food, natural raw materials, and others). The increasing scarcity of those goods shows that human needs are almost becoming social attributes in the full sense. The simplest example is people's needs for water. It is increasingly rare to see people taking water directly from the nature. Water has long been accepted by people as a social product. To meet people's needs, we have to possess and enjoy social products enabled by social labor. Interests reflect social relations. Interest relations among people are mainly the distribution of social products based on productivity and under social production relations, and the relations of distribution in terms of ideology.

(4) Seeing interests as "abilities." Such a viewpoint believes that the realization of interests is determined by people's abilities, which makes interests possible. The most basic definition of power is people's dominance over objects and people. To further define "interest," the meaning of power should be included. As such, "interest" should be further defined as the realization of people's reliance on the nature and society based on their certain dominance over objects and people. Power is the second element of "interest."[1] Here, power means people's dominance over objects and people and is a form or major form of ability. In certain social production relations, people's ability directly determines the amount of interests he can realize. For a whole society, in most cases, such a kind of dominance is related to productivity and equals to productivity in some circumstances. The level of productivity directly

---

[1] Yu Zheng, *On Interests in Integrated Economy*, Shanghai: Fudan University Press, 1999, p. 29.

determines the level of overall social benefits.

Summing up the above-mentioned viewpoints, we have a general understanding of the essence of interests. The essence of interests is manifested in three aspects: needs, social relations, and ability.

First, needs are the necessary foundation of interest forming. Without needs, there are no interests. Certain needs are needed to stimulate people's pursuit of certain interests. Needs are the necessary foundation of interests, and people's natural physiological needs of matter constitute the natural foundation of interests, particularly material interests. Human needs reflect people's objective reliance on the material and spiritual living conditions, as manifested in people's conscious pursuit of and desire for material and spiritual objects. That reflects the emotional desire of people (as subjects) for social living conditions (as objects). The contents of needs are objective, and the formation of needs is subjective. Human needs are the internal motivations of people's historical activities and the primary driving force behind the development of social production. The necessity of interests originates from needs, which constitute the primary and most fundamental basis of interests.

Second, social relations enable interests and serve as their social foundation. On one hand, people's social attributes socialize people's needs and make the formation of interests connect with certain social relations. People's interests can only be realized in a society. An object can become an interest only when it is connected with certain social subjects; otherwise, it is only a potential object of interest. Interests are the interests of people. Yet, people are not isolated but connected in a society. So interests cannot exist without a society. In essence, interests belong to the category of social relations and reflect social relations and the unity of opposites between needs and the objects of needs. If people's internal physiological needs constitute the necessary foundation of interest formation, then only the society makes interest formation possible and practical. Besides, the formation of various kinds of interests is based on the corresponding social conditions. Under different social conditions, people's needs are varied, as are the objects of needs, the relations between needs and the objects of needs, and finally the interests realized by people. On the other hand, interests can only be realized with the division of labor and co-production of the whole society. Even under the same social conditions, since people hold different positions according to the division of labor and social relations, their actually acquired interests are varied, at least in quantity; moreover, under different social conditions, whatever their positions in social relations are, the two positions *per se* are under different social conditions, hence the discrepancy with their corresponding interests in nature. Marx pointed out, "It is the interest of private persons; but its content, as well as the form and means of its realization, are given by social conditions that are independent of them all."[①]

Third, ability is an important condition that makes interests possible. Under certain social relations, despite the existence of needs, interests cannot be realized since it needs another important factor, namely ability. Those who want to acquire interests should have the basic ability of acquiring interests, which is the minimum requirement for the realization of interests. Without the factor, interests are only desires or needs. In certain social relations, ability is mainly manifested as dominance over objects and people, called as natural ability and social ability respectively. Natural ability refers to people's position in the nature and people's resources and abilities of developing and using natural resources. Social ability refers to people's abilities in politics, culture and other areas of social life. Natural ability and social ability are related to natural needs and social needs respectively and are the basic conditions for realizing natural interests and social interests. Individually, people's social abilities are mainly determined and endowed by the basic rules of social activities, consisting of viability and development ability. In a broad sense, these abilities are subject to

---

① Karl Marx and Frederick Engels, *Marx & Engels Collected Works Vol. 28: Marx: 1857 – 1861*, London: Lawrence & Wishart, 1986, Electric Book, 2010, p. 94.

certain social relations, the natures of which determine the natures of those abilities. Therefore, in terms of natural abilities alone, ability means people's capability of conquering the nature and acquiring natural interests. The declining amount of natural resources and the mounting complexity of natural environment has added to the difficulty of acquiring natural interests, hence higher demands for abilities. As the society develops, the level of overall abilities is on the rise. When other factors are almost the same, differences in people's abilities will surely lead to differences in interests.

To sum up, we can define interest as the sum of material and spiritual wealth that can meet people's own needs and other needs.[①] Such a definition embodies three factors: needs, society, and abilities. Needs are manifested as "meeting one's own needs"; society is manifested as "the society's material and spiritual wealth"; and abilities are manifested as "can." Acquired interests do not necessarily coincide with needed interests. Finally, acquired interests are actually acquired interests based on abilities.

II. Composition of Interests

The essence of interests is explored in the above sections. In terms of interest *per se* or its concept, an interest consists of several elements. An analysis of the composition of an interest can help us see through the essence of interests and grasp the internal laws of the phenomenon of interests. Belonging to the category of social relations, an interest consists of the subject, object, and intermediary.[②] The three elements hold different positions and play their unique roles.

The first element is the subject. The subject of an interest is the owner of the interest. As a contradictory relationship between the subject of needs and the object of needs, any interest is a unity of opposites between certain subject

---

① Hong Yuanpeng, *General Theory on Economic Relations*, Shanghai: Fudan University Press, 1999, p. 2.
② Zhang Yuying, *On Interests—Research on Interest Conflicts and Coordination*, Wuhan: Wuhan University Press, 2001.

of needs and object of needs. Therefore, interests are relative to certain subjects of interests. There is no interest that does not belong to any subject or have no subject. Here, subjects of interests are socialized subjects of needs. In many cases, they are directly unified. In a real society, subjects of interests are people in the real society, within certain social structure and certain groups. They can be individuals, certain groups, or organizations. There are varied groups in the human society, mainly including families, collectives, ethnic groups, and nations. In a class society, class is the most important group organization and one of the major subjects of interests. In today's world, with the advent of globalization and the ever-challenging global issues, the whole human society has become a subject of interest in the real world. Of course, individuals are the most basic ones among all subjects of interests. A group is formed by individuals in an organized manner; individuals are the basis of groups, and no groups can exist without individuals. However, it does not mean that individuals are the only subjects of interests, nor that the stressing of individuals' practical significance will cancel out, or dissolve the actual existence of other subjects of interests in human society. In today's world with increasingly complex social division of labor and the fast socialization and globalization, the role of groups and even mankind as subjects of interests is becoming ever more important.

People have already known and transformed into social products through social labor and objects that people have not yet known and touched. Of course, in terms of reality, many objects are only potential objects of interests, not real objects. As people's cognitive and practical ability gets improved, those potential objects of interests will be transformed into real objects of interests. That is to say, in the real world, any possible object of knowledge and practice will only become a real object of interest only when it is understood by people and stamped with the imprint of human beings.

The third element is the intermediary. Intermediaries of interests are the intermediary elements that connect subjects of interests with objects of interests, i.e., people's activities. Theoretically, all objects of knowledge and practice are possible objects of interests. However, in reality, not all objects are real objects of interests. The fundamental way of objects becoming real objects of interests lies in the fact that a contradictory relationship between objects and people's needs can only be formed through people's activities. To be specific, on one hand, people's activities separate the otherwise animal-style directly unified people's needs and the process of needs being met, thus forming a contradictory relationship. Other living things can acquire abilities directly from the nature to sustain their survival and development. Their needs, if any, are directly unified with the process of their needs being met. For human beings, the direct unity of needs and the process of needs being met is broken, and an intermediary link appears between needs and the process of needs being met, namely production. Just as Lenin said, "the world does not satisfy man and man decides to change it by his activity."① On the other hand, people can only meet their own needs with active activities. Marx pointed out that people are "actively behaving, availing themselves of certain things of the outside world by action, and thus satisfying their needs."②

It is people's active activities that communicate the relationship between objects and the needs of subjects and transform potential objects into real objects. Without the participation of subjects' activities, no objects can be related to people's needs, nor will they become real objects of interests, and people's interests will not exist. Therefore, people's social activities are not only the means that resolve the contradiction between needs and the process of needs being met, but also an intermediary link enabling the existence of the contradiction. All in all, mankind's practices are the intermediary link enabling and highlighting the existence of interest relations.

---

① V. I. Lenin, *Lenin Collected Works Vol. 38*, Moscow: Progress Publishers, 1976, p. 213
② Karl Marx and Frederick Engels, *Marx & Engels Collected Works Vol. 24: Marx and Engels: 1874 - 1883*, London: Lawrence & Wishart, 1989, Electric Book, 2010, p. 538.

Section Ⅱ The Meaning and Characteristics of Common Interests

Ⅰ. Meaning of Common Interests

Interest is a value judgment on the relationship between subject and object. Interest is manifested as the significance of certain (spiritual or material) objects to subjects and viewed, reasonably assumed, or recognized by the subject or other valuators as valuable to the existence of relevant subjects (useful, necessary, and worth being pursued).[①] People's needs generate interests, which combine needs and means to meet those needs and reflect social relations. That is how various kinds of interests are generated in human society, such as economic interests, political interests, cultural interests, individual interests, group interests, national interests, class interests, hierarchy interests, and state interests. Interest is a social phenomenon affected and restricted by subjects and objects, nature and society, production and relations of production, and many other factors. Therefore, interests feature a variety of contradictions and complexities. Different relations of interests happen among different subjects of interests. The selfness of interests means that differences and contradictions exist among subjects of interests that form relations of interests. The social nature of interests means that there is common ground among different interests in relations of interests, hence the intercommunity of relations of interests. The connotations of common interests are very rich and uncertain, with the following five viewpoints.

(1) Neumann classified interests into subjective intercommunity and objective intercommunity. Subjective intercommunity refers to the interests

---

[①] Hans J. Wolff, Otto Bachof and Rolf Stober, *Administrative Law*, Beijing: The Commercial Press, 2002, p. 324.

shared by an uncertain majority based on cultural relations; objective intercommunity refers to important objectives and goals based on the needs of a nation or a society, namely the objective (task) of a state.①

(2) Jeremy Bentham believed that common interests are by no means special interests independent of personal interests. The community is a fictitious body, composed of the individual persons who are considered as constituting as it were its members. The interest of the community then is, what is it? —the sum of the interests of the several members who compose it. It is in vain to talk of the interest of the community, without understanding what is the interest of the individual.②

(3) Alfred Verdross believed that common interests are neither the sum of interests that individuals desire for nor the interests of human beings as a whole. They are the sum of the value of things created through cooperation of individuals in a society; such cooperation is quite necessary and the objective is to enable people to build their own lives through hard work and labor and to make their life consistent with their individual dignity as human.③

(4) Edgar Bodenheimer explained common interests from the perspective of the outer boundary of individual rights. The concept of "common interests" ("common good") "is a useful conceptual tool for designating the outer limits which must not be transgressed in the allocation and exercise of individual rights." "The term 'outer limits' is meant to suggest that the granting of a substantial sphere of individual rights is in itself an essential condition of promoting the common good."④

(5) Friedrich August von Hayek defined common interest as an abstract

---

① Chen Xinmin, *Basic Theories of German Public Law*, Ji'nan: Shandong People's Publishing House, 2001, p. 185.
② Jeremy Bentham, *An Introduction to the Principles of Morals and Legislation*, Beijing: The Commercial Press, 2000, p. 58.
③ Edgar Bodenheimer, *Jurisprudence: The Philosophy and Method of the Law*, Cambridge: Harvard University Press, 2013, p. 242.
④ Ibid.

order. "The conception of the common welfare or of the public good of a free society can therefore never be defined as a sum of known particular results to be achieved, but only as an abstract order which as a whole is not oriented on any particular concrete ends but provides merely the best chance for any member selected at random successfully to use his knowledge for his purposes."[①]

The word "common" in "common interests" is explained as collectively owned, used, shared by or collectively affecting all or almost all members of a group or society.[②] Therefore, this book argues that common interests refer to objective interests in one or many aspects shared by at least two people or groups, the majority of a society, or two or more subjects in a certain period.

II. Characteristics of Common Interests

1. Universality

Common interests reflect horizontal interest relations of the subjects of interests. Since interests are the unity of selfness and sociality, any relation of interests contains a third interest, namely the "intersection" of interests formed through the combination of the interests of two original subjects of interests in relations of interests, namely the so-called common interests. In a sense, a common interest is a third interest in relations of interests.[③] Above all, common interests refer to the interests of the majority, which may be two people, the majority, or even all people. Those people may all benefit from common interests, which means the relative universality of common interests.

2. Shareability

Since "common interests" are collectively owned, shared, and undertaken, they are related to the common ground and collective actions of members of a society. They cannot be limited to an individual or owned by an individual, which means the inalienability of common interests. These two characteristics

---

① Friedrich A. Hayek, "The Principles of a Liberal Social Order," *Il Politico*, 1996, 31(4): 601-618.
② Yu Zuhua, "Thoughts on Harmony in Ancient China," Guangming Daily, March 7, 2005.
③ Su Baomei, "My Concept of Harmonious Ethics," *Journal of University of Ji'nan*, 2003(3): 1-10.

determine that competition subjects formed based on the common interests of members of a society have unified, common interest demands. Based on individual interests, common interests are the common parts of the respective interests of people in the same social relations and social status. Potential unified economic objectives only exist among economic individuals. Only when economic individuals realize according to common interests that the potential or expected benefit-cost ratio of collective actions is greater than the benefit-cost ratio of individual actions, scattered individual actions can be pooled together to form collective actions, so as to share the returns of collective actions.

3. Heterogeneity

During the formation of the relations of common interests, the differences in the natures of the original subjects of interests mean that the generated "common interests" may come with different natures. That is to say, under certain social and historical conditions, different relations of interests will certainly generate different common interests, hence the heterogeneity of common interests. The heterogeneity of common interests means that the real carrier of common interests may be an organization, a community, a region, a country, or even the whole human society. Their spontaneous or organized behaviors can form different organizations based on common interests. The contents of such common interests determine the composition and number of members of these organizations. Such organizations of common interests show a complex net structure.

4. Independence

The independence of common interests means that once a common interest is formed, it will become a third kind of interest in relations of interests, thus gaining a unique position among interests. Under some circumstances, common interests dominate over other interests in the same relation of interests. Common interests have rich meanings and are multi-layered. Vertically, the whole human society has common interests, each country has its own common interests, and different regions of a country also have their regional common interests. Horizontally, subjects of interests at the same level may have different common interests. In terms of coverage, there are common interests of the following levels: collective interests, group interests, hierarchy interests, class interests, national interests, and state interests.

The above sections expound on the four major characteristics of common interests. However, they fail to cover all features of common interests and should contain more rich practical contents and more diversified manifestations. What's more, the above-mentioned characteristics are not isolated, but interlinked and interactive. Yet, in view of the limitations of space, other features of common interests will not be expounded here.

Section III   Theoretical Origin of Common Interests

The issue of interests is the most basic issue of Marxism. The relation of interests is the basic focus of Marx's analysis of social relations. Marx and Engels used historical materialism to make a scientific analysis of interests and common interests.

I. Interests Originate from People's Needs for Survival and Development

Interest is the sum of material and spiritual wealth that can meet people's own needs and other needs. Interest represents the realization of a value relationship. The realization of interests relies on a subject's possession of his desired object. Different interest subjects have different needs and acquire and possess their desired objects through different activities, thus having different interests. Since each subject lives under certain social and historical conditions, their demands for interests bear specific historical imprints. As social animals, human beings never simply adapt to the nature but transform it consciously and purposefully to make objects meet their interest needs and serve themselves. People's pursuit of survival and development must be realized through certain social methods and social relations. That is to say, people's production activities of transforming objects and obtaining material subsistence must be carried out through interpersonal intercourse and connection. Only when people form certain relations (material production relations and ideological relations) can they play a dynamic role in their relations with the nature. Just as Marx said, "Human beings ... achieved their own development only in and through society."① So society is the prerequisite for people's survival and development, and such social relations should first manifest as interest relations. "The economic relations of a given society present themselves in the first place as interests."② Interests pursued for survival and development are also transformed into interests constrained by certain social and historical conditions.

II. Social Reasons of Interest Conflicts

In a society, interests pursued by people are manifested psychologically as people's motivations and wills. People's understanding of interests is manifested as motivations, intention and consciously proposed purposes. People's pursuit of interests is manifested in the process of pursuing objects purposely when people are driven by motivations. Thus, we can see that people's conscious and purposeful vitality come from the pursuit of interests, and interests drive people's activities. Different interest subjects show different wishes and actions based on different interests, hence the contradictions and conflicts among different interest subjects. Among those contradictions and conflicts, those between personal interests and common interests constitute an important aspect of interest contradictions and conflicts. Yet, an analysis according to the basic viewpoints of Marxism shows that the contradictions between personal interests

---

① Karl Marx and Frederick Engels, *Marx & Engels Collected Works Vol. 05: Marx and Engels: 1845 - 1847*, London: Lawrence & Wishart, 1976, Electric Book, 2010, pp. 214-215.
② Karl Marx and Frederick Engels, *Marx & Engels Collected Works Vol. 23: Marx and Engels: 1871 - 1874*, London: Lawrence & Wishart, 1988, Electric Book, 2010, p. 379.

and common interests are not always there, but are generated when the development of human history has reached a certain stage and become evident with the evolving social division of labor. Marx pointed out, "the division of labor also implies the contradiction between the interest of the separate individual or the individual family and the common interest of all individuals who have intercourse with one another."[①]

First, personal interests gradually split from common interests as the division of labor develops. With the development of division of labor, each person has certain division of labor, scope of activities, and specific purpose of labor. In the real world, each person pursues the special, partial interests within one's division of labor. This way, the interests formed among people who interact with each other in the different activities of different people have become some kind of alien and external force for individuals. Because of division of labor and because people can only act within the division of labor, "individuals always proceed from their own interests." The split between personal interests and common interests and the concept that people should pursue their own interests are the internal reasons of interest contradictions and conflicts.

Second, the failure to realize common interests has intensified interest contradictions. As the division of labor develops, the nature of common interests has been distorted. The original consistency between common interests and personal interests is broken down. On one hand, the split between personal interests and common interests is produced; on the other hand, with the deepening of division of labor, common interests are gradually separated from personal interests and gain some kind of independence, namely the existence of common interests independent of personal interests. Meanwhile, as the division of labor develops, some specialists appear to engage in social organization, management, and other matters related to common interests. At the same time,

---

[①] *Marx & Engels Collected Works Vol. 05*, p. 46.

the majority of people among social community gradually lose their right to the participation of common interests. This way, public servants organizing and managing common interests gradually become the undertakers, defenders and representatives of common interests. Therefore, the common interests that gain independence from single individuals will certainly evolve into special interests of the undertakers of common interests, which seem to be common interests on the surface but are actually the special interests of some specific subjects, namely the "shadowy common interests." As to how common interests become shadowy common interests, Marx and Engels conducted insightful analysis in their book *The German Ideology*, "it is precisely because of the contradictions between private interests and public interests that public interests take an independent form separated from practical interests (whether individual or collective) in the name of the state, namely a form of illusory community." The expounding of Marx and Engels not only explains the structure of the evolution of common interests in the social progress but also reveals the fundamental reasons behind the contradictions and conflicts between the illusory common interests and group interests and personal interests.

Ⅲ. Position of Common Interests in People's Interest Relations

Marx and Engels believed that common interests "do not exist in concept as a 'universal thing' but firstly exist in the reality as the relation of interdependence between individuals who divide work among themselves." People's social existence is firstly the existence of each specific person, connected with people's demands for interests and pursuits. It is firstly manifested as the demands for and pursuits of interests on the part of each individual. For each individual to realize their goals and wishes, they have to form mutual relations and societies, and cooperate with each other. People engage in activities through their connections and exchanges with other people, and they can only create their desired material interests and realize survival and development through cooperation. That is to say, people form a society only to realize their own interests. People's interests gain subjectivity only when social connections are created. Then, we can see that interest relations are the contents of people's social existence. As subjects of interests, people always show two kinds of interests: personal interests and common interests with others. Common interests bear their own features in people's interest relations.

First, common interests originate from inter-personal relations and interdependence among people. As subjects of the society, each individual has his own special interest needs and is driven by his own interests. Therefore, different individuals show mutual exclusion, mutual restriction, and mutual negation in terms of interests. However, the interests of any individual can only be realized through his connection with and reliance on others. So personal interests inevitably feature the interconnection with other people's interests and the reliance on and recognition of other people's interests. The interconnection, mutual reliance, and mutual recognition between personal interests and other people's interests is the basis of common interests.

Second, common interests are generated in the realization of personal interests. On one hand, just as analyzed above, common interests originate from the social connection and social reliance happened when people pursue their own interests. Common interests will not exist without personal interests. That is why we can say that common interests are generated in the realization of personal interests and originate from personal interests. On the other hand, personal interests cannot be realized without common interests as the prerequisites and conditions. "The point is that private interest is itself already a socially determined interest and can be attained only within the conditions laid down by society and with the means provided by society, and is therefore tied to the reproduction of these conditions and means." ①

---

① *Marx & Engels Collected Works Vol. 28: Marx: 1857 – 1861*, p. 94.

Third, common interests are the fundamental factor when people choose socialized survival. The fundamental reason lies in the social relations formed among people, which offer a more powerful force and a broader development space than individuals. That shows the most fundamental common interest for people's survival and development. MacIntyre noted that in terms of social practice, common interests cannot be understood as the sum of personal interests. Paul Heinrich Dietrich also believed that people form society to meet their own interests. Of course, only in this process can practical common interests be generated. For that, MacIntyre conducted an insightful analysis: If I do not cooperate with others and do not consider the motivation of others in obtaining their own interests, I will not obtain anything of my own interests except the most transitory interests. So I have found a kind of common interest in my cooperation with others, which is a tool to realize our own interests and thus is defined by our own interests.

IV. Common Interests Are the Core of Socialist Economics

According to Marxism, in the future society of socialism, all social members will freely form a socialized economic community, or a "community of free individuals." In the economic community, production materials are the common property jointly owned by all social members, labor process is joint labor with democratic management participated by all social members, and labor products are common goods owned by the society. To sum up, the view of interests of the founder of Marxism is to realize and enhance the common interests of all social members, and the view of common interests is the core of classic socialist economics. In the theoretical system of classic socialist economics, the common interests of all social members hold a dominating position and play a leading role. The common possession of production materials is both the basis of all social members' common interests and their fundamental common interests. The joint participation and democratic governance of the production process is the condition and guarantee for the realization of all social members' common interests. The collective allocation and common use of new social products is the realization of all social members' common interests. Therefore, classic socialist economics is a system of economic theory built centering on all social members' common interests.

Chapter III
Theory of Common Interests: Literature Review

Section I Bibliometric Analysis of Research Literature on Theory of Common Interests

"Common interests" has become a hot topic between China and other countries and even among countries worldwide today. Based on this, starting from current events, in order to better understand the status and progress of common interests in today's world, and summarize the trend of national development based on common interests, this book uses the periodical literature of China National Knowledge Infrastructure (CNKI) as the data source to sort out the relevant literature on the research of common interests in China. Based on Citespace visual analysis, this book summarizes the hot issues, main viewpoints and development trends of common interests from various perspectives, providing reference for future research on common interests.

I. Data Statistics of Research Literature on Common Interests

Our data source includes the relevant documents on the theme of common interests in China from 1929 to 2019. The retrieval database is of all the CNKI periodicals and the retrieval papers are classified as "Philosophy and Humanities," "Social Science I," "Social Science II" and "Economic and Management Science."

By analyzing the number of research literature on common interests from 1979 to 2019, the results show that there are 2,850 related articles published in periodicals and that the number of papers published shows an overall upward trend, but there is a significant decline in 2013. The number of articles published was 188 in 2010, 132 in 2011, 117 in 2012, 106 in 2013, 109 in 2014, 116 in 2015, 122 in 2016, 165 in 2017, and 125 in 2018.

According to the analysis in Figure 3-1, from the perspective of the number of published articles, the number in 2019 is not of reference value because the research is now being conducted in 2019. Since 1995, the number of articles studying common interests has started to rise, indicating that with the deepening of international exchange, more and more scholars have begun to study international relations and common interests. Since 2003, the number of articles published has fluctuated occasionally, but the total number is above 100. In recent years, the number of articles rises and falls, showing an irregular fluctuation.

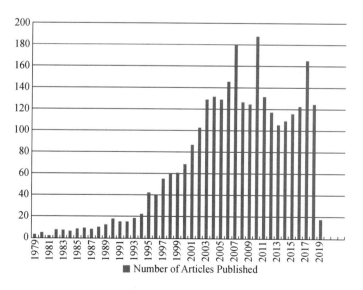

Figure 3-1 Annual Distribution of Research Literature on Common Interests from 1979 to 2019

II. Data Processing and Research Methods

The Citespace software is used to analyze the data, and the relevant data downloaded from CNKI are formatted and converted according to the operation requirements of the software.

1. Co-word analysis

First appeared in the 1980s, co-word analysis is a content analysis and scientific mapping method introduced into the intelligence field by Callon and others of the French National Center for Scientific Research (CNRS). Co-word analysis method puts forward the basic theory and application examples of co-occurrence analysis. It is a common co-occurrence analysis method and is a kind of content analysis. It is used to analyze the co-occurrence relationship and co-occurrence intensity of a group of words in the same document, to reflect the relationship between words, and to reveal the internal structure and trend of change in a certain research field. This method can not only describe the knowledge structure of the discipline but also reveal the evolution of the discipline structure in combination with time series. Skotov and others extracted multi-word phrases according to word frequency analysis and applied the adjacent phrase analysis algorithm to find representative research topics and the relationship between topics and between topics and subtopics. Finally, they calculated the link strength between phrases by using the equivalent index, and the co-occurrence of keywords was limited to about 50 words. Co-word analysis was mainly used in the fields of artificial intelligence and scientometrics in the early days. After years of development, experts and scholars at home and abroad have applied co-word analysis to many other fields, such as information systems, energy materials, libraries and information sciences, fuel cells, and medical fields. The common feature is to use words to represent the main contents of the literature and to reveal the hot spots, frontiers, and development trends in this research field by analyzing the relationship and intensity of co-words. The steps of co-word analysis include: (1) determining the high-frequency keywords of documents in the field of information resource management; (2) establishing a co-word matrix, a dissimilarity matrix, and a similarity matrix; (3) selecting cluster analysis, multi-dimension analysis, and network analysis based on co-word matrix to draw mapping; (4) conducting data analysis.

2. Cluster analysis

Cluster analysis refers to the analysis process of dividing the collection of physical or abstract objects into multiple classes composed of similar objects. It is an important human behavior.

The goal of cluster analysis is to collect data for classification on the basis of similarity. Clustering originates from many fields, including mathematics, computer science, statistics, biology, and economics. In different application fields, many clustering techniques have been developed. These techniques are used to describe data, measure the similarity between different data sources, and classify data sources into different clusters.

III. Visual Analysis Results of Research Literature on Common Interests

The Citespace software is used to obtain a visual mapping of keywords in research literature on common interests.

1. Keyword mapping

The purpose of keyword analysis is to confirm the number of articles published in the field of common interests and the key research areas and to determine hot topics by analyzing the keyword frequency together with the content analysis. Based on the statistics of the literature related to common interests from 1979 to 2019, the keyword co-occurrence knowledge mapping and the keyword frequency chart in the research of common interests are generated through the operation of the Citespace software.

In the literature on common interests, the words "the United States of America," "the People's Republic of China," "China-U.S. relationship," "ideological system," and "a community with a shared future for mankind" appear frequently, which shows that studies on common interests have focused on these hot issues in recent years. For visual manifestation, see Table 3-1 for details.

Table 3-1 Keywords Frequency of Appearance

Frequency	Year	Keyword
488	1980	Common interests
99	1999	Globalization
97	1997	China-U.S. relationship
94	2000	National interest
90	1995	U.S.
83	1995	The People's Republic of China
80	1995	Common interests of mankind
77	1982	Ideological system
74	1995	The United States of America
74	1995	North America
74	2001	Public interests
73	2000	Interests
65	2016	A community with a shared future for mankind
63	1982	Socialism
49	1983	Economy
48	1985	Enterprise
47	1985	Enterprise management
42	1995	Interest group
42	1990	Politics
40	1993	Marx
39	2005	Harmonious society
36	2003	China
34	1983	Personal interests
34	2003	International law
33	1993	Market economy

(To be continued)

		(Continued)
Frequency	Year	Keyword
29	1995	Deng Xiaoping
28	1980	Economic benefits
28	2003	Stakeholders
24	2002	Community of shared interests
24	2013	Global governance
23	2015	Xi Jinping
23	2014	A community with a shared future
22	1999	Common interests of all mankind
22	2005	Collective action
21	2006	Harmonious world
20	1997	Collectivism
20	2004	Marxism

This shows that the China-U.S. relationship is a very important topic in the study of common interests, which is also linked to current events.

Moreover, analysis by the Citespace software also shows that the Belt and Road (B&R) Initiative—China's proposal to build a Silk Road Economic Belt and a 21st Century Maritime Silk Road—is a new hot topic in the research of common interest research. The Belt and Road Initiative is also a cooperation initiative put forward by China in recent years. Co-constructing the Belt and Road Initiative conforms to the fundamental interests of the international community, demonstrates the common ideal and the beautiful aspirations of the human society, represents an active exploration of new modes of international cooperation and global governance, and will add new positive energy to the peaceful development of the world. With these key words as the core, a complete knowledge network in the research field of common interests is formed.

2. Mapping of research institutions

The Citespace software is used to generate the mapping of scientific research institutions engaged in research of common interests from 1979 to 2019. In the field of research on common interests, there are mainly four high-yield institutions in China. Among them, the research institution with the largest number of articles published is Wuhan University Law School, which has published 14 articles, followed by International Institute for Strategic Studies of Party School of the the Central Committee of the Communist Party of China (C.P.C.) (12 articles published), Party School of the Central Committee of C.P.C (11 articles published), Institute of World Economics and Politics of Chinese Academy of Social Sciences (CASS) (10 articles published), Renmin University Law School (10 articles published), China Institute of International Studies (9 articles published).

Ⅳ. Conclusions & Suggestions

Based on the mathematical statistics of the research literature on common interests in China from 1979 to 2019, this book uses the Citespace software to measure the relevant articles published on CNKI and presents the main issues in the research on common interests and the contributions of research institutions through visual mapping.

Through co-occurrence analysis of keywords, the keywords with the most frequency in recent years are extracted, including "globalization," "China-U.S. relationship," "a community with a shared future for mankind," "economy," and "global governance." This shows that scholars have done a lot of thinking on common interests, conducted considerable research from the perspective of state-to-state relations, especially the China-U.S. relationship and the economy, and made some achievements.

Through the visual analysis of research institutions, it can be found that colleges and research institutes of key schools related to politics and law have conducted relevant research.

Based on the above bibliometric analysis of the literature on common interests, the following four brief suggestions are put forward.

(1) Attaching importance to the education of the "ideological system" (this is a keyword with a rather high frequency of appearance).

(2) Attaching importance to China–U.S. relationship. From the the visual mapping analysis, it can be seen intuitively that a lot of the literature on common interests has focused on the relationship between the United States and China, involving topics such as the Taiwan region, the Asia-Pacific Economic Cooperation, etc. Considering the previous China–U.S. trade friction, the China–U.S. relationship is still a core aspect.

(3) According to the analysis of the types of research institutions for common interests, it is found that the nature of research institutions is relatively uniform and that the frequency of "economy" as a keyword is very high. However, there is almost no "institute of economics" among the research institutions which are basically related to law and politics. It is hoped that diversified research can be conducted.

(4) Attaching importance to "globalization." "Globalization" has a very high degree of correlation with other key words, almost all of which are related to globalization. Moreover, "globalization" is the word with the highest frequency. Since the 1990s, with the expansion of its influence on human society, globalization has gradually attracted the attention of various countries in the fields of politics, education, society, culture, and other disciplines and has caused a research upsurge in succession.

Section Ⅱ   Marxists' Discussion on Interests

Ⅰ. *Capital*, a model for analyzing relationship between economic interests

The representative work of Marxist economics is Marx's *Capital*. The object of *Capital* is capitalist production relations (i.e., economic relations), which is actually the study of capitalist relations of economic interests. The whole theoretical system of *Capital* reflects the objectively existing economic interest relations in capitalism.

All economic relations are essentially economic interest relations. *Capital* studies the capitalist economic relations, and, in fact, it studies the capitalist economic interest relations.

Marx, the founder of Marxism, was born in Germany on May 5, 1818. Marx's father, a well-known legal adviser, was eager for his son to inherit his career. Therefore, after finishing high school, Marx was admitted to the Law Department of University of Bonn according to his father's suggestions, and he later transferred to Berlin University. When he was studying in university, he's major was law, but he was especially interested in philosophy. He once said, "I had to study law and above all felt the urge to wrestle with philosophy."① In 1841, when Marx graduated from Berlin University, he received PhD in Philosophy from the University of Jena with his excellent paper "The Difference Between the Democritean and Epicurean Philosophy of Nature." That is to say, during his college years, Marx "knew absolutely nothing about political economy."② What caused Marx to turn to political economy? In July 1841, Marx returned to Bonn after graduating from Berlin University. In April 1842, he began to write for *Rheinische Zeitung*. From October 1842 to March 1843, Marx served as editor-in-chief of *Rheinische Zeitung*. He had extensive contact with social and economic issues and often encountered difficulties in expressing opinions on issues of economic interest, which prompted Marx to study economics. Lenin said, "Marx's journalistic activities convinced him that he was insufficiently acquainted with political economy, and he zealously set out to study it."③ Engels mentioned, "Marx always used to tell me that it was precisely his preoccupation with the law on thefts of wood and the condition of the Mosel wine-growers that led him from politics pure and simple to economic

---

① *Marx & Engels Collected Works Vol. 01*, p. 11.
② Karl Marx and Frederick Engels, *Marx & Engels Collected Works Vol. 49: Engels: 1890 – 1892*, London: Lawrence & Wishart, 2001, Electric Book, 2010, p. 550.
③ V. I. Lenin, *Lenin Collected Works: Vol. 21*, Moscow: Progress Publishers, 1974, p. 47.

conditions and thus to socialism."① The debate on wood theft happened due to the fact that at that time, according to the traditional customs in Germany, peasants could cut down trees and pick up dead branches in the forest. However, with the development of capitalism, forest trees were occupied as private property by landlords. Through the parliament that debated the economic interests of landlords in Rhine Province, a bill was promulgated, stipulating that peasants were not allowed to cut down trees and pick up dead branches without permission. Otherwise, they would be punished for stealing trees and be fined and detained. In this debate, Marx published "Debates on the Law on Thefts of Wood" to fight against the Rhine Provincial Parliament in order to protect the economic interests of poor peasants. At that time, however, he was mainly defending from the legal aspects of justice for peasants. He said, "In these customs of the poor class, therefore, there is an instinctive sense of right; their roots are positive and legitimate, and the form of customary right here conforms all the more to nature."② The debate over the situation of Mosel peasants started from a report on the living conditions of peasants in Mosel published in *Rheinische Zeitung*, describing their plight. The report was criticized by Rhine Governor von Schaper. Through his own investigation in Mosel, Marx wrote the article "Justification of the Correspondent from the Mosel," pointing out that the reason why the peasants are poor and the small-scale peasant economy is bankrupt and destroyed is Prussia's bureaucratic political system. Through these debates, Marx deeply felt that everything people fought for was related to their interests. Marx pointed out in his article "Proceedings of the Sixth Rhine Province Assembly" published in 1842 in *Rheinische Zeitung* that "everything for which man struggles is a matter of his interest."③ People engage in material production activities in order

---

① Karl Marx and Frederick Engels, *Marx & Engels Collected Works Vol. 50: Engels: 1892–1895*, London: Lawrence & Wishart, 2004, Electric Book, 2010, p. 497.
② *Marx & Engels Collected Works Vol. 01*, p. 234.
③ Ibid, p. 171.

to obtain material benefits; people's social integration is to achieve common interests; revolution is also for the interests. As Engels pointed out, "it will be interests and not principles that will begin and carry through the revolution."[1] However, the study of the relationship between economic interests should not be based only on legal analysis but should also be based on economic analysis. Therefore, he was urged to focus on economics and write *Capital*. From 1843 onwards, Marx began to systematically collect data to study political economics. At first, he planned to write a magnum opus criticizing the capitalist system and bourgeois political economics. At that time, Marx planned to publish the book *Critique of Political Economy* in six volumes, namely, capital, real estate, wage labor, state, foreign trade, and world trade and world market. The first sub-volume of "capital" is about commodities and currencies (equivalent to the first part of the first volume of the current *Capital*), which was completed in January 1859 and published in June. After that, Marx immediately set about sorting out and writing the second sub-volume of "capital." In the process, Marx did a lot of research work on political economy and wrote *Critique of Political Economy* (*Manuscript 1861 – 1863*). It was in the process of writing this manuscript that he changed his plan and decided to publish all his economic works in four volumes, with *Capital* as the title and *Critique of Political Economy* as the subtitle. Only with Marx's *Capital* can political economics truly acquire a scientific status and become a proletarian science. As Engels pointed out, *Capital* "is the political economy of the working class, reduced to its scientific formulation. This work is concerned not with rabble-rousing phrase-mongering, but with strictly scientific deductions."[2] *Capital* "is often called, on the Continent, 'the Bible of the working class.' That the conclusions arrived at in this work are daily more and more becoming

---

[1] Karl Marx and Frederick Engels, *Marx & Engels Collected Works Vol. 02: Engels: 1838–1842*, London: Lawrence & Wishart, 1975, Electric Book, 2010, p. 374.

[2] Karl Marx and Frederick Engels, *Marx & Engels Collected Works Vol. 21: Marx and Engels: 1867–1870*, London: Lawrence & Wishart, 1985, Electric Book, 2010, p. 63.

the fundamental principles of the great working-class movement, ... nobody acquainted with that movement will deny."①

The process of production of capital in the first volume of *Capital* is actually to study the production of economic interests and the relationship between economic interests. First, Marx concluded that the creation of economic benefits is the product of the combination of human labor and things. Marx pointed out, "Whatever the social form of production, labourers and means of production always remain factors of it. But in a state of separation from each other either of these factors can be such only potentially. For production to go on at all they must unite."② However, "A machine which does not serve the purposes of labour, is useless. In addition, it falls a prey to the destructive influence of natural forces. Iron rusts and wood rots. Yarn with which we neither weave nor knit, is cotton wasted. Living labour must seize upon these things and rouse them from their death-sleep, change them from mere possible use values into real and effective ones."③ Therefore, economic benefits are actually created by labor. On the one hand, all labor as abstract labor forms commodity values; on the other hand, as specific labor, it produces use-values. However, in a capitalist society, the economic benefits created by the labor of the workers, apart from the part that compensate for the value of labor force, are occupied by the capitalists for free in the form of surplus value by virtue of the capitalist ownership. Second, Marx analyzed in great length the economic interest relation of depriving and being deprived between capitalists and workers in a capitalist society. Finally, Marx pointed out the development trend of the economic interest relations: the squeezers will be deprived. In capitalist society, a small number of squeezers deprive the broad masses of the

---

① Karl Marx and Frederick Engels, *Marx & Engels Collected Works Vol. 35: Karl Marx Capital: Volume 1*, London: Lawrence & Wishart, 1996, Electric Book, 2010, p. 35.
② Karl Marx and Frederick Engels, *Marx & Engels Collected Works Vol. 36: Karl Marx Capital: Volume 2*, London: Lawrence & Wishart, 1997, Electric Book, 2010, p. 42.
③ *Marx & Engels Collected Works Vol. 35*, p. 193.

people of their economic benefits. In future socialist societies, the broad masses of the people deprive a small number of squeezers of their economic benefits.

The second volume of *Capital*, the process of circulation of capital, is essentially an analysis of the realization of economic interests or the reproduction of economic interests. How can the economic interests possessed by capitalists in the form of surplus value be realized? First, in the first and second parts, Marx examined from a microscopic point of view that only by maintaining the continuity of capital circulation—that is, the balance of supply, production and sales, can economic interests be realized, and accelerating capital turnover can realize more economic interests. Second, from a macro perspective—that is, from the point of view of the whole society—economic interests can only be realized if the two major categories of social production, the production of means of production and the production of means of consumption, maintain an appropriate proportion—that is, the economic structure is reasonable.

The third volume of *Capital*, the process of capitalist production as a whole, focuses on the distribution of surplus value, which is actually the distribution of economic interests. Part Ⅰ to Part Ⅲ study the economic interest relations between industrial capitalists and between industrial capitalists and workers in the form of average profits; Part Ⅳ studies the economic interest relations between merchant capitalists and industrial capitalists as well as the relationship between these capitalists and industrial workers and commercial clerks in the form of commercial profits; Part Ⅴ studies the economic interest relations between functional capitalists and loaning capitalists, as well as industrial workers, commercial clerks, and bank employees, which are expressed by interests; Part Ⅵ studies the economic interest relations among landowners, capitalists, and workers in the form of land rent; Part Ⅶ reveals that the distribution of economic interests is determined by the relations of production. Marx pointed out, "The so-called distribution relations, then, correspond to and arise from historically determined specific social forms of the process of production and mutual relations entered into by men in the reproduction process of human life."①

The theory history of surplus value in the fourth volume of *Capital* is actually a development history of the theory of relationship of economic interests. It can be seen that Marx's *Capital* takes surplus value as the center. In fact, it takes the analysis of capitalist economic interests as the center, and it is an economic theory that serves the interests of the proletariat.

Marx also revealed in *Capital* that the class nature of economics originates from economic interests. Bourgeois economics is an economic theory that serves the interests of the bourgeoisie. Marx noted, "in the domain of political economy, free scientific inquiry meets not merely the same enemies as in all other domains. The peculiar nature of the material it deals with, summons as foes into the field of battle the most violent, mean and malignant passions of the human breast, the Furies of private interest."② Marxist economics is an economic theory that serves the interests of the working class. Therefore, economics has a class nature and represents different economic interests. However, bourgeois economics often conceals the pursuit of class self-interests and likes to wear the mask of seeking the general interests of mankind or the social interests (national interests). In the early stage of capitalism where class struggles did not develop, Ricardo "consciously makes the antagonism of class interests, of wages and profits, of profits and rent, the starting-point of his investigations, naively taking this antagonism for a social law of Nature."③ However, Marxist economics has publicly stated that it seeks economic benefits for the working class. "[T]he Marxist analysis of ideological systems of thought reduces them to emulsions of class interests which are in turn defined in exclusively economic terms. According to Marx the ideologies of capitalist

---

① Karl Marx and Frederick Engels, *Marx & Engels Collected Works Vol. 37: Karl Marx Capital: Volume 3*, London: Lawrence & Wishart, 1998, Electric Book, 2010, p. 869.
② *Marx & Engels Collected Works Vol. 35*, p. 10.
③ Ibid, p. 14.

society are, to put it crudely, glorifications of the interests of what he styled the capitalist class, whose interests are made to turn on the hunt for pecuniary profits."①

II. Lenin and Stalin's Development and Supplement to Economic Interest Theory

Lenin once had a period of practice in socialist construction. He initially summarized some experiences in Soviet socialist construction and enriched the Marxist theory of economic interests.

(1) Developing productive forces is the most fundamental interest of socialist countries. Lenin pointed out, "Following its seizure of political power, the principal and fundamental interest of the proletariat lies in securing an increase in output, an enormous increase in the productive forces of society."②

(2) Care for the personal interests of the masses. He pointed out, "on the basis of personal interest, personal incentive and business principles, we must first set to work in this small peasant country to build solid gangways to socialism by way of state capitalism."③ He also pointed out that "every important branch of the economy must be built up on the principle of personal incentive."④

(3) People who do not work cannot obtain economic benefits. On the basis of Marx's principle of distribution according to work, Lenin further put forward the principle that he does not work and neither shall he eat.

(4) Socialist social and economic benefits may also take the form of bonuses and profits. Lenin believed that socialism could not do without bonuses. He pointed out, "we must not reject the system of paying bonuses for the most

---

① Joseph A. Schumpeter. *History of Economic Analysis*, 2nd edition, Oxford: Oxford University Press, 1996, p. 36.
② V. I. Lenin, *Lenin Collected Works Vol. 42*, Moscow: Progress Publishers, 1971, p. 378.
③ V. I. Lenin, *Lenin Collected Works Vol. 33*, Moscow: Progress Publishers, 1965, p. 58.
④ Ibid, p. 70.

successful work, particularly organisational work; bonuses would be impermissible under a full communist system but in the period of transition from capitalism to communism bonuses are indispensable, as is borne out by theory and by a year's experience of Soviet power."① Furthermore, socialism still needs profits. "Profit also satisfy social needs. ... Surplus products do not belong to the private class but to all the workers, and only to them."②

(5) Exploring the appropriate degree of subordination of private interests to common interests. Lenin pointed out, "we have now found that degree of combination of private interest, of private commercial interest, with state supervision and control of this interest, that degree of its subordination to the common interests which was formerly the stumbling-block for very many socialists."③

Stalin made an important supplement to the theory of relations of economic interests. This is the theory of "advanced profit" of socialism. If profitableness is considered not from the stand-point of individual plants or industries, and not over a period of one year, but from the standpoint of the entire national economy and over a period of, say, ten or fifteen years, then the temporary and unstable profitableness of some plants or industries is beneath all comparison with that higher form of stable and permanent profitableness which we get from the operation of the law of balanced development of the national economy and from economic planning, which save us from periodical economic crises disruptive to the national economy and causing tremendous material damage to society, and which ensure a continuous and high rate of expansion of our national economy.④ Stalin's theory of advanced socialist profits tells us that in a socialist society, we should examine not only individual micro interests but also overall

---

① V. I. Lenin, *Lenin Collected Works Vol. 29*, Moscow: Progress Publishers, 1972, p. 114.
② V. I. Lenin, *Remarks on Bukharin's "Economics of the Transformation Period,"* Beijing: People's Publishing House, 1958, pp. 41-42.
③ *Lenin Collected Works Vol. 42*, Moscow: Progress Publishers, p. 468.
④ Joseph Stalin, *Economic Problems of Socialism in the U.S.S.R.*, Beijing: People's Publishing House, 1971, p. 4.

macro interests, not only short-term interests but also long-term interests.

III. Contribution of Chinese Communists to Marxist Theory of Economic Interests

In the process of leading China's socialist construction and reform, the Chinese Communists, guided by the Marxist theory of relations of economic interests while also absorbing useful elements of western theories of economic interest relations and combined with China's socialist reality, greatly enriched and developed the Marxist theory of economic interests.

1. Mao Zedong's thoughts on economic interests

Mao Zedong was a great Marxist. In his many works, especially "On the Ten Major Relationships" and "On the Correct Handling of Contradictions among the People," Mao Zedong's thoughts on economic interests made great contributions to the theory of economic interests.

(1) Economic benefits must be created by hard work. In "On the Correct Handling of Contradictions among the People," Mao Zedong pointed out, "We must help all our young people to understand that ours is still a very poor country, that we cannot change this situation radically in a short time, and that only through the united efforts by our younger generation and all our people, working with their own hands, can China be made strong and prosperous within a period of several decades. The establishment of our socialist system has opened the road leading to the ideal society of the future, but to translate this ideal into reality needs hard work. Some of our young people think that everything ought to be perfect once a socialist society is established and that they should be able to enjoy a happy life ready-made, without working for it. This is unrealistic."[1]

(2) We should care for the actual interests of the masses. Mao Zedong pointed out, "We have always advocated plain living and hard work and opposed putting personal material interests above everything else. At the same

---

[1] Mao Zedong, *Collected Works of Mao Zedong Vol. 7*, Beijing: People's Publishing House, 1999, p. 226.

time we have always advocated concern for the livelihood of the masses and opposed bureaucracy, which is callous to their well-being."①

(3) We should achieve the overall consideration and proper arrangement of various economic interests. Mao Zedong put forward an important thought in dealing with contradictions among the people in socialist society—that is, overall consideration and appropriate arrangement, which also applies to the relationship among economic interests. In dealing with the relationship between the central government and the local government, he said, "if we are to promote socialist construction, we must bring the initiative of the local authorities into play. If we are to strengthen the central authorities, we must attend to the interests of the localities."② In dealing with the relationship between the state, cooperatives and peasants, he said, "Our policies towards the peasants differ from those of the Soviet Union and take into account the interests of both the state and the peasants. ... Similarly, the relationship between the co-operative and the peasants should be well handled. What proportion of the earnings of a co-operative should go to the state, to the co-operative and to the peasants respectively and in what form should be determined properly."③ On the issue of distribution, "we must take account of the interests of the state, the collective and the individual."④ "In short, consideration must be given to both sides, not to just one, whether they are the state and the factory, the state and the worker, the factory and the worker, the state and the co-operative, the state and the peasant, or the co-operative and the peasant."⑤

(4) The internal relationship of economic interests within socialism is a contradiction among the people. In "On the Correct Handling of Contradictions

---

① *Collected Works of Mao Zedong Vol. 7*, p. 28.
② Ibid, p. 31.
③ Ibid, p. 30.
④ *Collected Works of Mao Zedong Vol. 7*, p. 31.
⑤ Ibid, p. 30.

among the People," Mao Zedong pointed out, "Our People's Government is one that genuinely represents the people's interests, it is a government that serves the people. Nevertheless, there are still certain contradictions between the government and the people. ... All these are also contradictions among the people. Generally speaking, the people's basic identity of interests underlies the contradictions among the people."①

2. Deng Xiaoping's theory on economic interests

Deng Xiaoping was a great contemporary Marxist. Deng Xiaoping's economic theory is the inheritance and development of Marxism and Mao Zedong Thought and is an important result of summarizing the positive and negative experiences of socialist construction. Deng Xiaoping's theory about economic interests is an important part of Deng Xiaoping's economic theory.

(1) The theory of people's interests being fundamental. Comrade Jiang Zemin said in his report to the 15th National Congress of the Communist Party of China that Deng Xiaoping "dedicated his entire life to the Chinese people, and made their interests the starting point and objective in everything he did."② All for the fundamental interests of the people, which is the main theme of Deng Xiaoping's theory and practice, constitutes Deng Xiaoping's major contribution to the theory of economic interests.

Deng Xiaoping believed that the socialist revolution is for the interests of the people. The interests of the people determine the victory of the revolution. Therefore, the interests of the people are fundamental to the socialist revolution. As early as during the War of Resistance Against Japanese Aggression, he pointed out, "experience has shown that we are bound to fail if we resort to oversimplified and rigid work methods in enemy-occupied and guerrilla areas and that we must consider the local circumstances, do everything to protect the people's interests, and put forward appropriate methods for the

---

① *Collected Works of Mao Zedong Vol. 7*, p. 205.
② Jiang Zemin, *Selected Works of Jiang Zemin Vol. II*, Beijing: Foreign Languages Press, 2012, p. 11.

struggle against the enemy, if we want to win the support of the people and achieve victory. In particular, experience has shown that leaders who care about the people's problems and help them find ways to combat the enemy and protect their interests will enjoy popular support."① During the War of Liberation, he also pointed out that we should never learn from Han Xin. In dealing with the issue of life and death, he noted, "We are not cowards. We have only one choice between life and death. We must fight for the people and force the enemy to jump into the Yellow River."②

Deng Xiaoping believed that socialist construction and reform are also for the interests of the people. The interests of the people determine the fate of constructions and reforms. Therefore, interests of the people are fundamental to socialist modernization and reform. In 1979, at the Party's theory-discussing meeting on theoretical work, he pointed out that "at the present time, socialist modernization is of supreme political importance for us, because it represents the most fundamental interest of our people."③ In 1980, in "On the Reform of the System of Party and State Leadership," he pointed out, "We have before us the extremely arduous and complex task of socialist modernization. While many old problems still remain to be solved, many new ones are emerging. Only by consistently relying on the masses, maintaining close ties with them, listening to what they have to say, understanding their feelings and always representing their interests can the Party become a powerful force capable of smoothly accomplishing its tasks."④

(2) The theory of common prosperity. Common prosperity is the ideal state that the Chinese people have been striving for for thousands of years. As the embodiment of the fundamental economic interest relations of the people, this ideal also constitutes an important part of Deng Xiaoping's theory of building

---

① Deng Xiaoping, *Selected Works of Deng Xiaoping Vol. I*, Beijing: Foreign Languages Press, 1995, p. 51.
② Deng Rong. *My Father Deng Xiaoping — The War Years*. Beijing: Foreign Languages Press, 2008, p. 447.
③ Deng Xiaoping, *Selected Works of Deng Xiaoping Vol. II*, Beijing: Foreign Languages Press, 1995, p. 172.
④ Ibid, p. 340.

socialism with Chinese characteristics.

Deng Xiaoping believed that common prosperity is one of the essential characteristics of socialism. In his south tour talks in 1992, Deng Xiaoping not only discussed the important theoretical topic of the relationship among planning, market, and socialism but also clearly put forward that "[t]he essence of socialism is liberation and development of the productive forces, elimination of exploitation and polarization, and the ultimate achievement of prosperity for all."① In this important theoretical proposition, he placed common prosperity at such a high level that it is not only the essential feature of socialism but also the ultimate goal of a socialist society. Common prosperity is the fundamental characteristic of a socialist society that is different from all other exploitative societies. "[P]redominance of public ownership and common prosperity are the two fundamental socialist principles that we must adhere to."②

Deng Xiaoping's idea of common prosperity first came into being in 1978. At that time, his specific idea was put forward as the following: "In economic policy, I think we should allow some regions and enterprises and some workers and peasants to earn more and enjoy more benefits sooner than others, in accordance with their hard work and greater contributions to society. If the standard of living of some people is raised first, this will inevitably be an impressive example to their 'neighbours', and people in other regions and units will want to learn from them. This will help the whole national economy to advance wave upon wave and help the people of all our nationalities to become prosperous in a comparatively short period." ③ He not only put forward the goal of common prosperity but also clearly put forward the specific forms, methods, and steps to achieve this goal, which clearly had great guiding significance by providing the aim and methods of the later economic system reform.

---

① Deng Xiaoping, *Selected Works of Deng Xiaoping Vol. III*, Beijing: Foreign Languages Press, 1994, p. 361.
② Ibid, p. 117.
③ *Selected Works of Deng Xiaoping Vol. II*, p. 161.

In the gradual process of economic system reform, Deng Xiaoping's thoughts on common prosperity have gradually deepened with the deepening of practice. Shortly after the reform began, there appeared a trend of thought denying socialism in the society. Deng Xiaoping realized that the political guarantee of common prosperity must be emphasized and the socialist road must be adhered to. "Capitalism can only enrich less than 10 percent of the Chinese population; it can never enrich the remaining more than 90 per cent. But if we adhere to socialism and apply the principle of distribution to each according to his work, there will not be excessive disparities in wealth."① Therefore, afterwards, he repeatedly stressed the truth that "[o]nly socialism can bind the people together, help them overcome their difficulties, prevent polarization of wealth and bring about common prosperity."②

With the gradual advancement of economic system reform and economic development, the policy of common prosperity gradually exerted its power. Some people got rich first through legal means. Then new problems arose in economic life, mainly manifested as the widening income gap causing unstable factors. Ideologically, people also had doubts about "polarization." In order to safeguard the overall situation and ensure the smooth progress of the reform, Deng Xiaoping clearly pointed out, "The aim of socialism is to make all our people prosperous, not to create polarization. If our policies led to polarization, it would mean that we had failed; if a new bourgeoisie emerged, it would mean that we had strayed from the right path."③

So, how should we view the sensitive fact that the income gap is widening? As he pointed out, in encouraging some regions to become prosperous first, we intend only that "they should inspire others to follow their example and that all of them should help economically backward regions to develop." The same holds

---

① *Selected Works of Deng Xiaoping Vol. III*, p. 73.
② Ibid, p. 344.
③ Ibid, p. 116.

true for encouraging some individuals to become prosperous first.① In response to the specific phenomenon of the widening income gap, he proposed to levy income tax and encourage individuals to develop education and road construction. However, he also pointed out that we were still in the primary stage of socialism and that the fundamental task was to develop the productive forces, which should not be subject to too many restrictions. "We keep to the socialist road in order to attain the ultimate goal of common prosperity, but it is impossible for all regions to develop at the same pace." He firmly believed that as long as we stick to the socialist road, there would be no polarization. He observed, "The living standards of the people, with a few exceptions, have improved to varying degrees. Naturally, some negative phenomena are bound to appear in the process of reform. As long as we face them squarely and take firm steps to deal with them, it will not be difficult to solve these problems."② He believed that various means must be taken to develop the productive forces at the time, and to develop the productive forces, we must adhere to the road of reform. "China has no alternative but to follow this road. It is the only road to prosperity."③

The idea of common prosperity is of great theoretical value and practical significance. First, the development of human society is essentially the development of material living conditions. Socialism, as a new stage in the development of human history, cannot be based on poverty. Using all means to develop productive forces, to accumulate rich social wealth, to provide more economic benefits to the people as much as possible, and to expand the range of material products that can be distributed and consumed by the people is the prerequisite for common prosperity. Second, common prosperity is the fundamental goal of socialism as well as the essential feature and target of a

---

① *Selected Works of Deng Xiaoping Vol. III*, p. 116.
② Ibid, p. 145.
③ Ibid, p. 152.

socialist society. The concept of common prosperity is strictly scientific, pointing out not only the goal but also the way to achieve it and not only the content but also the form. Third, Deng Xiaoping pointed out the concrete steps to realize common prosperity. On the one hand, it is a process to provide more economic benefits to the people. Some regions and some individuals getting prosperous first is the first step to achieve common prosperity, and the purpose is to achieve common prosperity faster. On the other hand, the regions and individuals that become rich first have the obligation to help economically backward regions and individuals. This is the fundamental way to avoid polarization and the emergence of the bourgeoisie.

(3) The theory of unity of opposites. Under the condition of socialist market economy, subjects of economic interests are diversified, and there are complex relations of economic interests. These economic interests are both unified and opposite and must be properly handled in accordance with the correct principles. First, the various economic interests under the socialist system are unified. Deng Xiaoping pointed out that "in the final analysis, under the socialist system there is a unity of personal interests and collective interests, of the interests of the part and those of the whole, and of immediate and long-term interests."[1] This unity is based on the socialist system and the socialist public ownership of the means of production.

Second, the various economic interests under the socialist system are also opposing to each other in some aspects, and conflicts may occur. Deng Xiaoping believed that it is necessary to recognize and respect individual economic interests. He said, "As far as the relatively small number of advanced people is concerned, it won't matter too much if we neglect the principle of more pay for more work and fail to stress individual material benefits. But when it comes to the masses, that approach can only be used for a short time—it won't work in the long run. ... revolution takes place on the basis of the need for material

---

[1] *Selected Works of Deng Xiaoping Vol. II*, p. 183.

benefit. It would be idealism to emphasize the spirit of sacrifice to the neglect of material benefit."① Idealism in practice is a stumbling block to the development of productive forces. In response to a foreign reporter's question on whether communists also recognize personal interests, Deng Xiaoping answered in the affirmative and pointed out, "At the higher stage of communism, when the productive forces will be greatly developed and the principle 'from each according to his ability, to each according to his needs' will be practised, personal interests will be acknowledged still more and more personal needs will be satisfied."② However, he also made it clear that "we should guard against unthinking action, and particularly against the spontaneous and destructive tendency to seek gains for oneself or one's unit at the expense of the state and the people."③

How should we correctly handle the contradictions between various economic interests under the socialist system? Deng Xiaoping pointed out, "Under this system, personal interests must be subordinated to collective ones, the interests of the part to those of the whole, and immediate to long-term interests. In other words, limited interests must be subordinated to overall interests, and minor interests to major ones. Our advocacy and practice of these principles in no way means that we can ignore personal, local or immediate interests. ... We must adjust the relations between these various types of interests in accordance with the principle of taking them all into proper consideration. Were we to do the opposite and pursue personal, local or immediate interests at the expense of the others, both sets of interests would inevitably suffer."④ Deng Xiaoping also put forward some preventive measures. For example, he said, "We must teach Party members and the masses to give top priority to the overall

---

① *Selected Works of Deng Xiaoping Vol. II*, pp. 155–156.
② Ibid, p. 348.
③ Ibid, p. 358.
④ Ibid, p. 183.

situation and the overall interests of the Party and the state."① Deng Xiaoping said, "By upholding the principle 'to each according to his work' and by recognizing material interests we intend to increase the material well-being of the entire people. Everyone is bound to have material interests, but this in no sense means that we encourage people to work solely for their personal material interests without regard for the interests of the state, the collective and other people, or that we encourage people to put money above all else. ... We have maintained all along that in a socialist society there is a basic community of interests between the state, the collective and the individual. If they clash, it is the individual interests which should be subordinated to those of the state and the collective. Where necessary, all people with a high level of revolutionary consciousness should sacrifice their personal interests for those of the state, the collective and the people."②

When dealing with various economic interests under the socialist system, Deng Xiaoping stressed the importance of national interests and collective interests while also highly respecting personal interests. This is not only of great theoretical significance but also of great practical significance. In order to implement socialist market economy, we must not only ensure the independence of all stakeholders in decision-making, continuously improve the people's living standards and meet the people's growing material and cultural needs, but also make great efforts to safeguard national interests and collective interests and prevent the loss of state-owned assets and collective assets. In particular, we should take practical measures against misappropriation of state property.

(4) The theory of equality and mutual benefit. The socialist modernization must adhere to the principle of independence and self-reliance. However, independence and self-reliance are not the same as self-seclusion. Opening to the outside world is an objective requirement of China's socialist modernization.

---

① *Selected Works of Deng Xiaoping Vol. II*, p. 162.
② Ibid, pp. 335-336.

Opening to the outside world involves relationships between our country and foreign countries, which are essentially relationships between our own interests and foreign interests. Deng Xiaoping believed that equality and mutual benefit are essential in international exchange. At the opening ceremony of the 12th CPC National Congress in 1982, he proposed increasing "our exchanges with foreign countries on the basis of equality and mutual benefit."[①]

Deng Xiaoping believed that national interests should be taken into consideration first in foreign exchanges on the basis of equality and mutual benefit. He pointed out that "while the Chinese people value their friendship and cooperation with other countries and other peoples, they value even more their hard-won independence and sovereign rights. No foreign country should expect China to be at its vassal or to accept anything that is damaging to China's own interests. ... We, the Chinese people, have our national self-respect and pride. We deem it the highest honour to love our socialist motherland and contribute our all to her socialist construction. We deem it the deepest disgrace to impair her interests, dignity or honor."[②]

Deng Xiaoping believed that when opening to the outside world, we should also respect the interests of foreign countries. In 1989, he told Prime Minister Chatichai Choonhavan of Thailand, "China will safeguard its own interests, sovereignty and territorial integrity. It also maintains that a socialist country should not infringe upon other countries' interests, sovereignty or territory."[③] In the same year, when talking about international relations with former President Richard Nixon of the United States, he said that it is important for each country to "proceed from its own long-term strategic interests, and at the same time respect the interests of the other. Each country, whether it is big or small, strong or weak, should respect others as equals."[④]

[①] *Selected Works of Deng Xiaoping Vol. III*, p. 15.
[②] Ibid, pp. 14–15.
[③] Ibid, p. 318.
[④] Ibid, p. 320.

Deng Xiaoping believed that while opening to the outside world is beneficial to foreign businessmen, it is more beneficial to China. Therefore, we should gather our courage to open to the outside world. Opening to the outside world and introducing foreign capital, advanced technology, and management experience would definitely bring profits to foreign investors. "No one would come here and invest unless he got a return on his investment."① Excess capital and narrow market are the main problems restricting the development of developed capitalist countries. They have to seek outlets for their capital and expand their trade and markets.② China's low cost of labor, raw materials, and land use, coupled with its tax incentives and huge market, can bring higher profit margins to foreign investors. This is the fundamental reason that China attracts foreign capital. China, on the other hand, has benefited more from it. Deng Xiaoping noted that "we shall take more than half of the earnings of joint ventures," and he reassured the people, "So, don't be afraid. It is the country and the people who will benefit most from them, not the capitalists."③ When a foreign-funded enterprise is set up, "workers get wages and the state collects taxes, and part of the income of the joint and cooperative ventures goes to the socialist sector. An even more important aspect of all these ventures is that from them we can learn managerial skills and advanced technology that will help us develop our socialist economy."④ In Deng Xiaoping's south tour talks, he added that "we can get information from them that will help us open more markets." Therefore, "subject to the constraints of China's overall political and economic conditions, foreign-funded enterprises are useful supplements to the socialist economy, and in the final analysis they are good for socialism."⑤ In opening to the outside world, "[t]he Council should make its determination to open wider

---

① *Selected Works of Deng Xiaoping Vol. III*, p. 173.
② Ibid, p. 111.
③ Ibid, p. 97.
④ Ibid, p. 142.
⑤ Ibid, p. 361.

known abroad; it has to have the courage to do that. In general, it should allow enterprises to make less profits and should not be afraid of losses. It should be prepared to do anything as long as it is in our long-term interest."①

Deng Xiaoping strongly opposed the hegemonic interests of developed countries in bullying the weak. In response to the sanctions imposed on China by western countries after June 1989, he noted, "Actually, national sovereignty is far more important than human rights, but they often infringe upon the sovereignty of poor, weak countries of the Third World. Their talk about human rights, freedom and democracy is only designed to safeguard the interests of the strong, rich countries, which take advantage of their strength to bully weak countries, and which pursue hegemony and practice power politics."②

Section Ⅲ   Discussion on Common Interests in Marxist Classics

Marx studied the conditions for the realization of community and common interests with the scientific standpoint, viewpoint and method. Marx's research did not ignore the analysis of personal interests and put forward that personal interests are always influenced by their class, thus illustrating the essence of community and common interests.

Ⅰ. Essence of Community and Essence of Common Interests

What is the essence of a community? This is the key to correctly understanding common interests. Because of their concern for this issue, Marx and Engels divided communities into "illusory communities" and "real communities." What kind of communities are "real communities" and what kind

---

① *Selected Works of Deng Xiaoping Vol. III*, p. 303.
② Ibid, p. 334.

of communities are "illusory communities"? Marx and Engels believed that in an illusory community, everyone is only pursuing their own special interests, which they think are incompatible with the common interests and thus consider to be "alien" and "independent." Not only that, these special interests (personal interests) have actually always been opposed to the common interests and the illusory common interests. The actual conflicts among these special interests make it necessary for illusory "universal" interests appearing in a national manner to actually interfere with and restrict special interests. Therefore, Marx and Engels scientifically explained the essence of a community.

First, a community is made up of individuals with freedom and independence. Not all organizations and groups are communities. The meaning of a community is different from that of a group or a collective. In groups or collectives, individuals have neither independence nor freedom.

According to Marx's division of social states, human society experiences three social states—"human dependence," "material dependence," and "human independence." The community states under these three social states are different. A mass society characterized by "human dependence" is the initial state of individual-society relationship. Later, with the development of productivity and the commodity economy, individuals gained independence. Only under such conditions can a community consisting of independent individuals be formed. Therefore, if the replacement of "human dependence" by "human independence" is a great progress of the human society, then accompanying this progress is the emergence of "communities." However, "communities" can be categorized as "illusory communities" or "real communities." In other words, "communities" in the human society also went through a process of continuous development.①

What is a "community of free individuals"? Marx and Engels made this

---

① Zhu Yiting, et al, *Moral Value Orientation in Contemporary China*, Shanghai: East China Normal University Press, 1994, p. 153.

statement in Manifesto of the Communist Party: "In place of the old bourgeois society, with its classes and class antagonisms, we shall have an association, in which the free development of each is the condition for the free development of all."① Thus, the individual freedom to be realized in a communist society is not the freedom of some people but the freedom of each and every person in the social community, and the free development of each person is not a hindrance to the free development of others but a condition for the free development for all. Thus, the realization of this principle is "the genuine resolution of the conflict ... between man and man."②

Second, Marx and Engels revealed the class nature of communities. Marx and Engels divided communities into communities of the proletariat and communities of other classes. In a proletarian community, "Only within the community has each individual the means of cultivating his gifts in all directions; hence personal freedom becomes possible only within the community."③ In other words, the relationship between a proletarian community and an individual is not antagonistic. Individual interests can only be realized in a community. Communities are the means to develop individuals and safeguard the interests of each member.

It is different in the classes before the proletariat. "In the previous substitutes for the community, in the state, etc., personal freedom has existed only for the individuals who developed under the conditions of the ruling class, and only insofar as they were individuals of this class."④ Marx and Engels further pointed out, "The illusory community in which individuals have up till now combined always took on an independent existence in relation to them, and since it was the combination of one class over against another, it was at the same time for the oppressed class not only a

---

① Karl Marx and Frederick Engels, *Marx & Engels Collected Works Vol. 06: Marx and Engels: 1845 - 1848*, London: Lawrence & Wishart, 1976, Electric Book, 2010, p. 506.
② *Marx & Engels Collected Works Vol. 03*, p. 296.
③ *Marx & Engels Collected Works Vol. 05*, p. 78.
④ Ibid.

completely illusory community, but a new fetter as well."①

According to the views of Marx and Engels, in a class society, the national interests and class interests represented by the ruling class are a kind of "illusory" common interests that run counter to the interests of most people. Marx and Engels pointed out, "The social power ... appears to these individuals, since their co-operation is not voluntary but has come about naturally, not as their own united power, but as an alien force existing outside them, of the origin and goal of which they are ignorant, which they thus are no longer able to control."② This is actually a kind of externalization and alienation. To eliminate this alienation requires revolution, and only communism can make common interests universally meaningful. Marx and Engels pointed out, "The class making a revolution comes forward from the very start, if only because it is opposed to a class, not as a class but as the representative of the whole of society, as the whole mass of society confronting the one ruling class."③

II. Solving Contradiction between Personal Interests and Common Interests

Classical writers of Marxism use the cohesion effect of class consciousness and ideology to solve the contradiction between personal interests and collective interests. Marx pointed out, "In its struggle against the collective power of the propertied classes, the working class cannot act as a class except by constituting itself into a political party, distinct from, and opposed to, all old parties formed by the propertied classes."④ Lenin revealed the importance of class consciousness. "Only when the individual worker realises that he is a member of the entire working class, only when he recognises the fact that his petty day-to-day struggle against individual employers and individual government officials is a struggle against the entire bourgeoisie and the entire government, does his

---

① *Marx & Engels Collected Works Vol. 05*, p. 78.
② Ibid, p. 48.
③ Ibid, p. 60.
④ *Marx & Engels Collected Works Vol. 23*, p. 243.

struggle become a class struggle."① Whether it is organizing itself into an advanced political party or strengthening the cultivation of class consciousness, the aim is to make the proletariat act as a whole class.

Here, Marx and Lenin actually put forward the idea of awakening the subjective consciousness of members of the community and making them realize the consistency of their own interests and the common interests of their own class through education and training so that they would take joint actions consciously. However, there must be at least two conditions: first, members of the community have a high degree of identification with the community—that is, they trust and are attracted by the community ideologically; second, there must be genuine common interests as the basis.

Lenin spoke directly of the term "common interests." When discussing the "degree" of the relationship between personal interests and common interests, he believed that interest relations are the essence and foundation of all problems. Among them, the relationship between common interests and individual interests—that is, the interest relationship between the state or society and individual members of society—is a relationship of interdependence and mutual struggle. An important idea in Lenin's new economic policy is to realize the transformation and harmony of common interests and personal interests and pursue their accordance while recognizing the rivalry and difference between the two. Lenin pointed out, "The difficulty lies in creating personal incentive. We must also give every specialist an incentive to develop our industry."② The "difficulty" Lenin mentions here refers to how to organically combine people's concern for personal interests and their concern for common production to realize the common development of personal interests and common interests. In Soviet Russia, which was established after the October Revolution, the relationship between personal interests and

---

① V. I. Lenin, *Lenin Collected Works Vol. 4*, Moscow: Progress Publishers, 1964, pp. 215-216.
② V. I. Lenin, *Lenin Collected Works Vol. 33*, Moscow: Progress Publishers, 1965, p. 69.

common interests actually reflected the interest relationship among private capitalism, small-scale peasant economy, and socialist economy. Through arduous exploration, Lenin found a way to solve the difficult problem of how to achieve the harmony between personal interests and common interests and guide, regulate, and supervise personal interests so as to make them subordinate to common interests in socialism. In "On Cooperation," he said, "we have now found that degree of combination of private interest, of private commercial interest, with state supervision and control of this interest, that degree of its subordination to the common interests which was formerly the stumbling-block for very many socialists."① The "degree" proposed by Lenin is to guide small-scale production to the track of serving socialist construction through cooperatives based on commodity economy. At the same time, Lenin proposed to organically combine personal interests with common interests on the premise that the state regulates the circulation of commerce and money and to make personal interests subordinate to common interests to be conducive to the guidance and supervision of the individual interests by the state.

Section Ⅳ Chinese Communists' Thoughts on Common Interests

Chinese Communists' thoughts on common interests include thoughts on common interests in domestic development and thoughts on common interests in international economics and politics.

I. Chinese Communists' Thoughts on Common Interests in Domestic Development

Chinese Communists' thoughts on common interests in domestic development is

---

① *Lenin Collected Works Vol. 33*, p. 468.

embodied in the theory of "common prosperity." In the history of the development of Marxism, Mao Zedong explicitly expounded the issue of common prosperity for the first time. On the basis of inheriting Mao Zedong's correct thoughts on common prosperity, Deng Xiaoping systematically expounded the scientific approach to common prosperity and found a realistic way to realize common prosperity. For the first time, Deng proposed to allow and encourage some regions and some people to get prosperous first, gradually driving all the people and the whole country towards common prosperity, and took it as a major policy to realize the three-step development strategy of China's modernization. At the turn of the century, according to Deng Xiaoping's proposition of the "three-step" and "two-overall-situation" strategies. The third generation of the central collective leadership, with Comrade Jiang Zemin as its core, made the strategic decision of large-scale development of western China, inheriting, practicing, and innovating Deng Xiaoping's great idea of common prosperity. In the new era, Comrade Xi Jinping has put forward five concepts for development including "inclusive development."

1. Mao Zedong's thought of common prosperity and strategy of balanced regional development of common prosperity

Mao Zedong was extremely concerned about how to make the people of the whole country prosperous. In 1955, he explicitly put forward the concept of "common prosperity" for the first time and expounded the issue of common prosperity in China. Mao Zedong pointed out, "all the rural people will become increasingly well off together. We maintain that this is the only way to consolidate the worker-peasant alliance."[1] He proposed, "we have to lead the peasants onto the road of socialism, enabling them to attain collective prosperity; not only the poor peasants but all of them must prosper and, what is

---

[1] Mao Zedong, *Collected Works of Mao Zedong Vol. 6*, Beijing: People's Publishing House, 1999, p. 437.

more, they must become far better off than the present-day well-to-do peasants."[1] In his view, we would not get prosperous as an agricultural country, but now we have such a system and such a plan that we can grow more prosperous and stronger year by year. This prosperity is common prosperity, and this strength is common strength, which we all share. Thus, Mao Zedong's thought of common prosperity includes the following contents. First, the socialist system aims at the common prosperity of all people, and the achievement of common prosperity must be premised on socialism. Second, common prosperity is a gradual process. Third, common prosperity must be based on industrialization. Without national industrialization, there would be no common prosperity.

In the early days after the founding of the People's Republic of China, China's regional economic development faced a grim situation. Due to historical reasons, 70% of China's modern light industry and heavy industry are located in the coastal regions, with the other 30% in the interior. Noticing this, the Party and the state are committed to changing this unreasonable situation. Guided by the idea of reasonable and balanced development of the coastal regions and the interior, the Party and the state started to implement the "strategy of balanced development" of the coastal regions and the interior, which is essentially the strategy of focusing on the development of the interior (mainly the western regions), with the aim of narrowing the gap between the interior and the coastal regions. In "On the Ten Major Relationships," Mao Zedong was the first to propose the use and promotion of industry in the coastal regions to promote the development of industry in the interior and to make the distribution of productive forces more reasonable. Moreover, when "the international situation was quite tense" back then, Mao Zedong paid more attention to the construction of the interior and pointed out the following: "The coastal industrial base must be put to full use, but to even out the distribution of

---

[1] *A Chronicle of Mao Zedong (1949-1976) Vol. 2*, Central Party Literature Press, 2013, p. 449.

industry as it develops we must strive to promote industry in the interior."[1]

Therefore, during the period of the First Five-Year Plan, the Party and the state began to develop the western regions of China in a planned and step-by-step way. During this period, four-fifths of the 156 key projects nationally were in the western regions; during the period of the Second Five-Year Plan, the spatial distribution of productive forces was further tilted to the interior. However, regarding the tendency to neglect the original industries that once appeared, it was emphasized that both the development of the interior and the coastal areas should be taken into consideration; during the periods of the Third Five-Year Plan and the Fourth Five-Year Plan, the Third-Front Construction upsurge began, placing the focus of economic development entirely on the central and western regions; from the period of the Fifth Five-Year Plan to 1978, the strategy of balanced regional development has not changed. Therefore, for a relatively long period of time, the basic pattern of China's regional economy has been the promotion of balanced development of the coastal regions and the interior. The implementation of the strategy of balanced development lasted for about 30 years, having changed the extremely unreasonable spatial distribution of productive forces, having laid the material foundation for industrialization in the western regions of China, having maintained the social and political stability in the border areas, and having safeguarded ethnic solidarity and national unity. However, there are also some defects in this strategic layout: this strategy does not seek balanced development of regional economy based on the objective law of productivity development. The balanced allocation of productivity is highly subjective and one-sided, and what it pursues is actually a low-level balance; too much emphasis is placed on balanced regional development and social equity, and the principle of efficiency in economic development and regional productivity distribution is ignored, which leads to the loss of both national economic efficiency and social equity; the Third-Front Construction was particularly one-sided in highlighting the need for combat readiness, and the

---

[1] *Collected Works of Mao Zedong Vol. 7*, p. 25.

placement of many newly-built enterprises violate the principle of economies of scale and have extremely low economic efficiency; the strategy leads to the abnormal phenomenon of national average backwardness and common poverty, as it ignores China's basic national conditions while aiming to push forward the east and the west as a whole and achieve the same development level once and for all..

2. Deng Xiaoping's thought of common prosperity and strategy of unbalanced regional development of common prosperity

Deng Xiaoping summed up the experience and lessons in the spatial distribution of regional economic development since the founding of the People's Republic of China and rectified Mao Zedong's deviation on the issue of common prosperity. Deng Xiaoping put forward the idea of unbalanced development of regional economy—that is, allow some regions and some people to get prosperous sooner, and then achieve common prosperity through the inspiring effect of the regions and people who get prosperous first. This scientific thought has extremely rich connotations.

(1) Common prosperity is the essential characteristic of socialism that sets it apart from capitalism and all other exploitation systems. It is the fundamental principle and ultimate goal of socialism. "The greatest superiority of socialism is that it enables all the people to prosper, and common prosperity is the essence of socialism."[1] As Deng Xiaoping stressed, "To take the road to socialism is to realize common prosperity step by step." "The socialist system must and can avoid polarization."[2]

(2) Common prosperity is the long-term goal of socialism. Deng Xiaoping's "three-step" development strategy provides China with the short-term planning and long-term goals for achieving common prosperity. Now, the third step has been started—that is, by the mid-21st century, China's economy is expected to reach the level of a moderately developed country, further improving people's

---

[1] *Selected Works of Deng Xiaoping Vol. III*, p. 351.
[2] Ibid, p. 362.

well-being and basically realizing the goal of common prosperity of socialism.

(3) Common prosperity includes material and spiritual prosperity. Common prosperity is based on material common prosperity. However, if there is only prosperity in people's material lives but not in their spiritual lives, such prosperity is contrary to modern civilization. A high level of both material civilization and spiritual civilization is not only the important content of China's modernization but also the main content of China's common prosperity.

(4) The effective way to realize common prosperity is to allow and encourage some regions and some people to get prosperous sooner and finally realize common prosperity through the inspiring effect of the regions and people who get prosperous first. As Deng Xiaoping pointed out, "In economic policy, I think we should allow some regions and enterprises and some workers and peasants to earn more and enjoy more benefits sooner than others, in accordance with their hard work and greater contributions to society. If the standard of living of some people is raised first, this will inevitably be an impressive example to their 'neighbours', and people in other regions and units will want to learn from them."① Deng Xiaoping had consistently maintained that "some people and some regions should be allowed to prosper before others, always with the goal of common prosperity. If a few regions develop a little faster, they will spur the others to catch up. This is a shortcut we can take to speed up development and attain common prosperity."② "We keep to the socialist road in order to attain the ultimate goal of common prosperity, but it is impossible for all regions to develop at the same pace."③

Thus, Deng Xiaoping's series of theories and policies on the process from "partial prosperity" to the ultimate realization of common prosperity are clear. First, Deng Xiaoping's theories and policies have clearly drawn a strict line from egalitarianism both in degree and in process. Deng's proposed common

---

① *Selected Works of Deng Xiaoping Vol. II*, p. 161.
② *Selected Works of Deng Xiaoping Vol. III*, p. 169.
③ Ibid, p. 158.

prosperity is not equal prosperity, not the kind of prosperity where everyone steps forward in the same pace and reaches the destination at the same time, but the kind of prosperity achieved in sequences, with different paces, at different times, in different orders, and in different degrees. Second, Deng Xiaoping correctly handled the relationship of "prosper sooner," "prosper later," and "prosper together." According to him, the fundamental purpose of allowing and encouraging some regions and some people to get prosperous sooner is to achieve common prosperity, not to widen the gap in economic development and people's living standards between regions, between urban and rural areas, and between departments, nor is it to lead to polarization; we must admit that people get prosperous at different times and that there are differences in the degree of their prosperity; diligence and law-abiding are the prerequisites for some people to get prosperous first, and we are opposed to making profits and getting prosperous through illegal means; common prosperity should give consideration to fairness and efficiency, widening the income gap in a reasonable way, and focusing on the principle of common prosperity, the state should solve the problem of excessive income disparity through various regulation methods so that people can embark on a virtuous circle where people who are temporarily lagging behind unceasingly catch up with those who have prospered sooner.

On the basis of the theory of common prosperity, Deng Xiaoping put forward the strategic proposition of "two issues of overriding importance" to achieve common prosperity of the coastal regions and the interior and of the eastern regions and the western regions. He pointed out, "The coastal areas, which comprise a vast region with a population of 200 million, should accelerate their opening to the outside world, and we should help them develop rapidly first; afterwards they can promote the development of the interior. The development of the coastal areas is of overriding importance, and the interior provinces should subordinate themselves to it."[1] Compared with the central and

---

[1] *Selected Works of Deng Xiaoping Vol. III*, pp. 271-272.

western regions of the interior, the eastern coastal regions enjoy uniquely advantageous geographical locations and convenient transportation facilities and are relatively well-equipped with equipment, technologies, talents, and information. Thus, the first issue of overriding importance is to accelerate the opening of the eastern coastal regions to the outside world and let them take the lead in development.

At the beginning of China's reform and opening up, Deng Xiaoping specifically designed and organized the economic development of the eastern coastal regions. In 1979, according to Deng Xiaoping's suggestion, the CPC Central Committee and the State Council officially approved the establishment of four special economic zones, namely Shenzhen, Zhuhai, Shantou, and Xiamen. In 1984, according to Deng Xiaoping's proposal, the central government officially decided to open 14 coastal port cities such as Shanghai and Guangzhou. In 1985, a further three "Coastal Open Economic Regions" were established in the Yangtze River Delta, the Pearl River Delta and the "Xiamen-Zhangzhou-Quanzhou triangle" in Fujian Province. In 1986, the Seventh Five-Year Plan clearly divided the country into three major economic zones, namely the eastern, central, and western regions, and formulated a macro-regional economic development strategy with unbalanced development in tiers of the three major zones. In 1988, it was also decided to establish Hainan Province and implement in Hainan Province a policy more preferential than that implemented in the special economic zones. In the same year, many coastal cities of Liaodong Peninsula, Jiaodong Peninsula, and Bohai Rim were also designated as Coastal Open Economic Regions. The Hainan Special Economic Zone was established in April of 1988 so that a more flexible and open economic policy could be implemented. In the 1990s, the central government made another major strategic decision to develop Pudong in Shanghai and drive the economic development of the Yangtze River Delta and the entire Yangtze River Basin region, which marked the beginning of the development strategy of China's regional economy shifting from the coastal regions to the regions along Yangtze

River. At the same time, the state issued a series of policies to promote and speed up the opening up of the eastern coastal areas, which led to a new round of upsurge in opening to the outside world and a new trend of prospering sooner and prospering quickly in the eastern coastal areas. In 1992, the CPC Central Committee proposed to implement an all-round opening up strategy of "Seashore, Border-shore, Route-shore, and River-shore" opening-up, and approved 28 cities and 8 regions along the Yangtze River as well as 13 border cities in the northeast, southwest, and northwest regions to be opened to the outside world. All the provincial capitals in the interior were opened to the outside world, thus strengthening the horizontal connections between the interior and the coastal regions in opening to the outside world. Thus, a tiered pattern of opening-up and development has been formed with stepped promotion of "special economic zones—coastal open cities—coastal open economic regions—open cities along rivers, routes, and borders—special economic zones in the interior." In the meantime, Deng Xiaoping also attached great importance to the development of the central and western regions. He believed that the development momentum in the eastern region cannot be affected, nor can the gap between the eastern and the western regions be ignored. Thus, this is the second issue of overriding importance: "When the coastal areas have developed to a certain extent, they will be required to give still more help to the interior. Then, the development of the interior provinces will be of overriding importance, and the coastal areas will in turn have to subordinate themselves to it."[1] He has repeatedly discussed the great significance of the development and opening up of the central and western regions from different angles and put forward many important ideas on how to help and support the economic development of the central and western regions. He considered the situation and put forward a timetable for coastal areas to fully help the interior to resolve the development gap. Deng Xiaoping imagined that the right time to solve the problem "might be the end of this

---

[1] *Selected Works of Deng Xiaoping Vol. III*, p. 272.

century, when our people would be living a fairly comfortable life."① He also declared with confidence that country-wide, it was out of question that we would be able to gradually and successfully solve the problem of the wealth gap between the coastal areas and the interior areas.

3. Thought of common prosperity of third generation of central collective leadership and strategy for large-scale development of western China

The strategic proposition of "two issues of overriding importance" provides a scientific guiding principle for the coordinated economic development of the eastern and the western regions. At the turn of the century, under the circumstances that the strategic goal of the second step of China's modernization was about to be realized and that the gap between the eastern and the western regions was widening day by day, the third generation of the Party's central collective leadership with Comrade Jiang Zemin as its core started to consider the shift of the strategic focus of regional economic development from a comprehensive perspective and made the important strategic decision of large-scale development of western China, inheriting, practicing, and innovating Deng Xiaoping's thought of common prosperity. In June 1999, at the symposium on the reform and development of state-owned enterprises in the five provinces and autonomous regions of northwest China, Comrade Jiang Zemin explicitly put forward the concept of "large-scale development of western China" for the first time and explained incisively the great economic, political and social significance of large-scale development of the western regions. He pointed out that gradually narrowing the development gap among various regions in the country, realizing coordinated development of the national economic society, and ultimately achieving the common prosperity of all the people are the requirements of the essence of socialism and a major issue related to China's cross-century development strategy. In view of China's basic national conditions, he believed that it would be unrealistic to achieve synchronous and

---

① *Selected Works of Deng Xiaoping Vol. III*, p. 362.

equal prosperity in a certain time period. He pointed out that it was inevitable that some would become prosperous sooner and some would prosper later. Therefore, on the layout of regional development, we must have a comprehensive picture in mind. He also pointed out that accelerating the development of ethnic minority regions and promoting the common prosperity of all ethnic groups are the fundamental guarantee for strengthening ethnic solidarity and maintaining border stability. In 1999, the Decision of the Fourth Plenary Session of the 15th CPC Central Committee clearly stated that the country should implement the strategy for large-scale development of western China. In 2000, at the Third Session of the 9th National People's Congress, Comrade Jiang Zemin once again stressed the great significance of the implementation of the strategy for large-scale development of western China to the promotion of coordinated economic development among regions, the realization of common prosperity, the implementation of the strategic adjustment to the entire economic structure, the promotion of sustained, rapid, and healthy development of the national economy, the promotion of national unity, and the maintenance of stability and the consolidation of border defense. In the meantime, the Party's third generation of the central collective leadership put forward a series of guiding principles and decisions to narrow the regional gaps, develop the western regions, and coordinate the development of regional economies. First, we need to ease and narrow regional disparities and promote the coordinated development of regional economies. Comrade Jiang Zemin put forward the "two-step" policy. The first step was to ease the widening gap between the eastern and the western regions by the end of the 20th century; the second step was to actively move towards narrowing the gap and gradually narrow the gap after the year 2000. Jiang Zemin's report to the 14th CPC National Congress pointed out that we should promote the rational distribution and healthy development of regional economies under the unified guidance of the state and in accordance with the principles of adjusting measures to local conditions, rational division of labor, complementary advantages, and common development. According to the proposal of the CPC Central Committee, the Outline of the Eighth Five-Year Plan took promoting the rational division of labor and coordinated development of regional economies as a guiding principle for future economic development. The Fifth Plenary Session of the 14th CPC Central Committee pointed out that the widening gap in economic development between the eastern and the western regions must be treated seriously and correctly. Deng Xiaoping's idea that we should allow some people and some regions to become prosperous sooner and gradually realize common prosperity should be adopted to unify the understanding within the whole party; narrowing the regional gap should be regarded as an important policy to be adhered to in the long term; achieving common prosperity is the fundamental principle and the essential feature of socialism and must not be shaken; in order to understand and deal with the problem of regional disparity from a historical and dialectical point of view, it is necessary to understand that the unbalanced development of various regions is a long-term historical phenomenon, to attach great importance to the problem and take effective measures to correctly solve the problem of regional disparity, and to understand that it takes a process to solve the problem of regional disparity. The Outline of the Ninth Five-Year Plan formally established it as one of the important guiding principles to be adhered to for a long time to adhering to the coordinated development of regional economies and gradually narrowing the regional gap" as. Jiang Zemin's report to the 15th CPC National Congress proposed to promote the rational distribution and coordinated development of regional economies and gradually narrow the gap in regional development. The Outline of the Tenth Five-Year Plan further emphasized the implementation of the large-scale development of western China and the promotion of coordinated regional development.

In short, after the 14th CPC National Congress, the third generation of the Party's central collective leadership put forward the guiding principles of encouraging some regions and some people to get prosperous first, spurring the others to catch up, linking the eastern regions and the western regions, achieving common prosperity and insisting on coordination, regulating the gap, and unbalanced development. First, regard narrowing the gap as an important long-term policy and a strategic task in reform and development. It is believed that only when the western region develops in a large scale or even develop at a faster speed than the eastern coastal regions can we narrow the gap between the eastern and the western regions and eventually achieve common prosperity. Second, poverty alleviation and development should be regarded as a crucial task in the 21st century. In the 1990s, the third generation of the Party's central collective leadership summed up the experience and lessons in poverty alleviation in the past, began to combine poverty alleviation with development, and increased the intensity of development-oriented poverty alleviation. The state supports the development of the central and western regions through special discount loans for poverty alleviation and financial transfer payments. In addition, the central government has specifically made arrangements on how to adhere to the policy of development-oriented poverty alleviation and the measures to enhance the poverty alleviation development in poverty-stricken areas. Third, to speed up the development of the western regions, we must have new ideas, adapt to the requirements of building a socialist market economic system and the new internal and external opening environment, fully consider the new changes in the demands of the domestic and international markets, and act in accordance with objective economic laws. Fourth, it is believed that not only the eastern regions drive the development of the western regions, but the western regions also play a great role in the development of the eastern regions. New ideas for the linkage and cooperation between the eastern and the western regions have also been put forward.

  Furthermore, the CPC Central Committee has also identified the key areas for the large-scale development of western China: by making use of transportation lines such as the Eurasian Land Bridge, the Yangtze golden waterway, and the southwest China sea-bound waterway, we should give full play to the central cities' aggregation function and radiation function to link key areas of development and extend development from each key area into its surrounding areas, gradually form a cross-administrative economic belt with the characteristics of western China, drive the development of the surrounding areas, and promote the large-scale development of western China in a step-by-step and focused way. Meanwhile, the CPC Central Committee listed infrastructure, ecological environment, characteristic economy and agriculture, science and technology, and education as the key areas of the large-scale development of western China.

4. Xi Jinping's concept of "shared development"

Since the 18th CPC National Congress, the CPC Central Committee with Comrade Xi Jinping as its core has put the people above everything else, insisting that development is for the people, that development depends on the people, and that development achievements are shared by the people, and constantly pushing forward the cause of benefiting the people.

Xi Jinping has always attached great importance to common prosperity. On November 15, 2012, Xi Jinping pointed out in his remarks when members of the 18th Standing Committee of the Political Bureau of the CPC Central Committee met with Chinese and foreign journalists: "Our people have an ardent love for life. They want to have better education, more stable jobs, more income, reliable social security, better medical and health care, improved housing conditions and a beautiful environment. They hope that their children will have sound growth, good jobs and more enjoyable lives. The people's wish for a happy life is our mission. A happy life comes from hard work. Our responsibility is to bring together and lead the whole Party and the people of all ethnic groups to free their minds, carry out reform and opening up, further unfetter and develop the productive forces, solve the people's problems in work and life, and resolutely pursue common prosperity."[①] On December 29 – 30,

---

[①] Xi Jinping, *Xi Jinping: The Governance of China*, Beijing: Foreign Languages Press, 2014, p. 4.

2012, during a visit to the needy in Fuping County, Hebei Province, Xi Jinping pointed out, "It is the essential requirement of socialism to eradicate poverty, improve the people's livelihood and achieve common prosperity."① On March 17, 2013, in his speech at the First Session of the 12th National People's Congress, Xi Jinping pointed out, "All the Chinese who live in our great country in this great age share the opportunity to pursue excellence, realize our dreams, and develop ourselves along with our country."② On October 29, 2013, when Xi Jinping was chairing the 10th group study session of the members of the Political Bureau of the 18th CPC Central Committee, he stressed, "Accelerating housing supply is important for meeting the people's basic need for housing and ensuring that all of them have access to housing. It is a requirement for social fairness and justice as well as an important measure so share the fruits of reform and development."③ From May 25 to May 27, 2015, Xi Jinping stressed during his inspection and survey in Zhejiang that "social construction should take co-construction and sharing as a basic principle and make systematic designs of institutional mechanisms and policies."④

At the Fifth Plenary Session of the 18th CPC Central Committee, Xi Jinping put forward the concepts of "innovation, coordinated, green, open and inclusive" Development. He mentioned that for development for all, we must uphold the principle of development for the people, development by the people and development achievements shared by the people, achieve governance systems that can more effectively give the entire population an increased sense of shared gain, increase development momentum, and unite the people further toward a shared goal of common prosperity.⑤ Sharing means that the fruits of

---

① *Xi Jinping: The Governance of China*, p. 209.
② Ibid, p. 40.
③ Ibid, p. 212.
④ "Xi Jinping stressed during his research in Zhejiang that hard work requires endless efforts and we should seek new path to guide our development," *People's Daily*, May 28, 2015.
⑤ "Communiqué of the Fifth Plenary Session of the 18th CPC Central Committee (Excerpts)," China.org.cn, Nov. 30, 2015.

development should be shared by the broad masses of the people to eliminate the disparity between the rich and the poor and avoid polarization, and the direction and the goal are to realize common prosperity. The five concepts for development put forward by Comrade Xi Jinping, which take sharing as the aim and the standpoint of development, specify the value orientation of development, grasp the law of scientific development, and flow with the trend of development of the times, are important development concepts for making scientific arrangements to achieve the well-being of the people and the long-term stability of the country, which fully embody the essence of socialism and the purposes of the Communist Party.[1]

Shared development focuses on resolving the issue of social fairness and justice. Letting the broad masses of the people share the fruits of reform and development is the essential requirement of socialism, the concentrated embodiment of the superiority of the socialist system, and the important embodiment of the Party's fundamental purpose of serving the people wholeheartedly. Once problems in this regard are resolved, the enthusiasm, initiative, and creativity of all the people to promote development will be fully mobilized, and the country's development will have a steady stream of new impetus. Xi Jinping pointed out the following: "Comprehensively furthering the reform must be the guarantee of building a more equitable and just social environment, addressing breaches of equity and justice, and bringing more of the benefits of development to all the people in a fairer fashion. If we cannot deliver tangible benefits to the people, and create a fairer social environment, and, worse still, if we cause more inequality, then our reform will lose its meaning and cannot be sustained."[2] Our co-construction is co-construction of all people and overall co-construction; our sharing is sharing among all people, and

---

[1] Ren Lixuan, "Adhering to Shared Development: 'Five Concepts for Development' Interpretation No. 5," *People's Daily*, Dec. 24, 2015.

[2] *Xi Jinping: The Governance of China*, p. 108.

comprehensive sharing; co-construction and sharing are both complex issues.①

The CPC Central Committee regards poverty alleviation as the bottom-line task and the symbolic index for building a moderately prosperous society in all respects, and has launched the all-round battle against poverty. To complete the building of a moderately prosperous society in all respects by 2020 and achieve the first centennial goal is a solemn commitment that the Party has made to the people and to the history. To build a moderately prosperous society in all respects, we must ensure that the entire population is well covered. Xi Jinping has pointed out the following multiple times: "Without all the people living moderately prosperous lives, there will be no moderately prosperous society in all respects"; "the measurement for moderate prosperity lies in the rural areas"②; "To build a moderately prosperous society, no ethnic group can be left out." On December 29-30, 2012, Xi Jinping pointed out during a visit to the needy in Fuping County, Hebei Province that "[w]e cannot say we have realized a moderately prosperous society if the rural areas, especially the backward parts of the countryside, are left behind."③

Since the 18th CPC National Congress, China has put forward the targeted approach to alleviating poverty.④ China's battle against poverty and China's traditional virtues of "an able fellow needs the help of three other people" and "people from far and near help those in need" complement each other, mobilizing all social forces to participate in poverty alleviation and carry out work in accordance with the national strategy of targeted poverty alleviation. The state has promulgated relevant preferential policies and measures to enable poor households to receive real preferential subsidies and has continuously and vigorously increased investment in poverty alleviation, thus having greatly improved the infrastructure in poor areas and greatly changed the production

---

① "Implementing Shared Development is a Complex Issue," *People's Daily*, May 14, 2016.
② Xi Jinping, *Xi Jinping: The Governance of China II*, Foreign Languages Press, 2014, p. 4.
③ *Xi Jinping: The Governance of China*, p. 209.
④ "Xi Jinping Offers China's Solution to Poverty Elimination," *Xinhua Daily Telegraph*, Aug. 18, 2017, p. 4.

and living conditions of poor households. Over the past 40 years of reform and opening up, more than 700 million poor people in China's rural areas have been lifted out of poverty. The poverty incidence has dropped from 97.5% in 1978 to 3.1% at the end of 2017, creating a Chinese miracle in the human history of poverty reduction.① U.N. Secretary-General Antonio Guterres spoke highly of China's achievements in "eradicating poverty." China's development has kept hundreds of millions of people away from poverty, and China is committed to completely eliminating extreme poverty in the country by 2020. Therefore, this is China's greatest contribution to global poverty reduction. In addition, China's policy of win-win cooperation and common development towards developing countries such as African countries is another major contribution of China to poverty reduction. Furthermore, Guterres also believed that, on the whole, these two major contributions are important contributions made by China to fulfill its commitments and fulfill the (U.N.) 2030 sustainable development agenda and goals.②

II. Chinese Communists' Thoughts on Common Interests in International Politics and Economy

From Mao Zedong's theory of "three worlds," Deng Xiaoping's idea of "establishment of a new international political and economic order," Jiang Zemin's "new security concept," Hu Jintao's concept of "harmonious world" to Xi Jinping's concept of "a community with a shared future for humanity," Chinese Communists' thoughts on common interests come down in one continuous line and keep pace with the times. In particular, standing at China's new historical starting point and starting from the long-cherished wish of promoting a better world development and China's future strategic orientation of diplomacy, the concept of "a community with a shared future for mankind"

---

① "In Past 40 Years, Poverty Incidence in China Has Dropped From 97.5% to 3.1%," Xinhua News Agency, Dec. 8, 2018.
② "Guterres: China's Elimination of Extreme Poverty by 2020 Is Greatest Contribution to Global Poverty Reduction," China Network, Sept. 5, 2018.

proposes a new development path in line with the common interests of mankind. While respecting the diversity in development globally, this concept has comprehensively promoted the development of party diplomacy. It not only starts a new journey for China's diplomacy in the new era but also provides the Chinese Approach to the establishment of a stable international order which embodies the outstanding civilization and wisdom of the Chinese people.

1. Mao Zedong's thought of common interests

Mao Zedong's thought of common interests mainly represented the common interests of weak countries, poor countries, and small countries and reflected the historical process of the emergence, development, and increasing prominence of multipolarization in the world. This was mainly reflected in his in-depth analysis and accurate judgment of the development and changes of the international situation and his subsequently putting forward the theory of "three worlds" and "a strategic line of defense."

In the early 1950s, China implemented a strategy of "leaning to one side," focusing on befriending socialist countries. In the late 1950s, China's focus in making friends gradually shifted to the newly independent countries in Asia, Africa, and Latin America. Mao Zedong believed that China and the vast Asian, African, and Latin American countries "stand on the same front."[1] And he has repeatedly proposed that "the peoples of the Asian, African and Latin American countries should unite."[2] Therefore, strengthening the solidarity and cooperation between China and the vast number of Asian, African, and Latin American countries has gradually become the top priority of China's foreign strategy. In his talk with Ahmed Sukarno, President of Indonesia, Mao Zedong said, "Where do you suggest we put our emphasis in our work and effort to win friends? I believe it should be the three continents of Asia, Africa and Latin America, plus the larger half of Europe."[3] Mao Zedong said affectionately

---

[1] Mao Zedong, *Mao Zedong on Diplomacy*, Beijing: Foreign Languages Press, 1998, p. 311.
[2] Ibid, p. 391.
[3] Ibid, p. 208.

many times that "our closest friends come from three places, namely, Asia, Africa and Latin America" and "when we meet with you, we feel equality."[1] Mao Zedong also stressed that China and Latin America have a lot in common. "First, we both want independence. It is not only you who have the problem of independence; we have it too. ... Second, both our economies are not developed. Your desire for economic development is pressing, and so is ours. All Asian, African and Latin American countries is facing this common historical task of fighting for national independence and developing national economies and cultures."[2]

In order to implement the policy of "putting emphasis in our work and effort to win friends on Asian, African, and Latin American countries," China not only firmly supports third world countries and people in their struggles for national independence but also actively supports them in developing their national economy and consolidating their national independence.

After the founding of the People's Republic of China, Mao Zedong and the CPC Central Committee made a strategic decision that "we must give active support to the national independence and liberation movements in countries in Asia, Africa and Latin America as well as the peace movement and just struggles in all the countries of the world."[3] He told his friends in Asia, Africa, and Latin America many times that "the Chinese people regard the victory of the people in Asia, Africa and Latin America in their struggles against imperialism as our own victory and give them warm sympathy and support in all their struggles against imperialism and colonialism."[4] "The people who have

---

[1] Pei Jianzhang, *Research on Mao Zedong's Diplomatic Thought*, Beijing: World Affairs Press, 1994, p. 295.
[2] *Mao Zedong on Diplomacy*, p. 262.
[3] *Collected Works of Mao Zedong Vol. 7*, p. 116.
[4] "When receiving foreign guests from Asia and Africa, Chairman Mao expressed his deep sympathy and support for the people of all countries in their struggles against imperialism. Chairman Mao severely condemned U.S. imperialism for invading Cuba, pointing out that the Kennedy administration can only be worse rather than better than the Eisenhower administration. In the struggle against imperialism, victory is possible if we take the correct path and keep closely connected with the masses." *People's Daily*, Apr. 29, 1961.

triumphed in their own revolution should help those still struggling for liberation." "Earlier independent countries have the obligation to help later independent countries."① He also said, "We are always willing to give a helping hand to all Asian, African and Latin American countries whenever they need one."②

In January 1959, the Cuban Revolution won victory and overthrew the pro-U.S. regime. However, the threat of U.S. armed intervention ensued, and Mao Zedong advocated supporting Cuba and opposing the U.S. In 1961, when the danger of America invading Cuba was approaching, Mao Zedong said to the Cuban ambassador to China, "the Chinese people are determined to take all necessary measures from all sides to support the Cuban people's patriotic and just struggle."③ In early 1964, the people of Panama launched an anti-American struggle to recover sovereignty over the Panama Canal zone. On January 12 of the same year, Mao Zedong published "The Chinese People Resolutely Support the People of Panama in Their Patriotic and Just Struggle," pointing out that the Panamanian people were waging a struggle to defend their national sovereignty against U.S. aggression. "The Chinese people firmly stand by the Panamanian people and whole-heartedly support their just action of opposing the U.S. aggressors and recovering sovereignty over the Panama Canal zone."④ In April 1965, the United States invaded the Dominican Republic. On May 12, Mao Zedong issued "Statement in Support of the Dominican People Opposition to U.S. Armed Aggression," pointing out that the U.S. crackdown on the Dominican Republic was "a serious provocation by U.S. imperialism against the Dominican people, and also against the people of the Latin American countries and of the world as a whole."⑤ This statement greatly

---

① Pei Jianzhang, *Research on Mao Zedong's Diplomatic Thought*, Beijing: World Affairs Press, 1994, p. 283.
② *Mao Zedong on Diplomacy*, p. 261.
③ Han Nianlong, *Contemporary Chinese Diplomacy*, Beijing: Contemporary China Publishing House, 2009, p. 113.
④ *Mao Zedong on Diplomacy*, p. 390.
⑤ Ibid, p. 432.

inspired the Latin American people in their struggle against U.S. aggression. Mao Zedong also said many times to his Latin American friends, "We are on the same front, which is opposing imperialism and striving for national liberation. We support national liberation movements throughout Latin America."[1]

China also actively supported the development of Third World countries. Mao Zedong believed that China should strengthen its economic and technological exchange and cooperation with Third World countries to help them develop their national economies. He mentioned that "all Asian, African and Latin American countries is facing this common historical task of fighting for national independence and developing national economies and cultures."[2] He also believed that we must not forget our friends in the Third World who helped China to resume its seat in the United Nations.[3] Accordingly, China, in accordance with its own situation and the requirements and conditions of Third World countries, has continuously strengthened its economic and technological exchange and cooperation with Third World countries and has provided assistance within its capacity. Before 1954, the People's Republic of China mainly assisted Democratic People's Republic of Korea (DPRK), Vietnam, and other neighboring countries. After 1955, China began to aid the vast number of independent countries in Asia, Africa, and Latin America. 1964 – 1977 was the peak period of China's foreign aid. The amount of aid increased nearly five times compared with the foreign aid provided in 1950 – 1963. During this period, China's economic and technological cooperation with African countries developed particularly rapidly. In the 1960s, China signed economic and technological cooperation agreements with 13 African countries. In the 1970s, China signed similar agreements with 31 other

---

[1] Wang Taiping, *Diplomatic History of People's Republic of China Vol. 2*, Beijing: World Affairs Press, 1998, p. 484.
[2] *Mao Zedong on Diplomacy*, p. 262.
[3] Party Literature Research Center of the CPC Central Committee, *Mao Zedong Biography (1949 – 1976)*, Beijing: Central Party Literature Press, 2003, p. 1364.

countries. By the end of the 1980s, China had sent medical teams to more than 50 Third World countries, with a total of more than 10,000 medical personnel.① Mao Zedong also personally approved the construction of the Tanzania-Zambia Railway, which became a symbol of China-Africa friendship. The Chinese government and people firmly support the efforts of the Third World countries and people to defend their national independence, revitalize their own economies, and build their countries.

In the 1970s, major changes took place in the international situation. The military power rivalry between the two superpowers of the United States and the Soviet Union is developing in a direction favorable to the Soviet Union. The United States adjusted its foreign policy, implemented a retrenchment strategy in Asia, opened the door to China-U.S. relationship, and sought to extricate itself from the Indo-China Peninsula in order to focus on Europe as its priority. In order to promote the continuous development of the international situation towards peace and stability and towards a direction favorable to people of all countries, Mao Zedong put forward in 1973 when meeting Kissinger that "as long as we have the same goals, we will not harm you, nor will you harm us."② This is the "strategic line" of united opposition to Soviet hegemony.

2. Deng Xiaoping's thought of common interests

First, Deng Xiaoping's thought of common interests is embodied in his persistence in upholding the independent foreign policy of peace to safeguard world peace. In the field of handling international relations and foreign affairs, Deng Xiaoping has always insisted on the idea that "first priority should always be given to national sovereignty and security" in national interests. Deng Xiaoping was the first Chinese leader to explicitly put forward national interests as the starting point of China's diplomacy. In his talk with Nixon in October

---

① Pei Jianzhang, *Research on Zhou Enlai: Diplomatic Thought and Practice*, Beijing: World Affairs Press, 1989, p. 142.
② *A Chronicle of Mao Zedong (1949-1976) Vol. 6*, Central Party Literature Press, 2013, p. 468.

1989, he pointed out that "in determining relations between two countries, each party should proceed from his country's own strategic interests."① In August 1982, when meeting with Javier Pérez de Cuéllar, then Secretary-General of the United Nations, Deng Xiaoping said, "China's foreign policy is consistent and can be summed up in three sentences. First, we oppose hegemonism. Second, we safeguard world peace. Third, we are eager to strengthen unity and cooperation, or what might be termed 'union and cooperation,' with other Third World countries."②

While proposing that socialist modernization was China's greatest national interest at the time, Deng Xiaoping clearly pointed out that "for the interest of our own country the goal of our foreign policy is a peaceful environment for achieving the four modernizations."③ After that, he reiterated this view multiple times. In particular, when talking with the the president of Brazilian in May 1984, he made the point more clearly by saying the following: "The aim of our foreign policy is world peace. Always bearing that aim in mind, we are wholeheartedly devoting ourselves to the modernization programme to develop our country and to build socialism with Chinese characteristics."④

China adheres to an independent foreign policy of peace in order to safeguard world peace in terms of the world and to create a peaceful and favorable international environment for socialist modernization in terms of its national interests. China adheres to an independent foreign policy of peace and strives for a peaceful international environment to realize modernization, which is conducive to safeguarding world peace. Therefore, "[t]his is a vital matter which conforms to the interests not only of the Chinese people but also of the people in the rest of the world."⑤ China regards the maintenance of peace, the

---

① *Selected Works of Deng Xiaoping Vol. III*, p. 320.
② *Selected Works of Deng Xiaoping Vol. II*, p. 407.
③ Ibid, p. 242.
④ Ibid, p. 66.
⑤ Ibid, p. 242.

promotion of friendly cooperation with other countries, and the realization of common development and prosperity as the fundamental objectives of its diplomacy, which conforms to China's national interests by seeking a peaceful and stable international environment for China's modernization, the trend of the times with the theme of peace and development, and the common wishes and interests of people all over the world.

Second, Deng Xiaoping's thought of common interests is reflected in his handling of the territorial disputes with neighboring countries. In the late 1970s, China, which had just embarked on the road of reform and opening up, was facing severe international challenges and pressure from its neighbors. Against this background, Comrade Deng Xiaoping seriously pondered a new way to solve international disputes and strengthen the security of the neighborhood, and he gradually formed a strategic thinking in solving neighborhood disputes. In 1978, when China and Japan were conducting negotiations on a peace and friendship treaty, Comrade Deng Xiaoping put forward a proposal to set aside the sovereignty dispute over the Diaoyu Islands, thus enabling the two sides to get rid of the obstacles and reach an agreement smoothly. In the following years, the idea of "joint development" was put forward on the basis of "setting aside disputes." For example, regarding the question of Diaoyu Islands, he proposed that "such places be exploited jointly." He said, "This would only mean joint exploitation of the offshore oil resources. We could have a joint venture that would profit both sides."[1] When it comes to the question of Nansha Islands, he also advocated setting aside the dispute and seeking joint development. In 1984, China and the U.K. reached an agreement on the return of Hong Kong to China. Comrade Deng Xiaoping has said the following on many occasions: "Many international disputes may reach the flash point if they are not handled properly. I asked our guests whether the 'one country, two systems' solution could not be applied in some cases and the 'joint

---

[1] *Selected Works of Deng Xiaoping Vol. III*, p. 94.

development' solution in others."①

The South China Sea dispute involves five countries and six parties and is rather complicated. China has long adhered to the principle of "putting aside disputes and working for joint development" and has patiently and carefully coordinated and communicated with all parties, finally leading to the signing of the Declaration on the Conduct of Parties in the South China Sea. In the meantime, under the condition that it was difficult to solve the South China Sea dispute in a short while, China and Vietnam signed the Treaty of Land Border under the spirit of setting aside disputes and accomplishing the easy before the hard and made the China-Vietnam land border a peaceful and friendly boundary. Under the spirit of "setting aside disputes and working for joint development," China and India signed the Agreement on Political Parameters and Guiding Principles for the Settlement of the India-China Boundary Question to maintain the status quo of the border and jointly promote trade and economic development in the border area until a final settlement is reached.

The important connotation of this strategic thinking is "maintaining our claims to sovereignty, setting aside disputes, and working for joint development." The so-called "setting aside disputes" mainly includes two levels of meanings that are both in opposition and in unity. The first is the level of principles, which means that we adhere to the principle of safeguarding national sovereignty and core interests in the process of resolving disputes without denying the objective existence of disputes; the second is the level of flexibility, which means that we recognize the complexity and difficulty of resolving the disputes and that in order to avoid the intensification of conflicts caused by endless disputes, we can put the disputes aside for the moment and resolve them when the time is ripe. The so-called "joint development" means cooperative exploitation, benefit sharing, and common development on the

---

① *Selected Works of Deng Xiaoping Vol. III*, p. 94.

basis of "setting aside disputes."①

In the 21st century, some scholars have put forward many propositions and positions that Deng Xiaoping had not put forward during his time, such as safeguarding the common interests of all mankind, developing together with neighboring countries, constructing and promoting free trade and common market between China and East Asian countries, etc., which are all the results of Deng Xiaoping's diplomatic philosophy being applied in the new era.②

3. Jiang Zemin's thought of common interests

Adhering to the harmonious unity of national interests and the common interests of all mankind is also China's basic principle in handling foreign relations. China's foreign strategy must take into account both the national interests and the common interests of all mankind and handle the relationship between them. Upholding the unity of the common interests of all mankind and the national and ethnic interests is also the basic content of China's principle of national interests. Comrade Jiang Zemin put forward a foreign relations strategy that consists of three aspects "three focuses" in October 2001: manage our relations with major powers in light of the international strategic pattern, constructively manage our affairs with neighboring countries in light of the geopolitical strategic situation, and do all we can to develop multilateral diplomacy in light of the need to expand our strategic space.③ Comrade Jiang Zemin said, "China is a member of the international family. It cannot do without the world. China's reform, opening up and modernization require a long period of international peace and the development of friendly relations and

---

① Wen Hang, "A Complete Understanding of Deng Xiaoping's Strategic Ideas for Solving Maritime Disputes," *Study Times*, Jan. 7, 2011; Lin Dong, "Only Through Joint Development can Disputes be Shelved: Deng Xiaoping's Strategic Thinking on the South China Sea Question is not Outdated," *Study Times*, July 4, 2011; Pan Guang, "Revisiting Deng Xiaoping's Strategic Thinking in Solving Neighboring Disputes," *Jiefang Daily*, Sept. 13, 2010.
② Ye Zicheng, "Deng Xiaoping's Diplomatic Heritage and Its Influence," *International Herald Leader*, Aug. 16, 2004.
③ Jiang Zemin, *Selected Works of Jiang Zemin Vol. III*, Beijng: Foreign Languages Press, 2013, pp. 343-346.

cooperation with other countries. The world needs China, and world peace and development need China to be stable and prosperous."① On the eve of Jiang Zemin's visit to the United States in 2002, he pointed out that it was very important for China and the United States to maintain the healthy and stable development of their economic and trade relations, which was in line with the common interests of the people and businesses of the two countries.②

"Since ancient times the Chinese nation has observed the fine traditions of honesty, harmony and good faith. China has always adhered to these values in its relations with other countries. The aim of China's foreign policy is to safeguard world peace and promote common development." Jiang Zemin mentioned the above in his speech at the George Bush Presidential Library in College Station, Texas, in 2002.③

Comrade Jiang Zemin pointed out the following in "Harmony without Uniformity is an Essential Aspect of the Balanced Development of Cultures" in October 2002: "The more developed, more open and more intimately connected China becomes with the world, the more it needs an international environment of lasting peace and stability. Promoting world and regional peace and development is in line with China's fundamental interests. Since ancient times the Chinese nation has observed the fine traditions of honesty, harmony and good faith. China has always adhered to these values in its relations with other countries. The aim of China's foreign policy is to safeguard world peace and promote common development." Jiang Zemin pointed out that "[w]e advocate that the world's cultures, social systems and development models should interact and learn from each other, learn from each other's strong points to make up deficiencies amid competition and comparison, and develop together by seeking

---

① Jiang Zemin, *Selected Works of Jiang Zemin Vol. I*, Beijing: Foreign Languages Press, 2010, p. 470.
② Qi Bin, "President Jiang's Prospect of His U.S. Visit: Promoting Trust and Understanding and Seeking Common Interests," China News Service, Oct. 19, 2002.
③ "Jiang Zemin Expounds China's Values in Handling International Relations: Sincerity, Harmony and Faith," chinanews.com, Oct. 25, 2002.

common ground while putting aside differences."①

During his visit to Germany, Comrade Jiang Zemin stressed in his speech at the German Council on Foreign Relations (DGAP) that the correct way to safeguard world peace and promote common development is to conform to the trend of the times and the wishes of the people of all countries, make the best use of the situation, and actively promote the establishment of a just and reasonable new international political and economic order; governments and people of all countries should make joint efforts to actively push the world towards multipolarization, promote the democratization of international relations, respect the diversity of the world, correctly guide economic globalization, promote common development of all countries, and establish a new security concept with mutual trust, mutual benefit, equality, and cooperation as its core.②

In his report to the 16th CPC National Congress, on the basis of upholding and developing the principle of national interests, Comrade Jiang Zemin pointed out, "We stand for conforming to the tide of history and safeguarding the common interests of mankind." He also said, "The purpose of our foreign policy is to maintain world peace and promote common development. We are ready to work with all nations to advance the lofty cause of world peace and development."③

Jiang Zemin pointed out the following in his report to the 16th CPC National Congress when analyzing the issue of common interests: "Peace and development remain the themes of our era. Preserving peace and promoting development are important for the wellbeing of all nations and are common aspirations of all peoples. This is an irresistible trend of history." "Regardless of how the international situation changes, we will always pursue an independent

---

① *Selected Works of Jiang Zemin Vol. III*, p. 506.
② Jiang Zemin, "Jointly Create a Peaceful and Prosperous New Century," people.cn, Apr. 10, 2002.
③ *Selected Works of Jiang Zemin Vol. III*, p. 552.

foreign policy of peace. The purpose of our foreign policy is to maintain world peace and promote common development. We are ready to work with all nations to advance the lofty cause of world peace and development."

In analyzing the issue of "safeguarding the common interests of all mankind," Jiang Zemin pointed out, "We stand for conforming to the tide of history and safeguarding the common interests of mankind. We are ready to work with the international community to promote world multipolarization, encourage the harmonious coexistence of diverse forces and maintain stability in the international community. We will push economic globalization in a direction conducive to common prosperity and make the most of its advantages while avoiding its disadvantages so that all countries, particularly developing countries, can benefit from the process."

Jiang Zemin noted, "We will continue to improve and develop relations with the developed countries. Proceeding from the fundamental interests of the peoples of all countries concerned, we will expand the converging points of common interests and properly settle differences on the basis of the Five Principles of Peaceful Coexistence without haggling over differences in social systems and ideologies. We will continue to strengthen our friendly ties with our neighbors and persevere in building good-neighborly relationships and partnerships with them. We will increase regional cooperation and raise our exchanges and cooperation with surrounding countries to a new level. We will continue to enhance our solidarity and cooperation with other Third World countries, increase mutual understanding and trust, strengthen mutual help and support, and expand the scope and increase the results of cooperation. We will continue to take an active part in multilateral diplomatic activities and play our role in the United Nations and other international and regional organizations. We will support other developing countries in their efforts to safeguard their legitimate rights and interests. We will continue to develop exchanges and cooperation with political parties and organizations of all countries and regions on the principle of independence, complete equality, mutual respect and noninterference in each other's internal affairs. We will continue to carry out extensive people-to-people diplomacy, expand cultural exchanges with the outside world, enhance the friendship between the Chinese people and the peoples of other countries, and further the development of China's relations with other countries."[1]

The above thoughts are based on the requirements of the Party's work in international relations under the situation of world multipolarization and economic globalization and are mainly formed from the perspective of the relationship between countries under the new situation or the social relationship between human groups in different regions of the world. Although the report did not elaborate on the connotations of "common interests of all mankind," the above discussion has clearly told us that there is an imbalance of interests between different countries in globalization. Therefore, it is necessary to "push economic globalization in a direction conducive to the realization of common prosperity" for all mankind so that "all countries, particularly developing countries, can benefit from the process." Although the report did not further discuss the common interests of all mankind from the perspective of the relationship between human beings and the nature, the above discussions must have contained the meaning that efforts should also be made towards "the realization of common prosperity for all mankind" regarding the relationship between human beings and the nature.

4. Hu Jintao's thought of common interests

With regard to the changes in the pattern of international relations, the CPC Central Committee with Hu Jintao as its general secretary made major theoretical innovations and put forward the theories of profound transformation, a harmonious world, common development, shared responsibility, and active participation.[2] The main thread running through

---

[1] *Selected Works of Jiang Zemin Vol. III*, p. 553.
[2] Zhang Xiaotong, "China's Proposition Based on Hu Jintao's Concept of the Times," Outlook, 2009 (47): 32–36.

these theories is the idea of common interests.

Since the CPC Central Committee proposed to build a harmonious society at the 16th CPC National Congress, it has created favorable external conditions for building a harmonious socialist society. The third generation of the collective leadership of the Party and the State, in light of the development and changes in the international situation, solemnly put forward to the whole world the strategic thought of building a harmonious world of lasting peace and common prosperity. This kind of thinking on foreign strategy, as Hu Jintao expressed at the summit commemorating the 60th anniversary of the founding of the United Nations, has the following connotations: "We should respect every country's right to independently choose its own social system and path of development, and encourage countries to go for mutual emulation instead of deliberate exclusion, for mutual learning of respective strong points instead of making fetish a particular model, thus succeeding in their rejuvenation and development in line with their national conditions. We should enhance intercivilization dialogue and exchanges, allowing cultures to complement one another through competition and comparison, and to develop together by seeking common ground while putting aside differences. We should do away with misgivings and estrangement existing between civilizations and make humanity more harmonious and our world more colorful. We should endeavor to preserve the diversity of civilizations in the spirit of equality and openness, make international relations more democratic and jointly build towards a harmonious world where all civilizations coexist and accommodate each other."[1] Building a harmonious world is a new concept in China's international strategy, which reflects the development trend and objective requirements of peace and development as the theme of the times, expresses the common wishes of the people of all countries in the world, and reflects the common interests of

---

[1] Hu Jintao, "Written Speech by H.E. Hu Jintao President of the People's Republic of China at the High-level Plenary Meeting of the United Nations' 60th Session," Qiushi, Sept. 16, 2005 (updated Sept. 22, 2011).

all mankind.

On April 22, 2005, at the Asian-African summit in Jakarta, Hu Jintao called on all countries in the world to "promote the friendly coexistence, equal dialogue, development and prosperity of different civilizations and jointly build a harmonious world" and put forward the idea of building a harmonious world for the first time. On July 1, 2005, the heads of China and Russia met and wrote the concept of a harmonious world into the Joint Statement of the People's Republic of China and the Russian Federation on the International Order of the 21st Century, which for the first time got the concept of a harmonious world confirmed as a consensus between the two countries. On September 15, 2005, Hu Jintao delivered a speech entitled "Build Towards a Harmonious World of Lasting Peace and Common Prosperity" at the summit commemorating the 60th anniversary of the founding of the U.N. and comprehensively elaborated on the rich connotations of "a harmonious world."① The basic content of building a harmonious world is as follows: first, uphold multilateralism to realize common security; second, uphold mutually beneficial cooperation to achieve common prosperity; third, uphold the spirit of inclusiveness to build a harmonious world together; fourth, promote U.N. reform actively and prudently.

In September 2009, Comrade Hu Jintao pointed out in his speech at the General Debate of the 64th session of the U.N. General Assembly, "we should view security in a broader perspective and safeguard world peace and stability. … we should take a more holistic approach to development and promote common prosperity. … we should pursue cooperation with a more open mind and work for mutual benefit and common progress. … we should be more tolerant to one another and live together in harmony."②

---

① Hu Jintao. "Written Speech by H.E. Hu Jintao President of the People's Republic of China at the High-level Plenary Meeting of the United Nations' 60th Session," *Qiushi*, Sept. 16, 2005 (updated Sept. 22, 2011).
② Hu Jintao, "Unite as One and Work for a Bright Future: Speech at the General Debate of the 64th Session of the General Assembly" (New York, USA, Sept. 23, 2009), Xinhua News Agency, Sept. 24, 2009.

Common Interest Theory

On January 20, 2011, Hu Jintao met with U.S. House Speaker John Boehner and U.S. Senate Majority Leader Harry Reid respectively in Washington. As he pointed out, China and the United States are different in history, culture, social system, and level of development, and that it is normal to have different views on some issues, but the common interests of the two countries should always come first. A good China-U.S. relationship not only conforms to the fundamental interests of the people of the two countries but also effectively promotes the peace, stability, and prosperity of the Asia-Pacific region and even the world.[1]

Hu Jintao pointed out that "in the long history of human development, the destinies of the people of all countries have never been so closely linked and shared" and that "our correct choice can only be to promote win-win cooperation." Win-win cooperation should adhere to the following basic principles: countries, big or small, strong or weak, rich or poor, are all equal; we should adhere to maintaining and developing common interests as the starting point and the purpose of cooperation; we should give full play to the comparative advantages of different countries, strive to expand the development space and promote common development; we should benefit from each other, learn from each other's strong points, continuously expand the convergence points of common interests of all parties, innovate cooperation methods, broaden cooperation fields, and enrich the contents of cooperation; we should take care of each other's legitimate concerns in cooperation and strive to achieve mutual benefits and win-win results. Hu Jintao advocated that we should take a more holistic approach to development and promote common prosperity and examine and deal with international relations with a broad and profound strategic vision and a win-win thinking of the times. Countries "should treat each other's development objectively. They should see each other as

---

[1] "Hu Jintao said that the common interests of China and the United States have always come first," China Network, Jan. 21, 2011.

partners that are mutually-beneficial through cooperation, rather than mere rivals. They should support each other's peaceful development."[1] We should strengthen the dialogues between developing countries and developed countries, increase the voices of developing countries regarding the form of the dialogues, agenda setting, and results of the dialogues, and establish a new global development partnership that is equal, mutually beneficial, and win-win. Developed countries should earnestly help and support developing countries in accelerating their development, starting with basic issues such as institutions and mechanisms. They should reform and improve the international economic, trade, and financial systems—build a sustainable international economic system, build an inclusive and orderly international financial system, build a fair and reasonable international trade system, and build a fair and effective global development system. Developed countries should honor their commitments and take actions in debt relief, market opening, and technology transfer. Developing countries should promote cooperation, continuously expand the fields of economic and trade cooperation, promote diversification of cooperation methods, and realize complementary advantages, mutual benefits and win-win results, and common development.

Building a harmonious world of lasting peace and common prosperity is a beautiful ideal of people all over the world. It is a new view of world order with rich connotations on politics, economy, culture, security, environmental protection, etc. Politically, all countries should respect each other and consult on an equal footing to jointly promote the democratization of international relations. Countries, big or small, strong or weak, rich or poor, are equal members of the international community and should be respected by the international community. All countries should abide by the purposes and principles set forth in the Charter of the United Nations, abide by the international law and commonly recognized norms of international relations,

---

[1] "Hu Jintao Delivers Speech at Waseda University," CCTV.com, May 8, 2008.

and promote the spirit of democracy, harmony, cooperation, and win-win in international relations. People of all countries have the right to choose their own social system and development path. Economically, countries should cooperate with each other and use their advantages to complement each other to jointly promote economic globalization towards a balanced, inclusive, and win-win development. Efforts should be made to establish a fair, open, reasonable, and non-discriminatory multilateral trade system so that the fruits of economic globalization can benefit all countries in the world. Culturally, countries should learn from each other, seek common ground while reserving differences, and respect the diversity of world cultures. There should be intercivilization dialogue and exchange to do away with misgivings and estrangement existing between civilizations and jointly promote the prosperous development of the human civilization. In terms of security, all countries should trust each other, strengthen cooperation, persist in settling international disputes by peaceful means instead of war, and jointly safeguard world peace and stability. In terms of environmental protection, all countries should help each other and work together to protect the earth which we all depend on for survival. We should view from the perspective of the fundamental interests of mankind, advocate innovative development models, take the path of sustainable development, and promote the harmonious development of human beings and the nature. Promoting the building of a harmonious world of lasting peace and common prosperity is an enrichment and development of the Party's diplomatic thought of peaceful development. It is in line with the current trend of world development and the common interests and aspirations of people around the world and reflects the firm faith of the Chinese government and people in their commitment to world peace and progress.[1]

---

[1] Sun Cunliang, "Building a Harmonious World of Lasting Peace and Common Prosperity," *People's Daily*, Nov. 3, 2012.

5. Xi Jinping's thought of common interests in the New Era

Since the founding of the People's Republic of China, it has been striving to seek opportunities to integrate into the international community and make its contributions. On the domestic front, after decades of development, China's overall strength has continuously improved, and its international status has changed significantly. Internationally, economic globalization has brought countries closer together, making it possible for countries to cooperate and develop together; meanwhile, environmental pollution and other global issues are becoming more and more prominent. In the face of these global issues, countries around the world are interconnected and share weal and woe, becoming an intermingled, interconnected, and interdependent community with a shared future.

In the face of changes at home and abroad, Chinese Communists, based on China's national conditions and the world as a whole, put forward the important concept of "a community with a shared future for mankind" on the basis of the Marxist idea of a "community," drawing on the excellent ideas in Chinese traditional culture and combining the Marxist theory with the actual situation in China.

In September 2011, the white paper China's Peaceful Development first proposed the concept of "a community of common destiny"; in November 2012, Hu Jintao explained the concept of "a community of common destiny" for the first time in his report to the 18th CPC National Congress: "In promoting mutually beneficial cooperation, we should raise awareness about human beings sharing a community of common destiny. A country should accommodate the legitimate concerns of others when pursuing its own interests; and it should promote common development of all countries when advancing its own development. Countries should establish a new type of global development partnership that is more equitable and balanced, stick together in times of difficulty, both share rights and shoulder obligations, and boost the common interests of mankind."① It paved the way for the enrichment and development of the concept of a community with a shared future for mankind and provided theoretical preparation for the initiative to build a community with a shared future for mankind. In March 2013, Xi Jinping delivered a speech, conveying his understanding of a community with a shared future for mankind to the world for the first time; then, Xi Jinping mentioned a community with a shared future for mankind many times on major international occasions② and endowed it with a clear meaning of the times. In October 2017, Xi Jinping proposed to promote the construction of "a community with a shared future for mankind" in his report to the 19th CPC National Congress, which was also written into the Constitution of the Communist Party of China. In March 2018, the concept of "a human community with a shared future" was written into the Constitution of the People's Republic of China at the 13th National People's Congress. "A community with a shared future for mankind" transcends the boundaries between countries and nations, implicates the concept of win-win cooperation among countries around the world, and has important theoretical and practical values.

In 2017, General Secretary Xi Jinping pointed out in his report to the 19th CPC National Congress the following: "Our world is full of both hope and challenges. We should not give up on our dreams because the reality around us is too complicated; we should not stop pursuing our ideals because they seem out of our reach. No country can address alone the many challenges facing

---

① Hu Jintao, "Firmly March on the Path of Socialism with Chinese Characteristics and Strive to Complete the Building of a Moderately Prosperous Scociety in All Respects" (Report to the Eighteenth National Congress of the Communist Party of China), China.org.cn, Nov. 18, 2012.

② For example, in September 2015, Xi Jinping elaborated on the connotation of "a community of shared future for mankind" at a series of summits on the 70th anniversary of the founding of the United Nations; in September 2016, at the opening ceremony of the B20 summit, he called for the establishment of the consciousness of "a community of shared future for mankind"; in January 2017, Xi Jinping made a keynote speech at the United Nations Office in Geneva titled "Work Together to Build a Community with Shared Future for Mankind" and proposed to firmly establish the consciousness of "a community of shared future for mankind."

mankind; no country can afford to retreat into self-isolation."①"The future of the world rests in the hands of the people of all countries; the future of mankind hinges on the choices they make. We, the Chinese, are ready to work with the people of all other countries to build a community with a shared future for mankind and create a bright tomorrow for all of us."②"We call on the people of all countries to work together to build a community with a shared future for mankind, to build an open, inclusive, clean, and beautiful world that enjoys lasting peace, universal security, and common prosperity."③ A community with a shared future for mankind is not only a community of shared interests but also a community of shared values, which fully expresses the interest relations and pursuit of values common to all mankind. A community with a shared future for mankind is a form of community that is moving towards a real community and a transitional form between a illusory community and a real community in an era that economic globalization is deepening and that capitalism and socialism will coexist for a long time to come.④

Xi Jinping's thought of common interests is based on his concept of "common values of humanity." On September 28, 2015, in his speech at the 70th session of the U.N. General Assembly, President Xi Jinping first proposed, "Peace, development, fairness, justice, democracy, and freedom are common values of humanity."⑤ Xi Jinping's idea of "common values" focuses on human happiness and world harmony and is based on the construction of a community with a shared future for mankind, which puts forward China's solution and proposition to the question of what kind of world we human beings want to build and how to build it, and points the path forward to solve the survival and

---

① *Xi Jinping: The Governance of China Ⅲ*, Beijing: Foreign Languages Press, 2020, p. 62.
② Ibid, p. 65.
③ Ibid, pp. 62-63.
④ Peng Bingbing, "On the Essence, Connotation, and Significance of 'A Community with a Shared Future for Mankind,'" *Guizhou Social Sciences*, 2017 (4): 11-16.
⑤ *Xi Jinping: The Governance of China II*, Beijing: Foreign Languages Press, 2017, p. 570.

development problems facing mankind in the 21st century. "Common values" are the greatest common divisor of all human values, reflecting and representing the fundamental overall interests of all mankind, taking into account the interests of the state and individuals, promoting the universal realization of human freedom and well-being, and providing basic guarantee for human peace and security.[①] This thought has far-reaching social and historical influence and is of great theoretical and practical significance to the deconstruction of the capitalist cultural hegemony, the construction of a new order of international values, and the enhancement of China's international voice.

Xi Jinping also proposed the Belt and Road (B&R) Initiative, a realistic way to realize common interests. The Belt and Road Initiative—China's proposal to build a Silk Road Economic Belt and a 21st Century Maritime Silk Road in cooperation with related countries—was unveiled by Xi Jinping during his visits to Central and Southeast Asia in September and October 2013. This initiative coincides with the United Nations' promotion of the 2030 Agenda for Sustainable Development, opening up a new realm for China to participate in and lead global cooperation and is of milestone significance in the history of world development.

Since 2013, the construction of BRI has gradually progressed from concept to action and from vision to reality, with fruitful results. President Xi Jinping attaches great importance to BRI and has repeatedly talked about the initiative on various important occasions. At the policy level, programs, plans, and opinions on BRI have been issued intensively by the state, the ministries, and commissions. On March 28, 2015, the National Development and Reform Commission, Ministry of Foreign Affairs, and Ministry of Commerce of People's Republic of China jointly issued Vision and Actions on Jointly Building Silk Road Economic Belt and the 21st Century Maritime Silk Road, emphasizing

---

[①] Jiang Chang, "On the Construction of Human System of Shared Values," *Culture Development Review*, 2016 (3): 3-17.

the strengthening of the Five-Pronged Approach and implementing the approach in specific international cooperation projects. In June 2017, the National Development and Reform Commission and the State Oceanic Administration jointly issued Vision for Maritime Cooperation under the Belt and Road Initiative and proposed to use China's coastal economic belt as its support, adopt the theme of sharing a blue space and developing the blue economy, and embark together on a path of green development, ocean-based prosperity, maritime security, innovative growth, and collaborative governance. This was also the first time that the Chinese government put forward the Chinese Approach to promoting maritime cooperation under the Belt and Road Initiative.

Section V Literature Review on Common Interests in International Economic Relations

I. Literature Review on Common Interests in International Trade

Common interests in international trade are mainly embodied in the theory of division of labor. The theory of division of labor in international trade discusses the causes of division of labor, trade benefits, and changes in trade patterns in international trade. Dating back to Adam Smith's *An Inquiry into the Nature and Causes of the Wealth of Nations* (i.e., *The Wealth of Nations*, first published in 1776), the theory of division of labor in international trade has been developed for more than 200 years, during which it has gone through the classical stage, the neoclassical stage, and the new trade theory stage, reflecting the characteristics of different stages in the development of international trade.

The founding stage of the theory of labor division in international trade—that is, the classical stage—lasted for years from the theory of absolute cost advantage proposed by Adam Smith in *The Wealth of Nations* in 1776 to the theory of comparative cost advantage proposed by David Ricardo in *On the Principles of Political Economy and Taxation* in 1817.

Adam Smith's theory of absolute cost advantage is based on his theories of division of labor and international division of labor. Smith extended his theory of division of labor to the field of division of labor in international trade and established the theory of absolute cost advantage, convincingly demonstrating that as long as a country specializes in producing products whose costs are absolutely lower than the costs of other countries' products, in exchange for products whose domestic production costs are higher than those of other countries' products, this will lead to the most efficient use of resources of all countries as well as the benefits of increasing total output, enhancing the consumption level, and reducing labor time.① Smith not only demonstrated that the basis of division of labor in international trade is the existence of differences in absolute advantages between commodities of different countries, but also further pointed out the reasons for the existence of those differences. Smith believed that every country has favorable conditions suitable for producing specific products, so its costs of producing these products will be lower than such costs in other countries. Generally speaking, a country's absolute cost advantage comes from two aspects. The first aspect is natural advantages, i.e., advantages in geography, environment, soil, climate, minerals, and other natural conditions; the second aspect is advantages in unique skills and techniques, which is acquired through training and education. If a country has one of these two kinds of advantages, its labor productivity of a certain commodity will be higher than that of other countries, and thus its production cost of this commodity will be lower than that in other countries.②

Smith's theory of absolute cost advantage is of epoch-making significance.

---

① Adam Smith, *An Inquiry into the Nature and Causes of the Wealth of Nations*, in *The Glasgow Edition of Works and Correspondence of Adam Smith Vol. II*, edited by R. H. Camphell and A. S. Skinner, Oxford: Oxford University Press, 1976, pp. 456-457.
② *An Inquiry into the Nature and Causes of the Wealth of Nations*, p. 458.

Based on the principle of division of labor, it demonstrates the principle of mutual benefits of trade for the first time in the history of human cognition (i.e., obtaining common interests), overcoming the mercantilists' one-sided view that international trade is only beneficial to one side (i.e., gains of one country will inevitably lead to losses of another country). This "win-win" concept of division of labor in trade and mutual beneficiality are not outdated yet, and it will never be. In a sense, this "win-win" concept is still the guiding principle for all contemporary countries in the expansion of their opening up to the outside world and their participation in the division of labor in international trade. An introverted country or nation will definitely fall behind, and a beggar-thy-neighbor trade protectionism policy will only lead to a "lose-lose" result; this is still the most important enlightenment left to us by Smith's trade theory of division of labor. As for how and to what extent countries should participate in the division of labor in international trade to gain benefits, it is a problem of another level that has to be decided according to each country's national conditions and economic development.

Furthermore, Smith's argument that "the very different genius which appears to distinguish men of different professions ... is not upon many occasions so much the case, as the effect of the division of labour"[①] was also a foundation for the new classical trade theory established by Professor Yang Xiaokai and others. According to Yang Xiaokai's trade model of endogenous division of labor and specialization, with the continuous improvement of transaction efficiency, there will be an evolution in the division of labor, and changes in economic development, trade, and market structures are all different aspects of this evolution process.[②] The development of the new classical trade theory provides a unified foundation for the interpretation of

---

① *An Inquiry into the Nature and Causes of the Wealth of Nations*, p. 28.
② Yang Xiaokai, Zhang Yongsheng, "New Achievements in New Trade Theory, Theory of Comparative Advantage, and the Empirical Research: Literature Review," *China Economic Quarterly*, 2001(1): 19-44.

domestic and international trade.[①] Its perfect theoretical framework and explanatory power in practice are appealing, making the new classical trade theory an important school of contemporary theories of division of labor in trade and a definite proof of the vitality of Smith's theory of trade division.

However, regarding specific trade patterns, Smith confined mutually beneficial trade within the scope of absolute cost advantage, which is an obvious limitation of the theory. The famous theory of comparative cost advantage, put forward by English classical economist David Ricardo, demonstrated with incomparable logic for the first time that the basis of division of labor in international trade is not limited to the absolute cost difference. As long as there are relative differences (i.e., "comparative advantage" differences) in production costs between countries, the countries can participate in the division of labor in international trade. Every country, based on international division of labor according to the differences in comparative advantages, can obtain comparative benefits through producing and trading products with comparative advantages of their own. The idea of "choosing the best from the good and the least from the worst" is the "reasonable core" or "essence" of the theory of comparative cost advantage.

Ricardo's theory of comparative cost advantage marked the establishment of the overall system of international trade theory. Samuelson, the famous contemporary American economist, called it the unshakable foundation of international trade. The theory of comparative cost advantage reveals the general principles and laws of economic operation objectively existing in international trade. If the theory of absolute cost advantage proves the principle of mutual benefitiality (common interests) in trade for the first time in the history of human cognition, then the theory of comparative cost advantage

---

[①] Yang Xiaokai, Zhang Yongsheng, "New Achievements in New Trade Theory, Theory of Comparative Advantage, and the Empirical Research: Literature Review," *China Economic Quarterly*, 2001(1): 19-44.

further generalizes this principle of mutual benefitiality in the division of labor in trade. In other words, Ricardo's principle of division of labor based on comparative cost advantage is more generalized than Smith's principle of division of labor based on absolute cost advantage. The theory of comparative advantage shows that no matter what stage of development a country is in, whether the country is strong or weak economically, it is possible to determine its comparative advantages. Even those at a disadvantage may find comparative advantages comparing with other disadvantaged countries and find their positions in the international system of division of labor and gain benefits from participating in the system. Philosophically speaking, the theory of comparative cost advantage reveals the "general principle" of division of labor, cooperation, exchange, and mutual benefit in the human society. Only from this perspective can we deeply understand the idea of division of labor revealed by the theory of comparative cost advantage.

Some economists (mainly from developing countries) believe that the theory of comparative cost advantage only focuses on immediate static advantages and does not pay attention to the cultivation of dynamic comparative advantages and benefits from long-term development. Thus, fixing the relative advantages in production on a few kinds of products for a long time, especially a few primary products, as suggested by Ricardo's theory, would be very unfavorable. Some people even consider the theory of comparative cost advantage to be the root of the old international division of labor and specialized production. As mentioned above, the theory of comparative cost advantage illustrates the general principle of mutual benefitiality in trade, not a specific "plan" for the pattern of international division of labor. That is to say, Ricardo had not intention to let some countries produce primary products for a long time, and he should not be held responsible for the unjust international economic order. The existing unreasonable international economic order is caused by various historical and realistic reasons and has nothing to do with the theory of comparative cost advantage itself.[1]

In the 1930s, Swedish economist Bertil Ohlin published the book *Interregional and International Trade*, putting forward the factor endowment theory, which replaced Ricardo's theory of single factor of production with the theory of multiple factors of production in interdependent production structures. Bertil Ohlin's factor endowment theory is called neoclassical trade theory and is regarded as the cornerstone of modern theories of division of labor in international trade. The factor endowment theory is also known as the Heckscher-Ohlin model, as Ohlin adopted the main arguments of an important paper by his teacher Heckscher published in Swedish in 1919.

The Heckscher-Ohlin model assumes that each country has the same labor productivity (that is, the same production function for each country). In this case, there are two causes for the differences in comparative advantages. First, the ratio of factor endowments varies from country to country. Factor endowments refer to the ownership of factors of production (i.e., economic resources) in various countries. Different countries have different ratios of factor endowments, which is an important determinant of the differences in comparative advantages. All countries produce and export commodities that use more factor endowments of their own countries and that are relatively cheap in price, thus benefiting both sides. Second, the combinations of factors of production adopted in the production of various commodities, i.e., the intensity of factors in commodity production, are different. According to the type of the most intensive factor of production contained in a commodity, commodities can be roughly divided into labor-intensive, capital-intensive, land-intensive, resource-intensive, technology-intensive, knowledge-intensive, and other commodities. Even when producing the same kind of commodity, the combination of factors of production used is not the same in different countries.

---

[1] Zhang Erzhen, *Research and Comparison of International Trade Policy*, Nanjing: Nanjing University Press, 1993, p. 75.

For example, in the production of rice, Thailand relies mainly on labor, while the United States relies mainly on capital and technology. Whether producing different or the same commodities, as long as the combination or proportion of the factors of production invested in the the production varies in different countries, there will be differences in comparative advantages, which further lay a basis for the division of labor in trade. Obviously, if a country makes the best combination of factors of production and applies more factors of production that have low prices during the production of a certain commodity, then the country can have a lower comparative cost in this country and thus obtain greater trade benefits.

The logic of Ohlin's demonstration of the factor endowment theory is as follows: differences in commodity prices are the basis of international trade, and differences in commodity prices are caused by differences in cost ratios of commodity production; differences in cost ratios of commodity production are caused by differences in price ratios of various factors of production, which result from differences in the factor endowment ratios of different countries. Therefore, differences in factor endowment ratios are the most important basis for international trade. According to Ohlin, the primary condition for trade is that the production cost of certain commodities in one region is lower than the production cost in other regions. In each region, exports of goods contain factors of production which are relatively cheaper in the region and of which the region has relatively large quantities, while imports of goods are those that can be produced with lower costs in other regions. In short, import those goods that contain a larger proportion of expensive factors of production and export those goods that contain a larger proportion of cheap factors of production.[①]

The Heckscher-Ohlin model inherits the traditional classical theory of comparative cost advantage, yet with new development. First, Ricardo explained the general principle of mutual benefit in trade with differences in

---

① Bertil Ohlin, *Inter-Regional and International Trade*, Beijng:The Commercial Press, 1986, p. 23.

comparative costs, while Ohlin and others further explained why there are differences in comparative costs with differences in factor endowments. Second, Ohlin expanded Ricardo's micro-analysis to aggregate analysis, not only comparing the unit labor expenditure of the two products from two countries but also directly comparing the total supply of factors of production factors in the two countries. He explained the foundation of division of labor in trade and the trade pattern with the most basic factors such as capital, land, and labor in a country's economic structure, promoting the theoretical development and innovation. Third, the Heckscher-Ohlin model can explain not only the determinants of comparative cost advantages but also the alterations in factor prices and income distribution. In the short period after trade starts, as there are only alterations in commodity prices without any flow of production factors between import and export departments, the remuneration for all the factors of production in industries with rising prices (export industries) in the two countries will increase, while the remuneration for all factors of production in industries with falling prices (import-competing industries) in the two countries will decrease. For a long period after trade starts, the changes in the relative prices of commodities will have led to the flow of production factors between import and export departments and the changes in the supply-demand relationship in the market of factors of production, thus resulting in alterations in the prices of production factors and affecting the remuneration to factor owners, i.e., increasing the remuneration for factors of production that are intensively used in industries with rising prices (i.e., export industries) while decreasing the remuneration for factors of production that are intensively used in industries with falling prices (i.e., import-competing industries). If all countries trade based on their differences in factor endowment ratios, the prices of factors that are relatively abundant before the trade will rise, and the prices of factors that are relatively scarce before the trade will fall. Such a process will lead to the international equalization of the factor price ratio. This is the so-called "factor-price equalization theorem." In 1949, Samuelson, a well-known

American economist and Nobel laureate in economics, demonstrated this theorem in his essay "International Factor-Price Equalisation Once Again."① The Heckscher-Ohlin model explains the trade pattern from the perspective of a country's economic structure, while the factor-price equalization theorem in turn helps analyze the influence of international trade on the economic structure. On the one hand, the occurrence of international trade increases the demand for relatively abundant resources, thus increasing their prices—that is, increasing their remuneration. On the other hand, international trade reduces the demand for relatively scarce factors, thus reducing their remuneration. International trade can change a country's economic structure and make the most efficient use of factors of production, thus increasing production output and income. Such analysis is undoubtedly of positive significance to how a country can take advantage of its natural resource endowment to participate in the division of labor in international trade to obtain trade benefits.

Marxist economics holds that the Heckscher-Ohlin theory meets the need of western economics to abandon the labor theory of value in international trade. Because the theory is obviously based on the three-factor theory, which is the famous "trinity formula" of land-ground rent, labor-wages, capital-interest/profits that was severely criticized by Marx.② Careful analysis shows that the Heckscher-Ohlin theory has nothing to do with the so-called "trinity formula." The three-element theory focuses on the creation of commodity value, while the Heckscher-Ohlin model analyzes the causes of the differences in comparative costs between the two sides of the division of labor in trade and does not touch on the creation of value. From the perspective of economic operation, it must be admitted that the conditions of the endowments such as land, labor, capital, and technology have played a significant role in determining the production

---

① Paul A Samuelson, *Internatioal Factor-Price Equalisation Once Again*, Cambridge: The MIT Press, 1996.
② Zhang Erzhen and Ma Yeqing, *International Trade*, Nanjing: Nanjing University Press, 1998, p. 74.

costs and the patterns of foreign trade in various countries. Marx said decades before Ohlin, "In the competition of individual capitalists among themselves as well as in the competition on the world-market, it is the given and assumed magnitudes of wages, interest and rent which enter into the calculation as constant and regulating magnitudes; constant not in the sense of being unalterable magnitudes, but in the sense that they are given in each individual case and constitute the constant limit for the continually fluctuating market-prices. For instance, in competition on the world-market it is solely a question of whether commodities can be sold advantageously with existing wages, interest and rent at, or below, existing general market-prices, i.e., realising a corresponding profit of enterprise. If wages and the price of land are low in one country, while interest on capital is high, because the capitalist mode of production has not been developed generally, whereas in another country wages and the price of land are nominally high, while interest on capital is low, then the capitalist employs more labour and land in the one country, and in the other relatively more capital. These factors enter into calculation as determining elements in so far as competition between these two capitalists is possible. Here, then, experience shows theoretically, and the self-interested calculation of the capitalist shows practically, that the prices of commodities are determined by wages, interest and rent, by the price of labour, capital and land, and that these elements of price are indeed the regulating constituent factors of price."[1]

The emergence of the Leontief Paradox has aroused heated yet meaningful debates on the Heckscher-Ohlin model in the international economic circle. In the mid-20th century, U.S. economist Wassily W. Leontief was surprised to find that what the U.S. exported were labor-intensive products and what the U.S. imported were capital-intensive products when he used the U.S. import and export structure as a case for verification and analysis. This conclusion, which is

---

[1] *Marx & Engels Collected Works Vol. 37*, p. 861.

contrary to the trade pattern inferred by the Heckscher-Ohlin model, is called the Leontief Paradox. Many economists believe on this basis that the Heckscher-Ohlin model has been overturned, because a large amount of "empirical evidence"[1] like the Leontief Paradox can be found. There is also a prominent "misreading" of the factor endowment theory. First, most of the explanations of the Leontief Paradox given by international economists, such as the factor intensity transformation theory, the factor heterogeneity theory, the trade barrier theory, the demand bias theory, and the natural resources theory, also depend on the basic analysis method of the factor endowment theory—that is, the method of using the factor endowment ratio to determine the comparative advantages and disadvantages of a country's industries (or products). It can be said that all the different kinds of theoretical analysis about the Leontief Paradox have supplemented and enriched the factor endowment theory and strengthened its explanatory power to international trade practice.[2] Second, the so-called "new factor theory of international trade" that emerged later believes that we should give the factors of production new connotations to involve more elements. Production factors not only include labor, capital, and land, as pointed out by the endowment factor theory, but also include technology, human capital, research and development, information, and management. These are invisible "soft" factors. These intangible "soft" factors are increasingly becoming the basis of trade and determine a country's pattern of comparative advantages. This new factor theory is undoubtedly a development of the factor endowment theory, but as far as analysis methods are concerned, the new factor theory is not fundamentally different from the traditional factor theory of trade. Third, a comprehensive review of the

---

[1] Yang Xiaokai and Zhang Yongsheng, "New Achievements in New Trade Theory, Theory of Comparative Advantage, and the Empirical Research: Literature Review," *China Economic Quarterly*, 2001(1): 19-44.
[2] Zhang Erzhen and Ma Yeqing, *International Trade*, Nanjing: Nanjing University Press, 1998, pp. 76-78.

literature in western economics on the theoretical falsification and empirical negation of the Heckscher-Ohlin model shows that the literature tampers with nothing more than the assumptions on which the Heckscher-Ohlin model depends on, claiming that the factor endowment theory only discusses the relationship between trade volume, trade pattern, and relative factor endowments and ignores factors such as demand and technological differences.[1] This is, to some extent, the result of a lack of sufficient understanding of the abstract methods that must be used to build economic models. British economist Joan Robinson said that the art of building models and deepening our understanding is to make the most thorough simplification possible without excluding the factors that are important to the relevant issues and that if a model takes into account all the factors in the real world, it will be no more useful than a map scaled at 1 : 1.[2] The series of assumptions that Ohlin made to establish the factor endowment theory is reasonable. Without scientific and reasonable assumptions and without abstract methods, almost no economic analysis can be carried out. As long as it is correct abstraction, the conclusion drawn will be more accurate, more general, and more universal.

If it is inter-industry trade that the classical and neoclassical trade theories analyze, then it is intra-industry trade that the new trade theory mainly focus on.

International trade can be roughly divided into two basic types in terms of product content: one is inter-industry trade where a country's imports and exports are produced by different industrial sectors; the other is intra-industry trade where a country both exports and imports some manufactured goods of the same type, and two countries import and export from each other manufactured goods that belong to the same sector or category.

---

[1] Yang Xiaokai and Zhang Yongsheng, "New Achievements in New Trade Theory, Theory of Comparative Advantage, and the Empirical Research: Literature Review," *China Economic Quarterly*, 2001(1): 19-44.

[2] He Liping and Shen Xia, *Methodology of International Economics and Basic Theory Research*, Beijing: Economic Science Press, 1989, p. 12.

For these new phenomena in international trade, it is difficult for the classical and neoclassical trade theories to give convincing explanations for inter-industry trade. A group of economists, represented by Paul Krugman, drew on the reasonable factors in previous international trade theories and established a new analytical framework, which is the so-called "new trade theory." These economists explain the new phenomena in international trade with the theories of industrial organization and market structure, construct new trade theoretical models with concepts and ideas including imperfect competition, increasing returns to scale, and product differentiation, analyze the basis of intra-industry trade, and has drawn a series of brand-new conclusions.[①]

On the causes of trade, the neoclassical trade theory holds that the differences in relative factor endowments between two countries are the fundamental reason that international trade happens. The new trade theory, however, holds that due to the existence of economies of scale, the joint effect of the differences in relative factor endowments, the degree of economies of scale, and the extent of monopoly is the fundamental cause of trade. The relative factor endowment difference is no longer the only reason for international trade. Conversely, even if there is no difference in relative factor endowments between two countries, trade may still happen because of economies of scale and monopoly.

On the pattern of commodity trade, according to the $2 \times 2 \times 2$ (2 countries, 2 commodities, 2 factors) model, the neoclassical trade theory concludes that countries with relatively abundant labor force export labor-intensive commodities while importing capital-intensive commodities. The new trade theory holds that after introducing economies of scale and imperfect competition and breaking through the limitation of the $2 \times 2 \times 2$ model, the above conclusions need to make the following revisions. (1) The existence of

---

① Elhanan Helpman and Paul R. Krugman, *Market Structure and Foreign Trade*, Cambridge: MIT Press, 1985, p. 1.

different products makes intra-industry trade possible. Under the condition of self-sufficiency, the economies of scale and the varieties become a pair of contradictions. With the limited resources, the more varieties there are, the smaller the scale of production is, and the more difficult it is to give full play to economies of scale. The number of varieties will remain at a level after balancing with economies of scale. After trade develops, the markets of the two countries are integrated, resource restrictions are relaxed, and it is more accessible to adjust the contradictions between the economies of scale and the varieties. In order to pursue economies of scale, each country specializes in producing several varieties, which do not coincide with each other. Then, through trade, parties can obtain the varieties that each other produces and improve the social welfare. As a result, intra-industry trade—that is, trade among products with similar factor intensity—comes into being. (2) Economies of scale and monopoly factors. Due to the monopoly of economies of scale, the relative price difference of factors is no longer the only reason for the relative price difference of commodities. Differences in countries' conditions in applying economies of scale and different reasons for the existence of monopoly factors can also cause the relative price difference of commodities. Therefore, in the pattern of commodity trade, it is possible to witness countries with relatively abundant capital exporting labor-intensive commodities or countries with abundant labor exporting capital-intensive commodities. It is also possible to witness countries with low production costs becoming net importers of this commodity and two-way trade being caused by mutual price discrimination. (3) Multi-commodity multi-factor model. After a variety of commodities and factors are introduced, if there are more types of trade commodities than types of factors, even without the influence of economies of scale and market structure, there is still uncertainty in the two countries' commodity production and commodity trade. In other words, there are many equilibrium points in production and trade.

  On trade interests, the traditional trade theory holds that, regardless of the dynamic benefits generated by trade, when two countries with differences in relative factor endowments carry out incomplete specialized production respectively, give full play to their comparative advantages, and trade with each other, then both sides can make profits. Such static trade benefits come from the improved production efficiency of specialized production. Free trade is the best choice for trade policy, as all trade parties can benefit from it. The new trade theory, however, points out that under the market structure of economics of scale and imperfect competition, economies cannot achieve the best allocation of resources as in a perfectly competitive market and can only operate in a state of sub-optimization. For a country, trade might reduce its welfare. This happens when trade makes domestic industries that produce on an increasing scale and that are highly monopolized shrink (losing to foreign monopolies in competition), while other benefits brought by trade are not sufficient to compensate for the loss of economies of scale and monopoly profits caused by such shrinkage (at this time, some monopoly profits are obtained by foreign manufacturers). Ralph E. Gomory and William J. Baumol applied the classical trade model to the analysis of the modern world economy. Their analysis shows that in the modern world economy, the improvement of a country's production capacity to a certain point usually damages the overall welfare of other countries. Therefore, international trade may lead to major conflicts of interest rather than the overall improvement of the welfare of trading countries.[①] Therefore, free trade policy is not necessarily the best policy. It is necessary for a government to properly intervene and support industries with economies of scale, which is the basis for implementing the so-called strategic trade policy.

The new trade theory attaches great importance to the role of companies. This is because in intra-industry trade, the competitive advantages of each

---

[①] Ralph E. Gomory and William J. Baumol, *Global Trade and Conflicting National Interests*, Cambridge: MIT Press, 2001.

country are mainly manifested as the specific competitive advantages of companies, which is different from the situation under inter-industry trade where competitive advantages are primarily manifested as the national competitive advantages. The specific advantages of a company are its monopoly advantages over other competitors, which mainly include two types: one is the advantage of knowledge assets, and the other is the advantage of savings through economies of scale. The so-called knowledge assets include all intangible skills such as technologies, management and organization skills, and sales skills. If a company owns and controls these knowledge assets, it can produce differentiated products to compete in the international market. At the same time, it is usually easy for such companies to expand production rapidly, gain benefits from the scale effect, and enhance their international competitiveness. Whether it is a developed country or a developing country, as long as the country has companies with monopoly advantages, it can produce differentiated products to compete in the international market of intra-industry trade.

According to the constantly changing global economic and trade situation, contemporary international economists have revised, supplemented, and modified the classical and neo-classical theories of the division of labor in international trade and put forward some new theories, which is a challenge to the traditional theories. This is because with the general development of intra-industry trade, it is difficult to stick to the analysis method of factor endowment ratio to effectively explain the new trade phenomena. The traditional trade theory takes a country as the basic unit of analysis and is based on the premises that the international market is a perfectly competitive market and that the factors of production cannot flow freely among countries. The real market, however, has already become a market of monopolistic competition. The international flow of production factors has become a common phenomenon, and the influence of multinational corporations' decisions on trade and investment patterns cannot be ignored. Contemporary international economists have put forward various new opinions to illustrate these new phenomena of the division of labor in international trade. Economies of scale, increasing returns, and market structure theories are widely adopted to explain intra-industry and intra-company trade. The analysis of a company's behavior and specific advantages is considered to be abler to explain the evolution of contemporary trade patterns, intra-industry trade, and foreign direct investment, considering the incomplete connection of market structures, the monopoly advantages of companies, and new products and technologies. People have begun to devote themselves to establishing a general theory of international trade division and foreign direct investment to replace the traditional theory of division of labor in international trade.

The new theory of international trade, however, is not a total negation of the traditional theory. It still shares an inseparable theoretical origin with the traditional comparative costs theory and factor endowment theory. Its main viewpoints and analysis methods have not gone beyond the category of comparative advantages and disadvantages. Instead, they can be said to be the specific application of the analysis method of comparative advantages and disadvantages in a new situation. Ricardo's and Ohlin's analysis started from inter-industry trade, studying how to choose between different industries to find their own industries with comparative advantages to participate in international exchange. Intra-industry trade, in contrast, enlightens people on how to take advantage of the monopoly advantages of domestic enterprises such as knowledge assets to participate in international competition. Therefore, it can be said that the new trade theory is nothing more than studying how a country can obtain comparative benefits by participating in the international division of labor and international exchange under the circumstances that the pattern of division of labor in international trade has changed since the end of the Second World War. The comparative benefits under the traditional trade pattern come from the differences in comparative costs caused by different endowment ratios of production factors. When the horizontal international division of labor increasingly develops and becomes the dominant form of division of labor, comparative benefits come from the monopoly advantages and economies of scale of a country's enterprises. This does not mean that there is no difference between the new theory of division of labor in trade and the traditional one; rather, as the trade patterns studied by the two are different, their theoretical forms are naturally different. However, they are the same in terms of studying how a country can expand the division of labor in international trade and gain benefits through it according to the actual situation and its own comparative advantages. From this point of view, the new theory is not completely opposed to the traditional one; rather, it inherits and develops the latter.

II. Literature Review on Studies of Common Interests in International Capital Flow

Although Marx did not specifically discuss the issue of international capital flow in *Capital* and other works, his classic works still reflect abundant thoughts on international capital flow. The Marxist theory of international capital flow scientifically reveals the dual nature of international capital flow and its economic effects on the world economic pattern, the monetary effects, and the international transmission of economic crisis, laying a theoretical foundation for analyzing and studying current international capital flow.

1. Nature of international capital flow

(1) The duality of the nature of international capital flow. From the perspective of the theory of surplus value and the theory of socialized mass production, Marx profoundly revealed the dual nature of international capital flow. On the one hand, capital's essential attribute of pursuing surplus value inevitably leads to the expansion of capital across national borders. Capital is seeking to proliferate and develop in its continuous movement, featuring a tendency to expand indefinitely. Therefore, the process of capital circulation and proliferation is bound to extend beyond a country and form an international flow of capital. The growing demand for markets, raw materials, and capital "chases the bourgeoisie over the whole surface of the globe. It must nestle

everywhere, settle everywhere, establish connexions everywhere."① On the other hand, international capital flow is an objective requirement for socialized mass production.

With the progress of science and technology, the social division of labor is bound to go deeper. The combination of the deepening of the division of labor and the accumulation of capital will inevitably lead to the improvement of labor productivity and the expansion of commodity exchange. When the development of international exchange and international division of labor turns domestic production into international production, the world capitalist commodity production system, which is based on the international division of labor, is formed. A remarkable feature of the capitalist mode of production, which is different from previous modes of production, is the international nature of production. "[I]t made all civilised nations and every individual member of them dependent for the satisfaction of their wants on the whole world, thus destroying the former natural exclusiveness of separate nations."② The internationalization of production will inevitably lead to the internationalization of capital. Through commodity capital export and loan capital export, capitalist countries integrate all countries in the world into their own production systems. In Marx's view, international capital flow is the internationalization of commodity capital in the rotation of capital, and it extends across national borders to foreign countries as an important link in socialized reproduction— that is, part of the surplus value is realized through the world market. Therefore, it is also an important method of capital accumulation.

(2) The law of capital export and surplus capital. Marx believed that "surplus capital" is the material basis and necessary condition for capital export, while the latter is the only way out for surplus capital. Surplus capital refers "to a plethora of the capital for which the fall in the rate of profit is not

---

① *Marx & Engels Collected Works Vol. 06*, p. 487.
② *Marx & Engels Collected Works Vol. 05*, p. 73.

compensated through the mass of profit ... or to a plethora which places capitals incapable of action on their own at the disposal of the managers of large enterprises in the form of credit."① The full realization of the law of capitalist accumulation inevitably leads to a decline in the average profit rate, resulting in some capital having to accept a lower profit rate to continue its operation or losing its ability to operate independently and leaving it to others for control and use in the form of credit. These two types of capital are called "surplus capital." From the historical process of capitalist development, the process of capital accumulation and concentration has always been accompanied by the improvement of the organic composition of capital—that is, overpopulation occurs while there is already a surplus of capital. The coexistence of capital surplus and overpopulation will lead to the intensification of various contradictions inherent in capitalism. "If capital is sent abroad, this is not done because it absolutely could not be applied at home, but because it can be employed at a higher rate of profit in a foreign country. But such capital is absolute excess capital for the employed labouring population and for the home country in general."② It shows that Marx revealed the inevitable connection between capital export one the one hand and the law of the decline in the average profit rate of capital and the law of capital surplus on the other hand.

(3) Lenin's development of Marx's international capital flow theory. At the end of the 19th century and the beginning of the 20th century, when capitalist free competition turned to monopoly and state-monopoly capitalism, Lenin further developed Marx's international capital flow theory on the basis of the achievements of Marx's theory. Lenin, distinguishing commodity export from capital export, believed, "Typical of the old capitalism, when free competition held undivided sway, was the export of goods. Typical of the latest stage of capitalism, when monopolies rule, is the export of capital."③ He

---

① *Marx & Engels Collected Works Vol. 37*, pp. 249–250.
② Ibid, p. 255.
③ V. I. Lenin, *Lenin Collected Works Vol. 22*, Progress Publishers, 1964, p. 240.

further pointed out that capital export has two primary forms, namely, production capital export and loan capital export. Lenin believed that capital export needs to meet two conditions: first, there is surplus capital in a few developed capitalist countries; second, underdeveloped countries can develop capitalism. The two conditions are indispensable. "As long as capitalism remains what it is, surplus capital will be utilised not for the purpose of raising the standard of living of the masses in a given country, for this would mean a decline in profits for the capitalists, but for the purpose of increasing profits by exporting capital abroad to the backward countries. In these backward countries profits are usually high, for capital is scarce, the price of land is relatively low, wages are low, raw materials are cheap. The export of capital is made possible by a number of backward countries having already been drawn into world capitalist intercourse; main railways have either been or are being built in those countries, elementary conditions for industrial development have been created, etc. The need to export capital arises from the fact that in a few countries capitalism has become 'overripe' and (owing to the backward state of agriculture and the poverty of the masses) capital cannot find a field for 'profitable' investment."[①] Neither international commodity capital flow nor international monetary capital flow can get rid of the "original sin" of international capital flow—that is, driven by the motive to profit.

2. Economic effects of international capital flow

(1) International capital flow and world economic pattern. Marx not only examined the international capital flow from the perspective of production but also revealed the essence of international capital on the level of productive relations. This is because in Marx's view, capital not only manifests as a combination of production technologies but also reflects the social relations among people. The dual nature of international capital flow determines the duality of the capitalist world system formed by the international capital flow.

---

① *Lenin Collected Works Vol. 22*, pp. 241-242.

On the one hand, every process of international capital flow and capitalist development is accompanied by corresponding political, economic, and cultural changes. International capital flow has replaced the local and national self-sufficiency in the past with the interdependence and interconnection of nations. "The further the separate spheres, which act on one another, extend in the course of this development and the more the original isolation of the separate nationalities is destroyed by the advanced mode of production, by intercourse and by the natural division of labour between various nations arising as a result, the more history becomes world history."① "It produced world history for the first time, insofar as it made all civilised nations and every individual member of them dependent for the satisfaction of their wants on the whole world, thus destroying the former natural exclusiveness of separate nations."②

On the other hand, according to the needs of capitalist economies to develop the world market, international capital flow controls and reforms colonies and semicolonies and incorporates them into the capitalist development system, thus ending these countries' own process of economic and social development to a greater extent. Lenin not only regarded capital flow as one of the important economic characteristics of the monopoly capitalism period but also pointed out that the inevitable result of capital export would be the world being carved up by the capitalist alliance. "[U]nder capitalism the home market is inevitably bound up with the foreign market. Capitalism long ago created a world market. As the export of capital increased, and as the foreign and colonial connections and 'spheres of influence' of the big monopolist associations expanded in all ways, things 'naturally' gravitated towards an international agreement among these associations, and towards the formation of international cartels."③

Lenin believed that the economic division of the world by the monopoly

---

① Marx & Engels Collected Works Vol. 05, pp. 50–51.
② Ibid, p. 73.
③ Lenin Collected Works Vol. 22, p. 246.

alliance is an inevitable trend and result of the free competition and development of capitalism in the world. Of course, the monopoly alliance can take different forms of international capital flow to divide the world market, but no matter which form they take, it is a method of exploitation and enslavement of people by financial oligarchs in imperialist countries. Lenin further pointed out that capital export would inevitably bring about two consequences: first, capital export would cause some stagnation in the development of exporting countries to some extent; second, capital export always affects the capitalist development of the importing countries, greatly accelerating the development of capitalism in importing countries.

(2) Monetary effects of international capital flow. In the international market, once money flows out of the domestic circulation field, it loses the local forms of price standard, coins, fractional currency, and value symbols obtained in this field and restores its original form of precious metals. "One national currency is expressed in another, and thus all of them are reduced to their content of gold or silver, while the latter, being the two commodities circulating as world money, are simultaneously reduced to their reciprocal value ratio, which changes continually."①

Marx believed that the inflow and outflow of precious metals in a country are related to its trade balance; they may also be, however, the manifestations of the import and export of precious metals themselves that are not related to commodity transactions. First, the leading cause of changes in exchange rates is the balance of international payments. No matter what causes the balance of international payments, it will bring about changes in the supply and demand for foreign exchange: when there is a favorable balance of international payments, international capital inflow occurs, and the local currency value will rise if foreign currency supply exceeds demand; on the contrary, when there is an adverse balance of payments, international capital outflow occurs, and it

---

① *Marx & Engels Collected Works Vol. 37*, p. 317.

may lead to devaluation of the local currency. Second, under the condition of the commodity economy, inflation causes increases in prices and declines in the internal value of money. Furthermore, it also leads to the long-term falling trend of exchange rates until the internal value of money is in line with its external value. In examining the impact of international capital flow on exchange rates, Marx pointed out, "If this export is made in the form of precious metal, it will exert a direct influence upon the money market and with it upon the interest rate of the country exporting this precious metal ... since it is precious metal and as such is directly loanable money capital and the basis of the entire money system. Similarly, this export also directly affects the rate of exchange. ... In the long run, such a shipment of precious metal to India must have the effect of increasing the Indian demand for English commodities, because it indirectly increases the consuming power of India for European goods. But if the capital is shipped in the form of rails, etc., it cannot have any influence on the rates of exchange ... it need not have any influence on the money market."[1] It can be seen that, in Marx's view, only the output of precious metals will have a direct impact on exchange rates, while under normal circumstances, the output of ordinary commodities will not have any direct impact on exchange rates because the commodity importers do not need to pay.

(3) International capital flow and international transmission of economic crisis. Marx examined currency circulation under the capitalist credit system around the world, pointing out that the comprehensive crises in reality always broke out when the inflow of precious metals exceeded the outflow. International credit makes it possible for all countries to be drawn into a crisis successively—that is, international capital flow acts as an accelerator to the outbreak of financial crises. This is because international commercial credit and capital credit may create false demand and prosperity around the world, prompting all countries to export and import excessively and thus leading to

---

[1] *Marx & Engels Collected Works Vol. 37*, p. 572.

overproduction. Under the gold standard system, the flow of precious metals is closely connected with the industrial cycle. During the period of economic prosperity, as commodities are overproduced, the illusory prosperity is completely maintained by credit. At this time, precious metals outflow occurs, leading to higher interest rates and credit expansion and resulting in excessive inflation—that is, precious metals outflow promotes the outbreak of credit crises. "[A] drain of metal is generally the symptom of a change in the state of foreign trade, and this change in turn is a premonition that conditions are again approaching a crisis."① The outflow of gold does not necessarily lead to a credit crisis, but if it occurs at a difficult time in the industrial cycle, it may lead to the outbreak of a credit crisis. "[A] drain, a continued and heavy export of precious metal, takes place ... as soon as a greatly increased demand for loan capital exists and the interest rate, therefore, has reached at least its average level. This period, therefore, precedes the crash."② Therefore, international capital flow itself does not necessarily lead to a financial crisis, but it often facilitates the outbreak of a financial crisis when affected by other factors. In fact, the root cause of economic crises lies in the economic system itself—the fundamental contradiction between the inherent socialized production in capitalism and the capitalist private ownership, which further leads to the contradiction between the unlimited expansion of social production and the relatively reduced effective demand. International capital flow is only the means and a manifestation of capitalism in trying to resolve the conflicts and crises by expanding the external scope of production. "Capitalist production seeks continually to overcome these immanent barriers, but overcomes them only by means which again place these barriers in its way and on a more formidable scale."③ On the one hand, international capital flow has temporarily eased the inherent contradictions in capitalism; on the other hand, it has pushed the

---

① Marx & Engels Collected Works Vol. 37, p. 565.
② Ibid, pp. 565-566.
③ Ibid, p. 248.

contradictions to a greater space, increasing the possibility of crises breaking out and spreading internationally. Different countries' economies are linked by international capital flow, which means that as long as one country on the chain has a credit crisis, the crisis will spread to all the relevant countries in turn.

3. Practical value of Marx's thought on international capital flow

When Marx's was writing *Capital*, capitalism was in the period of free competition, with a relatively low level of productivity and a narrow range of the international division of labor. Although international capital flow (mainly capital exports) have already appeared, it is small in scale and have not become a regular phenomenon, and the capital flowing overseas is mainly commodity capital. Marx mainly revealed the essence of international capital flow from the perspective of production relations and thus focused on capital exports from developed countries to colonial countries, which was also in line with the international capital flow at that time. Under the historical conditions at that time, whether it is the flow of loan capital or production capital, it is always accompanied by the transfer of actual resources.

However, since the mid-1980s, with the in-depth development of economic financialization and the overall advancement of economic globalization, the international capital flow has become increasingly complicated. On the one hand, international capital flow exists not only between developed and developing countries but also among developed countries. For example, the United States absorbs a large amount of international capital inflow while exporting a huge amount of capital. What is more complicated is that when developing countries open up their domestic markets to attract foreign investment, they also begin to invest abroad and actively participate in international capital markets. On the other hand, with the development of financing securitization and the continuous emergence of innovative financial tools, international capital flow is increasingly breaking away from the operation of physical economy and is increasingly manifested as pure virtual capital flow, featuring more complex motives. In addition to differences in expected profit margins, risk differences in different markets, changes in policies in various countries, changes in investors' psychological expectations, and even the irrational "Herd Effect" can all bring about international capital flow. Needless to say, from today's reality of international capital flow, Marx's theory does have certain historical limitations. However, the Marxist theory of international capital flow scientifically reveals the dual nature of international capital flow and lays a theoretical foundation for scholars today to analyze and study the current international capital flow.

First of all, although the modern forms of international capital flow are more diversified with increasingly complex influences, from a comprehensive and historical perspective, Marx's analysis of capital outflow shares common essential characteristics with today's complex international capital flow. Whether it is highly speculative international hot money or international direct investment with certain stability, it is always profit-oriented, only different in the means and methods of pursuing profits. If the decision-making of international capital flow is incorporated into the analysis framework of utility optimization for investors from a micro perspective, we will find that the utility function of the Marxist theory is unitary, i.e., the surplus value rate or profit rate is the only independent variable, while the utility function of modern international capital flow is an extension of the former, showing diversified characteristics: on the one hand, the variable of profit rate is subdivided into several specific variables such as the interest rate, the expected exchange rate, etc.; on the other hand, the risk variable increases, enabling investors to find an asset portfolio with maximum utility when balancing risks and returns. It can also be simply put that the study of modern international capital flow needs to extend the Marxist principle of profit maximization into the principle of utility maximization so as to expand its theoretical interpretation to adapt to the reality of modern international capital flow. However, the extension of the theoretical interpretation does not constitute a negation of the essence of international investors which is the pursuit of maximum profits. On the contrary, it is a more adequate and comprehensive disclosure of this essence.

Second, historical international capital flow reflects the exploitation of colonies and semicolonies by western developed countries, while today's international capital flow is more reflected in the relations of equality and mutual benefits between sovereign countries, at least in form. This fact can also be explained by the duality of international capital flow proposed by Marx. In Marx's era, capitalism invaded the colonial and semicolonial countries with powerful weapons, while today, developing countries actively introduce foreign capital and actively participate in the international capital market against the background of economic and financial globalization. On the one hand, although different forms of international capital flow have different impacts on the mechanisms of capital formation and thus have different effects on the economic growth of these developing countries, there is one thing that cannot be denied—that is, international capital flow plays a huge role in promoting the economic development of developing countries. For example, in addition to directly increasing the domestic capital supply and resolving the cash flow gap and foreign exchange gap of the capital-inflow country, the inflow of international direct investment can also introduce advanced management experience and production technology and produce positive technology spillover effect and market spillover effect on other economic sectors of the capital-inflow country. Besides, securities investment and international bank loans can directly make up for the capital accumulation gap, increase the foreign exchange supply, improve the scope and depth of the financial market, promote the organic combination of capital and labor, and also advance the economic growth of the capital-inflow country. The free flow of international capital strengthens the discipline of the macro-economic policies of capital-inflow countries, which brings benefits similar to those brought by the opening up of trade in goods and services. On the other hand, it is precisely because of capital's profit-seeking nature that large-scale international capital flow will also bring huge risks to the real economy and financial system of developing countries. Income growth and improved trading conditions will have a further positive impact on investment and savings, and capital inflow and foreign debt increase will have a negative impact, while the impacts of interest rates and the depth of financial markets on investment and savings remain uncertain. According to the standard model of an open economy, the increase in consumption and investment will bring appreciation to the actual exchange rate, which will lead to an upward pressure on the price of non-trade goods, thus stimulating inflation. International capital inflow will result in an excessive expansion of the aggregate demand in the capital-inflow country, which is mainly manifested as inflationary pressures, appreciation of the actual exchange rate, and widening current account deficits. This feature of concurrent opportunities and risks is also rooted in the duality of international capital flow.

Finally, under the gold standard system, the international capital flow was realized by promoting the growth of social real wealth to exploit surplus value (profits). At that time, the international capital flow was limited to the growth of real wealth, and capital proliferation was always limited by gold, the "metal." However, when the monetary system is transformed into a standard system of pure credit, capital proliferation breaks through almost all possible restrictions. International capital can be built on the huge storage of abstract wealth, and international capital flow itself breaks further and further away from the actual production process. The financialization of international capital enlarges and spreads the instability and volatility in capital flow, laying financial risks and even financial crises in the process of international capital flow. The current economic globalization has made the crisis transmission effect of international capital flow more obvious, which can be divided into the spillover effect and the contagion effect. The spillover effect means that a country's financial fluctuation or crisis may affect another country's macroeconomic foundation, causing the same fluctuation. In international capital flow, this phenomenon is realized through creditors' adjustment of asset portfolios. The contagion effect means that due to investors' tendency to invest in different securities portfolios to obtain stable returns, under the condition that returns from financial assets resemble the risk structures in emerging market economies, investors will sell assets of neighboring countries that they believe have similar risks when a country has a crisis, thus causing contagion of the crisis.

III. Literature Review on Studies of Transfer and Diffusion of International Technological Interests

International technology diffusion plays a vital role in the process of economic development. As productivity is the main determinant affecting a country's economic growth, international technology diffusion exerts effects on the long-term economic growth of a country by affecting its productivity. Therefore, international technology diffusion is the main determinant of the difference in per capita income among countries. Since the 1990s, driven by transportation and information technologies, the world is gradually moving towards economic globalization, featuring an increasingly great influence of international technology diffusion on the economic development of various countries.

1. Research on international technology diffusion models

A large number of scholars such as Richard R. Nelson and Edmund Phelp (1966), Krugman (1979, 1993), and Grossman and Helpman (1991)[1] have made contributions to the study of technology diffusion models. Raymond Vernon, who proposed the product life cycle (PLC) theory, was the pioneer in this field. The theory holds that new products and technologies that are developed in developed countries will only be transferred to developing countries after standardization. Krugman developed Vernon's hypothesis into a general equilibrium model based on Vernon's PLC theory. In this model, each product is invented in the North and then exported and transferred to the South. Dollar made an important extension of the Krugman model and developed it

---

[1] G. Grossman and E. Helpman, *Innovation and Growth in the World Economy*, Cambridge: MIT Press, 1991.

into a two-element neoclassical dynamic equilibrium model. Dollar's model focuses on the dynamic process of technological innovation, capital flow, and the transfer of product production from developed countries to developing countries and analyzes both short-term and long-term equilibrium. Jensen and Thursby put forward a dynamic game model in 1986, simulating the process of North-South trade and technology transfer as the game result of both sides' optimal decision-making while internalizing the technological innovation and transfer in the first-generation model. They introduced the concepts of imitation cost and innovation cost, in which the scale of technological imitation in countries of the South depends on the number of monopoly technologies currently possessed by the developed countries of the North. Grossman and Helpman (1991) also discussed the relationship between innovation in the North and imitation in the South under the framework of the new growth theory. Based on their research, Barro[1] further improved the technology diffusion model. In his leader-follower model, the leader countries develop new products through investment in research and development; then the follower countries only imitate and absorb the products invented and produced by the leader countries at certain costs without inventing any intermediate product. Thus, under certain conditions, the technology diffusion in the follower countries will expand at a higher pace than the leader countries. After the follower countries have learned all the innovations in the leader countries, the technology diffusion in the two groups will expand at the same pace, but they will not converge to the same per capita output and wage level. Barro[2] developed the model again in 1997, combining the new growth model with the neoclassical growth model's feature of convergence inference, resolving the adjustment mechanism problem of technology diffusion that had not been solved before, and emphasizing the importance of intellectual property protection. R. van

---

[1] Barro and Sala-I-Martin, *Economic Growth*, New York: Mcgraw-Hill, Inc., 1995.
[2] Robert Barro and Jong-Wha Lee, "Technology Diffusion, Convergence and Growth," *Journal of Economic Growth*, 1997(2): 363-394.

Elkan (1997) further pointed out that the possible improvement in production efficiency that may be brought about by technological imitation depends on the technological gap between the countries, while the effectiveness of technological innovation depends on a country's ability to "learn by doing" and the accumulation of experience. Because of the existence of technology diffusion, the increase in investment in any country may affect the economic growth of the country itself and other countries at the same time. Enric Detragiache[1] established a macroeconomic model of income convergence caused by technological gaps: developing countries pay a certain amount to introduce advanced foreign technologies, and the first adopters have certain externalities to the following adopters, as they have reduced the costs of trial and error. The adoption of a technology is a gradual process in a balanced situation. Because of the existence of externalities, minor differences in adoption costs may lead to substantial differences in the long-term income. These models provide a theoretical framework for technology diffusion between developed and developing countries and among developed countries, laying a foundation for subsequent empirical research.

2. Determinants of the effect of international technology diffusion

(1) The level of human capital in the host country. Keller (1996) pointed out that for developing countries, trade liberalization has brought about advanced technologies and products which can only be applied after the domestic labor force have learned the corresponding skills. There are high-level and low-level human capital. Human capital at higher levels (such as scientists and engineers) is conducive to the digestion and absorption of introduced technologies, the resolution of technical problems encountered in production, and giving full play to the production capacity of these technologies. Moreover, high-quality technicians are also needed to carry out imitation and innovation on

---

[1] Enric Detragiache, "Technology Diffusion and International Income Convergence," *Journal of Development Ecnomics*, 1998 (56): 367-392.

the basis of digestion and absorption to develop independent innovation capability. Human capital (skilled workers) at the lower levels is helpful in giving full play to the productivity of advanced equipment and the application of introduced advanced technologies. For foreign direct investment (FDI), it is easier for human capital at the higher levels to attract capital-intensive multinational companies and increase the potential space for technology diffusion. The conclusion drawn from the empirical test of FDI also demonstrates the importance of human capital.

(2) R&D investment from the host country. First of all, in order to adapt the introduced technologies to local production, it is necessary to adjust and transform the technologies to a certain extent, which requires corresponding research in the technology-introduced country. Second, in order to imitate foreign technologies, the host country must master the foreign technologies, which also requires research. The purpose of much of the R&D investment in Japan, for example, is to digest and absorb introduced foreign technologies. The study of Republic of Korea (RoK) also shows that the rapid improvement of its technology level has benefited from its emphasis on the digestion and absorption of introduced technologies. Finally, independent research and development in the host country can improve its technology level, which will in turn enhance its ability to absorb, digest, and innovate advanced technologies, thus increasing the possibility of technology spillovers.

(3) Technology gap. There needs to be a certain gap between foreign technologies and domestic technologies; otherwise, there is little to learn. However, the gap cannot be too large; otherwise, enterprises from the host country will be unable to use the introduced technologies.[①] Research by Teece (1980) and Kumar (1994) shows that the cost of technology transfers decreases with the increase in the age of the technology. The longer the technology has

---

[①] Magnus Blomstrom and Fredrik Sjoholm, "Technology Transfer and Spillovers: Does Local Participation with Multinationals Matter," *European Economic Review*, 1999 (43): 915-923.

been invented, the easier it is for the host country to digest and absorb. Japanese management scientist Kiyoshi Kojima, who proposed the theory of ordered technology transfer, holds that the smaller the technology gap between the technology exporter and the importer is, the better the effect of the technology transfer is.

(4) The similarity in technologies. Only when the technologies used by different regions and countries have certain similarities can technology diffusion be effective. Taking agriculture as an example, Schultz (1964) and Hayami and Rutan (1985) noted that the process of international diffusion of agricultural technology is more difficult than that of technologies in the manufacturing industry. This is because agricultural technology is highly localized, and in most cases, technological development in developed countries is not directly spread to underdeveloped countries with different climate and resource characteristics.

(5) Share of the host country in joint ventures. For FDI, it is generally believed that the host country's participation in joint ventures makes technology more likely to spill over. Many countries have imposed restrictions on foreign equity shares and forced multinational companies to sign joint venture agreements. In the face of this restriction, however, multinational companies can choose not to invest, or they can choose not to introduce advanced technologies into joint venture subsidiaries. Faced with profit incentives, the larger the equity is, the more willing the multinational parent company is to transfer advanced technologies, which expands the scope of potential spillovers. However, in empirical studies, Magnus Blomstrom's research on Indonesia shows that equity share has little effect on technology spillover.

(6) Intellectual property protection. The impact of intellectual property protection on technology diffusion is twofold: on the one hand, better intellectual property protection prompts foreign companies to transfer advanced technologies, enlarging potential diffusion; on the other hand, strengthening the protection of intellectual property rights is unfavorable to the imitation by domestic enterprises, restricting, for example, reverse engineering and

technology diffusion.

(7) Market environment and policies of the host country. Competition among multinational companies is conducive to their introduction of advanced technologies, thus expanding the space for technology spillovers. In countries with a low degree of marketization, enterprises have insufficient motivation to improve their technology level and do not pay attention to the introduction, digestion, and absorption of technologies, leading to a poor technology diffusion effect. Most countries have formulated a series of policies on technology diffusion, which have had a great impact on the effect of technology diffusion. For example, many countries have technology transfer regulations for FDI, forcing multinational companies to transfer technologies. Subsidies are given to enterprises that take the lead in introducing technologies and R&D cooperation is carried out between the government and enterprises to reduce the total introducing costs and increase the welfare of the country. Japan and Republic of Korea are both successful examples in this regard.

Research on the effect of international technology diffusion on economic growth emerged in the late 1980s. Scholars have carried out detailed discussions on the mechanism, channels, and constraints of technology diffusion and put forward many useful policy suggestions. Although many issues have not yet been settled, from the above analysis, we can draw the following three conclusions. ① International technology diffusion plays a huge role in global economic growth, especially for developing countries. ② The main channels for international technology diffusion are international trade, FDI, and international exchange. Trade as a channel for technology diffusion has been basically uncontroversial, and sufficient evidence has been found under various methods. However, for FDI, a consensus has not been reached. Generally speaking, the diffusion effect of FDI is more significant in developed countries than in developing countries. One important reason emphasized by scholars is the difference in absorbing abilities. ③ Technology diffusion does not naturally lead to technological progress in the host country but faces a series of constraints. Therefore, the host country must have a certain absorbing ability and adopt some policies to promote the diffusion of technology in order to obtain greater benefits.

IV. Literature Review on Studies of Interests in International Human Capital Flow

The 1970s and 1980s had seen the introduction and rise of the human capital theory, but thoughts on human capital can be traced back to ancient Greece. Plato believed that national managers should receive education and training, having not only cultural knowledge such as mathematics, geometry, and astronomy but also a strong body. Aristotle also mentioned many times the role of knowledge and skills in production activities and in determining one's social status. William Petty, the founder of British classical political economy, once stated that "labor is the Father and active principle of wealth, as lands are the Mother." A country's economic strength is closely related to its population and people's physique and skills.

After the Industrial Revolution in Europe in the mid-18th century, human beings entered the great industrial age, and three fundamental changes took place in productivity: first, natural forces replaced human beings, and mechanical production replaced manual production; second, science and technology replaced experience and technical routines, and the interaction between science and technology and production was increasingly strengthened; third, professional technological training replaced workshop mentoring, and human knowledge and technologies played an increasingly important role in production. The rise of classical economics at that time began to focus on the significance of education in promoting the development of production and increasing wealth from the perspective of the different roles of laborers in the production process. Adam Smith, representative of the famous classical school, made a profound exposition of human capital and the significance of education in his monumental work *The Wealth of Nations* published in 1776. He pointed out that among the fixed capital of the society, the projects that can provide revenue or profit include, in addition to material capital, the acquired and useful abilities of all the inhabitants or members of the society. The improved dexterity of a workman may be considered in the same light as a machine or instrument of trade which facilitates and abridges labor, which is fixed capital of the society. It can be seen that Smith's thoughts have approached the core of modern human capital theory to some extent. A large number of famous economists in the period of classical economics had thoughts on human capital, including Sismondi and David Ricardo, who have all realized that human knowledge and skills are the source of wealth and an important factor of production. Friedrich List of the German Historical School proposed the concept of "mental capital," believing that "mental capital" is formed by the convergence of intellectual achievements. The level of a country's productivity depends on its utilization of the mental capital. Therefore, he advocated that teachers should be included in the list of producers because teachers "can make the next generation become producers." He also believed that mental capital is the mental strength and physical strength possessed by individuals or obtained by individuals from social and political environments and that the current situation in various countries is the result of all the discoveries, inventions, improvements, and efforts made by many generations before us, which are the mental capital of modern human beings.

Marx founded Marxist economics on the basis of the labor theory of value put forward by the masters of classical economics. Marx expounded from a philosophical point of view that man is the subject of labor and that natural resources are the object of labor. He divided labor into simple labor and complex labor, which is also enlightening for contemporary human capital theorists.[1]

However, thoughts on human capital were set back because of the

---

[1] Liu Chunyang, "Development of Western Human Capital Theory," *Journal of Shandong Agricultural University (Social Science Edition)*, 2004 (6): 1-4.

opposition of Marshall, famous representative of English neoclassical economics in the late 19th and early 20th centuries. Marshall pointed out that from an abstract and mathematical point of view, there is no denying that people are capital, but regarding them as capital in actual analysis is not consistent with the actual situation of the market. On the one hand, Marshall carefully studied the economic value of education and advocated viewing education as a national investment that could bring huge profits. He believed that human talent is as important a means of production as any other kind of capital and even reached the conclusion that the most valuable capital is investment in people, holding that investment in education will bring much greater benefits than the investment itself. On the other hand, in actual analysis, Marshall objected to viewing human as capital because he held the belief that human beings are not for trading and objected to the concept of "human capital."

In 1935, Professor Walsh of Harvard University published an article entitled "Capital Concept Applied to Man." He was the first to put forward the concept of human capital and studied the issue of the economic income of education in universities with quantitative methods. However, the actual formation of the theoretical system was in the 1950s and 1960s. The economic phenomena after the Second World War could not be explained by traditional economic theories. For example, why is economic growth always higher than the growth of factor investment? Why could resource-poor countries such as Germany and Japan recover quickly and rise again after the war? Some economists got rid of the the narrow view of traditional economics which was limited to the study of material capital and shifted their focus from materials to human, conducting in-depth research and discussions on the problems mentioned above from the perspectives of education, health, and workers' skills and providing convincing answers, thus directly promoting the formation of modern human capital theory.

In 1960, Theodore W. Schultz, Nobel laureate in economics and famous American economist, delivered a famous speech entitled "Investment in Human

Capital" at the annual meeting of the American Economic Association. Human capital theory in the modern sense was thus formally formed, and Schultz was also praised as the "father of human capital" by later generations. The theory was immediately accepted by western theorists the moment it was put forward.

1. Connotations and characteristics of human capital

In Schultz's view, human capital is a concept in contrast to material capital or non-human capital, which refers to the knowledge, ability, and health embodied in the human body and is a kind of capital that can be used to produce future income. Human capital exists in the forms of scientific knowledge and labor skills. It has the following four characteristics when compared with material capital.

First, from the perspective of production time, material capital is a production factor that is produced in a relatively short period of time, while human capital cannot be produced until workers have studied and been trained for a relatively long period of time. With the development of science and technology and the progress of social productivity, workers are required to have a more extended study time. Therefore, the production time of human capital will be further extended.

Second, as far as the characteristics of property rights are concerned, the property rights of material capital can be transferred in the process of circulation; however, only the right of use of human capital can be transferred, not its ownership.

Third, from the perspective of the number of uses, although material capital can be reused many times, the use value, function, or utility of material capital will also gradually decrease or disappear with the increase in the number of uses. It is not the case with human capital. Not only can human capital be reused, but its use value, function, and utility also do not decrease with the increase in the number of uses. On the contrary, human capital will be added new functions and utilities in the process of each usage or application.

Fourth, from the perspective of the functional efficacy, the exertion of the functions or utilities of material capital is carried out uniformly, while human capital can be utilized under non-uniform conditions—that is, it has the characteristics of creating new products and more value.

2. Scope and content of human capital investment

Schultz not only discussed the importance of human capital and its investment but also elaborated on the specifics of its investment. There are mainly five points.

The first is investment in formal education, which refers to investment in primary, secondary, and higher education. Education is a kind of "quality investment" and is an important way to improve the general quality of citizens and the abilities of workers. School education includes primary, secondary, and higher education. Educational costs refer to the expenses that students directly use for education and the income that students give up during their schooling.

The second is investment in on-the-job training, which is adult education for on-the-job workers, aiming to improve their labor skills, adapt them to new technologies, and promote new experiences. In this regard, off-campus learning and training in agricultural technology are particularly effective. On-the-job personnel training, including the traditional apprenticeship in enterprises, is a considerable expenditure, which leads to an important question: who is going to pay the costs? Gary S. Becker once put forward a point of view in this regard that in a competitive market, employees themselves pay all the training fees, which may initially reduce their net income but will substantially increase their income later.

The third is health investment, which refers to investment to improve the physical quality of the population, which includes expenditures on health care, maternal and infant health, nutrition, rest, and other aspects related to physical health. Health investment contributes to the increase in "health capital stock." As a result of improved health status, the average life expectancy of people of different ages has increased by 30%. Medical treatment and health care, including all the expenses affecting a person's life span, strength, endurance, energy, etc., have both quantitative and qualitative requirements, which will inevitably improve the quality of human resources.

The fourth is migration investment, which refers to the investment that individuals and families make to adapt to changing employment opportunities through migration in order to seek a better life or greater benefits.

The fifth is investment in scientific research. Schultz defined scientific research as a special activity that requires special skills and facilities to discover and develop special forms of new information and believed that such new information is both appropriate and of certain economic value.

As the founder of the human capital theory, Schultz has made pioneering contributions to the human capital theory. First, on the basis of explaining human capital, he clearly identified the scope and content of investment in human capital, providing an important framework for future research. Second, he conducted analysis of many economic phenomena that cannot be explained by the traditional capital theory, which has provided a new way of thinking for economic research. Third, he conducted economic analysis on the time value of human beings and observed that there was a considerable gap in the time value of human beings between low-income countries and high-income countries. Fourth, based on the human capital theory, Schultz initiated the theory of "the economics of being poor." He pointed out that the root cause of poverty lies not in the proliferation of the poor but in the lack of human capital.

Another scholar who made a fundamental contribution to the human capital theory is Gary S. Becker, who laid the microeconomic foundation of human capital theory. In 1964, Becker's monumental work *Human Capital* was regarded as the starting point for the revolution of human capital investment in economic thought by the western academia. Becker's contribution to the human capital theory mainly lies in his microeconomic analysis of human resources and his analysis of the economic decision-making and cost-effectiveness of family childbearing behavior. The concepts put forward by Becker of direct cost and indirect cost of children, time value and time allocation of families, and market activities and non-market activities in families are refreshing. He emphasized the importance of education and training in the formation of human capital, analyzing the expenditure and income of formal education, on-the-job training, and other human capital investment, the age-income curve, and other issues. Becker's research methods and achievements are quite groundbreaking, laying a good foundation for the development of the human capital theory.

In general, from the perspective of the research paradigm, there are two trains of thought for research on the human capital theory. The first is from a macroscopic perspective, which takes economic growth problems into consideration, discusses in depth the role of human capital in economic growth, and uses the human capital theory to explain the observed economic phenomena that cannot be interpreted with traditional theories. The second is from a microscopic research perspective. It tries to use economic methods to analyze individual and family behaviors and incorporate issues such as education, marriage, fertility, health, and migration into the input-output analysis framework.

3. Direction of international human capital flow

The flow of talents has long been a controversial worldwide problem, whose impacts on the entire world economy and the outflow and inflow countries have not yet been determined. Since the second half of the 20th century, international migration has been characterized by diversity. The most prominent feature is that the proportion of senior talents, who mainly flow from developing countries to developed countries, in international migration has increased. With economic globalization, the proportion of high-quality population migration will continue to expand.

Allan M. Williams (2005) classified the international flow of human capital according to the static influence of the international distribution of intelligence, dividing international flow of human capital into brain exchange, brain drain, brain overflow, brain waste, brain circulation, etc. Among them, brain drain is the most controversial focus in international flow of human capital because the permanent flow of human capital from developing countries to developed countries will bring far-reaching and complex impacts on the balanced development of the entire world economy.

Since the 1990s, there is no exact data on the international flow of highly skilled talents, but there is evidence to indicate that more and more talents are flowing from developing countries in Asia, Africa, and South America to developed countries in North America and Europe. Brain drain has become the main form of international human capital flow. Specifically, it has the following two characteristics.

First, developed countries are the major inflow countries of human capital, among which the United States is the largest. In addition, Canada, Germany, France, and the U.K., as well as some emerging industrial countries in Asia, such as Singapore, are also net inflow countries of human capital. By 2000, highly skilled foreign immigrants had accounted for a significant proportion of the total number of highly skilled workers in developed countries.

Second, developing countries are the main outflow countries of human capital. Africa is the region with the most serious brain drain. In 1999, in 40% of African countries, more than 35% of their college graduates settled abroad. Small countries in Central and South America and the Caribbean have lost nearly one-third of their highly skilled talents. Asia is the region with the largest population of brain drain, and India is the main outflow country. Other Asian countries such as Pakistan, China, Thailand, Sri Lanka, and Vietnam also face various problems brought by brain drain.

4. Main causes of international human capital flow

From a macro perspective, the international human capital flow is caused by the imbalanced supply and demand for human capital in different countries. With the economic growth and progress of developed countries, many jobs and positions requiring high skills are also emerging. These countries are facing a shortage of senior talents and are actively looking for suitable talents in the international labor market to fill these vacancies.

From the micro perspective, economic incentives are the most direct cause.

Senior talents can usually find jobs with much higher salaries in developed countries than in their own countries. In developing countries in Africa and the Caribbean, such as Jamaica, South Africa, and Ghana, a large proportion of their well-trained professionals are attracted by employment opportunities with high salaries in developed countries. Besides, other non-economic factors are also important reasons for people to choose to emigrate. Some people choose to emigrate because there are no suitable jobs in their own countries to give full play to their special skills and to provide the conditions needed for work and research, including hardware facilities and a supportive environment of colleagues. In addition, many other people are trying to escape from the high crime rate, AIDS, the high unemployment rate, and the political oppression in their own countries. Some scholars believe that non-economic factors have a more severe impact on the international flow of human capital than economic incentives and often lead to permanent brain drain.

V. Impact of International Human Capital Flow

1. Impact of international human capital flow on welfare of entire international community

The loss of human capital will lead to a permanent decrease in the growth rate of per capita income in the outflow country while the impact on the economic growth of the inflow country is not clear as it will change along with the ratio of the two countries' average human capital level. Further research shows that the flow of human capital will cause permanent differences in economic growth rates among countries.

Some scholars also proposed to use the S-shaped production function model to analyze the impact of brain drain on the overall international welfare. This model describes the different marginal rates of return of human capital at different levels of development, which can be increasing, decreasing, or negligible. Developing countries are at the bottom of the S-shaped production function model, which means that the marginal rate of return will increase when a new senior talent is added. On the contrary, as developed countries may be at the top of the S-shaped production function model, under the premise that they already have a large number of high-quality talents, an additional talent may bring about a diminishing marginal rate of return. In extreme cases, the least developed countries (LDC), at the very beginning of the S-shaped production function, own a tiny number of senior talents and do not meet the minimum threshold for generating the marginal rate of return. In this case, the marginal rate of return of human capital is insignificant. However, adding a certain quantity of senior talents to exceed the "threshold" of human capital can bring about significantly increased rate of returns. Therefore, senior talents are more valuable in developing countries than in developed countries. The decrease in the number of talents in developing countries may even cause their production function to regress to the beginning of the S-shaped model, thus making them fall into the trap of scarcity of human capital. Brain drain cannot bring about a "win-win" result, and to a large extent, it is a "lose-win" situation, which means that the improvement of one side's welfare is based on the reduction of the other side's welfare. Developing countries are the victims of brain drain, whose negative impacts are not limited to the economy but also involve all aspects of the social life. The widening wealth gap between developing and developed countries and the various serious social problems in developing countries are not good for developed countries as well.

2. Impact of international human capital flow on welfare of outflow countries

For developing countries, the benefits of human capital outflow mainly depend on the talents that went broad bringing back the advanced ideas and technologies they have learned in other countries and applying the ideas and technologies to practice in their homeland. However, in fact, the talent flow between developing countries and developed countries is mostly one-way—that is, migrants from developing countries are more inclined to stay in developed countries to work and live. For example, from 1990 to 1991, 79% of the Indian students studying in the United States and 88% of the Chinese students studying in the United States continued to stay in the United States after obtaining their PhD degrees. In contrast, only 11% of the RoK students and 15% of the Japanese students studying in the United States chose to work in the United States after obtaining their PhD degrees in science and engineering. Therefore, for developing countries, brain drain may bring great negative effects.

(1) Impacts on the fiscal revenue. Brain drain has a relatively great impact on the fiscal revenue of developing countries. On the one hand, brain drain will reduce the tax base of tax revenue; on the other hand, senior talents are often the objects of the highest tax rate. Therefore, the national fiscal revenue will decrease with the loss of senior talents. According to statistics, although Indian Americans make up only 0.1% of India's total population, their income in the United States is equal to 10% of India's national income. Relevant research shows that nearly one-third of India's personal income tax has vanished with the departure of emigrants. Other developing countries are also facing similar problems.

In addition to the direct impact on personal income tax, brain drain also has indirect impacts on other types of taxes. The loss of high-quality talents makes direct taxes more difficult to collect, and the government relies more on indirect taxes. Like many developing countries, India relies on indirect taxes to a greater extent, with about 65.6% of its revenue coming from indirect taxes. Furthermore, brain drain will also distort taxation. In order to retain talents, governments reduce the marginal tax rate of personal income tax, making low-income earners bear heavier burdens accordingly and thus weakening the significance of tax revenue as a social regulator.

(2) Impacts on the education system. In most countries, the state will allocate a large amount of the fiscal revenue to finance part of the education expenses, which comes almost exclusively from taxpayers. Brain drain means that when talents from developing countries leave their countries after completing their higher education with taxpayers' aid. On the one hand, they

have not devoted the knowledge they have accumulated back to their own countries for the benefits of their own people; on the other hand, they have not fulfilled their obligation to pay taxes to their homeland to finance the education of the next generation. As brain drain has taken away a large part of the government's fiscal revenue, the government will have insufficient funds for civic education. What is more serious is that because previous investment in education has vanished with the brain drain, the government and taxpayers will have increasingly fewer incentives to further invest in education, thus increasingly weakening a country's education system. At the same time, due to the lack of favorable educational conditions in their homeland, more students will choose to receive education and live abroad, thus plunging the country's education into a vicious circle: brain drain leads to a lack of incentives for educational investment, which reduces educational investment and deteriorates educational conditions, and this leads to a further outflow of students and brain drain, thus further deteriorating educational conditions.

(3) Impacts on establishment of the talent system. Mihir Desai, a professor at Harvard University, believes that the loss of a large number of the "best and brightest" talents will bring incalculable negative impacts to a country. These losses will hurt the so-called "facilitating factors"—the integration of highly skilled talents, ordinary workers, entrepreneurs, and capital providers. Furthermore, the massive loss of highly educated talents may even result in a country's inability to meet the minimum need to form a "critical pool" of talents, and the country would not be able to form a complete domestic talent system. After studying the theory of "critical pool," economist Thomas Schelling pointed out that brain drain may lead a country into a vicious circle: the loss of high-quality talents will bring about more and more brain drain. This is because talents need the group's assistance and cooperation. First of all, talents themselves need the cooperation of other talents to complete their work, thus contributing to the society. The characteristics of modern science and technology such as diversification, wide range, comprehensiveness, and

marginalization determine that it is difficult for a single person to complete a scientific research project with his or her own limited energy, ability, and knowledge structure. Second, people need a sense of belonging. A highly educated person needs to belong to a group with a higher level of knowledge. He expects that people around him have the similar abilities and knowledge structures as him. When these conditions are not met, he needs to leave and go abroad to look for such groups. Therefore, there is a chain reaction of everyone's leaving and staying. The number and scale of such groups become smaller and smaller as individuals leave. Therefore, the loss of human capital will aggravate itself, thus affecting the establishment of a country's complete talent system.

(4) Impacts on reform of the national system. Becker, an economist, believes that the loss of human capital in developing countries is not only a "loss of intelligence" but also a "loss of change" as these intellectuals should have helped the country to reform and revitalize. Their departure, to a certain extent, takes away the stable and powerful influence of the middle class on politics. Meanwhile, economic, social, and educational progress depends especially on a sufficient number of high-quality talents to find the most effective use of human capital and a basic outlook on the system applicable to the country in the future. The loss of human capital undoubtedly restrains the pace of national system reform.

3. Positive effects of brain drain on outflow countries

In recent years, some studies have shown that the aggregation of immigrants will form a "network effect," which will have a positive impact on the bilateral trade between inflow countries and outflow countries. After examining the bilateral trade of the United States using the gravity model of migration, some economists have found that a 10% increase in migrants will lead to a 4.7% increase in exports and an 8.3% increase in imports. Similar results were found when the model was applied to Canada, only with a less obvious variation. The migrant network can also act as an important credit intermediary and form credit enhancement mechanisms, playing an especially important role in the field of intellectual property rights. An empirical analysis of India's IT industry shows that the success of Indians in Silicon Valley has an important positive impact on the international image of India's IT industry. The "spillover" of the accumulated reputation of Indian immigrants brought a brand effect to India's IT industry and spread the information indicating its reliable quality to the outside world in advance.

Chapter IV
Analysis of Common Interests in International Trade

Section I Interest Analysis in International Trade Theories

I. David Ricardo's Theory of Comparative Advantage

In April 1817, Ricardo's *On the Principles of Political Economy and Taxation* was published. In this epoch-making book, Ricardo gave a systematic and comprehensive account of his economic thoughts, pushing the classical bourgeois political economics to the highest peak. Building on this, he creatively put forward the theory of comparative advantage, which laid the theoretical foundation for the development of international trade and economy and promoted the spread of the capitalist system in Britain and the rest of the world while making him one of the most prominent economists in history.

Ricardo's theory of comparative advantage derives from Adam Smith's theory of absolute advantage. The theory of absolute advantage has a premise that there is a natural division of labor among countries in the world in production due to constraints of nature and other conditions. International trade is beneficial to all countries as both sides of an exchange can save labor by exchanging needed goods. However, in the view of Smith, the commodities exported by a country must have absolute advantage in production—the production cost required must be absolutely less than that of other countries.

However, Smith's theory is often inconsistent with the reality and does not meet the need of the British industrial bourgeoisie to develop and expand foreign markets. From the invalidity of the law of value in international trade, Ricardo analyzed the causes of this invalidity and put forward the theory of comparative advantage and revised Smith's theory of absolute advantage.

Ricardo believed that value theory is invalid in international trade. He argued that the law governing the relative value of goods within a country cannot govern the relative value of goods exchanged between two or more countries because the free transfer of capital and labor between countries is not absolute. He points out that the ideal commercial freedom postulates not only absolute free circulation of goods but also absolute free transfer of capital and labor. Based on the postulate, international exchange of goods will proceed in accordance with the law of exchange, just like domestic exchange of goods, and the territorial division of labor in international trade can only be based on the absolute advantage of production costs of goods. However, Ricardo pointed out that due to complicated reasons, absolute free transfer of capital and labor from a country to another is impossible in reality. This leads to the invalidity of the law of value in international trade on the one hand and changes in the principle of territorial division of labor in international trade. Against this backdrop, countries in the world will produce goods with relative advantage for exchange rather than goods with absolute advantage, and the value of goods is determined by the exchange rate when exchanging them with goods of other countries, not the labor time for production. Ricardo came to the conclusion that under a system where absolute free commerce is ensured, each country will inevitably put its capital and labor to uses most beneficial to itself. This pursuit of individual interests is well integrated with that of the universal good. Encouraging diligence, rewarding ingenuity, and making the most effective use of various special forces endowed by nature, it allows the most effective and economical division of labor. In the meanwhile, as it can increase total production, it benefits all and unites peoples worldwide into a unified society bound by common ties of interests and mutual exchange. In short, maximizing benefits and minimizing loses is the core of the theory of comparative advantage.

II. Marx's Theory of International Value

The theory of international value is a significant contribution made by Marx to the theories of division of labor in international trade. Marx's theory of international value depicts the general law of productivity development and has great guiding significance for revealing the essence of contemporary international production relations. Till today, its ideas of mutual benefit and equivalent exchange in the theory of international value can still provide convincing explanation to contemporary international division of labor and international trade. Along with the deepening of international division of labor, the theory of international value is also constantly being enriched and developed, which reflects the vitality of this theory brought forward by Marx.

The theory of international theory is an integral part of Marxist theory of political economy. With more than a century of evolution, the fundamental principles of this theory can still provide potent explanations for contemporary international trade and even economic globalization, bearing great guiding significance for China in building an open economy. The essence of Marxism— and the reason of its vitality—is that it develops and improves with practice. Marx's theory of international value is not unchangeable. Instead, its connotation and function are being enriched and expanded along with the constant development of the world economy.

Marx put forward this theory when criticizing the capitalist mode of production. Marx believed that the law of value applies to international division of labor and international trade too, only in a different form. Domestic law of value dominates domestic exchanges, while international law of value dominates international exchange. The proposition of international value is of profound theoretical significance. It answers the questions that British classical political economy fails to answer and solves the difficult problem of determining commodity value in international exchange. We can derive from Marx's international value theory that under the condition of relatively equal international economic relations, international division of labor and international trade among countries with different economic development levels can achieve economic win-win. Many scholars always emphasize the exploitation of developing countries by developed countries in their analysis of Marx's theory of international value. Their reason is that developed countries can produce more use value of the same kind in the same time than developing countries and the labor or value contained in unit use value produced by developed countries is lower than that of less developed countries because developed countries have higher labor productivity than less developed countries. However, under the condition that the law of value is at full play (i.e., there is no supra-economic compulsion or monopoly), in international exchange based on international value, the use value containing less labor produced by developed countries has equal international value with the different use value containing more labor produced by less developed countries. This way, less socially necessary labor time of developed countries is recognized as more international socially necessary labor time, while the more socially necessary labor time of less developed countries is recognized as less international socially necessary labor time. When conducting exchanges, developed countries exchange less labor for more labor with less developed countries, meaning that less developed countries are exploited by developed countries. According to this view, exchange between developed countries and developing countries is not equivalent, and developing countries should develop their own industrial systems and promote closed import substitution. However, this is a misunderstanding of Marx's theory of international value.

(1) According to Marx's theory of international value, under the condition of relatively equal international economic relations, exchange between developed countries and less developed countries is not equivalent in form but

equivalent in substance. On the surface, developed countries exchange less labor for more labor with less developed countries in international exchange, but the nature of the labor exchanged is different and cannot be simply compared. In Marx's value theory, there is an important constraint condition of international social "average degree of skill and intensity." Based on this condition, developed countries actually invest more labor than the less developed countries in the same labor time because the developed countries have more abundant workforce, higher labor proficiency, and stronger labor intensity. This is how Marx distinguishes skilled labor and simple labor. From the perspective of efficiency, skilled labor in the same time should be regarded as more simple labor. Therefore, according to Marx's theory of international value, a country with higher labor productivity is believed to create greater value in the world market. Although the amount of materialized labor obtained by the two sides of the exchange varies, an exchange should be regarded equivalent as long as it is based on the amount of international socially necessary labor amount, namely the international value. We believe that whether international exchange based on international value is equivalent or not involves the issue of research method in Marxist economics. From the view of criticism and class struggle, we may find the exploiting role of developed countries to be prominent and reach the conclusion that international exchange based on international values is "equivalent in form but not in substance." However, from a constructive perspective and considering the nature of Marx's theory of international value, they would become "equivalent in substance but not in form." In form, it is an exchange of inequivalent amount of labor, but in substance, it is an exchange of "standard labor" containing the same amount of value. Therefore, while an exchange of inequivalent country value, it is an exchange of equivalent international value. In international exchange, as long as the principle of equivalent exchange of international value is adhered to, there will not be one party occupying the labor of another party for free, and thus there will not be the so-called exploitation. International exploitation is not normal in international exchange and only appears in inequivalent exchange of international value.

(2) International division of labor and international trade based on international value are beneficial to both developed and developing countries. Under the condition of equivalent exchange based on international value, if the country value of a product in a country is lower than the corresponding international value, then the country can steadily obtain much higher excess profits in the international market than in the domestic market. In international trade, it is possible that both sides have a commodity whose country value is lower than its international value. Generally speaking, developed countries have high labor productivity, resulting in more commodities whose country value is lower than their international value, and thus can obtain more trade benefits from exchanges. As Marx said, "[T]he law of value in its international application is yet more modified by this, that on the world market the more productive national labour reckons also as the more intense, so long as the more productive nation is not compelled by competition to lower the selling price of its commodities to the level of their value. In proportion as capitalist production is developed in a country, in the same proportion do the national intensity and productivity of labour there rise above the international level. The different quantities of commodities of the same kind, produced in different countries in the same working time, have, therefore, unequal international values."[1] From the point of view of countries with lower labor productivity, they are at a disadvantage when trading with developed countries because the difference between their country value (i.e., individual value) and international value is relatively small, or their country value may be equal to or higher than their international value. However, this does not mean that they cannot obtain benefits from trade. Marx pointed out that underdeveloped countries in trade with developed countries "may offer more objectified labour *in natura* than it

---

[1] *Marx & Engels Collected Works Vol. 35*, p. 559.

receives, and yet thereby receive commodities cheaper than it could produce them."① This is because the value realization of commodities in international trade is also different from that in domestic trade. Every commodity participating in international trade has to be exchanged in the international market as well as the domestic market before they reach consumers and thus there are two opportunities for value realization. This is a significant difference from commodities circulating only in the domestic market. In other words, the creation and realization of international value is different from that of domestic value. No matter a country is developed or underdeveloped, having been exchanged twice in the international and the domestic market, the commodities' realized value will be greater than the actual labor time consumed in the export commodities or save the labor time to be consumed in domestic production of similar products in the future. For less developed countries exchanging with developed countries based on international value, although the labor time contained in the commodities they export is much more than the actual labor time contained in the commodities they import, the value of the commodities will be realized again in the market according to the domestic production conditions after the commodities are imported. The reason that some commodities are imported is not that the importing country can not produce the commodities on its own but that the production costs are too high. Therefore, the value of imported commodities in less developed countries realized in the domestic market will still be greater than or at least equal to the actual labor time consumed. Thus, less developed countries can benefit from participating in the international division of labor. Moreover, trade with developed countries can make less developed countries see their gap with the world's advanced level and thus inspire them to improve labor productivity, reduce individual (country) value, and strive for a favorable position in international competition. In fact, by making full use of their strengths to produce

---

① *Marx & Engels Collected Works Vol. 37*, p. 236.

commodities with lower-than-international-level production costs, many underdeveloped countries or regions have ventured into international markets and some even drove commodities of the same kind produced by developed countries out of the market. As a result, these underdeveloped countries have gained huge trade benefits, promoted the economic growth, and narrowed their gap with developed countries.

(3) Marx's theory of international value is a theory of economic globalization by nature and has great guiding significance for understanding economic globalization. "Commodity" is the logical starting point of Marxist political economy, and the world market is the logical destination. Commodity has two constituent elements: "value" and "use value." Value, as a general form of undifferentiated, abstract human labor condensed in commodities, can only be fully displayed on the premise of a full comparison of social attributes of labor—that is, in the world market covering economic activities of all peoples. Only in the world market can the law of value regulating commodity production be at play in a universal manner, and only against the backdrop of economic globalization can the law of value be at full play.

Section II National Interests in International Trade

I. Absence of "National Interests" in Theory of Free Trade

Traditional theories of international division of labor and free trade pioneered by Adam Smith and David Ricardo are still the cornerstone of western trade theory. However, free trade systems and policies have not been really established and implemented in any country or region so far. As history tells us, trade protectionism played a dominating role in the United States and Germany becoming major economic powers. In today's world, both developing countries that are economically backward and developed countries that are strong in economy are using trade protection measures, not only to protect their infant but also to protect their competitive industries, which cannot be explained by the theory of free trade.

The theory of free trade cannot provide accurate explanations for the nature and causes of international trade, nor can it provide a convincing theoretical explanation for today's actual international trade landscape. This is not caused by the natural differences between theory and practice but the inherent fundamental defect of the theory itself. This defect is that it ignores the objective existence and the irreplaceable role of nations as the sovereign units in international trade, which results in the absence of national interests in its theoretical system.

The research subjects of the theory of free trade are private parties, and the scope of its theoretical analysis is the whole world, so the analysis of trade benefits develops on two levels—the private level and the worldwide level. In Ricardo's 2x2 model, although the trade partners are Portugal and the United Kingdom, the actual participants and beneficiaries in the trade are private parties in the two countries rather than the two countries as a whole. Ricardo's analysis shows that if both sides of the trade benefit, the output of the whole world also increases. In his view, the analysis is good enough to reach this conclusion, and there is no need to delve further into the distribution of trade benefits among countries. Since Quesnay, the western mainstream economics has been extended to study all mankind and do not consider the concept of "nation" any more. From their perspectives, national interests are the sum of private interests, which means that when private interests are realized, national interests are naturally realized subsequently and that there is no conflict between the two. The concept of "nation" only exists in the framework of political geography and does not belong to the scope of analysis in economic theories. Therefore, the analysis of the nature, causes, and laws of operation of international trade in the theory of free trade has always been carried out centering on private acts. How to increase the private trade benefits and the welfare of the whole world has become the core of the theoretical research on free trade.

Building on Jeremy Bentham's philosophy of utilitarianism, the theory of free trade defines private individuals as the subjects of economics and international trade research. Taking personal interests as the highest moral criterion and emphasizing that public interests will be subsequently realized if everyone can freely pursue their personal interests, the theory holds that there is not any conflict between private and public interests. On this basis, it considers "laissez-faire" as the best economic policy in which transactions between private parties are not interfered by the state in any form, and it considers free trade as the best trade policy. When extending his theory of division of labor suitable for activities within a state to the international level, Adam Smith ignored the objective existence of states as the actors and their national interests. The conclusion thus reached was that the same economic efficiency could be achieved through international division of labor as the domestic division of labor and that increase in world output and trade volume can be realized through free trade, maximizing the private interests of all trading parties. Since then, all western orthodox theories of international trade have evolved along this line. When western welfare economics uses "economic welfare" and "Pareto optimality" to regulate the meanings of "economic benefit" and "economic efficiency," the increase or decrease in human "economic welfare" has become the criterion in western orthodox theories of international trade for calculating international trade benefits, and "Pareto optimality" has become their eternal goal. However, private interests and world interests are not equal to national interests, which has been proved by the research of modern philosophy and economics. It is because it defines the actors in international trade as private parties, confuses private acts with national acts as well as private and world interests with national interests, and fails to properly integrate the actor of "state" into its theoretical system that the theory of free trade has an inaccurate understanding of the nature and causes of international trade, fails to correctly reveal the development rules of international trade, and cannot provide useful guidance for countries in the world on their foreign trade activities. List once pointed out the three major defects of the traditional theoretical system of free trade: endless cosmopolitanism, rigid materialism, and fragmented and narrow-minded selfish departmentalism and individualism. Due to these three defects, the theory neither recognizes national principles nor considers national interests.

II. State as "Shadow Body" in International Trade Activities

The direct actors in international trade or the specific operators of trade activities are private parties or economic blocs, but their acts and the realization of their interests are not of independent significance but subject to a kind of sovereign force behind them, i.e., the states. In the operation of international trade, it can be felt everywhere at any time that the force is ubiquitous like a shadow, making an effect. It can be said that states are the "shadow bodies" in international trade.

(1) As the shadow bodies in international trade, states have their own independent interests. This kind of interests is different from overall world interests and is not a simple sum of the interests of blocs or private parties. Instead, it represents the overall interests of a sovereign unit and has significance in its independent existence. The goal of this kind of interests is ultimate and at a higher level than the interests of blocs and private parties. All trade activities of private parties and blocs cannot deviate from this goal. When the goal of a private party's interests conflicts with that of the state, the state may leverage the control power of the state apparatus to impose its will on the private party by a multitude of economic or non-economic means and achieve effective transformation or forcible exclusion of the interests and demands of the private party. Thus, the state becomes able and will realize its own goal.

(2) States are the controllers of international trade activities. This kind of control is reflected in both internal and external policies. The internal policy decides what commodities are supplied to the international market, and the

external policy decides whether and how to trade with other states. A state may use political and diplomatic means to open up channels and provide guarantees for trade with other states on the one hand, and may suspend the trade due to political, diplomatic, and military strategies on the other hand.

Therefore, without realizing the status of states as the "shadow bodies" and the objective existence of national interests in international trade, one cannot correctly understand the essence of the operation of international trade and the reason that a free trade system cannot be established in today's world.

III. Interests in National Foreign Trade

Since the establishment of states by mankind, no state would pursue interests beyond its national interests. Even in today's world of increasing interdependence, national interests are still above all. The foreign trade policy of any state is based on its own national interests. So, in international trade, what are the national interests in foreign trade from a state's point of view? Generally speaking, like private interests, national interests of a state, big or small, tend to be manifested as the pursuit of its own existence and development. In the meanwhile, a state's pursuit of its own existence and development reflected in national interests also involves a multitude of levels. Structurally, national interests can be divided into three interdependent parts: economic interests, political interests, and security interests. While nominally, security interests have been regarded as paramount by states, as they are related to the existence of states, from the historical perspective, economic interests are actually the basis of national interests because only by maximizing the growth of national wealth can political and security interests of a state be guaranteed to the maximum extent. As a tradition in economics, attention to the growth of national wealth has remained a basic proposition in this science, which is also determined by the law of productivity development. Of course, as rules in international political and economic exchange are far from complete and as all kinds of violent and hegemonic attempts are still common, sometimes political interests and security interests may seem more important than economic interests. At least, a state's efforts to seek economic interests may sometimes be subject to the needs of its political and security interests. As far as the actual national interests are concerned, a state's principle of national interests depends on the following three main aspects.

(1) The state's strategic goals and strategic thinking. They not only reflect the state's expectations regarding social and economic development in a certain period of time but also often serve as the benchmark against which we measure the state's social and economic realities as well as the evolution of its state influence under a specific international backdrop. Therefore, if the relevant evolution trajectory fits well with the predetermined track towards achieving the national strategic goals, then it means that national interests have been maintained and promoted relatively well. On the contrary, if the actual evolution is far from expectations, then undoubtedly one would make the judgment that national interests have been severely damaged.

(2) The state's ideology and cultural tradition. Generally speaking, there are two aspects. ① The degree of states' compromises regarding differences or even contradictions in international ideology will determine the basic judgment of the parties having differences or contradictions on other states and thus affect the orientation of their own interests, e.g., the extreme emphasis on security interests during wartime. ② Specific nationalist tendencies. Nationalism is a common phenomenon in international relations, but the degree and manifestations of nationalism vary from state to state, thereby affecting states' judgment on and the orientation of their respective national interests.

(3) The degree of the state's identification with the international political and economic order. It mainly refers to the state's judgment regarding two aspects: ① whether to accept the "normal" damage of vested interests under the actual international political and economic order or whether to recognize it as "normal" damage of interests; ② whether to accept the "normal" distribution of benefits determined by the actual international political and economic order

or whether to recognize it as "normal" acquirement of benefits in the process of international distribution of added benefits.

IV. Choice of Trade Policies as an Embodiment of Principle of National Interests

As an embodiment of the principle of national interests, the choice of trade policies in the reality must strive to maximize benefits from foreign trade activities on the one hand and avoid harm to the state's own interests by specific policies of other states on the other hand. Due to different historical backgrounds and economic development levels, developing countries and developed countries have different views on how to realize national interests through trade policies, thereby having different focuses on trade policy choices.

Developed countries have relatively high economic development levels, relatively sound domestic market mechanisms, and relatively internationally competitive products, so their needs and expectations for trade policies are much lower than those of developing countries. By and large, their trade policies have two features. On the one hand, they expect an increasingly open international market so as to sell their own competitive products and further promote domestic economic growth through trade activities. On the other hand, they are on high alert to trade polices of other countries. Once there is a change against their national interests, they will fight back with a firm resolution. Due to these two features, developed countries generally remain stable in their choice of trade policies. They seldom substantially revise their trade policies unless there are drastic changes in the internal or external economic environment. As far as the whole national economic policy system is concerned, developed countries generally assign relatively more importance to domestic policies.

Due to special historical backgrounds and relatively backward economic development levels, developing countries generally attach much more importance to trade policies than developed countries. From the perspective of historical backgrounds, the vast majority of developing countries today had a history of being enslaved by foreign powers. This past often makes the nationalism tendency more prominent in developing countries. On the other hand, the successes of developed countries have inspired a strong desire in developing countries to accelerate economic growth to catch up with and surpass developed countries. Therefore, speeding up the industrialization process has remained the common choice of developing countries. As a result, realizing the goal of industrialization has become the most direct embodiment of the national interests of developing countries. In the process of accelerating industrialization in developing countries, trade policies are generally regarded as a core component of the whole industrialization strategy.

There are two reasons for this phenomenon. First, under the traditional international division of labor, developing countries always appear in the international market as producers of primary products, but compared with manufactured goods, trade in primary products is often at a disadvantage. Transforming the industrial structure and the trade structure through accelerating industrialization is no doubt a correct choice in the economic sense. However, the long-established landscape of international division of labor cannot be completely changed overnight, and developing countries' efforts to realize their own industrialization are bound to be restricted by developed countries. Faced with the need to accelerate industrialization and the reality to compete with foreign products, it is natural that developing countries choose to use trade policies to protect their domestic markets. In this regard, even the United States, Japan, and Germany, which have now become the world's top three economies, chose to use trade policies to support the realization of their own development goals in the process of their industrialization and economic take-off. Their successes have undoubtedly enlightened many developing countries.

Second, even purely from the perspective of economic factors, it is still reasonable for developing countries to choose highly protective trade policies in the process of accelerating their industrialization. The reasonableness is reflected in two aspects. ① The domestic market mechanisms of developing countries are far less complete than those of developed countries, which means that there are a relatively large number of defects in the domestic markets of developing countries. It is obviously unrealistic for them to wait for the perfection of their domestic market mechanisms before developing industrialization. Therefore, appropriate policy intervention is quite necessary for the industrialization process of developing countries to offset the distortion, although according to the explanation of the distortion theory, the most effective policies to eradicate domestic defects are domestic policies that directly point to the root causes of the defects, such as using financial subsidies to support the development of domestic infant industries. However, for a developing country constrained by both general distortion and national financial shortage, the choice between domestic policies and trade intervention policies is very obvious after a comparison of their respective advantages and disadvantages. ② When choosing the targets of intervention, developing countries face much less information constraints than developed countries. In the early stage of industrialization, developed countries had little experience to learn from regarding which industries governments should focus on and provide support for. Consequently, developed countries also paid a heavy price in the process of exploring a right path towards industrialization. However, for developing countries, the situation is different. Although different types of countries have different characteristics in the process of industrialization, the transformation of industrial structures in the process of industrialization share some common rules. The successful industrialization experiences of developed countries have provided developing countries with models for imitation. Developing countries can fully learn from these experiences and lessons of developed countries in industrialization to serve their own industrialization. ③Because the share of developing countries in the world market is generally small, changes in their trade policies have relatively small impacts on other countries. Even if developing countries adopt relatively protective trade policies, the possibility of incurring foreign retaliation is relatively small. This indicates that in the early stage of industrialization, developing countries are generally under less external pressure in the process of formulating trade policies.

V. List's Theory of National Economy

The theory of state intervention and the theory of trade protectionism are the cornerstones of List's theory of national economy.

Friedrich List was a skeptic and critic of classical economics and a forerunner of the German Historical School of economics. List's goal was to promote the economic convergence in Germany, which determined that his economics served national and social interests. Unlike Adam Smith who put forward economic liberalism, List believed that the state should play an important role in the economic life. Deeply influenced by Alexander Hamilton and the American School of economics, List's main ideas include state-led industrialization, trade protectionism, etc. By virtue of concrete actions, List's theory facilitated the establishment of German Customs Union and the abolishment of customs duties of member states, enabling the economic harmonization in Germany, and had an impact on the later unification of Germany.

From the perspective of the special national conditions, low development levels, and special national interests of underdeveloped countries, List put forward the idea that it is necessary to intervene in private economy. List notably stressed that it would be especially necessary for a country to rely on the power of state intervention when the country is expanding its national economy and at the stage of transition towards an economic power with the agriculture industry co-existing with the manufacturing industry or with the manufacturing industry and the commercial industry. He even believed that state intervention in this period should be intentional and purposeful so that the country's economy could develop towards "a man-made direction." List did not agree with the laissez-faire economic theory of English classical economics. For this reason, he urged to improve the existing system of economics by adding national economics to it. In order to highlight the theoretical importance of the theory of state intervention, he even wrote that "state" is the feature that sets the system he created apart. He pointed out that states are the intermediary between private parties and the whole humankind and that therein lied the basis of the overall structure of his theory.

So, how should a state intervene in the economy? List did not consider economy-wide intervention in all fields to be wise and held that state intervention or control should be limited only to some areas. In other words, there is no need to utilize state intervention in areas where citizens know better and are more skilled; instead, state should concentrate on matters that individuals cannot accomplish by themselves even if they have some relevant knowledge. List also specifically mentioned things that a state needs to do, including: protecting its merchant ships through naval forces and maritime laws and regulations; constructing roads, railways, bridges, canals, seawalls, and other infrastructure; formulating autocratic laws and various other laws and regulations conducive to production and consumption; practicing trade protectionism to promote the growth of domestic manufacturing industry; etc. In short, the mission of a state is to promote the growth of wealth and productivity, thereby transforming itself from uncivilized to civilized and from weak to powerful.

In a sense, List's theory of trade protectionism is an extension of his theory of state intervention. Building on a review of the history of trade, he proposed three stages of trade development, roughly in line with the stages of economic development he proposed. During the first stage, economically backward countries should conduct free trade with economically developed countries as a way to get rid of the uncivilized state and develop the agriculture industry. During the second stage, trade protectionism should be implemented to develop the domestic manufacturing, shipping, and commercial industries. During the third stage when the state's manufacturing, agriculture, and commercial industries as well as the overall economic strength have been highly developed, free trade should be restored step by step, with its products competing with the products of other countries without restriction in both domestic and foreign markets. According to List, free trade can be implemented in the fields of agriculture, raw materials, and science and technology, but implementing free trade regarding industrial products is detrimental to the development of domestic industry, so state intervention in economic development is necessary. For a relatively economically backward country, it should establish a protective rather than fiscal tariff system with conditions and time restrictions. He believed that the tariff level should be raised amid rising productivity so that domestic commodities can occupy domestic markets. List believed that the targets of tariff protection should be key industrial sectors that can compete with foreign products after development and that there should be a specific focus on technology sectors. For less important economic sectors, only low-level protection is required, while no protection is required for infant sectors without competitions. Furthermore, a state should adopt import bans or tariff regulations on industrial products according to its unique environment and industrial conditions. Bans and tariffs should be placed on exports, but free tariff should be introduced for imports of natural products; tax refund should only be applied to semi-finished products that still need to be imported from abroad; the use of incentives to make domestic industrial products more competitive in a third country should not be encouraged. Tariffs imposed should remain within a reasonable range. List pointed out the following: tariffs should not restrict import and consumption, otherwise it would not only weaken domestic productivity but also frustrate the purpose of tax increase; if a technology industry cannot be established under the protection of the previous 40%～60% tax rate and cannot last for a long time under the constant protection of a 20%～30% tax rate, then it lacks the basic conditions of industrial strength; tariff protection measures should be carried out step by step; tariffs should only increase according to the growth rate of capital, technological talent, and entrepreneurial spirits at home or attracted from abroad and the progress of transforming surplus raw materials and natural products from being specifically for exports to being utilized by the country itself. List replaced cosmopolitanism in the classical economics with nationalism, as he saw the conflicts of interests between different countries in international trade and analyzed the impact of tariff policies on domestic industries. He examined not only the static benefits brought by international division of labor but also the impact of trade on the dynamic adjustment of a country's industrial structure. Later, List's theory became an important theoretical basis for various kinds of trade protectionism. There is a huge difference in nature between trade protection adopted by developing countries and trade protection adopted by developed countries. Developing countries adopt trade protection measures because of the intrinsic needs of their economic development, which is necessary unless they give up their economic development. Trade protection policies are the only choice for developing countries to realize industrialization. Moreover, one of objectives of such policy is to rectify a series of unequal factors arising from the different elasticity of demand in international trade and reduce the difference in income demand between manufactured products and primary products, so it would not hinder the growth of world trade. However, developed countries adopt trade protection policies for their manufactured products to expand the difference in income demand between manufactured products and primary products, and if developed countries also protect their primary products, it will exacerbate the inequality of trade between manufactured products and primary products. Therefore, trade protection by developed countries not only is unnecessary but will also reduce the scale of world trade and its growth rate. If developed countries reduce or abolish their trade protection policies, developing countries will export more, thereby expanding world trade. Moreover, due to the high elasticity of demand for industrial product imports in developing countries, trade would thus enjoy the feature of "reciprocity."

Section III Common Interests of China and Developed Countries in Trade

This section takes the United States as an example of developed countries. The United States is the largest developed country and the largest market in the world, while China is the largest developing country and the largest potential market. Sustained and rapid economic development in China and the United States is an important condition for the continuous expansion of the economic and trade relationship between the two countries. The mutually beneficial economic and trade relationship between China and the United States has not only brought tangible economic benefits to the people of the two countries but also become an important foundation and a powerful driving force for the development of China-U.S. relationship. However, some contradictions have arisen as the China-U.S. economic and trade relationship makes rapid progress. It is conducive to the joint promotion of sustained, rapid, and healthy development of China-U.S. economic and trade cooperation and the establishment of a new prospect for China-U.S. trade cooperation that the two sides objectively analyze the contradictions and common interests in the China-U.S. bilateral economic and trade relationship and carry out equal and sincere dialogues and negotiations.

I. Status Quo of Development of China-U.S. Economic and Trade Relationship

Since the establishment of diplomatic relations between China and the United States 40 years ago, the political and economic relationship between the two countries has experienced ups and downs, but the economic and trade cooperation between them has maintained rapid development. Following

China's accession to the WTO, China-U.S. economic cooperation has made historic breakthroughs in field, scope, breadth, and depth. According to statistics from China's customs, the China-U.S. bilateral trade volume in 2006 reached more than $262.6 billion, 107 times that of the 1979 level of $2.45 billion. According to U.S. statistics, the China-U.S. bilateral trade volume in 2002 was $147.3 billion and rose to $343 billion in 2006. This shows that the China-U.S. economic and trade relationship occupies a very important position in both countries' respective foreign trade relations. As the two sides build more and more common grounds where they share common interests, China and the United States have forged ever closer and more interdependent relationship in their economic and trade cooperation. China and the United States are each other's largest trading partner and important originating country of investment. In 2018, the China-U.S. bilateral trade volume in goods and services exceeded $750 billion and the two-way direct investment approached $160 billion. China-U.S. economic and trade cooperation has brought tangible benefits to people of both countries.[1] In terms of bilateral trade, according to statistics from China's customs, the China-U.S. trade volume in goods has increased by more than 252 times from less than $2.5 billion in 1979 when the two countries first established diplomatic relations to $633.5 billion in 2018. In 2018, the United States was the largest trading partner, the largest export market, and the sixth largest importing country of China. According to statistics from the U.S. Department of Commerce, in 2018, China was the largest trading partner, the third largest export market, and the largest importing country of the United States. China has been the major export market for U.S. planes, soybeans, automobiles, integrated circuits, and cotton. During the decade from 2009 to 2018, China was one of the fastest growing export markets for U.S. goods, with

---

[1] State Council Information Office of the People's Republic of China, "Facts and China's Position on China-U.S. Trade Friction," Box 2: The Chinese and American economies are interlinked and bilateral trade and investment are mutually beneficial, website of the State Council Information Office, Jun. 2, 2019.

an average annual growth rate of 6.3% and a cumulative growth rate of 73.2%, higher than the average growth rate of 56.9% in the rest of the world.[①]

China-U.S. trade in services maintained rapid growth and became highly complementary, carrying out extensive, in-depth, and beneficial cooperation in tourism, culture, intellectual property, and other fields. China has become the largest tourist destination for the United States in the Asia-Pacific region, and the United States the largest destination for Chinese students to study abroad. According to Chinese statistics, China-U.S. trade in services increased by 3.6 times, from $27.4 billion in 2006 (the starting year of the statistics) to $125.3 billion in 2018. In 2018, China's trade deficit in services with the United States reached $48.5 billion.

Although China-U.S. economic and trade relationship has made great progress since the two countries established diplomatic relations, numerous conflicts have also arisen along the way, mainly regarding issues such as trade imbalance, trade frictions, RMB exchange rate, product quality, food safety, and so on. Trump's administration who pursues the "America First" policy has adopted a series of unilateralism and protectionism measures towards foreign countries and has used tariffs as a regular means to impose its own interests and demands on other countries. The United States started to use again many tools such as the "Section 201 Investigation" and the "Section 232 Investigation" which have laid dormant for many years to act against major trading partners, disrupting the global economic and trade landscape. The United States also targeted China. In August 2017, it launched the "Section 301 Investigation" which has a strong sense of unilateralism, ignoring China's unremitting efforts and huge progress in strengthening intellectual property right protection and improving the business environment for foreign investors over the years. Despite these facts, the United States made many negative and nonobjective remarks of

---

[①] Website of the U.S.-China Business Council (USCBC): 2019 State Export Report, https://www.uschina.org/reports/ 2019-state-export-report, May 1, 2019.

Chapter IV Analysis of Common Interests in International Trade

China and adopted economic and trade restrictive measures such as levying tariffs and restricting investment, provoking China-U.S. economic and trade frictions. Since the beginning of July 2018, the United States has imposed in three tranches a 25% tariff on $50 billion worth of Chinese goods exported to the United States and a 10% tariff on $200 billion worth of Chinese goods exported to the United States. On May 9, 2019, the United States announced to increase the tariff rate on the listed $200 billion worth of Chinese goods exported to the United States from 10% to 25% from May 10.① The United States also threatened to impose tariffs on all remaining Chinese goods exported to the United States, quickly escalating the already intense economic and trade friction between the two countries. In order to safeguard the national dignity and people's interests, China had to make necessary responses, imposing tariffs on $110 billion worth of U.S. goods exported to China.

1. Trade imbalance

Trade imbalance is the most noticeable problem in the China-U.S. economic and trade relationship. According to statistics from China's customs, China's trade surplus with the U.S. had increased 31.1% annually on average from 2005 to 2005 and increased from $29.74 billion to $114.17 billion, accounting for 152.5% of China's total surplus. According to statistics from the U.S. Department of Commerce, the U.S. trade deficit with China increased 19.65% annually on average from 2000 to 2005 and increased from $83.88 billion (excluding trade in services) to $201.74 billion, accounting for 25.8% of the United States' total deficit against 18.5% in 2000. China is the country with which the U.S. had the largest trade deficit. The United States is the country with which China had the largest trade deficit in services, and the deficit is widening rapidly. According to U.S. statistics, in 2007 - 2017, U.S. service exports to China increased by 3.4 times, from $13.14 billion to $57.63

---

① On Jun. 1, 2019, the Office of the United States Trade Representative (USTR) announced to extend the deadline to enter the U.S. before the goods would be subject to an additional 25% tariff rather than the previous 10% to Jun. 15, 2019.

billion, while U.S. service exports to other countries and regions in the world increased by 1.8 times. In the same period, the U.S. annual trade surplus in services with China increased by 30 times to $40.2 billion. The United States is the country with which China has the largest trade deficit in services, accounting for about 20% of China's total trade deficit in services. China's trade deficit in services with the United States concentrated in three areas, i.e., travel, transportation, and intellectual property royalties. According to statistics from the U.S. Department of Commerce, as of 2016, the number of U.S.-bound tourists from China's mainland has increased for 13 years in a row, 12 years of which witnessed a growth rate of double digits. Statistics from China's Ministry of Commerce show that in 2017, U.S.-bound Chinese visitors spent a total of $51 billion for travel, study, medical care, and other purposes. Notably, the United States received 3 million visits from Chinese tourists in the year, whose travel expenditures in the U.S. reached $33 billion. In terms of education, the United States is the largest destination for Chinese students to study abroad. In 2017, there were about 420,000 Chinese students studying in the United States, contributing about $18 billion to the country's revenue. According to statistics from the United States, China's trade deficit in travel services with the United States widened from $430 million in 2006 to $26.2 billion in 2016, with an average annual growth rate of 50.8%.①

2. Trade friction

Since the establishment of diplomatic relations in 1979, bilateral trade between China and the United States gradually went back to the normal track, and the two countries started to carry out equal and mutually beneficial economic and trade exchange, which has been rapidly developing through the years. In 1979, the China-U.S. bilateral trade volume was $2.5 billion, and it surged to $583.7 billion in 2017, increasing by more than 230 times. Especially

---

① The State Council Information Office of the People's Republic of China, "Facts and China's Position on China-U.S. Trade Friction," website of the State Council Information Office, Sep. 24, 2018.

after China opened wider to the outside world in 1992 and joined the World Trade Organization in 2001, China-U.S. bilateral trade saw a sharp acceleration, bringing tangible benefits to both Chinese and American people and enterprises. However, rapid development was accompanied by trade frictions. On July 2, 1980, the United States launched an anti-dumping investigation against menthol from China, raising the curtain for the United States' anti-dumping actions against China. In the 1980s, the United States conducted 17 anti-dumping investigations against China. During the period, China was not the main target country of the United States' anti-dumping actions, but the average tariff rate levied by the United States on China reached 44.4% in these 17 anti-dumping investigations, which speaks volumes about how hard China was hit by the United States' anti-dumping investigations. In the 1990s, China's trade with the U.S. was overshadowed by "Section 301" of the U.S. In April 1991, the United States launched an investigation into China's intellectual property rights under "Section 301," which was the first time that "Section 301" appeared in the China-U.S. trade battle. The investigation concluded that China's Patent Law failed to secure effective protection for intellectual property rights, thereby putting the commercial interests of American enterprises at risk. Based on this conclusion, the United States planned to levy 100% retaliatory tariffs on $2.8 billion worth of Chinese goods exported to the United States. In 1992, the two sides negotiated an agreement under which China promised to improve its protection of intellectual property rights. In October 1991, the United States launched another "Section 301 investigation" against China regarding the issue of market entry. In 1992, the United States proposed to impose punitive tariffs on $3.9 billion worth of Chinese goods exported to the United States. In the end, the two sides reached a settlement after China promised to reduce trade barriers to goods imported from the United States for a period of five years. In June 1994 and April 1996, the United States conducted another two "Section 301 investigations" against China, accusing China of not properly enforcing its intellectual property right protection measures. As before, China promised to further strengthen its domestic legislation. In 2003, the United States intensified again its anti-dumping actions against China due to imbalanced China-U.S. trade. The United States successively ruled that China was dumping to the U.S. color TV sets, malleable cast iron pipe fittings, and other products, announced that it would implement special safeguard measures against Chinese textiles, and ruled that Chinese furniture enterprises dumped products into the United States. In October 2010, the United States undertook a "Section 301 investigation" for the fifth time, which looked into China's new energy subsidies and which was also the first time that China had been hit by a "Section 301 investigation" after joining the WTO. This "Section 301 investigation" showed that the United States worried about the rapid development of China's new energy industry. It tried to relieve the competition pressure on its domestic relevant industries by suppressing China's new energy industry. These previous "Section 301 investigations" were all resolved through negotiations: the United States agreed to withdraw its retaliatory measures, while China made corresponding policy adjustments and improvements, including further improving its laws related to intellectual property right protection such as Patent Law, Copyright Law, and Trademark Law, strengthening the enforcement of relevant laws, agreeing to amend the contents suspected of prohibited subsidies in Interim Procedures on the Management of Special Funds for the Industrialization of Wind Power Generation Equipment, and further reducing relevant trade barriers. Statistics show that China-U.S. bilateral trade has maintained development despite all these trade frictions and investigations, and after several slight adjustments, the bilateral economic and trade cooperation between the two countries would always drive again into the fast lane.[①] Since 2018, a trade friction has broken out between China and the United States. According to the statistics from the

---

[①] The historical data mentioned above are quoted from: Hong Junjie and Yang Zhihao, "China-U.S. Trade Friction from a Historical Perspective," *Financial Minds*, 2018 (4).

customs, in the first quarter of 2019, China's foreign trade volume with the United States was 815.86 billion yuan, registering a year-on-year decrease of 11%. Within this trade volume, the export volume from China to the U.S. was 622.43 billion yuan, down by 3.7% year on year, and the import volume was 193.43 billion yuan, down by 28.3% year on year. In March, China's foreign trade volume with the United States was 291.35 billion yuan, up by 0.1% year on year, within which the export volume was 214.99 billion yuan, up by 10.6% year on year, and the import volume was 76.36 billion yuan, down by 21% year on year. The China-U.S. economic and trade friction has also brought certain impacts on business operations, but by and large, the impact is still controllable. Economic and trade cooperation still plays the important role of a "ballast stone" in the China-U.S. relationship. With the concerted efforts of the two countries, the China-U.S. economic and trade relationship is bound to deliver mutually beneficial and win-win results.

3. RMB exchange rate

Since 1990, the U.S. government has accused China of undervaluing RMB for a long time. In terms of actions, there were three upsurges in the history when the United States put pressure on the RMB exchange rate through both official and unofficial subjects.[1] The first upsurge occurred in 1990 – 1994. During this period, the United States claimed that China acquired an unfair advantage in trade through the dual exchange rate system for RMB. But the pressure did not last long and weakened along with the reform of the RMB exchange rate system and the outbreak of the Asian financial crisis.

The second upsurge occurred in 2003 – 2007. During this period, the main subjects exerting pressure were the parliament, the administration departments, and interest groups, and the methods of exerting pressure also diversified. The undervalued exchange rate of RMB was regarded as the "culprit" of the China-U.S.

---

[1] Guo Wei and Yan Haiming, "Analysis on the Behavior and Motivation of U.S. Pressure on RMB Exchange Rate," *Seeker*, 2018 (3): 83-89.

trade imbalance. In order to lift U.S. enterprises from their weak positions when competing in the international market, the United States has been demanding RMB appreciation, even by the U.S. Congress threatening to levy special tariffs. Congressional bills and acts became important means of pressure, and the first bill focusing on the RMB exchange rate (the Schumer-Graham Bill) appeared at this period. In July 2005, China abandoned the system of having RMB pegged to U.S. dollar and announced a 2.1% appreciation, putting off the strong demand for RMB appreciation by the United States. Since 2006, amid the resurgence of protectionism in the United States, more people in the U.S. became dissatisfied with the slight appreciation of RMB. Recently, the United States has used international institutions and multilateral cooperation mechanisms to increase the pressure on China for RMB appreciation and prompted the IMF to strengthen supervision of exchange rate systems in emerging markets. However, China has made it clear that it will handle the issue of RMB exchange rate in its own way, which means that it will be a long time before the dispute between China and the United States regarding the RMB exchange rate is resolved.

The third upsurge started in 2009 and has lasted till now. During this period, the United States has further upgraded its pressure on China to adjust the RMB exchange rate. On October 11, 2011, despite strong opposition on the Chinese side, the Currency Exchange Rate Oversight Reform Act of 2011 went through the procedural vote of the Senate of the U.S. Congress. The act used "currency imbalance" as the excuse and further escalated the dispute over the exchange rate, seriously disturbing the China-U.S. economic and trade relationship. Since the RMB exchange rate entered the track of continuous fluctuation and devaluation in February 2014, there have been less incidents where the United States exerts pressure (including congressional incidents and executive incidents), but the success rate has been rising.[1] In 2017, the newly-

---

[1] Guo Wei, "Study on the Impact of U.S. Political Pressure on RMB Exchange Rate (2005 – 2016)," *World Economy Study*, 2017 (1): 28-40.

elected U.S. President Donald Trump publicly accused the Chinese government many times both before and after his election of "manipulating" the RMB exchange rate to gain an unfair advantage in China-U.S. trade.

4. Product quality and food safety issues

Product quality and food safety are new issues arising in the China-U.S. economic and trade relationship. Since March 2007, a large number of reports on the product quality and food safety in China have been published on the U.S. media. Some successive incidents including the "U.S. Melamine Pet Food Recall," the "toxic cough syrup incidents," and the "Mattel recall of toys with lead paint" have incited great concern over "made-in-China" in the international community. Some fake news in the United States targeted "made-in-China" and took the opportunity to fuel distrust of Chinese products. The essence of denigrating "made-in-China" is trade protectionism. Under the underlying background of trade protectionism, the safety issue of Chinese products has been unduly exaggerated. On the evening of July 13, 2007, the General Administration of Quality Supervision, Inspection and Quarantine of the People's Republic of China announced on its website that due to food safety problems, the products of several major American meat processors would be excluded from the Chinese market from then on. Among others, even the frozen poultry and meat products of the world's largest meat processor Tyson Foods were found to be contaminated with salmonella. On July 12, Carlos Gutierrez, then the U.S. Secretary of Commerce, took a tough stance by saying that "China is responsible for the safety of its exports." China's exports to the United States, especially food products, are undergoing unprecedented strict inspections. Regarding the dispute on food safety between China and the United States, both sides should adopt appropriate economic and trade policies and measures to avoid politicizing the issues of product quality and food safety. In fact, China today is the third largest market for American pork. According to statistics, in 2017, the total agricultural export volume of the U.S. was $140.5 billion, of which $22 billion worth of goods (including $1.1 billion worth of goods from the U.S. pork industry) were exported to China. Also in the year, the United States exported $200 million worth of wine to China, with a year-on-year increase of 10%. Wine exports to China from California alone have increased by 450% in the past few years.[①]

II. Common Interests in China-U.S. Relations

In addition to the aspects where China and the United States have disputes, the China-U.S. relations also have many aspects where the two countries have a lot to offer and cooperate with each other. China and the United States have common interests in various matters, especially in safeguarding global and regional security and protecting the international environment, as well as in economic and trade, scientific, technological, and cultural exchange. Minimizing contradictions and safeguarding and developing common interests is the key to the China-U.S. relationship embarking on a track towards healthy development. With the smooth progress of the China-U.S. Strategic Economic Dialogue (SED) and the official launch of negotiations on the bilateral investment treaty, the two sides could deal with the deep-seated issues existing in both economies through rational negotiations and joint efforts, which would help to ease the contradictions and maintain the stability of the bilateral economic and trade relationship to some extent.

1. China-U.S. common political interests

Political interests are the needs with social contents and social characteristics that people realize with the help of public power in the political process. Security interests are the basis for determining whether the China-U.S. relationship could develop normally. As the world's influential powers and permanent members of the U.N. Security Council, China and the United States have broad and important common interests in safeguarding the peace and

---

[①] The data is quoted from: "Achilles' Heel of the United States: Why would soybean, pork and other agricultural products hit Trump hardest?" *The Paper*, Mar. 30, 2018.

stability in the Asia-Pacific region and the whole world and in combating international crimes. The Cold War was over, but the world has not been in peace. While some old issues have not been resolved, new conflict hotspots have already emerged. Security factors still play an important role in the China-U.S. relationship. With the relative decline in national power, the United States needs China's cooperation to deal with a host of international and regional issues. This point has been demonstrated by the Gulf Crisis and the political settlement of the Cambodia Conflict. In preventing nuclear proliferation and global environmental pollution, the United States also needs China's cooperation to the proper extent. In the field of military security, China, on behalf of the Association of Southeast Asian Nations (ASEAN), opposes the U.S. attempts to seek hegemony in the Asia-Pacific region. In addition, on many other issues, ASEAN also has contradictions with the United States, which is the representative of developed countries. For example, in the field of economic cooperation, ASEAN opposes APEC being led by the U.S. and APEC focusing only on trade and investment liberalization while ignoring economic aid and technical cooperation, and ASEAN is also strongly dissatisfied with developed countries' attempts to use human rights and labor conditions as excuses to suppress the economic development of developing countries. Recently, the United States has intensified its struggle for the leadership of the ASEAN Regional Forum (ARF) and has demanded that ASEAN give up part of its control over ARF, thus exacerbating the contradiction between ASEAN and the United States on the issue of ARF leadership. On the issue of human rights, there are also contradictions and differences between ASEAN and the United States as well as Europe. All these constitute a threat to American interests in the Asia-Pacific region. China's development is also inseparable from the security and stability of the Asia-Pacific region, so China is committed to the maintenance of friendly relations with all the countries in the Asia-Pacific region. As a neighboring country of ASEAN, China has political and economic influence beyond the Asia-Pacific region and takes the same stance as ASEAN in opposing hegemonism and power politics. Therefore, ASEAN attaches great importance to the development of its relationship with China and advocates to give play to China's "constructive role" in dealing with regional issues. The U.S.-China relationship has become the cornerstone of the Asia-Pacific policy of the United States. If the United States wants to maintain its interest relationship with the Asia-Pacific region in the long term, it is impossible for it not to cooperate with China. Obviously, China and the United States have common political interests.

2. China-U.S. common cultural interests

Cultural interests are the satisfaction of spiritual needs by human beings in their material and spiritual activities. Specifically, cultural interests are not only the satisfaction of spiritual needs that the subjects pursue as a means to obtain economic benefits but also the direct satisfaction of the subjects' own needs in the spiritual and cultural field (such as ideas and ideologies, literature and art, education and science, etc.). The former shows that cultural interests are a means for the subjects to pursue economic interests, while the latter shows that cultural interests are the objective pursued by the subjects in the spirit and culture field. Economic interests determine cultural interests, and conversely, cultural interests also affect economic interests. However, in a certain period of time, cultural interests may remain relatively independent and stable, unaffected by changes in economic interests. It is generally believed that the subjects of cultural interests include micro subjects (individuals and enterprises) and macro subjects (regions and countries).

China and the United States have carried out extensive cooperation in science and technology, education, and other cultural fields. The China-U.S. bilateral science and technology agreement involves more than 30 departments and agencies. More than 100,000 Chinese students and scholars have visited the United States to receive advanced training and to conduct research. The United States is the largest destination for Chinese students to study abroad. In 2017, there were about 420,000 Chinese students studying in the United States, contributing about $18 billion to the country's revenue. According to statistics from the United States, China's trade deficit in travel services with the United States widened from $430 million in 2006 to $26.2 billion in 2016, with an average annual growth rate of 50.8%. According to data from Open Doors Report 2017, the number of Chinese students studying in the higher education institutions in the U.S. increased to 350,755 in the 2016 – 2017 academic year, up 6.8% from the previous academic year. In the meanwhile, many U.S. students and scholars have also visited China to study, engage in language research, participate in cooperation projects of scientific research, or teach in Chinese universities. In 2017, 489,200 foreign students studied in China's higher education institutions. Among the top 10 origins of overseas students in China, the United States ranked fourth in terms of the number of students studying in China. The scientific and technological cooperation and the cultural and educational exchange between China and the United States has not only promoted the technological and economic development of both countries and enhanced the understanding between the experts and scholars from the two countries, but it has also given a major boost to the development of the political relationship between the two countries.

3. China-U.S. common economic interests

As the world's largest developing country and the world's largest developed country respectively, China and the United States both have vast markets. With quite different industrial and consumption structures, the Chinese and American economies complement each other very well. China has abundant labor resources and vast market potential, while the United States has advanced technology and equipment, advanced management experience, and solid financial strength. The combination of these factors will surely promote the rapid economic development of the two countries. In terms of trade structure, the Chinese economy and the U.S. economy are highly complementary. With the abundant labor resources and low wage level, China has an edge in developing labor-intensive productions. The United States gradually transferred its labor-intensive industries overseas after the Second World War, and China's labor-intensive products supplement the mass market of the United States. What China needs most from the United States are technical products. China is the major sales market for U.S. wheat, phosphate fertilizer, and timber, the fourth largest client of the Boeing Company of the U.S., and one of the largest buyers of U.S. computers, industrial machinery, and other products. China's imports from the United States are increasing year by year. In addition, the trade in services between the two countries is also becoming increasingly important. In the field of investment, in recent years, due to the rapid growth of the bilateral trade volume, the U.S. paid-in investment in China has been expanding, making the United States one of the largest investors in China. Over the past 40 years since the resumption of diplomatic relations between China and the United States, two-way investment between the two countries has increased from almost zero to a total of nearly $160 billion and the cooperation has delivered fruitful results. According to statistics from China's Ministry of Commerce, by the end of 2018, the direct investment in the United States by Chinese enterprises reached $73.17 billion. The booming investment by Chinese enterprises in the United States has contributed a lot to the local economic growth, job creation, and tax revenue. According to statistics from China's Ministry of Commerce, by the end of 2018, the U.S. paid-in investment in China was $85.19 billion. In 2017, the annual sales revenue of the U.S.-funded enterprises in China was $700 billion, with their profits exceeding $50 billion.[1]

The China-U.S. Strategic Economic Dialogue is a new mechanism to adjust the China-U.S. relationship. Both China and the United States attach great importance to the dialogue mechanism and consider it to be a major strategy.

---

[1] State Council Information Office of the People's Republic of China, "Facts and China's Position on China-U.S. Trade Friction," Box 2: The Chinese and American economies are interlinked and bilateral trade and investment are mutually beneficial, website of the State Council Information Office, Jun. 2, 2019.

Established by the leaders of the two countries, SED has created a mechanism for dialogue between two big countries in the world—in particular, a major developing country that is rising and one of the largest developed countries—which is of great significance in today's international relations. This innovation has given more substance to the China-U.S. strategic partnership. The common interests between China and the United States require mutual economic cooperation. The United States' global strategy needs China's cooperation, and China's development is beneficial to the United States. Therefore, common interests are the basis for dialogue. The United States needs China's cooperation on issues of global and regional security in the first place. In fact, the United States also face many economic issues where it is in a disadvantaged position, such as the signing of the Kyoto Protocol, the U.S.-E.U. negotiations on trade in agricultural products, and the WTO negotiations. China also needs the United States. For China, the reason that it considers stability and cooperation as common interests is that China needs a favorable external environment for sustained economic development. To become a major country in the world in the real sense, China must interact with the United States. The outcomes of the several dialogues reflect the common interests of the two countries. No doubt there have also been some disputes in these dialogues, but we see the fruits in the first place. These fruits include three aspects. The first is the recognition of the mechanism. Both sides believe that this is a useful mechanism and have attached great importance to it. Since the second dialogue, more attention has been paid to the responsibilities of China and the United States on global common issues. This positioning is not only correct and but also what a strategic dialogue should have. The United States pays close attention to issues like China's domestic system reform and model of development, such as issues regarding pensions, which are indeed closely related to deepening cooperation between the two countries. The potential cooperation between the United States and China in environment, energy, and other fields fully meets China's needs. The second is the establishment of the cooperation principles on major international issues, which reflects the international role of the two major countries. The third is the arrangement on the two countries' markets opening wider to each other, which, of course, currently still focuses on opening China's market of specific financial service to the United States. Through several dialogues, the strategic role of this mechanism has gradually become the consensus of both sides. Objectively speaking, SED is becoming more institutionalized and strategic. This is a consensus gradually reached between China and the United States, especially through China's efforts. After several dialogues, the dialogue mechanism has been formed and its positioning function has been clarified. This was reflected in the Joint Fact Sheet on the second China-U.S. Strategic Economic Dialogue. The United States began to realize that some of China's problems in foreign economic relation arose when its domestic system reform had not been completed. This attention to China's institutions is correct and is also in line with China's interests and needs. Only through the further deepening of reform is the opening of some sectors possible, especially the financial sector. The United States has also noticed that the main reason for China's insufficient domestic demand is the immaturity of its social security system, so it has chosen to promote the building of China's social security system as a way to gain access to a larger market in China, which is also in China's interests. The U.S. government is now paying more attention to long-term institutional issues. David Dollar, former World Bank country director for China, believed that although Paulson was still discussing issues such as flexibility of the RMB exchange rate with senior Chinese officials, the more important task for him was to maintain the excellent tendency of the Chinese and U.S. senior officials to communicate over issues in the economic relations, which was a step towards deepening the economic and trade relations between the two countries. The China-U.S. Joint Fact Sheet issued after the second China-U.S. Strategic Economic Dialogue reflected the international obligations of China and the United States as the world's major countries. The Joint Fact Sheet pointed out that building on the consensus reached at the first SED, China and the United States agreed to the following principles. ① Promoting balanced economic growth in a manner compatible with sustained development is a shared responsibility of the two sides. ② China and the United States recognized the importance of innovation in creating a prosperous economy and encouraging market-oriented fair competition, effective property rights, and, specifically for small and medium enterprises, the development, management, and application of innovation. ③ China and the United States would strengthen cooperation on meeting respective goals in energy security, conservation, and efficiency, on developing clean sources of energy, on environmental protection, on clean development, and on addressing climate change. ④ China and the United States would cooperate and exchange information on transparency to enhance predictability for market participants, promote confidence in their economies, and increase their international obligations.

Chapter V
Analysis of Common Interests in International Capital Flow

Section I Interest Analysis in Theory of International Capital Flow

As economic and financial globalization keeps deepening, the role international capital flow plays in the economic development of all countries in the world is becoming increasingly important, bringing about changes to the common interests and the distribution of interests between developed and developing countries.

I. Views on Benefits of International Capital Flow before Second World War

The early international capital theories, be it the theory of neutrality of money in mercantilism or the quantity theory of money in classical economics, all expressed their views on whether cross-border capital flow was beneficial or harmful to a country when discussing whether to use precious metal currency as a means of international flow or as a purpose of international trade. For example, the early mercantilists took the accumulation of currency as a way to enrich a country, believing that the export of currency would decrease national wealth. However, the late mercantilists believed that the export of currency would promote the development of trade, thus achieving the purpose of increasing currency through the expansion of trade. If loans were provided for foreign countries, then a large amount of interest income could be obtained, thus increasing the stock of domestic currency. Hume (1752), who was the main representative of English classical economics, believed that the amount of currency would not matter if a country was examined alone. As an exchange tool, money could make the gears of trade move more smoothly and freely. Ricardo (1820) made it clear that if capital was allowed to flow freely like commodities, it would benefit not only the owners of the capital but also consumers all over the world, thereby bringing maximum benefits to human society.

From the second half of the 19th century to the 1930s, foreign studies on the effects of international capital flow have further developed. Lenin (1916) clearly expressed his view on the economic consequences of international capital flow. He believed that the export of capital may tend to a certain extent to arrest development in the capital exporting countries. Monopoly countries export a large amount of capital to foreign countries in order to obtain high monopoly profits, resulting in a reduction in domestic investment and subsequently inevitable certain stagnation in their economic development. However, "[t]he export of capital influences and greatly accelerates the development of capitalism in those countries to which it is exported."[1] Building on an examination of the shift in purchasing power and the change in trade terms caused by international capital flow, Ohlin (1929) held that the result of international capital flow was increasing the purchasing power and the income level of borrowing countries and declining the purchasing power and the income level of lending countries. Based on a comprehensive study of the short-term capital flow after the end of the First World War, Kindleberger (1937) pointed out that the economy of an inflowing country of short-term capital would expand by increasing its short-term net assets abroad or reducing its short-term net liabilities abroad, while the economy of an outflowing country would shrink

---

[1] *Lenin Collected Works Vol. 22*, p. 243.

by increasing its net short-term liabilities abroad or reducing its net short-term assets abroad.

II. Research on Benefits of International Capital Flow from Second World War to the End of 1970s

1. Theories on developing countries utilizing foreign capital

In the wake of the Second World War, a large number of developing countries emerged. These countries all attached high priority to developing national industries and promoting industrialization, but their efforts were faced with a host of problems such as weak industrial foundation, serious shortage of funds, and abnormal economic structures. Against this background, American economist Nurkse (1953) put forward the theory of capital formation in underdeveloped countries. Nurkse pointed out that capital formation was the core of the development of underdeveloped countries. In order to break the vicious circle of capital supply and demand caused by poverty and solve the problem of the low capability of savings in underdeveloped countries, foreign capital, especially direct investment from enterprises, should be used to contribute to domestic capital formation directly. Rostow (1958) put forward the "take-off theory." He believed that if a country was to take off, it would need the safeguard of "social overhead capital." For underdeveloped countries, it is a necessary road to take to use foreign capital to accumulate social overhead capital. Chenery and Strout (1966) put forward the famous "two-gap theory," holding that due to the lack of capability of savings in developing countries, there would be a gap in the capital needed for the investment scale scheduled by the economic plan, while the savings gap originates from the foreign exchange gap, and the internal economic imbalance in developing countries originates from the external economic imbalance. The savings gap restricts economic growth because of the low capacity to earn foreign exchange through exports and the low foreign exchange earnings. Therefore, foreign capital and foreign aid should be introduced to fill the foreign exchange gap.

Some western economists develop theories on developing countries utilizing foreign capital from other perspectives. For example, the "Debt Cycle Theory" first proposed by Fisher and Frenkel (1972) holds that a country's international balance of payments is related to its economic development level. Along with economic growth, a country's borrowing status will change dynamically. This theory focuses on studying how a country could improve domestic productivity, increase exports, and promote foreign trade surplus by borrowing overseas. Lewis put forward the theory of urbanization rate in the 1970s to discuss the importance of introducing foreign capital from the perspective of the constantly accelerating process of urbanization. He believed that with the progress of industrialization and the number of cities and the urban population increasing, a great deal of the rural labor force would transfer to cities, which would inevitably lead to the decline of labor price (wages) and the rise of capital price (interest rates), thus causing the import of capital.

The above theoretical research focuses on whether it would be necessary for developing countries to introduce and utilize foreign capital and the role of foreign capital. While conducted from different perspectives and from relatively macro viewpoints, their conclusions have something in common—that is, across-border capital flow in the form of direct investment and loan funds is beneficial to developing countries which are host countries in most cases because they can obtain benefits such as increasing investment and promoting economic development.

2. International direct investment theory

If the theories on developing countries utilizing foreign capital reflect the benefits of international capital flow to the host countries, whether the capital flow is beneficial to the investing countries can be seen from theories on international direct investment. Hymer (1960) proposed in his "monopolistic advantage theory" that under the condition of imperfect competition, manufacturers could overcome various unfavorable factors when investing in the host countries because of their monopolistic advantages such as capital, technology, management level, and sales system, produce high-quality and high-tech products, control the market of host countries, and seek high monopoly profits. According to him, the process of foreign direct investment is exactly the process in which multinationals use and exert their monopoly advantages. Buckley and Casson (1976) proposed in their "internalization theory" that through international direct investment, enterprises could transform transactions in external markets into transactions between internal enterprises of their companies, thus reducing the time lag and transaction costs (such as bargaining, uncertainty of buyers, and government intervention) caused by market defects and other reasons and ensuring that trade secrets of the enterprises would not be leaked so that the enterprises could put their technological advantages into full play abroad at a lower cost. Vernon (1966) classified the product life cycle into three stages: innovation, maturity, and standardization. He believed that enterprises should determine whether to produce at home or to produce by investing in foreign countries according to the stage the product is in, the degree of technological monopoly, and the main factors affecting the profits. From the perspective of international division of labor, Kiyoshi Kojima (1973) proposed that relatively less competitive industries with higher factor prices should be transferred to countries with lower factor prices and the resource advantages of the host countries should be leveraged for production, which would be beneficial to both countries. Dunning's (1976) "eclectic theory of international production" holds that only with ownership-specific advantages, internalization-specific advantages, and location-specific advantages would a multinational make outward direct investment. Otherwise, the multinational would be unable to internalize the advantages, have no suitable investment location, or cannot take advantage of the factor endowments of host countries and can only adopt the form of export or technology transfer.

　　The above theories focus on the causes and mechanisms of international direct investment and do not directly discuss the effects of international direct investment on investing countries and host countries. The research objects are the outward direct investment activities of the multinationals of developed countries. In other words, the theories study how the multinationals could obtain high profits through direct investment activities in host countries by making use of various specific advantages and selecting specific regions at specific stages. Therefore, from another perspective, we can say that theories on international direct investment study the effects of outward direct investment in international capital flow from a micro level. Thus, we can draw an indirect conclusion: under the condition of making effective use of various advantages, outward direct investment can bring high profits to multinationals and is thus beneficial to the home countries (i.e., the investing countries) where the multinationals are located.

3. Theory on global effect of international capital flow

In the early 1960s, MacDougall (1960) established a general model of international capital flow. Later, Kemp (1966) and Jones (1967) further refined MacDougall's analysis. The model holds that the differences in interest rates and expected profits among countries in the world cause international capital flow. Under the condition of perfect competition, capital flows freely from capital-rich countries to capital-poor countries, making the marginal productivity of capital move towards uniformity and thereby enhancing the world's total output and the welfare of all countries. Based on static analysis, MacDougall's model highly simplifies the international movement of monetized capital without distinguishing between direct investment and indirect investment which are sharply different from each other. As a highly abstract theoretical analysis, this model discusses for the first time the overall effect of cross-border capital flow from a global perspective and draws a clear conclusion: cross-border capital flow can make capital allocation more effective and capital gains more equal, thus improving the utilization efficiency of world resources. Investing countries can get higher returns by investing part of their capital in host countries with higher marginal productivity of capital, while host countries can make more effective use of other domestic resources and increase net gains through utilizing foreign capital. Therefore, international capital flow can bring both outflow countries and inflow countries an increase in income, which is beneficial to both sides.

III. Research on Benefits of International Capital Flow and Their Distribution Since 1980s

Since the 1980s, the economic and financial globalization has maintained rapid development. One of its remarkable characteristics is the unprecedented prosperity and the ever prominent role of international capital flow in the global economic system. Economists have conducted a lot of research on the effects of international capital flow with a specific focus on the effect of direct investment on economic growth and the harm of short-term capital. Some also study issues such as the differences in national status and income between developed and developing countries and the uneven distribution of benefits within the framework of economic and financial globalization and discuss the reasons behind these issues. Economic and financial globalization is the main feature of the economic development in today's world, and international capital flow is the core of globalization. When they study globalization, especially the global distribution of benefits, economists always analyze international capital flow as the main factor. Therefore, conclusions drawn from the research under the framework of globalization can explain to a certain extent the distribution of benefits of international capital flow.

1. Research on role of foreign direct investment in economic growth

Because it is rapidly growing, foreign direct investment has gradually become the main way for developing countries to introduce foreign capital. Many scholars have conducted a great deal of research on the promotive effect of foreign direct investment on the economic growth of host countries and have achieved fruitful results. For example, V. N. Balasubamanyam, M. Salisu, and David Sapsford (1996) examined the role of foreign direct investment in the economic growth of developing countries that adopt different trade policies and systems within the framework of the "new growth theory." Studies have proved that foreign direct investment has promoted the economic growth of host countries to a certain extent and that its effect is stronger in countries adopting outward-looking trade policies than those adopting inward-looking trade policies. M. Obstfeld (1992) believed that capital flow could disperse investment risks, make production more professional, and promote the rational allocation of capital, thus contributing to economic growth. Borensztein, DeGregorio and Lee (1998) found an obvious connection between foreign direct investment and economic growth by studying the capital flow from industrial countries to 69 developing countries between 1970 and 1989. M. Klein and G. Olivei (2000) put forward the theory that the free flow of capital enables capital to flow to countries that lack capital and has a positive effect on the output of these countries. Some Chinese scholars have also carried out research in this field, taking into consideration China's practice in utilizing foreign direct investment, and have come to the conclusion that foreign direct investment can promote the economic growth of developing countries (including China). Luo Yunyi (1999) studied investment as a demand element and the contribution rate of investment in economic growth according to the characteristics of China's current macroeconomic policies and operations. Research shows that foreign investment has a certain promotive effect on China's economic growth. Li Jingping (2001) used the cointegration and error correction model to analyze the relationship between economic globalization and China's economic growth and concluded that while globalization (including foreign investment) had a positive effect on China's economic growth, domestic investment was still the main driving force for China's economic growth. Dou Xiangsheng (2002) drew the following conclusion through a concrete analysis of the impact of international capital flow on factors of economic growth in the host countries such as capital accumulation, technological progress, human capital upgrading, and institutional changes: under the condition of an open economy, international capital flow would have an important impact on the structural changes of economic growth factors such as capital, technology, human capital, and institution and would subsequently play an important role in the economic growth. Of course, there are also foreign scholars (Steven J. Most & Hendrik Van Den Berg,1996; Hai J. Edison, Ross Levine & LucaRicci, 2002) that have studied the promotive effect of foreign investment on the economic growth of host countries through different methods and have reached an opposite conclusion: foreign direct investment has no obvious effect on the economic growth of host countries, while domestic savings seem to play a more important role in promoting economic growth than foreign direct investment or foreign aid.

2. View on unbalanced distribution of benefits of international capital flow

Since the rapid development of economic and financial globalization, issues such as the irrational landscape of international capital flow, several financial crises, and the huge gap between developed and developing countries in the benefits they gain and the risks that they undertake have attracted the attention of the academic circles of countries all over the world. Some scholars at home and abroad began to shift the focuses of their research to the influence of international capital under the control of financial hegemony and the imbalance between the benefits and the risks of international capital within the current international financial system. Building on a comprehensive and in-depth analysis of the economic cycle of the capital appreciation of multinationals, Chesnais (1994) revealed the operating mechanism of contemporary capitalism and has pointed out that the imperfect financial globalization nowadays provides a good speculative environment for cross-border capital flow. Through investment, interest-eating capital absorbs the wealth created by the production sector of the recipients of the investment, thereby becoming an independent center and force of financial profit accumulation. Stiglitz (2003) has pointed out that the current global financial system dominated by the U.S. does not realize effective allocation of international funds, which is not conducive to the stability of the world economy. According to him, the global financial system should allocate global savings to the poorest countries so that these countries could use the savings to invest and develop. On the contrary, the existing system allocates global reserves to the richest countries where the living standards have far exceeded the imagination of citizens in developing countries. The "world systems theory" represented by Wallerstein divides the modern world system into core, periphery, and semi-periphery areas, namely the richest countries, the poorest countries, and the countries and regions in between. The theory holds that the core countries are mainly engaged in monopolistic and profitable production, while the production activities of the periphery countries have the characteristics of low monopoly and low profit. This hierarchical structure of the modern world system ensures a redistribution of world wealth that is in favor of core countries at the cost of the interests of periphery countries. On the basis of an in-depth analysis of the various phenomena of globalization, Hans-Peter Martin and Harald Schumann (1998) pointed out that the result of the development of globalization was a "20 : 80" distribution pattern—that is, the richest countries accounting for 1/5 of the world's population determined 84.7% of the global gross social product, 84.2% of the total global trade volume, and 85.5% of the total domestic savings of all countries around the world. Many domestic scholars have also studied the distribution of benefits between developed and developing countries. Building on a brief analysis of the net international capital flow, the issuance of various bills and securities in the international financial market, and international reserves, Li Chong (2001) argued that in the process of financial globalization, developed countries gained most of the benefits while developing countries had borne most of the risks, demonstrating the imbalance between developed and developing countries in the benefits they gain and the risks they undertake. He Fan and Zhang Ming (2005) held that the current U.S. dollar hegemony was embodied in the "core-periphery" framework under the Jamaican system. The United States, which is a core country, has received seigniorage and benefits from currency stability, while periphery countries have borne more of the costs of inflations and financial crises. According to Chen Zhi'ang (2005), financial globalization has led to the redistribution of global wealth and the loss of welfare in developing countries, while increasing the property income in the U.S., stimulating its consumption and investment, and widening its international balance of payment deficit. In the view of Wang Chuanrong (2005), the income from division of labor is extremely asymmetric in today's international division of labor. Developed countries in the upper reaches obtain most of the income from division of labor, while developing countries which have put in a great amount of labor only reap small benefits barely enough for survival. Additionally, there are also some scholars who, while not having directly studied the role of international capital flow in income distribution, have studied the disparity in income distribution around the world under the framework of economic globalization, and they believe that with the development of economic globalization, income distribution among countries worldwide has become more and more unequal. Margaret E. Grosh and E. Wayne Nafziger (1986) calculated the Gini coefficient of world income distribution to be 0.67 based on data from 117 countries, indicating that there was a relatively big disparity in world income distribution. Based on an investigation of the income distribution around the world from 1988 to 1993, Branko Milanovic (1999) reached the conclusion by analyzing the changes of Gini coefficient that the degree of income inequality in the world was very high and that this inequality experienced a remarkable increase from 1988 to 1993, largely due to the differences in the average income of countries. This increase in inequality took place both between countries and within countries, but the inequality between countries was much greater. Branko Milanovic and Shlomo Yitzhaki (2001) divided the world into three parts (i.e., the first class, the middle class, and the third class) to explain the unequal distribution of global income. According to this division, 76% of the world's population live in poor countries, 8% in middle-income countries (defined as countries with an average income between that of Brazil and that of Italy) and 16% in rich countries. Francois Bourguignon and Christian Morrisson (2002) investigated the income changes in countries over the world from 1820 to 1992 and pointed out that the income inequality in the world had been exacerbated sharply in the past two centuries.

3. Explanations for unequal distribution of benefits under framework of economic globalization

(1) Effect of the market. Samir Amin (1996) argued that neoliberalism economics was too keen on privatization, advocating "market omnipotence" and opposing state intervention but losing its direction as a result, causing worldwide polarization between the rich and the poor and impoverishment of the vast majority of the population, and bringing about world financial crises and political turmoil. Lu Xinde (2003) held that the main reason for uneven distribution of benefits under the framework of economic globalization was that globalization had been rooted in marketization. The allocation of world resources and the distribution of income have been based on the market mechanism, but what a market mechanism seeks is not "social equity" but "profit maximization," which will inevitably lead to polarization. Developed countries possess huge capital and the monopoly over advanced high technology, which are bound to bring them huge benefits. Zhong Chao (2005) presented that there were two transmission mechanisms in the process of marketization: the price mechanism and the competition mechanism. In the process of economic globalization, the international economic rules that industrialized countries at different levels must abide by when participating in the competition are formulated by the developed countries and correspond to their economic level.

(2) The theory of factor income distribution. Based on the factor endowment theory and from the perspectives of enterprise management and global economic operation, Zhang Youwen (2002) redefined factors of production as including not only labor and capital but also, more importantly,

international sales channels, international operation management, and global enterprise networks and analyzed the distribution of factor income on this basis. According to him, under the background of globalized economy and knowledge economy, the international flow of factors has increased, and factor earnings obey the law of scarcity, which determines the distribution mechanism of benefits under economic globalization. Differences in the structure of factor endowments lead to the disadvantaged positions of developing countries, and the differences in factor endowments determine the size of benefits that countries gain by participating in the globalization system. From the international division of labor determined by factor endowments, we can see that the more international investment develops, the greater the income distribution gap becomes. In a globalized economy, the distribution of factor income is transformed into a distribution among countries. As a globalized economy follows the principle of distributing benefits according to the scarcity of factors, developed countries obtain higher benefits because they possess the main scarce factors while developing countries are at a disadvantage. Yu Shiliang and Qin Fengming (2002) have also pointed out that developed countries are the main owners of capital and advanced technologies, and this comparative advantage gives them dominance over price setting and thus enables them to obtain more benefits when exchanging with developing countries, which is the main factor that leads to the uneven income distribution among countries.

(3) Research on institutional economics. Xie Hao (2004) has argued that marketization of the global economy is the main manifestation of economic globalization, but the market may also have failures and defects. Therefore, global rules and systems should be established. However, rules and regulations fundamentally determine the distribution of economic benefits by regulating the economic activities of economic subjects. The root of the uneven distribution of benefits under economic globalization lies first in the fact that developed countries have controlled the economic and trade rules under the institutional

arrangement, thus maximizing the benefits in the international capital, technology, labor, and other markets. When analyzing the essence of economic globalization, Zhao Xueqing and Gao Yulin (2000) have pointed out that the establishment of international economic organizations, the signing of international economic agreements, and the formulation of international economic laws and regulations are virtually all carried out under the control of developed countries, thus putting developing countries at a disadvantage when sharing the benefits of economic globalization. According to Jay Mazur (2000), the power to formulate global trade and investment rules is possessed by developed countries and entirely serves multinationals that possess capital factors. Jiang Dan (2003) has concluded from studies on the distribution of benefits in globalization that one of the reasons for the inequality of benefits during the process of globalization is the lack of democracy-based rule-making power. Because of the inability of developing countries to participate in the rule-making, IMF, the World Bank, and the WTO have become the rule makers in globalization and when making rules, they have taken the developed countries as models, refining the domestic rules of these countries and extending them to the whole world. Based on an analysis of the intervention of institutional factors, Lu Genxin (2000) has argued that although it could be beneficial to leverage the comparative cost advantage to participate in the process of economic globalization, the magnitude of the benefit is related to institutional factors—that is, as long as a country influences or even dominates and controls the international economic and political system, its institutional benefits can be internalized while its institutional costs can be externalized.

IV. Comments on Relevant Theories

After reviewing the development of relevant theories on international capital flow, comparatively speaking, research on benefits of international capital flow has made great progress, while research on the distribution of benefits has been obviously insufficient. Early views on whether international capital flow would be beneficial or harmful were confined by the issue of whether it would be conducive to increasing a country's foreign trade and wealth. Under strict postulates, Ohlin, Kindleberger, and others used the two-country model to conduct abstract analysis, ignoring the factors that lead to the actual differences in economic structure and development level between exporting and importing countries. No developing country has made use of the foreign capital theories or the international direct investment theories to further study the distribution of benefits. MacDougall's highly abstract model describes the process of equalization of the benefits of international capital flow, which hardly matches the reality. Since the 1980s, research on the promotive effect of foreign direct investment on economic growth has been conducted purely from the perspective of developing countries and has not put developing countries and developed countries on the same platform to study the distribution of benefits. Most of the views on the unequal distribution of benefits between developed and developing countries were put forward in research on economic and financial globalization, and the reasons were also analyzed under the framework of globalization. These conclusions have explained to some extent the distribution of benefits of international capital flow, but they are studies carried out in a wider scope, rather than special analyses based on textual research on the practice of international capital flow.

Section II Analysis of Common Interests in Outward Direct Investment

Against the backdrop of a more and more globalized economy, outward direct investment (ODI) as the most dynamic factor in the development of the world economy has a comprehensive, profound, and complex impact on investing and host countries and even the whole world. Lenin once pointed out, "The capital-exporting countries are nearly always able to obtain certain 'advantages,' the character of which throws light on the peculiarity of the epoch of finance capital and monopoly."[1] Introducing foreign direct investment will remain the main way for China, which is a developing country, to participate in international direct investment for a long time to come. However, at the same time, we should also see that as China is opening wider and wider to the outside world and as the international economic connections are being increasingly strengthened, expanding the scale of outward direct investment will play a more profound role in promoting the sustainable and healthy development of China's national economy.

I. International Direct Investment and Sharing of Benefits

In 1960, American economist MacDougall published a paper entitled "The Benefits and Costs of Private Investment From Abroad: A Theoretical Approach" and established an interest distribution model of international investment. Later, Kemp and others developed the model into a general theoretical tool for analysis of the distribution of national interests in international capital flow. The model holds that free international capital flow will internationally equalize the marginal productivity of capital, thus increasing the utilization rate of world resources and enhancing the global production and the welfare of countries around the world.

The interest distribution model of international investment has the following postulates: ① the world is made up of investing countries and recipient countries, and capital flows only from absolutely rich countries to absolutely poor countries; ② capital gains decline progressively; ③ capital can flow freely internationally. The model is shown in figure 5-1. If A is a capital-poor country and B is a capital-rich country, Country A has capital MA and Country B has capital NA. The model postulates: ① capital is governed by the law of diminishing marginal productivity—that is, if more capital is added

---

[1] *Lenin Collected Works Vol. 22*, pp. 243-244.

without changing other factors, the productivity of each unit of capital added decreases; ② there is complete competition in both countries and the rate of return on capital is equal to the marginal productivity of capital. In Figure 5-1, EO is the marginal product curve of Country A; FO is the marginal product curve of Country B.

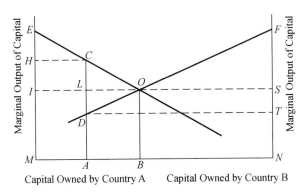

Figure 5-1　Model of Interest Distribution in International Investment

In a closed economy, if Country A invests all its capital MA domestically with a marginal productivity of MH, the total domestic output will amount to MECA, of which MHCA is capital income and HEC is income from other factors. Similarly, if Country B invests all its capital NA domestically, the total domestic output will be NFDA, of which NTDA is capital income and TFD is income from other factors. Since the capital productivity of Country B NT is lower than that of Country A MH, it shows that Country B is rich in capital and Country A is poor in capital.

In an open economy, because the rate of return on capital of Country A is higher than that of Country B, part of the capital of Country B flows to Country A. If we assume that AB amount of capital flow from Country B to Country A, then the capital income level of the two countries reaches equilibrium at point O (MI = NS). At this time, due to the inflow of foreign capital, Country A can make full use of other factors of production, increasing the total output from MECA to MEOB, of which MIOB is capital income and

IEO is income from other factors. Of capital income *MIOB*, *ALOB* is the income of foreign capital *AB*, and *LCO* is the additional income from other factors Country A actually obtains from additional output. Due to capital export, the total domestic output of Country B is reduced from *NFDA* to *NFOB*, but it obtains capital income *ABOL* from its investment in Country A. As a result, the total income of Country B increases by *LDO* instead. It can be seen that due to the international transfer of capital, both countries have gained additional profits. In the meanwhile, the world's total output has also increased because of the rational allocation of capital, and it has increased by *UDO* which is the sum of the added income of the two countries.

 Such transnational movement of capital will have a direct impact on the gross domestic product, the international balance of payments, and the national income distribution of the two countries. Due to the introduction of foreign capital, the production factors in Country A such as labor force and land are fully utilized, and the effective allocation of resources will increase the gross domestic product of Country A. However, the actual income Country A has obtained from the new gross domestic product is lower than the income it has obtained from foreign capital, which will affect the international balance of payments of Country A in the long run. Because of capital export, Country B has gained increased capital income from overseas investment, which puts Country B in a favorable position in terms of the international balance of payments.

 From the perspective of domestic income distribution, capital inflow reduces the rate of return of domestic capital in Country A, and the actual income of the original domestic capital also decreases correspondingly. However, the income of labor force, land, and other factors of production in Country A increases correspondingly, including both the national income transferred from the original capital income due to the reduction of the rate of return on capital and the newly added income from previously idle factors of production becoming fully utilized due to foreign capital investment. Due to the export of surplus capital, the rate of return on domestic capital of Country B increases, thereby resulting in a rise in the real income of domestic capital. Because of this rise coupled with the huge income from foreign investment, the total capital income of Country B sees a significant increase. In the meanwhile, due to the relative reduction of capital investment, other domestic factors of production are underutilized, leading to a relative decline in prices and a subsequent smaller share of them in the distribution of gross national income.

The contribution of the interest distribution model of international capital is that it clarifies the economic benefits brought by capital movement to both countries concerned, thus demonstrating the promotive effect of international investment with multinationals as the medium on the development of the world economy. Although the model has obvious theoretical defects, it can still be used as a general explanation for the widespread occurrence of international investment. By learning from the analysis of the interest distribution model of international capital, China should actively absorb foreign capital and proactively invest abroad at the same time in international capital movement so as to keep itself a country engaged in two-way capital movement. Through outward direct investment, China can transfer domestic capital and technology to countries and regions with better returns so as to reap net gains. This way, China can obtain double benefits from the outflow and inflow of capital.

II. Analysis on Benefits of China's Outward Direct Investment

1. ODI can help make resource allocation more reasonable

An open economy entails a global perspective to promote organic combination and sound utilization of domestic and foreign resources (including capital, technology, management, talents, and natural resources), thus realizing the best allocation of resources. If a country only imports foreign direct investment but does not export domestic capital and technology for outward direct investment, it could easily develop excessive dependence on foreign capital and technology, which will not only restrict its capability of domestic capital utilization and technological innovation but also hinder its efforts to achieve economical global resource allocation and increase its economic returns. If foreign preferential policies can be regarded as a kind of resources, then outward direct investment is virtually the only way to achieve maximum direct utilization of this resource.

2. ODI can help expand use of foreign capital

Through outward direct investment, especially in countries and regions with developed international financial industry, China can obtain financing facilitation. Due to the huge amount of international floating capital and the fierce competition in the financial industry, coupled with the unimpeded financing channels thanks to the close ties between Chinese enterprises engaged in outward direct investment and the international financial community, China has convenient access to fund-raising for domestic construction. For Chinese enterprises engaged in outward direct investment, only a small amount of investment is paid in cash, as most capital is raised locally or through the international market. Outward direct investment through fixing a price for tangible assets such as machinery, equipment, raw materials and intangible assets such as technical know-how also accounts for a certain proportion. It should be noticed that outward direct investment is also a form of utilizing foreign capital, only that it it takes place abroad rather than at home.

In the short run, outward direct investment may be considered capital outflow, but in the long run, under the combined effect of the recovery of investment capital, the investment returned to China, and the profit remitted back to China, it is conducive to promoting capital inflow. Instead of crowding out domestic capital, outward direct investment can increase China's capital to a certain extent, so it is an effective means of utilizing foreign capital and is conducive to promoting the adjustment and upgrading of China's industrial structure and boosting exports. In recent years, with the economic development, many traditional processing industries in China are faced with a saturated market and excess production capacity, which makes the adjustment of China's industrial and product structures a high priority. On the one hand, outward direct investment can digest traditional technologies and transferring excess production capacity and thus help promote the adjustment of the industrial and product structures. On the other hand, by extending traditional industries and labor-intensive technologies with comparative advantages to other developing countries, it is conducive to stimulating China's exports of technology, equipment, labor services, and commodities, advancing the traditional industries to develop to a higher level, and promoting the virtuous cycle economic development. It is especially worth mentioning that outward direct investment can also help increase the export ratio of China's manufactured products, especially the electromechanical products, thereby improving the commodity structure of China's exports. Practice has proved that outward direct investment can effectively promote China's exports of machinery, equipment, and intermediate products. Generally speaking, outward direct investment can promote the exports of equipment and intermediate products in three ways. The first is to appraise the value of equipment on the Chinese side and turn the equipment into shares. Among China's overseas investment, on average, about 50% is invested through equipment, giving a strong boost to China's equipment exports. The second is to drive exports through equipment renewal and supporting requirements, especially for overseas enterprises with long terms of operation which often have to make a considerable part of their purchase from domestic sources in the process of equipment maintenance and renewal. The third is to boost exports through supplying raw materials and intermediate products to overseas enterprises.

3. ODI can help cultivate international business talents

As a way of outward direct investment, setting up businesses overseas enables the management and technical personnel working overseas to get trained in the complex international market, thereby cultivating all kinds of talents in the fierce competition who are familiar with international business and can act in accordance with international practices.

4. ODI can help introduce advanced technology from foreign countries

Through direct investment in developed countries by acquiring local high-tech enterprises or setting up new technology development joint ventures with local leading high-tech enterprises, China can employ local engineers, researchers, managers, and skilled workers and use local advanced equipment, thereby gaining access to advanced technologies and management experiences that are difficult to obtain at home. In addition, these foreign branches established in hubs of information resources can timely, accurately, and directly transmit a large amount of information obtained locally about the technology market to their domestic headquarters. This helps domestic enterprises keep abreast of the world's leading technology trends and the international market conditions so that they can optimize their business activities. As a developing country whose economy is on track towards a take-off, China must bear in mind its own comparative advantages and find the source of technological innovation under the background of global technological integration. In the meanwhile, it is necessary for China to transfer foreign advanced technologies to itself through corresponding transfer mechanisms and increase the contribution made by technological progresses to economic growth. In this regard, some large enterprises in the developed coastal areas have taken the lead. Since the late 1990s, some enterprises in Shanghai have set up research and development enterprises in western developed countries with the main objective of acquiring advanced foreign technologies. For example, Shanghai Fudan Forward Science and Technology Co., Ltd. has set up high-tech joint ventures in the United States, Japan, and other countries to develop and produce UPS and computer software products and has transferred advanced technologies to China to accelerate the upgrading of domestic products. Shanghai Huali Microelectronics Corporation, China's largest integrated circuit manufacturer, has also set up research and development enterprises in western developed countries to improve the whole company's capacity of developing new products. As another example,

Wanxiang Group, a well-known private enterprise of China, bought UAI, a Nasdaq-listed company in the United States, aiming to acquire and track UAI's advanced brake technology.

Of course, if a country's outward direct investment is not in accordance with its own economic development in scale, structure, and mode, it will have negative impacts on the country's macroeconomic operation. Such negative impacts mainly include the following: first, if a country exports excessive capital abroad, there will be a sharp decrease in domestic investment, even resulting in industrial hollowing-out at home. In particular, developing countries have limited financial strength, and thus transferring excessive funds for overseas investment will definitely hinder the normal development of the domestic economy. Second, because the international investment environment is complex and volatile, many factors are difficult to predict, so outward investment faces greater risks than domestic investment, including political risks, commercial risks, and exchange rate and interest rate risks. If investors misjudge the nature and extent of these risks or fail to prevent them effectively, major losses will occur. Third, since domestic investment and production factors have been transferred overseas, domestic employment opportunities may be correspondingly reduced.

However, on the whole, vigorously developing outward direct investment will enable China to share more international economic benefits. Compared with its foreign capital inducement, China's outward direct investment lags behind obviously, which is not commensurate with China's economic development speed and its status in global economy. In order to change this situation, China should enhance its subjective understanding of the significance of transnational investment and understand that foreign investment inducement and outward direct investment are both means of utilizing international capital. China should put equal emphasis on "bringing in" and "going out" as "going out" is essentially a way of foreign investment inducement, only that it happens abroad. With China's outward direct investment lagging far behind its foreign investment inducement, China should make greater efforts to develop outward direct investment. The pessimistic view that China does not yet have the conditions or advantages to expand outward direct investment is meritless, while the unrealistically optimistic view that China should promptly develop outward direct investment with the same scale as its foreign capital inducement is also harmful. Given that China's outward direct investment is still in its initial stage, it takes time for the country to realize its transition towards a strategy that places equal emphasis on foreign capital inducement and outward direct investment, as such a transition overnight is unrealistic. China should make positive and solid efforts to implement the development strategy of outward direct investment, sharpen the competitive edge of overseas enterprises, motivate the domestic enterprises to invest overseas, and enhance their corporate strength in developing outward direct investment. The state should also establish corresponding departments to coordinate and guide outward direct investment activities, formulate corresponding policies to support multinational enterprises and create the domestic environment and objective conditions for outward direct investment. Only then can China take advantage of the opportunities, rise above the challenges brought by economic globalization, participate in the international division of labor, and share in the benefits from increased international capital movements.

Section Ⅲ National Interests and Common Interests of Countries amid Financial Crisis

The global financial crisis has made countries around the world solemnly realize the following fact: only by bearing in mind the big picture of global economic development and financial stability, earnestly strengthening international coordination in the formulation of monetary policies, and all countries bearing risks together can the countries pull through the hard times, realize the recovery of the global economy, and restore the stability of the international financial order, which are the roots of the common interests of all countries over the world. However, since the outbreak of the global financial crisis, there have been great differences in the coordination of monetary policies among countries in the world. The coordination in combating the financial crisis has been much worse than what people expected, and the contradictions between international coordination and independent national interests become more prominent. Under the current situation that the international financial crisis is still having implications and that the global economic landscape is becoming more volatile, how to deal with the relationship between international coordination and national interests in perspective, determine the orientation of monetary policies, and promote the reform of the international financial system are still major challenges facing countries around the world.

I. Game between International Coordination and National Interests

Since the outbreak of the global financial crisis, to prevent the financial crisis from spreading and worsening, countries around the world have strengthened and widened the scope of international coordination and cooperation in economic and financial fields. However, amid economic recessions and the financial crisis, the game between international coordination and national interests is a reflection of the objective realities. At the G20 London Summit in November 2008 and April 2009, the international community reached a consensus on strengthening international coordination to combat the financial crisis, opposing trade protectionism, and further strengthening the voting rights and the voice of developing countries such as China in the International Monetary Fund.[1] Moreover, China's proposals for countries to

---

[1] Wang Dong, "Game between National Interests and Common Interests of Countries around the World amid Financial Crisis," *Contemporary Economics*, 2009 (17), pp. 4-8.

jointly shoulder the responsibility for combating the financial crisis, to resolve the problem of unbalanced development of global economy, and to ensure that all developing countries can fully enjoy the opportunities presented by globalization were met with general recognition. Therefore, from the perspective of the common interests of global countries, international coordination is necessary in striking a balance in interests and rights among countries all over the world in the process of coping with the international financial crisis and promoting the reform of the international financial system. However, in the realistic international economic and financial environment, due to the fact that the national interests of some western countries have been infinitely "enlarged," when there are nearly irreconcilable major differences in national interests, international coordination has become more difficult, which has to a certain extent limited the effectiveness of international coordination, causing the game between international coordination and national interests. There is no denying the fact that the spread of the global financial crisis has objectively stricken a hard blow economically and financially to all countries in the world, hurting the national interests of every sovereign country. Under the background that the worsening of financial crisis and the exacerbation of economic recession are expected, it is not "overreacting" but extremely necessary to take appropriate countermeasures and actions. However, on the other hand, it would be a totally different issue if a country uses policy instruments for crisis transfer in confrontational competitions of national interests and adopt financial and monetary policies with a strong sense of protectionism that would harm other countries. According to the core views of game theory, the choice of different monetary policies by countries around the world is a game between different national interests of different countries against the backdrop of the current international financial crisis, At the same time, it is also a game action of common interests of the countries who are participants in international affairs under international coordination and cooperation. The goal of international coordination and cooperation is to realize the common interests of all countries in the world, and the game between national interests is to ensure that the core interests of countries are not harmed. Judging from the current interstate benefit game caused by the different orientations and frictions of monetary policies, if the game among different monetary policies is intensified to the extent that only national interests are taken into account without considering the common interests of countries around the world, international coordination will become more and more difficult, and the unbalanced situation of the international community will also be aggravated. As a result, some problems caused by the current mainstream orientation of the national monetary policies of relevant countries are very thought-provoking. Of course, from the point of view of game theory, the game between international coordination and national interests amid the financial crisis is not a specific product of the financial crisis but a common phenomenon taking place when countries strive to realize their respective national interests through mutual coordination and cooperation, which reflects the deep-seated relationship between national interests and the common interests of all countries around the world. Therefore, the game between international coordination and national interests in the international community not only can be traced far back but will also persist for ever.

After the U.S. subprime mortgage crisis broke out in 2007, the Federal Reserve System started the monetary policy of directly purchasing commercial paper and transferring its creditor's rights to the U.S. Treasury Department. Then, the Treasury Department will inject capital into enterprises and financial institutions to buy shares in the form of debt relief. It can thus be seen that the rescue plan of the United States partly relies on the joint actions of monetary and fiscal policies and are mostly implemented in the form of relief of debts such as bills and bonds. In particular, following the Federal Reserve System's announcement on March 18, 2009 to purchase $300 billion of long-term treasury bonds and $1.25 trillion of agency mortgage-backed securities, the United States launched a bank "detoxification" program on March 23 to deal with the "toxic assets" of financial institutions, with a goal of providing more liquidity and shifting the focus of the monetary policy towards "quantitative easing." At the same time that the Federal Reserve System launched a host of unconventional monetary policies to buy back government bonds and the "toxic assets," central banks such as the European Central Bank, the Bank of England, and the Bank of Japan have also issued their own monetary policies to buy corporate bonds. Thus, the shift of the focus of the monetary policies of western countries including the U.S. towards "quantitative easing" has become increasingly obvious. This monetary policy adopted by western countries including the United States aims to increase the supply of money to the capital market on a large scale and maintain the stability and liquidity of the financial sector on the surface by expanding the circulation of money, which is a typical "quantitative easing" monetary policy. The core of this policy is to relax the control on currency issuance to a certain extent, increase money supply in the money market, expand the scale of the capital market, and increase liquidity to ease the liquidity squeeze in the money market; the orientation of the policy is to "activate" the capital market and thus promote the recovery of the real economy through monetary policy instruments under both the financial and the economic crisis; the essence of the policy is "quantitative easing," which is actually an excuse used by monetary authorities for using the banknote printing machine and issue banknotes on a large scale. Since 2009, western countries represented by the United States have used the excuse of "quantitative easing" to issue currency to buy treasury bonds, which is the very essence of this monetary policy. Therefore, the monetary policy of "quantitative easing" is considered by some economists as a protectionist policy adopted by monetary authorities which is similar to trade protectionism as both belong to economic protectionism and reflects core national interests rather than the global concept of world economy and international finance.

By and large, the monetary policy of "quantitative easing" is a kind of policy that is adopted only when the economic and financial situation is deteriorating while there is no room for interest rate reduction and it is difficult for interest rate adjustments to make a significant effect. Since the beginning of this year, western countries have injected a large amount of liquidity into the money market by purchasing all kinds of bonds. This means of intervention is different from the conventional means of an interest rate lever adopted in the early stage and is a non-conventional means of monetary policy. It is a general consensus among the economist community that the current policy of "quantitative easing" adopted by western countries is an "extreme" choice when the "conventional means" adopted in the early stage failed to deliver effective results or even proved useless. Since the outbreak of the global financial crisis, the United States, Europe, Japan, and other western countries have fallen into a substantial all-round crisis. Interest rate reduction, as the conventional means of macro-economic regulation, was once frequently used by western countries, but up to now, there has been little effect, with little room for further interest rate reduction. This conventional means of macro-economic regulation which is interest rate reduction has been depleted. Therefore, faced with increasingly fewer choices of policies as the conventional means of an interest rate lever is being depleted, it is natural that the western world turns to the monetary policy of "quantitative easing." Therefore, most experts and scholars define this policy as a product of the current western economic and financial environment. On the one hand, this shows that western economy and finance is still deteriorating and that there are not many "antidotes" left available to stimulate the economy and activate the market. Once the policy of "quantitative easing" also becomes useless and cannot reach the policy goals, it is worrisome how the economic and financial landscape of the western countries will unfold. On the other hand, it also shows that the western countries are not completely aligned with each other in their current economic and financial policies and that "quantitative easing" is only a short-term or medium-term action taken by the countries according to their respective economic and financial realities. Once there is a change in the situation, the uncertainty in their economic and financial policies will be further reflected, and the economic and financial policies might lose orientation in their tracks. It is uncertain how western countries will coordinate economic and financial policies, and it is doubtful whether they will be able to reach a consensus.

As the global economic recession and financial crisis are still having implications currently, the financial policies and the "quantitative easing" monetary policies as part of the western countries' national economic stimulus plans are targeted to a certain extent and also heavily protectionist in their contents and nature, but the policy orientation in the game between national interests is more essential and provide much food for thought. In addition, if western countries such as the United States fail to keep the amount of money issued into the market within a reasonable range, it would be highly likely that a new round of asset "bubbles" will be "cultivated" and thus trigger new crises similar to inflations, currency crises, and credit crises. In fact, the spreading process of the financial crisis in western countries such as the United States is more like a constant process of "shifting" the crisis. The series of rescue plans and policy measures issued both have a sense of protectionism in "shifting" the crisis elsewhere and raise the suspicion of being irresponsible in monetary policies and allowing currency devaluation. Embodying the principle of putting national interests first to the full, they run counter to the ongoing international cooperation between countries. Judging from the connotations of game theory in economics, there is certain antagonism between different policies introduced, so game between different policies is omnipresent in real economic life. Therefore, in a sense, the game between different monetary policies in response to the financial crisis is more prevalent in the economic field against the current backdrop of financial crisis. Among them, the inclination towards the monetary policy of "quantitative easing" in the western world is a typical concept in game theory in economics, which has aroused heated debates in the international community. This shows that while the global financial crisis surpasses the scope of any state, making strengthening international coordination even more necessary, in the international coordination of a joint battle against the financial crisis, the game and collision between international coordination and national interests of monetary policies have actually become more prominent in the real international community because it involves interests of all parties and complicated international relations. To a certain extent, how the game and collision between international coordination and national interests on monetary policies will evolve in the current international environment depends on the development and changes of the international financial and economic situation. If the international financial and economic situation continues to deteriorate, especially if western countries are unable to get rid of the crisis in the foreseeable future, western countries will likely continue to expand the scope of their protectionist financial and monetary policies and strengthen their policies in the game for national interests. Subsequently, the global-scale game and collision between international coordination and national interests will become even more intense and may even "escalate" if the international financial crisis continues to aggravate. Moreover, the game and collision between international coordination and national interests is a universal and comprehensive phenomenon that takes place in every sector of the international community. It is relatively implicit and flexible, and it needs to be considered from all angles of international coordination and national interests to reflect the intricate international economic relations. Therefore, countries around the world should refrain from the unlimited expansion of and excessive attention to national interests to achieve the common interests of all countries but at the same time safeguard their own national interests to the greatest extent. This is an unavoidable and important choice that every country needs to make in today's world.

II. Game Between National Interests under Different Monetary Policies

Although all designed to deal with the financial crisis and stimulate economy, monetary policies around the world are totally different in nature.

The monetary policy of "quantitative easing" taken by western countries and the monetary policy of "moderate easing" taken by China, for example, not only have fundamental differences in nature but also reflect the countries' different choices in orientation under their respective strategies for the game between national interests. The biggest differences between the monetary policy of "quantitative easing" and the monetary policy of "moderate easing" lie in the following four aspects.

First, the two are different in nature. The monetary policy of "quantitative easing" is a "stimulant" that monetary authorities facing shrinking market liquidity adopt as a last resort when all other measures have proved useless in addressing the economic and financial crisis. The so-called "quantitative" refers to the "quantification" of currency issuance, which depends on whether the currency issuance can alleviate the deteriorating crisis without considering potential inflation risks. Unlike "quantitative easing," the monetary policy of "moderately easing" is to moderately increase the money supply from the perspective of macro-regulatory monetary policies, expand consumption, and inject vitality into the economy for its recovery. As a result, the adjustment is within a controllable range, with changes in the money supply being determined based on the changes and development of the market, and the factors of potential inflation risks can be timely tracked.

Second, the two are different in policy orientation. By adopting the "quantitative easing" policy, the monetary authorities aim to increase the amount of money in the market by printing banknotes, and the policy orientation is the acceleration of currency devaluation. If the amount of currency in circulation is far higher than the amount needed for commodity circulation, it will be difficult to control currency devaluation in a certain period of time. The policy orientation of the "moderate easing" monetary policy, on the other hand, is to increase monetary credit and remove the obstacles in putting currency into circulation, thereby expanding the scale and increasing the speed of money emission into circulation. Meanwhile, appropriate funds are taken out from banks' equity fund or fiscal revenue and injected into the market in a planned way.

Third, the two deliver different final effects. The final effect of the "quantitative easing" policy is mainly embodied as the "virtual" expansion of the economy, and it has little effect on the real economy and cannot deliver long-term results. On the other hand, the final effect of the "moderate easing" policy is mainly reflected in the real economy and is relatively long-term and stable.

Fourth, the two face different levels of potential risks. The potential risks of the "quantitative easing" policy are reflected in the fact that the money supply in the money market exceeds the actual money demand, which will inevitably lead to a decline in the market value or the purchasing power of money. The risks are essentially inflation risks caused by the scenario that the total social demand is greater than the total social supply, which has the potential to spread on a global scale. Although the "moderate easing" policy is also subject to potential inflation risks, which are usually manifested as a decline in fiscal revenue and an increase in fiscal expenditure in the financial sector and an excessive expansion of credit loans in the banking sector, the inflation risks are relatively small as long as the policy is properly implemented and flexibly regulated under the condition that the downward inflation trend has been established and that fiscal accumulation is sufficient.

Therefore, adopting the "quantitative easing" policy which now prevails in western countries is an irresponsible, short-term choice, while the "moderate easing" policy currently adopted by China is different from the "quantitative easing" policy in essence. The game between the two essentially different monetary policies may continue for quite some time.

Thus, as the global financial crisis and the western economic situation continue to deteriorate, the game between different monetary policies to protect and maximize national interests is an unavoidable new challenge facing all countries at present. Therefore, handling the relationship between international coordination and cooperation and national interests properly and strengthening necessary international coordination while safeguarding national interests are not only appeals of the international community and countries around the world to safeguard their interests but also where the countries' national interests lie. From the perspective of international relations, the same relationship of opposition and interdependence in interests exists between international coordination and cooperation and national interests. In the international community, sovereign countries can ensure neither their national interests nor their common interests without the existence and cooperation of each other. Common interests are realized both through international coordination and cooperation and through games. Especially amid the continuous development of economic globalization and the deepening of economic and financial interdependence among countries, international coordination and cooperation in economic and financial fields are increasing day by day. Against this backdrop, people have to accept the fact that it is impossible to create maximum value without extensive international coordination and cooperation, so countries around the world must learn to examine the relationship between international coordination and cooperation and national interests from a global perspective and safeguard the common interests of countries and the whole mankind while pursuing and realizing their own national interests.

III. Game in International Financial System Reform

At the two G20 London summits, countries have proposed to reform the system of international financial institutions such as the International Monetary Fund (IMF) to keep them in accordance with the current status of world economic development and increase the voices of emerging and developing economies. This proposal has brought calls for reforming the current system of international financial institutions to the fore again. Looking back on the history, virtually every major international economic and financial crisis is accompanied by great international economic and financial changes that have led to significant reforms or even restructuring of the international economic and financial system and landscape.

At the G20 London Summit held in early April 2009, the countries present pledged to add another $500 billion of loanable funds to IMF both as a measure to combat the financial crisis together and as an important step in preparation of the reform of the IMF Special Drawing Right (SDR) composition. On the eve of the G20 London Summit, Zhou Xiaochuan, governor of the People's Bank of China, proposed to create a "super-sovereign reserve currency" based on the existing SDR system of IMF. This proposal was not only a response to the monetary policy of "quantitative easing" adopted by western countries but also a proposition for the reform of the existing SDR system of IMF. Meanwhile, China also pledged to contribute more funds to IMF at the G20 London Summit, which also reflected China's efforts to establish positive interactions with international financial institutions, as well as the game in the international financial system reform.

Because of the comprehensive international economic and financial crisis, the international community has paid great attention to the international financial system reform with a specific focus on raising the voices and status of emerging and developing economies in the system. However, the United States, the Eurozone, and emerging countries will also definitely have fierce games with each other regarding issues such as the risk and cost sharing for the rescue of the market, the monetary policies to stimulate economic growth, and the reform of the international financial institution system.

Moreover, reforming the international financial system is bound to involve the interests of different parties and have an impact on the leading position of the western developed countries such as the United States in the international financial field. Therefore, the debate on the reform of the international financial system has gradually evolved into an international game. Additionally, judging from the establishment and evolution of the contemporary international financial system, the content and direction of the international financial system reform still depend on economic and financial strengths to a large extent. In other words, whoever has stronger economic and financial strength has more say and even controls the direction of the reform and dominates the international financial system. Based on the above-mentioned realities, the current game in the international financial system reform is mainly embodied in the contest of three forces in three aspects: the game regarding right and interest distribution within the developed countries of the United States and Europe that have long dominated the international financial system; the game between emerging and developing economies which demand to change the current order and developed countries which demand to maintain the current order; the game in international coordination between equally matched forces. As a matter of fact, because every country has its own national conditions, the financial crisis has different implications on different countries, so countries around the world focus on different issues when it comes to the international financial system reform. For example, the United States is relatively "indifferent" to the reform of current international financial system because it is more concerned with how to promote all the countries to work together towards expanding capital investment in the market to stimulate economic recovery; unlike the United States, European countries represented by Germany and France are more enthusiastic about the reform of the international financial system and economic structure, emphasizing the strengthening of financial supervision and the comprehensive reform of the American mode of laissez-faire capitalism in the international financial system; emerging and developing economies such as China, Brazil, India, and Russia are paying more attention to practical issues such as raising the voices and status of emerging and developing economies in the international financial system, improving the international financial and economic environment, opposing trade protectionism, and stimulating economic recovery.

  The international financial system reform depends on changes in the relative strength of major powers. However, under the conditions that there have not been fundamental changes in the current international economic and financial structure and especially that the United States has not lost its economic strength and its major influence on the financial market, there are still a host of challenges ahead for the international financial system reform. Looking back on the history, since the "Bretton Woods System" was established after the Second World War, the international financial sector has undergone many reforms but all in the form of either amendment or improvement, and none has ever shaken its foundation. In the meantime, financial crises have broken out several times in the international financial sector for various reasons, dealing a blow to all countries in the world. Western countries did not escape from the "fate" of recession after prosperity despite the "superiority" of capitalism, nor did they get exempt from financial turmoil despite their leading position in the international financial system. On the contrary, these countries were ridden by financial problems, even leaving their financial sectors on the verge of a breakdown. Meanwhile, emerging and developing countries did not remain unaffected either under the financial order dominated by the western system and got hurt again and again. In fact, problems in the international financial system has aroused the international community's attention for a long time. Especially after the Asian financial crisis broke out in 1998, relevant countries and regions and international financial institutions have assigned more importance to these problems and have repeatedly called for a comprehensive reform of the existing international financial system. However, western countries have turned up their nose on these calls until this global financial crisis hit them hard and made them become well aware of the seriousness of the problems in the existing international financial system and the urgency of international financial system reform. Against this backdrop, the reform was put on the agenda at long last. However, it is impossible to reform the international financial system without adjusting and integrating the voices and positions of members in the international financial authorities—IMF and the World Bank, which will change the unreasonable and unbalanced situation that has lasted for more than half a century. This will undoubtedly affect the actual interests of all parties, and the difficulty of such a reform is imaginable. For this reason, although there has been a consensus that we need relevant international financial conferences and the involved countries to adjust the voices and positions of members in IMF and the World Bank, it is predictable that once the reform enters the actual implementation stage in the future, the game between various forces on the distribution of rights and interests will become more intense.

At the moment, the hard nut to be cracked in the reform of international financial system remains to be how to redress the imbalance. Specifically, the current imbalance involves two important aspects. The first is global economic and financial imbalance. Such an imbalance is a normality, which is mainly manifested as imbalance in the international balance of payments. An effective international financial system must tackle the problem of the identification and allocation of adjustment responsibilities when there is a fundamental imbalance in the international balance of payments. Under the "Bretton Woods System" and even the "Jamaica System," the adjustment responsibilities are shared by the two parties of the imbalance. There are also some differences between the two systems. Under the "Bretton Woods System," the United States often assumed part of the adjustment responsibilities in substance when it was a party of the imbalance. However, under the "Jamaica System," the United States has never assumed such responsibilities. The second is the imbalance in the distribution of voices and positions in the international financial system. In the existing global economic and financial managing institutions, especially in IMF and the World Bank which are important managing institutions of the international financial system, emerging and developing economies have never gotten their opinions respected and their interests fairly reflected. As a result, emerging and developing economies have remained extremely passive in previous financial crises and even had to be "manipulated" by developed countries or accept harsh conditions in the "aid" clauses of international financial institutions. Therefore, in the current international financial system reform, emerging and developing economies hope to establish a financial system based on democratic principles and change the long-term imbalance in the distribution of voices and positions in the system through increasing the representation of developing countries. In addition, it should be noted that the current financial liberalization and excessive innovation of financial products have increased financial risks, adding more new uncertainties to the financial system. Governments of countries around the world must strengthen international cooperation and coordination to promote the reform of the international financial system while further improving their national monetary control and maintaining a stable financial order. Therefore, the international financial system reform should be a step-by-step process during which countries around the world need to strike a balance in national interests through coordination and cooperation and reconstruct an international financial system with a relatively reasonable composition which does not put sole emphasis on who should dominate the system.

Section Ⅳ International Capital Flow and Common Interests of Mankind

In the process of establishing an international investment order, it is necessary to coordinate the relationship between protecting the interests of investors and their investment and improving the investment treatment standards on the one hand and safeguarding the jurisdiction over foreign investment and the development goals of host countries on the other hand. To coordinate the interests among developed countries and between developed countries and developing countries, the only method is to establish multilateral investment rules on the premise of common development of mankind.

Chapter V Analysis of Common Interests in International Capital Flow

I. Principle of Common Interests of Mankind

Common interests of mankind refer to interests that transcend national boundaries, nationalities, and ideologies and reflect the concept of the overall value of mankind. An injury to such interests is a common injury to the survival of the whole mankind.

1. Importance of common interests of mankind against backdrop of globalization

Amid the globalization, international relations are becoming an interactive, intertwined, and interdependent system, and the international community is becoming a unity. Under this context, "global issues" have grown more and more prominent. The so-called "global issues" refer to a series of major issues that involve the interests of the entire humankind and require attention on a global scale and coordinated international actions. These global issues mainly include environmental issues, resource issues, population issues, international economic order issues and anti-terrorism issues. These issues that exist worldwide and need to be solved by all countries together reflect the importance of the common interests of mankind. As people have said, people all over the world are villagers of the global village and passengers on the same boat. Common interests have bound the whole mankind closely. On some common issues, people need to overcome the obstacles of different social systems and ideologies as well as the limitation of national interests and understand and examine these common interests in the international community that are related to the survival and development of the whole human society from a global perspective.

2. Coordination between common interests of mankind and national interests

In today's era, sovereign states are the basic theme of not only the international community but also the international law. The struggle and cooperation between sovereign states to safeguard their own economic, political, and military interests are the most important components of international relations in which national interests still play the dominating role. However, as mentioned above, when human beings enter the era of globalization, the co-existence and co-development of national interests and the common interests of mankind have become a reality. Therefore, what we are pursuing is the harmonious unity of national interests and the common interests of mankind. This laudable concept encourages all countries to consider the common interests of mankind and avoid the scenario that "injure one and you injure them all," thereby achieving "multi-win" and "win-win" results.

II. Evaluate Current International Investment Order Based on Principle of Common Interests of Mankind

In order to establish a unified international investment order, the international community has made long-term attempts and efforts. On the one hand, to coordinate the worldwide flow of international direct investment, the World Bank, the United Nations, and the WTO have made great efforts and reached some agreements on investment. Among them, the most effective one is the Agreement on Trade-Related Investment Measures (TRIMs) reached in the Uruguay Round. On the other hand, the Organization for Economic Co-operation and Development (OECD) initiated negotiations in 1995 – 1998 aimed at formulating a comprehensive high-level multilateral agreement on investment (MAI) but announced the failure of MAI in 1998. TRIMs and MAI have played a crucial role in the history of the establishment of a unified international investment order by the international community. Therefore, this book starts from these two international investment agreements and evaluate them based on the principle of common interests of mankind.

1. Evaluate TRIMs based on principle of common interests of mankind

After the start of the Uruguay Round, the United States advocated regulation over all investment measures under the General Agreement on Tariffs and Trade (GATT) in a radical manner to accommodate the needs for outward expansion of its domestic multinational enterprises and put forward a list of 13 types of trade-related investment measures. This was very beneficial for multinational enterprises from developed countries to enter the domestic markets of host countries, especially some developing countries that implement intervention policies on foreign direct investment, and carry out global procurement, production, and sales. Therefore, this proposal was met with support of some developed countries. However, developing countries cited Article XVIII of GATT which includes clauses on infant industry protection to justify their investment measures. Due to the tit-for-tat disputes between the two sides and disagreement within developed countries, the focus of the final negotiations was whether the nationalization requirements, foreign exchange balance requirements, and import requirements could be retained. Through intense negotiations, the two sides finally reached TRIMs, which prohibits member countries from setting investment measures such as local content requirements, export performance requirements, foreign exchange balance requirements, and local sales requirements for foreign investment access.

Thus, in the process of reaching TRIMs, there were conflicts of interests between different parties, mainly between developed and developing countries. To accept TRIMs, developing countries had to make major policy adjustments, but their efforts have not received commensurate repayments. In other words, developing countries did not get their due benefits in the Uruguay Round, and there was a serious imbalance in the distribution of benefits between developed and developing countries. The implementation of TRIMs has brought great challenges to developing countries. Among others, developed countries and developing countries had great disagreement on the prohibition of local content requirements. Many developing countries believe that this measure runs counter to their interests. Although many countries have reduced the use of such requirements in recent years, local content requirements are still in use in developing countries and industrial countries, especially in automation sectors which are mostly located in developing countries. Therefore, since the implementation of TRIMs, developed countries have raised many objections to developing countries regarding the automation sector.

In order to solve these problems encountered by developing countries in the implementation of TRIMs, the WTO conference in July 2001 extended the transition period under Article 5 to the end of 2001 and allowed it to be extended for another two years under certain requirements and conditions. Although this was effective in the short term, these extension clauses cannot solve the fundamental problem of TRIMs—that is, TRIMs did not give developing countries enough policy space to freely choose development policies that can add value, improve employment, and enhance competitiveness.

2. Evaluation of MAI based on principle of common interests of mankind

In the 1990s, OECD made an attempt on multilateral investment legislation and tried to formulate a global comprehensive multilateral investment agreement. However, the efforts to negotiate a multilateral investment agreement finally failed in December 1998, and after three years of hard efforts in negotiation by OECD member countries, only a daft of the multilateral agreement on investment (the MAI draft) was formulated. There were many reasons for the failure of the MAI negotiations, but the most important one was that the contents did not accurately reflect the investment policy needs of different countries and did not properly consider the balance of rights and obligations. Thus, we can see that the root cause of the failure of MAI negotiations was that it violated the principle of common interests of mankind as it did not reflect the interests of different countries or seek an appropriate balance of interests between different countries.

First, there was a conflict of interests between developed countries which would take some time to achieve interest coordination.

The proposed MAI was a high-level investment agreement, and OECD member countries were all developed countries. On the one hand, they called for the relaxing of investment control and put forward a host of highly liberalized rules. On the other hand, they were unwilling to completely abolish existing investment measures to protect their own interests, resulting in many lists of exceptions. For example, the United States put forward many highly liberalized rules such as encouraging free access and prohibiting performance requirements while also proposing various exceptions, many of which were opposed by the other side of the negotiations. These exceptions included national security exceptions, minority support exceptions, exceptions to ensure that the United States could fulfill its obligations under existing bilateral investment treaties and the North American Free Trade Agreement (NAFTA), exceptions regarding government subsidies and government procurement programs, etc. In addition to the United States, the problem of exception lists also existed in other OECD member countries. For another example, based on its own special interest needs, E.U. proposed the exception of regional economic integration organizations. The United States strongly opposed this exception, believing that this exception would create a huge loophole in national treatment and most-favored-nation treatment.

It can be seen from these exceptions and the contradictions they have caused that the problem of different economic development levels and different interest priorities also exist between developed countries. On a series of issues in the MAI draft, developed countries remained very careful and weighed the possible advantages and disadvantages that highly liberalized investment rules might bring them. Thus, at least at present, not all developed countries can accept highly liberalized investment rules, as differences in economic development levels determine that these countries cannot accept the same rules on the same level. The failure of MAI shows that the developed countries have not reached a consensus on what kind of comprehensive multilateral investment rules should be established.

Second, there was a conflict of interests between developed countries and developing countries because MAI ignored the interests of developing countries.

Although OECD intended to open MAI to developing countries when formulating the agreement, the core rules of the MAI draft only emphasized the protection of investors and their investment and did not stipulate the obligations that investors should undertake in host countries. As most of the recipients of direct investment from developed countries are developing countries, the MAI draft assigned excessive importance to the interests of developed countries at the cost of the interests of developing countries. Its high-level rules were obviously not in accordance with the economic development levels and the economic affordability of developing countries.

On the issue of treatment of investors and their investment, the draft stipulated that on joining the MAI, developing countries must implement national treatment immediately and apply it to the stage of foreign investment access. Obviously, this would severely limit the rights of host countries in determining which fields foreign investment could enter and examining the possible negative impacts of foreign investment to their national economies. On the issue of performance requirements, the types of performance requirements that the MAI draft prohibited far exceeded those stipulated in TRIMs. The MAI draft prohibited performance requirements in both service trade and non-trade areas, such as technology transfer. Additionally, the MAI draft's prohibition of performance requirements applied to all stages before and after an investment or a business setup. This thorough prohibition of performance requirements would have a major impact on the power of host countries to guide and manage foreign capital. Obviously, such stipulation cannot be accepted by developing countries at the current stage. On the dispute settlement mechanism, the MAI draft introduced an "investor-to-state" procedure, which would mean that investors could directly submit disputes to international arbitration without relying on the governments of their home countries and without the consent of the governments of the host countries, i.e., investors and international arbitration institutions are given the right to review and deny the legislative power of host countries, which is unacceptable to developing countries.

The above analysis shows that the core rules in the MAI draft did not accurately reflect the investment policy needs of different countries and did not take into account the interests of both developed and developing countries. In the process of pursuing maximum investment liberalization and more comprehensive and refined protection for investors, the MAI draft ignored the interests of host countries, requiring a degree of market openness and deregulation that exceeded the degree developing countries could provide, and did not practice the principle of common interests of mankind, which made it difficult for developing countries to accept.

Chapter VI
Analysis of Common Interests in International Technology Transfer

Section I Analysis of Common Interests of International Technology Transfer

Technology transfer is the process of transferring (disseminating) technology from the entity that owns or holds it to another. Vertical transfer refers to transfer of technology from scientific research institutes and universities to enterprises. Horizontal transfer refers to transfer of technology from one manufacturer to another. International technology transfer to developing countries has a long history. Multinationals possess a large proportion of the world's technologies, thus becoming an important player in international technology transfer. The study of international technology transfer has just emerged in recent decades. Since 1961, theories, experience, and case studies on international technology transfer have increased continuously. Technology is defined both in a broad sense and in a narrow sense, and there are many ways to classify it. However, the key is knowledge and production, and the most critical point is that useful knowledge in production is different from science. Science is a kind of knowledge that has not been applied to commercial processes (Smith, 1980). It is also difficult to define technology transfer. On the one hand, technology transfer may refer to the movement of technology from one geographic location to another, the shift from one use to another, or both (Smith, 1980); on the other hand, technology transfer must be a transfer of the ability to understand and develop the imported technology. The transfer of a technology is incomplete until the recipient is able to operate, maintain, absorb, improve, expand, and develop the original transferred technology completely without external assistance. In this sense, technology transfer is not only the acquisition of a productive knowledge but also the establishment of technological capacity in a country. The reason that technology transfer is hard to define is mainly that technology is knowledge, not a product. Therefore, different researchers conduct research on technology transfer for different purposes and and have different research scopes.

Theories of foreign direct investment (FDI) generally emphasize that a technology is a specific advantage of manufacturers, industries or countries that can be developed and utilized abroad. Thus, for new technologies, the partial equilibrium theory is generally adopted to explain the activities of multinationals and FDI, and therefore, no independent theory of international technology transfer has been formed. When harnessing their technological advantages, multinationals transfer their technologies to another country through FDI, subcontracts, licenses, or other means. It is enough to explain the international technology transfer behavior of multinationals based on the concepts of the oligopolistic market structure and transaction costs in the general theory of the firm. Three types of economists have extensively discussed the issue of international technology transfer using the partial equilibrium theory. The first type is the international trade economists, who regard multinationals as producers of technologies that trade the transferred technologies on the international market as commodities. Stephen Hymer, Burfers and G. K. Helleiner are this type of economists. The second type is industrial economists, who mainly conduct case studies on the alternative methods of international technology transfer of industries and multinationals based on the theory of the firm. The third type is development economists, many of whom are also experts in international trade. These economists study the applicability of technology transfer and the impact and significance of technology transfer on the financial flow, technology, and economic development of the host country.

"The Role of Multinational Corporations in the Less Developed Countries' Trade in Technology" (Helleiner, 1975) was the first paper that comprehensively discussed technology transfer and the concepts and problems of technology in multinational corporations. At the beginning, this paper analyzed the imperfect nature of the international technology market and its impact on the costs, conditions, and modes of technology transfer. Helleiner divided technology into two categories: technology for production and technology for consumption. He pointed out that transnational corporations were the main producers and transferors of production and consumption technologies. He argued that in technology transfer, the product life cycle theory was not applicable and that transnational corporations not only earned monopoly profits but also transferred inapplicable or unnecessary technologies to the host country.

Although most research on transnational corporations and technology transfer use the partial equilibrium theory on new technology, some theory-oriented international trade economists construct neoclassical dynamic models within the framework of general equilibrium to examine the impact of technology transfer on resource allocation and economic welfare. Ronald Findlay's "Relative Backwardness, Direct Foreign Investment, and the Transfer of Technology: A Simple Dynamic Model" (1978) and Sanghamitra Das's "Externalities, and Technology Transfer through Multinational Corporations: A Theoretical Analysis" (1987) explored these two issues in a different way. Findlay's paper assumed that the rate of technological change was an increasing function of the technology gap and the openness to foreign direct investment in developed countries and developing countries. Based on some assumptions about the growth rate of domestic capital and foreign capital, Findlay has drawn some interesting conclusions about the path for long-term and steady growth. For example, if the technology transfer rate is too high, the ultimate dependence on foreign technology will increase; if human capital investment is made, the dependence will decrease, and many models have discussed the dynamic trend of FDI in optimal growth. The basic idea is to set the aggregate production function whose independent variables include domestic capital and foreign capital. One technology transfer function captures the following idea: the contribution of FDI to output cannot be separated from the hard and soft new technologies associated with it; thus, a growth path is found at the same time that the optimal solution to a set of difference equations is found. The steady-state properties of the solution have also been studied. T. Koiznrni and K. J. Kopecky (1997) found that capital intensity became a strategic variable in the steady-state growth model because technology transfer was explicitly introduced in the production function (Koiznrni and Kopecky, 1977). They have proved that assuming that technology transfer takes the form of management input in the production function of transnational corporations, positive employment effects can be expected from FDI in the long run (Koiznrni and Kopecky, 1980). The article of Das has proved that although not all technology transfer through multinationals can benefit domestic manufacturers within the industry, there is no doubt that the host country will benefit. In 1989, it was concluded that foreign investment had produced two opposite forces on the aggregate production function, namely, the improvement of technology and the decline of marginal productivity of capital. Relative strength determines whether the host country should encourage more foreign direct investment (Tsai, 1989).

In fact, the effect of foreign direct investment and technology introduction on the domestic technological progress of the host country has the phenomenon of "antinomies." The introduction of foreign direct investment may not necessarily bring advanced technology. Many scholars have explored the research and development (R&D) activities of multinational corporations in developing host countries. Although most multinationals are R&D intensive enterprises, their overseas subsidiaries have not carried out R&D with great fanfare. In addition, overseas R&D is mainly aimed at developing technologies that meet the needs of the local market rather than developing basic research. There is a positive correlation between foreign R&D expenditure and the importance of sales for foreign subsidiaries. If foreign subsidiaries have registered large sales, they will be more motivated to locate production and development activities close to overseas markets.

There have been many case studies on technology transfer in specific industries or in individual countries. For example, Usui has studied in detail the technology transfer from Japanese manufacturers to some important industries in Latin American countries, and Balashon has conducted case studies on the technology transfer from American companies to 5 major industries in developed and developing countries. Regarding technology transfer to specific developing countries, a large number of articles and monographs have been published. However, most of these case studies focus on manufacturing, especially pharmaceuticals, petrochemicals, textiles, semiconductors, and automobiles. There have been few such studies on agriculture and even fewer on the service sector. It is quite difficult to identify and collect information on agricultural technology and service technology. However, agro-technology transfer is most important for the economic growth in developing countries and for the rapid growth and internationalization of the service sector, particularly telecommunications and finance. The transfer of financial institutions and financial instruments from developed countries to developing countries may be an interesting case study of international technology transfer.

International technology transfer includes the international transfer of social technologies (such as the military, postal, police and public education systems). International transfer of social technologies is more complex than international transfer of physical technologies (such as telecommunications systems) because this kind of technologies are less expressible and depend more on social environments and institutions. The study of international transfer of social technologies is conducive to deepening the study of international transfer of physical technologies. As for the international transfer of operational "proprietary technology," Korean Lee Chun-ju made an interesting study on the transfer of soft technology in 1983 based on a case study of ESSO in Singapore. The transfer process is divided into three phases. The first phase is the physical transfer of operational "proprietary technology" from the regional headquarter to the subsidiary in Singapore. The second phase is the localization process of the personnel and the management culture. The last phase is integration, absorption (i.e., being absorbed by and integrated into the society), and diffusion of the proprietary technology to other manufacturers. Technology transfer affects not only the recipient manufacturers but also the recipient economies. Some people have realized that international competitiveness is determined not only by technological progress but also by organizational innovation characterized by brand-new intra-firm and inter-firm organization and production management methods (Hoffman, 1986, 1990). Organizational innovation emphasizes flexibility, quality, and collaboration. Since the 1970s, microelectronics technology has developed rapidly, especially the scale of its production technology. Computer aided design (CAD) and computer aided manufacturing (CAM) have fostered new automation technologies and new flexible manufacturing system (FMS). This kind of systems features flexible production, "just-in-time systems," "make-to-order systems," "minimum idle time," "perfect quality and total quality control," "multi-skilled workers," and "cooperative manufacturer-supplier relationships."

The transfer of organizational innovation or software technology from one manufacturer to another or from one country to another is a much more complicated process than the transfer of product technology or process technology. This also reflects the differences in organizational culture. Some researchers have proved that the cost of cross-border transfer of organizational innovation is higher than the cost of technological innovation transfer, and it also takes more time than technological innovation cross-border transfer. The success of organizational innovation transfer in transnational corporations mainly depends on the form of such international transfer, the coordination of interpersonal relations, and the creation of a pleasant working environment (Kogut, 1993). Japan-based multinational corporations were the first to have demonstrated that in the process of improving efficiency and productivity, production management and organizational innovation is as important as or even more important than processing technologies or techniques. The key question is whether the advanced production management and organization systems of Japanese manufacturers are culturally specific. Earlier studies answered in the affirmative (MuraKama, 1983). However, recent experience suggests that Japan's production management and organization can be expressed and transferred (Hoffman, 1990). However, the evidence that leads researchers to this definitive conclusion is insufficient.

It may also be important for management scientists and professional managers to study the structures of real-life technology transfer. Economists who want to study the reasons for the successes or failures of international technology transfer may be interested in the results of such research. In the 1970s, the research of Berman and Warrender on the structure of technology transfer was representative. They examined the process of technology transfer from a multinational corporation to its foreign subsidiaries and put forward a technology transfer matrix (suggestions and plans, product design, factory design and construction, construction, value engineering and control, production development, and external support). The corresponding carriers of international technology transfer are culture, instructions, conferences, visits and exchanges, equipment, and communications.

In general, transnational corporations are the main players in international technology transfer. There are nearly 40,000 multinational corporations in the world, with nearly 300,000 subsidiaries overseas. These giants possess strong financial resources and advanced technology. Transnational corporations are pursuing the strategy of globalized development. In order to maintain the original ownership-specific advantages of ownership (especially the technological advantages), explore regional advantages, and cultivate new technological advantages, they all attach great importance to R&D. The world's 500 largest multinational corporations monopolize and control 90% of international technology trade. With the increase in overseas direct investment by multinational corporations, the internal international technology transfer within the multinational corporations accompanying the overseas direct investment has quickly become the most important form of international technology transfer. According to statistics, 80% of current U.S. technology income comes from technology transfer between U.S. multinational corporations and their overseas subsidiaries. Raymond Vernon's product life cycle theory, John H. Dunning's selection theory of technology transfer, and the internalization theory of international technology transfer proposed by Peter Buckley, Mark Casson, and Alan M. Rugman have discussed from different perspectives and angles the motivations for international technology transfer of multinational corporations.

Section II Analysis on Benefits of FDI Technology Transfer

I. Significance of FDI Technology Transfer to Host Countries

Transnational corporations are the products of modern management technology and organizational innovation. Their emergence and development cater to the development of modern science and technology and facilitate the spread and transfer of science and technology around the world. In order to maintain their ownership-specific advantages (especially the technological advantages), explore regional advantages, and cultivate new technological advantages, most multinational corporations attach great importance to R&D in the process of advancing their strategy of globalized development strategy. According to statistics, the world's 500 largest multinational corporations monopolize and control 90% of international technology trade, and multinational corporations have become important institutions for international technology production and dissemination. With the increase in FDI activities of transnational corporations, technology transfer has become an important part of the economic activities of these transnational giants.

For host countries, accepting the technologies brought by FDI is conducive to the promotion of their own technological progress, enhancing their technological capability, and accelerating their economic development. Especially for those less developed countries, if they rely on their own capabilities to develop and create new technologies, they will face limitations on time, capital, human resources, etc. Introduction of technology through FDI can avoid the greater risks brought by independent R&D, bring down costs, fill the domestic gaps in some technologies, and speed up the technological transformation of enterprises. More importantly, FDI technology transfer can also produce a "demonstration effect" in the host country, i.e., multinational corporations, as technology leaders, have a positive impact on the technological progress and the improvement of management level of host country enterprises in the process of technology transfer. This is external economics or the technology spillover effect. Paul Romer and Robert Lucas, representatives of the new growth theory, believe that the introduction of foreign investment can improve the level of technology and organizational efficiency of a country and generate positive externalities.①② The model established by Uwe Walz shows that through FDI, knowledge can be indirectly transferred across regions and become the key to economic growth in developing countries. According to calculations by American economists, from 1971 to 1990, for every $100 increase in the U.S. domestic R&D capital reserve, the GDP of 77 developing countries will increase by $22. If the economically developed countries are taken as a whole, the developed countries' R&D spillovers increased the GDP

---

① Uwe Walz, Innovation, Foreign Direct Investment and Growth, *Economics*, 1997(1): 24-25.
② Paul M. Romer, Increasing Returns and Long-Run Growth, *Journal of Political Economy*, 1986(5): 30-33.

of developing countries by $21 billion in 1990.

The technology spillover effects of FDI can be summarized into four situations: the various pressures brought about by the emergence of foreign-funded enterprises urge host country enterprises to give full play to the efficiency of existing technologies and improve the quality of product production; foreign-funded enterprises bring the pressure of competition and force their competitors in the host country to seek to improve their level of technology, carry out technological innovation, and carry out imitations; foreign-funded enterprises provide relevant technologies to upstream or downstream business clients; technology spillovers are realized through the flow of personnel with workers and managers trained by foreign-funded enterprises entering domestic-funded enterprises or self-establishing enterprises in the host country and becoming the driving force in promoting local technological innovation and disseminating management knowledge. As international technology transfer by transnational corporations becomes increasingly faster and also larger in scale, developing countries are likely to gain more spillover benefits from such technology transfer, which is conducive to the economic development of these countries.

II. Principles for Host Countries to Accept Technology Transfer

Technology transfer by multinational corporations through FDI is of great significance to the development of host countries, but this does not mean that technology transfer by multinational corporations is always beneficial to the host country. In the process of technology transfer, a host country should take the following aspects into consideration.

1. Technical applicability

The issue of factor proportions is very important to developing countries, so when introducing technologies, the developing country should consider the applicability of the technologies and introduce the appropriate technology according to domestic factors. If unskilled labor occupies a high proportion in a country, then the country should focus on introducing such technologies that need unskilled labor. If the projects introduced are capital-intensive, they will limit the degree of absorption of local labor and have a negative impact on local employment. However, developing countries still face considerable difficulties in introducing appropriate technologies because of the following reasons.

(1) The technology level of developed countries differs greatly from that of developing countries. Therefore, those technologies required by developing countries may have long been obsolete and eliminated in developed countries.

(2) In developing countries, for the purpose of expanding investment and strengthening social security, the government will, on the one hand, stimulate investment by lowering interest rates and, on the other hand, raise labor costs through policies to protect the interests of workers. These two measures objectively urge enterprises to introduce capital-intensive technologies that save labor.

(3) Compared with labor-intensive technologies, capital-intensive technologies can produce greater monopoly advantages and a higher benefit rates, thus leading multinational corporations to seek the development of new capital-intensive technologies and thus also inhibiting the introduction of technologies appropriate for developing countries.

(4) The production of labor-intensive products requires skilled labor and managers with strong self-restraint, which is relatively difficult for developing countries with abundant unskilled labor resources. This urges multinational corporations to choose capital-intensive technologies to the greatest extent for FDI projects and reduce the demand for skilled labor.

(5) As intransparency of information has led to the inefficacy and incompleteness of the technology market, the buyer (host country) of a technology cannot fully understand the technology to be purchased, and thus, multinational corporations have transferred many inapplicable technologies to developing countries.[1]

Despite the above difficulties, it is not unrealistic for host countries to seek the introduction of appropriate technologies. Empirical materials suggest that

---

[1] Wu Bin, *Economic Analysis of Transnational Corporations*, Hong Kong: Hong Kong Tianma Book Co., Ltd., 2002.

about half of the multinational corporations have improved their technologies when entering developing countries in order to adapt to the situations of the developing countries. Moreover, due to increased competitive pressure, more and more multinational corporations are consciously transferring more applicable technologies to developing countries.

2. Prices and conditions of technology transfer

Host countries often cannot get the ideal price and conditions when introducing the technologies of multinational companies. The reasons include two aspects. First, due to the incompleteness of the technology market, host countries lack some necessary information, such as the technology being supplied, the production and transaction costs faced by the suppliers, their opportunities to sell the technology or technical strength in other countries, and the conditions put forward by other countries for the same technology. Second, there is a great disparity in negotiation power between the buyer and the seller. The host country does not have enough information about the technology to be purchased, and undoubtedly, the multinational corporation as the seller will not provide sufficient information about the technology either before the technology transaction contract is signed. Incomplete market and asymmetric information put the host country in a disadvantageous position when negotiating the price of the transferred technology. In this regard, the host country should take active measures to get rid of this unfavorable position. Such policies to attract foreign technologies include providing high-quality professionals and well-motivated skilled labor, developing sufficient capacity of local suppliers, and paying attention to and satisfying the needs of multinational corporations to implement organizational methods that may not conform to the host country's resource allocation. At the same time, the ability of a country to purchase similar technologies or to purchase or create similar technologies through other channels will affect its negotiation ability and status.

In technology transfer agreements, multinationals may also impose restrictive conditions on host countries, such as restricting the receiving party from freely purchasing, selling, and using products of the technology. Host countries should clarify their rights and obligations when accepting technologies and implement unbinding or unbundling technology strategies accordingly. Therefore, host countries should, as far as possible, distinguish the technology factors (technical know-how and capital goods) from ownership and management and at the same time divide the technology factors into several parts. For example, we can divide the technology factors into core technologies and peripheral technologies, and the buyer can thus make better use of the comparative competitiveness of the peripheral or marginal technology market. Another unbundling strategy is to separate the pre-investment, investment, and operation of a project from each other and divide them into several phases with unique characteristics.① In order to minimize the probability of occurrence of restrictive business practices, host countries should mainly pay attention to export restrictions, bundled input clauses, output restrictions, and property rights after the expiration of licensed marks. Many host countries have developed policies to ensure the introduction of applicable technologies and have established specialized agencies to investigate and verify the technologies to be transferred or introduced. For example, one possible policy is to only allow introductions of technologies that are not available from local sources or supply sources; another is to stipulate that subsidiaries of foreign multinational corporations importing technologies must provide training services for local employees to ensure the transfer and adoption of the introduced technologies.②

3. The strategy of technology introduction

The industries that multinationals focus on in their investment are often inconsistent with the host countries' objectives in the adjustment and

---

① UNCNC, *Transnational Corporation & Technology Transfer Effects and Policy Issues*, New York: United Nation, 1987.
② Wang Xuehong, "Policy Choice and Effect Analysis of Host Countries on International Technology Transfer of Transnational Corporations," *Journal of Yunnan Institute of Finance and Trade*, 2001 (1): 20-23.

optimization of their economic structures. FDI tends to favor those industries with rich profits and quick returns rather than those industries and departments that have long cycles and high risks but are necessary for the development of national economy, further aggravating the imbalance and irrationality of host countries' industrial structures. Therefore, when a host country introduces technology, it should rationally allocate resources, avoid repeated introduction and construction, and actively transform traditional industries on the one hand and consider the needs of its domestic industrial structure adjustment from a long-term perspective on the other hand, choose FDI projects that are conducive to optimizing the industrial structure, promote the development of emerging industries, and further drive the upgrading of the industrial structure. The direct investment and technology transfer from transnational corporations in developed countries to the Four Asian Tigers were in line with the high-tech strategies pursued by these countries and regions and have pushed the transformation of their industrial structures from labor-intensive to capital-intensive and to technology-intensive, thus further promoting the upgrading of their industrial structures. Moreover, overseas direct investment has greatly pushed the technological transformation of the host countries' traditional industries, thus contributing to the adjustment of the host countries' industrial structures. In the 1990s, the revival of Britain's automobile industry was mainly dependent on the large-scale capital injection and technological transformation brought by U.S. and Japanese multinational corporations (such as GM, Honda, etc.).

FDI plays a dynamic and cumulative rather than static and individual role in the cultivation of host countries' technological upgrading, management skills, and entrepreneurship. As a result, this kind of technology transfer presents a potential risk: the incompleteness of technology transfer leads to a strong dependence of local enterprises on foreign technologies and makes it difficult for the enterprises to develop independent technology products with their own characteristics. In this regard, the host country should consider the following issues.

(1) Technology introduction should take the path of introduction,

improvement, absorption, and innovation and adopts the strategy of absorptive technological innovation. The experience of postwar technology introduction in Japan is as follows. It focused on production technology and practical technology in technology introduction and combined the new uncoordinated technologies with different conditions from different countries; it laid emphasis on soft technologies rather than hard technologies, thus introducing patent rights, design drawing methods, and related technical know-how; it paid attention to the industrialization and private application of technological research results and preemptively occupied the market of new products through research reform and innovations.

(2) One way to encourage indigenous development of technologies to take the place of the importation of technologies is that the importing country produces the technologies itself. Such practices may be costly, at least in the short term, but the policy is realistic if the home-developed technologies can ultimately improve the efficiency of resource allocation.

III. Factors Affecting Technology Transfer

The effects of the technology transfer of multinational corporations are subject to the limitations of the host country's human resources, policies and regulations, management level, etc. Some studies suggest that the catalytic effect of FDI to the growth of domestic technology and production is conditional. The model established by Rodriguez Clare shows that when the connections between multinational corporations and local enterprises are relatively weak, FDI is negatively correlated with domestic growth. One of the disadvantages of FDI technology transfer is that the technologies of multinational corporations are black boxes for local employees. Although the workers can pick up some production skills, they cannot obtain the corresponding technology because they are not involved in the entire process of production and design as well as the construction of hardware and software facilities. These studies prove that the effects of technology transfer tend to be affected by certain factors in the host country.

(1) The government clearly has a multifaceted role to play in influencing the transfer of technology from transnational corporations to host countries. To realize successful technology introduction, it is of vital importance for the host country to develop correct, scientific, and practical technology introduction policies. In addition, it is also very important to consider the actual enforcement measures and the performance of these policies and to make these policies and measures compatible with each other. Specifically, macroeconomic policies must be coordinated with specific management policies. Dunning, a world-renowned international economist and an expert on international investment and transnational corporations, listed 20 possible policy options for the host country to maximize the benefits of the introduced technologies.

(2) State-owned enterprises play an important role in the technology transfer and diffusion in the host country. When introducing a new technology, state-owned enterprises can establish joint ventures with foreign enterprises or multinational corporations or directly form strategic alliances with foreign enterprises to develop new technologies. Besides, in the process of purchasing large capital goods or introducing new technologies through license trade, state-owned enterprises have relatively strong negotiation abilities.

(3) The proportion and distribution of skilled labor, professional talents, and professional managers in human resources restrict the operational efficiency and the technology spillover effects after technology introduction. There are three ways for FDI to generate technology spillover effects: first, external pressure; second, technology transfer; third, the flow of personnel. Both the improvement in technology level and the enhancement of competitiveness are directly related to the quality of personnel. In a sense, the personnel factor is the most important factor affecting the technology spillover effects of FDI enterprises. It not only directly affects the technology spillover effects but can also influence the other two ways of technology spillover effect generation. Moreover, the differential pattern of domestic personnel flow and the unidirectionality of such flow in the host country will hinder the effective

diffusion of technology to some extent and weaken its spillover effects. If locals can only work for foreign capitalists as cheap labor, the benefits that foreign companies might bring to the country will be wasted.①

Transnational corporations, as technology exporters, can obtain high profits through technology transfer. In the meantime, they can expand the scope of application of the technologies and further develop new technologies with the ultimate goal of maximizing benefits. For the host country, however, the purpose of technology introduction is to realize its own economic and social development strategy, enhance its level of technology, and promote its technological progress. The principle is to obtain the greatest possible benefits with the lowest possible costs. In the process of technology transfer, the two sides carry out negotiations repeatedly until finally reaching a mutually recognized binding agreement to share the benefits of cooperation. In this process, the host country should keep a clear mind and a clear perspective of development, adopt a comprehensive approach to secure a relatively favorable position, reasonably and effectively utilize the technology introduced, and give full play to the external economics brought about by the technology spillover effects, with the purpose of maximizing the benefits of the introduced technology.

Section III Analysis of the Interests of Developing Countries in Participating in International Technology Transfer

I. Development Trend of International Technology Transfer under Open Economy

1. Systematization and networking of international technology transfer

According to the research of the Organization for Economic Cooperation

---

① Robert E. Lucas, On the mechanic of economic development. *Journal of Monetary Economics*, 1988 (10): 17-20.

and Development (OECD, 1993), under an open economy, important technological transformations mainly occur in the following aspects: the increase in product complexity, the diffusion of automation, the preference for standardized technology, the avoidance of congestion, the control of chemical compositions, and the diffusion and amplification of information. One result of this trend is the breakdown of complex processes, such as the separation of assembly and component production in the computer and automotive industries. As products become more complicated, manufacturers can only specialize in one area of production, such as component production or assembly. With this increasing degree of division of labor, it is difficult for a single manufacturer to master both core and non-core technologies. Because production can be broken down, manufacturers can import only certain parts for production, but the price is highly dependent on the designers and producers of core technologies. As the number of technologies an enterprise must master increases, enterprises have to move towards technological diversity. As it becomes more and more difficult for enterprises to master all the core and non-core technologies, enterprises must join an alliance in order to get access to the technologies and knowledge needed for development.

All these technological transformations have made technology transfer a more complex process. Because one-time technology introduction is very difficult to provide systematic benefits, enterprises need to keep in long-term contact with suppliers of core technologies, and it is especially important to continuously provide input and get feedback. The organizational foundation of this process is the innovation network (a form of organization between the market and the hierarchy). Although enterprises in the innovation network are independent in form, they are closely related. They exchange knowledge about design and process improvement, and such exchanges are not exchanges of technical information between buyers and sellers. With the operation mechanism of the innovation network functioning, the features of systematization and networking of international technology transfer are becoming increasingly evident.

2. Internalization of international technology trade and globalization of production networks

In the past 100 years, world trade has been growing at a faster rate than GDP. After entering the 21st century, driven by the global multilateral trade system, trade openness has increased at a faster rate and involved more and more developing countries. With the global economic integration, regional economic cooperation and the rapid development of information technology have also facilitated the processes of global trade in goods, international direct investment, and service liberalization. However, current trade liberalization mainly belongs to priority free trade zones, i.e., members within regional blocs enjoy a higher degree of freedom of trade, while countries outside the trade zones are subject to differentiated treatment under barriers. However, whether in the World Trade Organization or in regional blocs, trade liberalization has made it easier for technologies to flow within companies or industries. Therefore, it has also strengthened the business of multinational corporations. Due to the market power of multinational corporations and in order to maintain their monopolistic advantages, most international technology trade is controlled by multinational giants. According to the research report released by the United Nations Conference on Trade and Development (UNCTAD), about a third of international trade takes place within multinational corporations, and about two-thirds of international trade is related to the international production network of multinational corporations. On top of that, the ratio of transactions within an insecure distance to transactions within a secure distance rose from 1.6 in 1982 to 1.9 in 2002. As a result, this tendency has led to the emergence of transnational production networks. These transnational production networks have created forms of trade that can only be understood when the strategies of transnational corporations are taken into account. The shallow integration in economic globalization has been around in history, but as a process of deep integration, new types of procurement and trade have been created, which are entirely new contents.

The internalization of international technology trade by multinational corporations and the globalization of production networks play a very important role in the development of trade in host countries. Transnational corporations have made the connection between international direct investment and international technology trade become closer. This close connection has created a new situation of entering foreign markets via international direct investment rather than trade. Many cases show that types of trade and types of international direct investment are becoming increasingly closely related, and most international direct investment is located in the markets of technology exporting countries, which shows that international direct investment is also driven by international technology trade. Not considering the causal mechanism, the relationship between international direct investment and international technology trade seems to be becoming increasingly close. The increased importance of multinational corporations' strategies in determining the types of trade will affect a country's production types and export compositions, separating the two. The intensified interaction between international direct investment and international technology trade does not mean that there is harmony between the two.

3. Better protection of intellectual property rights for international technology transfer

The non-competitiveness during the process of technology use makes new technologies vulnerable to misappropriation. As it is easy to imitate technologies, it is required to strengthen the protection of technologies in the process of transfer. The technological and engineering characteristics of a new product determine the path that it will be imitated. Besides the technological characteristics, there are two other factors that affect the possibility of misappropriation and the transferability of the new technology, namely, the confidentiality of intellectual property rights and the structural characteristics of the national innovation system. These three aspects together seriously affect the technology transfer policies and determine the way developing countries use new technologies. The fact that new technologies rely more on tacit knowledge and/or standardized knowledge has an important impact on technology transfer. The knowledge base of new technologies can be categorized into two types: tacit and standardized. If the knowledge base is tacit, then the main way of learning the technology is learning while doing. If the knowledge base is standardized, the technology can only be mastered through a formal learning process. Some scholars believe that this dichotomy of the knowledge base of new technologies is wrong because tacit knowledge and standardized knowledge are not independent of each other but complementary to each other as a whole and new technologies also reflect this complementarity between the two. This complementarity is not static but dynamic. The relationship between them is always being reconstructed, and the complementary form of these two kinds of knowledge is always in a state of transformation. Others have proposed a third hypothesis that new technologies increasingly rely on standardized knowledge while new tacit knowledge is also needed for people to master the standardized knowledge. Tacit knowledge has not disappeared but is being repositioned.

In the past, developing countries generally focused on protecting the property rights of enterprises but overlooked the protection of the system of intellectual property rights. The protection of the property rights of enterprises is conducive to the process of industrialization, while the protection of intellectual property rights has not stimulated inventions or technology transfer. However, in the recent 10~15 years, an opposite trend has emerged—that is, emphasis on intellectual property rights between trading countries. Therefore, according to the WTO agreements on trade-related intellectual property rights, many developing countries have amended their laws on intellectual property rights, broadening the scope and duration of their protection of technologies. One view holds that emphasizing intellectual property rights will promote international direct investment and technology flow. For instance, patents are considered as an important incentive for inventors to engage in inventions and their commercialization. The opposite view holds that intellectual property should be in a loose state, based on the assumption that it is impossible for technological efforts to be completely misappropriated, spilt, or leaked out of control. Many economists are studying both views and have not reached a final conclusion yet. However, it is generally agreed that our understanding of the relationship between intellectual property rights and technological capabilities as well as technology transfer is still relatively fuzzy.

II. Impact of International Technology Transfer on Interests of Developing Countries

1. International technology transfer has spillover effects on developing countries

The impact of international technology transfer on host developing countries can be divided into two types, namely, the direct impact through the improvement of capabilities and productivity and the indirect impact generated by training domestic suppliers or by increasing competitive pressure or locally diffusing knowledge and technology to transmit the impact to other enterprises. The direct impact is usually a one-time change, not the most important. What is more important is its dynamic effect, which stimulates the restructuring of industries through the local diffusion of knowledge and technology. This means that studies of this issue should go beyond the general static cost-benefit framework and study the spillover effect.

The spillover effect is a kind of benefit loss for technological innovators that cannot be directly compensated for and can also be regarded as an involuntary technological diffusion. By definition, it creates a dichotomy between private returns and social returns. Social returns can be defined as private returns plus the reduction in marginal costs between firms due to spillover effects. Spillover effects occur when market prices cannot fully reflect the benefits of innovation investment or when one enterprise's idea is freely obtained by another. The spillover effect reflects to some degree the extent to which host country enterprises hitchhike and use the R&D technology and actual production knowledge of multinational corporations.

Based on the expectation that spillover effects can bring benefits to the local economy, many countries have facilitated foreign investors in many aspects, such as setting tax exemption periods, offering free import, providing infrastructure, etc., hoping to improve the economic efficiency of the host countries through the dynamic externality of technology transfer. There are few empirical estimates of the impact of spillovers on technology efforts, and most work has focused on the impact of spillovers on productivity. In all the cases in the literature survey, the social rate of return of R&D is higher than its private rate of return, which shows the extent of R&D spillover effects. Griliches concluded that the major problems in the field of spillovers still mainly existed in measurement. Most of the studies on spillover effects involve developed countries, and these studies have reached contradictory conclusions. Some studies have concluded that spillover effects have complementary effects on R&D of enterprises, while others have concluded that spillover effects have substitution effects. These studies have failed to reveal the nature of spillover effects in a profound way, but there is still plenty of evidence supporting the hypothesis of spillover benefits. Based on a comprehensive understanding of the spillover effect of R&D, Mohnen reached the conclusion that the spillover effect of international R&D can be transmitted between countries and that such transmission between the two countries is often unidirectional. Spillover effects within an industry are mainly realized through the influence of foreign investment on local consumers and suppliers. These spillovers happen because the competition brought by multinationals spur local firms to increase their competitiveness, and the trainings carried out by multinationals spill into local economies. This demonstration effect under local environmental conditions is crucial for local enterprises to imitate foreign investors.

2. Higher investment expenditures for developing host countries participating in international technology transfer

Because technologies involve a lot of tacit knowledge and because technological transformations have the feature of localization, technology transfer becomes more complicated. As Grant and Gregory pointed out, as technology matures, the manufacturing process becomes increasingly difficult to transfer. This is mainly because tacit knowledge exits in operation, error finding, process control, machine installation, problem solving, equipment design, equipment testing, etc. Success in technology transfer requires investment in learning to acquire tacit knowledge. Due to the localization of technologies, a new application of a technology is a kind of new investment, regardless of whether the technology is novel or not.

Technology transfer is not about moving hardware from one location to another, nor is it just about transferring information and rights to other vendors. The transferor must provide services relevant to the transferred technology to make the transfer more convenient and effective. As Ctractor pointed out, service rent enabling technology transfer, such as expenditures on technology, management, market, and R&D assistance, is an important component of technology transfer costs. Mansfield and Teece defined the costs of transmitting and absorbing all the relevant intangible knowledge as transfer costs, which are different from technical costs.

There are usually four types of costs: pre-project technology exchange costs; costs related to product design, techniques, and transfer engineering; R&D personnel costs during the process of transfer; costs of pre-start training, learning, and setting up. There has been little empirical research on the cost measurement of technology transfer. Therefore, when developing countries participate in international technology transfer, the transfer costs of patents and proprietary technologies will inevitably lead to an increase in the total project cost.

3. Promotion of accumulation of elements of human capital in developing countries by international technology transfer

Human capital is the main executor that transform technologies into products, and the accumulation of human capital's technological capabilities is the central issue in the process of catching up. It is evident, however, that developing countries have not taken this factor into consideration when conducting technology transfer analyses over the past many years. This particular nature of technology was overlooked mainly because, according to the view at that time, technologies are treated as commodities. The focuses of technology analysis are technology selection and R&D. The reason that R&D is important is that the view at that time believed innovation to be the linear result of R&D. Based on these views, the technology transfer policies at that time mainly focused on the transfer of R&D components and the control over technology transfer that comply with policy standards. Taking technologies only as commodities makes the policies underestimate the complexity of technologies. Technologies are embodied in the structure of human capital, and human capital is the main executor of innovative behaviors. With the emergence of research on technological capability, systematic research on technological accumulation at the level of human capital has also embarked on.

Many studies have shown that the main mode of human capital learning is adaptive learning. There are many different abilities and learning trajectories related to learning. The concept of technological capability is the sum of the large amount of knowledge and skills needed to acquire, use, adapt, change, and create technologies. Westphal and Kim defined technological capability as the ability to effectively use technological knowledge. One of the important concepts in technological capability is learning. Bell believes that through learning, human capital can acquire technological knowledge, as well as techniques and skills.

The technological capability approach, while valuable, has its limitations, focusing more on what technological capabilities are than on how the technological capabilities of human capital are acquired. The technological capabilities (management, market, organization, and finance) of human capital elements are an important part of enterprise capability. Enterprises need complementary capabilities and assets, such as organizational flexibility, finance, human resources, quality, service support, information management, and coordination capabilities, to create and improve their technological capabilities. With the development of international technology transfer, developing countries have paid more and more attention to the importance of human capital in absorbing foreign advanced technology and have stepped up efforts to strengthen human capital elements.

Section Ⅳ Realization of Common Interests in Technology Transfer between China and Developed Countries

Xi Jinping stressed, "Key and core technologies are crucial to a country and bear major significance for promoting China's high-quality economic development and maintaining national security. China must improve innovation capabilities for key and core technologies and keep a firm hold on the initiative in the development of science and technology to offer a strong technological guarantee for China's development.① The technology transfer system is the bridge and link connecting the knowledge innovation system and the technology innovation system, and it is also an important part of the national innovation system. The degree of perfection of the technology transfer system and the strength of its functions have become important constraining factors for the construction of China's national innovation system.

Ⅰ. Current Situation of Technology Transfer in China

In general, after more than 20 years of development, China has established primarily a relatively complete technology transfer system. In particular, since

---

① "Xi Stresses Improving Innovation Capabilities for Key, Core Technologies," Xinhua Agency, July 14, 2018.

the Ministry of Science and Technology, the Ministry of Education, and the Chinese Academy of Sciences jointly initiated the National Technology Transfer Promotion Action in 2007, the implementation of a series of policies and measures has effectively promoted the development of China's technology transfer. The legal framework for technology transfer has gradually taken shape. Promoting the transformation of scientific and technological achievements and technology transfer is a major issue in China's scientific and technological, economic, and social development and is also one of the important contents of the reform of the science and technology system reform. The Decision of the Central Committee of the Communist Party of China on the Reform of Science and Technology System, released in March 1985, clearly proposed to expand the technology market and promote the commercialization of technological achievements, which played a key foundational role in establishing the basic system and framework for China's technology transfer. Since then, laws such as the Law of the People's Republic of China on Progress of Science and Technology, the Law of the People's Republic of China on Promoting the Transformation of Scientific and Technological Achievements, the Contract Law of the People's Republic of China, the Patent Law of the People's Republic of China, etc., as well as regulations made by relevant departments and the regulations on the technology market developed by local governments, have continuously enriched the legal system and framework of China's technology transfer. Since the launch of the National Technology Transfer Promotion Action, development of the legal system for technology transfer has been obviously accelerated, and the legal framework for technology transfer has gradually taken shape. First, in order to strengthen the construction of technology transfer institutions, the Ministry of Science and Technology has formulated the Administrative Measures for National Technology Transfer Demonstration Institutions, which clearly stipulates the functions and the business scope of technology transfer institutions, as well as the evaluation, management, support, and promotion of these institutions. At the same time, to guide national technology transfer demonstration institutions towards the direction of specialized and large-scale development, the Torch High Technology Industry Development Center of the Ministry of Science and Technology has formulated the Evaluation Index System for National Technology Transfer Demonstration Institutions to strengthen the evaluation and assessment of the demonstration institutions. Second, tax incentives for technology transfer are strengthened. The Law of the People's Republic of China on Enterprise Income Tax, which came into effect on January 1, 2008, stipulates that for income from qualified technology transfer, the enterprise income tax may be exempted or reduced. For the income obtained by a resident enterprise from the transfer of technology in a tax year, the portion that does not exceed 5 million yuan shall be exempted from enterprise income tax; and the portion that exceed 5 million yuan shall be allowed a half reduction of enterprise income tax. Previously, the standard for enterprises to enjoy preferential tax treatment for technology transfer income was 300,000 yuan.

As a result, the scale and quality of technology transactions have improved significantly. According to statistics, the contract turnover in China's technology market registered only 700 million yuan when the market first opened, but the turnover reached 222.651 billion yuan in 2007. It took 17 years for China's technology contract turnover to exceed 100 billion yuan, but it only took 4 years for the turnover to increase from 100 billion yuan to 200 billion yuan. According to the National Technology Market Statistics Bulletin, 220,868 technology contracts were registered nationwide in 2007, up by 7.00% year on year. The transaction amount totaled 222.651 billion yuan, up by 22.00% year on year. The average transaction amount of each technology contract exceeded 1 million yuan, reaching 1.01 million yuan, up by 15.00% year on year. In 2008, the national technology market recognized 226,343 registered technology contracts with a turnover of 266.5 billion yuan, with a year-on-year increase of 2.50% and 19.70% respectively. The average transaction amount per technology contract rose to 1.18 million yuan from 1.01 million yuan in 2007. In 2008, the

Beijing technology market saw 52,742 technologies transferred, accounting for 24.41% of the total number within the country, and a turnover of 102.722 billion yuan, accounting for 38.47% of the national total. In 2009, hit by the financial crisis, 31,605 technology contracts were concluded in Beijing from January to September, with a year-on-year decrease of 3.61%. Turnover reached RMB 89.814 billion, up 15.00% year on year, of which 67.660 billion was turn over from technology transactions, up by 19.60% year on year, accounting for 75.33% of technology contract turnover. In Shanghai, from January to July 2009, 14,690 technical contracts were registered, up by 9.00% year on year; the turnover was 27.298 billion yuan, up by 19.50% year on year; the average turnover of individual technology contracts was 1,858,300 yuan, up 9.80% compared with the average turnover of all technology contracts in 2008. In 2017, according to the overall plan of implementing the innovation-driven development strategy, the liquidity of China's technology market increased and the scale and quality of technology transactions continued to improve steadily. That year, China saw a steady growth of turnover in the technology market. 368,000 technology contracts were signed with a turnover of 134,242 billion yuan, with an increase of 14.7% and 17.7% respectively. The proportion of contract turnover in the national GDP continued to increase, reaching 1.62%. The average transaction amount of each technology contract was 3.652 million yuan, up by 2.6% year on year. It can be seen that both nationally and locally, the scale and quality of China's technology transactions have improved significantly (as shown in Figure 6-1).

In 2017, the turnover of technology development and technology service contracts displayed a growth trend, while the turnover of technology transfer and consulting contracts decreased when compared with the previous year. Among the four types of contracts, the turnover of technology service and technology development contracts ranked first and second respectively, becoming the main types of technology transactions. Especially, the turnover of technology service contracts topped for five consecutive years, reaching 682.62

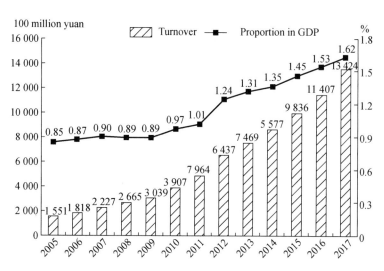

Figure 6-1　Turnover of National Technology Contracts and Its Proportion in GDP (2005 - 2017)

billion yuan, up by 16.7% over the previous year and accounting for 50.8% of the national turnover of technology contracts; the turnover of technology development contracts reached 474.85 billion yuan, up by 36.5% over the previous year, accounting for 35.4% of the national total. The number of technology service and technology development contracts signed and their turnover continued to hold more than 80% of the national total. Among various types of technology service contracts, general technology services dominated, with the turnover reaching 667.43 billion yuan, accounting for 97.8 percent of the total turnover of all technology service contracts, down slightly from the previous year. A total of 26,735 technology consulting contracts were concluded, up by 9.4% year on year, with a turnover of 44.93 billion yuan, down by 4.1% year on year, accounting for 3.3% of the total number of technology contracts concluded in the country.

　　In the meantime, the construction of technology transfer service institutions in China is advancing rapidly. For China, a developing country, international technology transfer is not only the introduction of technologies. It has the deeper connotations of mastering or even innovating technologies through the introduction, digestion, and absorption of advanced technologies and further achieving re-innovation and improvement on this basis. Since the reform and opening up, especially in the mid-1980s, China's economy has developed rapidly, and the international technology transfer in China has also witnessed great development. During that period, the country mainly focused on the introduction of technologies, with almost no technology export. However, since the end of 1990s, China's international technology transfer has really stepped onto the normal track. Not only has technologies been introduced, but technologies have also been exported. In 2006, Academician Li Guojie made the judgment that "technology transfer is the weakest link in China's innovation system."[①] China began to set up its first batch of technology transfer service agencies in the 1980s. After more than 20 years of development, nearly 100 technology markets of different scales have been built, including: China's Zhejiang Online Technology Market, Northern Technology Exchange Market, and other 10 permanent national technology markets; 10 national technology transfer centers relying on key domestic universities and scientific research institutions; 69 national university science parks. There are also 1,532 productivity promotion centers that provide intermediary services for small and medium-sized enterprises and more than 60,000 technology and trade organizations and scientific and technological consulting service companies, involving 1.3 million employees. As yet, domestic technology transfer service organizations have begun to take shape and is still growing. In particular, since the launch of the "National Technology Transfer Promotion Action," the establishment of technology transfer service agencies has developed rapidly. First, a number of demonstration institutions for technology transfer have been established. On August 7, 2008, the Ministry of Science and Technology identified 76 institutions, including Tsinghua University National Technology

---

① Li Guojie, "Technology Transfer Is the Weak Link in National Innovation System," *Bulletin of Chinese Academy of Sciences*, 2006 (5): 369-370.

Transfer Center, as the first batch of national technology transfer demonstration institutions. On September 24, 2009, another 58 institutions, including Taiyuan Technology Transfer Promotion Center and Wuhan University Technology Transfer Center, were listed as the second batch of national technology transfer demonstration institutions. So far, 134 institutions have been accredited as a national technology transfer demonstration agency. In 2016, the number of national technology transfer demonstration institutions increased to 453.[①] Second, regional technology transfer service alliances have witnessed rapid development. On the basis of the existing technology transfer alliances in the Yangtze River Delta, Northeast China, the Bohai Rim, and Beijing, new alliances in the Ji'nan Metropolitan Area, Shanghai, Guangxi Zhuang Autonomous Region, and the Pearl River Delta have emerged. Since the 12th Five-Year Plan, under the guidance of the Torch High Technology Industry Development Center of the Ministry of Science and Technology, China has formed primarily a "2 + n" overall pattern of 11 national technology transfer regional centers, including the national technology transfer agglomeration area, the national technology transfer centers in the south, in the east, in the central region, in the southwest, in the northwest, and in the northeast, the national technology transfer strait center, the national technology transfer southern Jiangsu center, the national technology transfer Zhengzhou center, and the national marine technology transfer center, which has played a huge role in exploring the technology transfer service model and realizing the transformation of regional scientific and technological achievements. Third, the construction of innovation relay centers has started. The Innovation Relay Center Network is a plan supported by the European Union for transnational technology transfer, international industry-university-research cooperation, and assistance to small and medium-sized enterprises in technological innovation. So far, 71 innovation

---

① Guo Man, Zhu Changhai, Shao Xiang and Shi Ningning, "Research on Development Strategies of China's Technology Transfer Institutions-Based on the Perspective of Capacity Upgrading," *Forum on Science and Technology in China*, 2018 (1): 16-23.

relay centers in 33 countries have been incorporated into the network. It has become one of the largest and best technology transfer networks in the world. In May 2007, the first innovation relay center in China, the Qingdao innovation relay center, was inaugurated at Qingdao Technology Property Rights Exchange, followed by the innovation relay centers in Qingpu District of Shanghai and Deqing County of Zhejiang Province. In 2017, colleges and scientific research institutions signed 104,836 technology contracts through technology transfer, technology shares, and industry-university-research cooperation, with a turnover of 122.26 billion yuan, increasing by 14.8%. Among them, universities, as sellers, saw a year-on-year decrease of 1.2% in the turnover of technology contracts, while scientific research institutions saw a year-on-year increase of 22.9%.

Ⅱ. China-U.S. Technology Trade

For reasons known to all, for a long time after the founding of the People's Republic of China, there was no economic and trade exchange between China and the U.S. It was not until the 1970s when President Nixon of the U.S. visited China that China-U.S. economic and trade exchange gradually resumed and expanded. However, for a long period of time, China-U.S. trade and exchange remained sluggish. It was not until 1979 when Chinese leader Deng Xiaoping visited the U.S. that the two countries established ambassadorial-level diplomatic relations. Moreover, China began to implement the policy of reform and opening up and actively introduced advanced foreign technologies and equipment. As a Chinese poem says, "It was as if a spring breeze had blown overnight." China-U.S. technology trade began to go on track. Judging from the China-U.S. technology and equipment import and export contracts and their amounts, an important statistical index of the level of technology trade between the two sides, the bilateral technology trade has maintained a trend of expansion over the past 30 years, while also having experienced many ups and downs. In terms of the U.S. technology exports to China, the number of contract transactions increased from 5 in 1979 to 1,804 in 1999, multiplying by more than 360 times. The total contract amount also increased from $18.3 million in 1979 to $3.3415 billion in 1999, increasing by more than 180 times. According to the contract amount, the U.S. ranks first among the major countries exporting technologies to China, up from the initial fifth place. Specifically, in 1979, the U.S. exports of technology and equipment to China accounted for 0.7% of China's total technology imports that year, ranking behind Japan, Germany, France, and Sweden; in 1985, the amount reached $710.8 million, accounting for 22.2% of China's total technology imports, ranking second only to Germany; in 1987, the amount decreased slightly to $673.5 million, accounting for 27.18% of China's total technology imports that year, ranking only behind Japan's $706.1 million; in 1990, the number and amount of U.S. technology export contracts to China saw a sudden drop, with the total amount decreasing to $322.7 million, less than half the amount of 1987, and accounting for 25.3% of China's total technology imports that year. As other countries experienced a greater decline, the U.S. technology exports to China ranked first for the first time; from 1991 to 1995, the growth of U.S. exports of technology and equipment to China was relatively stagnant, with 5-year exports to China amounting to $4,932.2 million, accounting for 14.8% of China's total technology imports during the same period, ranking second only to Japan. In 1996, the U.S. technology exports to China increased slightly to $2.13 billion. However, due to Germany's significant growth in technology exports to China, registering a record $4.907 billion, the U.S. ranking further dropped to the third place. In 1997, Canada's technology exports to China surged to $2,804.7 million, while the U.S. technology exports to China fell to $1,816.3 million, decreasing by about 15% compared with the previous year. However, as Germany's exports to China dropped by about three-quarters compared with the previous year, the U.S. retained its third position. In 1998, the U.S. technology exports to China increased by a large margin, reaching about $3 billion, accounting for 18.3% of China's total technology imports that year, ranking first again; in 1999, the U.S. exports of technology and equipment to China saw a year-on-year increase of about 11% and accounted for 19.5% of China's total technology imports that year, maintaining the top position. From 2001 to 2011, the total import and export trade of high-tech products between China and the U.S. increased from $17.11 billion to $134.86 billion, with an average annual growth rate of 22.9%. Specifically, China's exports of high-tech products to the U.S. increased from $7.79 billion to $105.88 billion, with an average annual growth rate of 29.8%; China's imports of high-tech products from the U.S. increased from $9.32 billion to $28.98 billion, with an average annual growth rate of 12.0%. Although the growth rate of China-U.S. trade in high-tech products is relatively high, it is lower than the overall growth rate of China's trade in high-tech products. From 2001 to 2011, the growth rate of China's exports and imports of high-tech products to the U.S. was lower than that of China's total exports and imports of high-tech products by 1.4 and 11.5 percentage points respectively.① Judging from China's position in U.S. trade in high-tech products, China has become the third largest market for U.S. high-tech products and the largest source of imports. In 2011, exports to China accounted for 6.1% of U.S. high-tech exports, with the ranking rose by 7 places, from 10th place in 2001 to 3rd place in 2011. China's share in U.S. high-tech exports also rose from 3.3% to 6.1%, up by 2.8 percentage points. In 2017, U.S. exports of technology to China exceeded $127 billion, the highest ever in the U.S. history. In the years from 2007 to 2017, the growth rate of U.S. exports to China reached 86%, while the growth rate of its exports to other parts of the world was only 21%. In 2016, U.S. exports of technology services to China exceeded $50 billion for the first time, with a total trade volume of more than $52 billion, only slightly lower than its exports of technology services to Canada that year. In the ten years from 2007 to 2016, the

---

① Gu Xueming and Cui Weijie, "Current Situation, Problems and Suggestions of China-U.S. Trade in High-tech Products," *International Trade*, 2012 (9): 23-30.

growth rate of U.S. exports of technology services to China exceeded 300%, while that to the rest of the world was about 50%. In 2016, the trade volume of U.S. technology services exported to China increased by 12%, while the trade volume of its technology services exported to other parts of the world decreased by 0.6 percentage point. According to Chinese statistics, the U.S. is China's largest source of copyright imports. From 2012 to 2016, China imported nearly 28,000 copyrights from the U.S. China's intellectual property royalties to the U.S. doubled over the six years, rising from $3.46 billion in 2011 to $7.2 billion in 2017. In 2017, China's payment to the U.S. accounted for one-quarter of China's total foreign payments of intellectual property royalties.① The U.S. has a huge competitive advantage in the trade of high-tech products. However, based on the Cold War mentality, the U.S. government has implemented strict export control restrictions on China for a long time, thus inhibiting the export potential of its products with comparative advantages to the Chinese market. As a result, the U.S. enterprises have lost a large number of export opportunities to China, widening the trade deficit of goods between the two countries. According to the analysis in the April 2017 report released by the Carnegie Endowment for International Peace, if the U.S. relaxes its export control restrictions on China to the level of those on Brazil, the U.S. trade deficit with China can be reduced by 24%; if it is relaxed to the level of those on France, this deficit can be reduced by 35%.②

In terms of China's technology exports to the U.S., although its overall technology level was relatively low in the beginning, due to China's active introduction and absorption of the advanced science and technologies of foreign countries, as well as its transformation and innovation in combination with its

---

① Data from: State Council Information Office of the People's Republic of China, "Facts and China's Position on China-U.S. Trade Friction" (September 2018), the website of the State Council Information Office, Sep. 24, 2018.

② Carnegie Endowment for International Peace, "Political Barriers to U.S. Exports to China and U.S.-China Trade Deficit," Apr. 10, 2017.

own advantages, China has greatly enhanced its technology level in recent years. China's foreign technology exports have increased rapidly, and the amount of technology exports has also reached a certain level in recent years. In connection with this, China's technology exports to the U.S. have also grown rapidly. The U.S. ranks second and fifth respectively among the major countries and regions importing technologies and equipment from China. However, China's technology exports still have a long way to go to catch up with developed countries and regions, as shown in the following aspects: first, the total scale of China's technology exports is not large; second, the scale of projects are generally small; third, the level of technology is relatively low (but in recent years, the export of high-tech has been growing rapidly). According to data from the U.N. database, the amount of China's high-tech exports to the U.S. was only $ 16.165 billion in 2002, while it climbed to $ 125.941 billion in 2015. In 2017, China's import and export trade of high-tech products totaled $ 125.75 billion. The top five trading partners in China's mainland's high-tech exports remained Hong Kong (China), the U.S., RoK, Japan, and the Netherlands, accounting for 23.8%, 19.9%, 5.9%, 5.3%, and 4.8% respectively. The top five high-tech importing partners were Taiwan (China), RoK, Japan, the U.S., and Malaysia, accounting for 19.4%, 17.8%, 9.1%, 8.2%, and 5.4% respectively.[1] In as early as 2003, China has become the largest source of imports of high-tech products for the U.S. and has remained at this position so far. From 2001 to 2011, China's share in the imports of high-tech products in the U.S. has also been on the rise year by year, increasing from 7.0% to 28.9%.

  Judging from the position of the U.S. in China's trade in high-tech products, the U.S. has become the second largest market for China's high-tech products and the largest source of imports. In 2011, the U.S. accounted for 20.0% China's total high-tech exports and 7.2% of China's total high-tech

---

[1] Data from: Ministry of Science and Technology of the People's Republic of China, *Analysis Report on Trade Status of High-tech Products in 2017*.

imports, ranking second and fourth respectively. In the past 10 years, the proportion and ranking of the U.S. market in China's exports of high-tech products have shown the characteristics of "rising before declining." The U.S. accounted for 20.9% of China's high-tech exports in 2001, and the proportion rose to 24.3% in 2003; its ranking also rose from second to first.[②]

Overall, the technology trade between China and the U.S. features the following characteristics: first, the U.S. enjoys evident advantages in technology exports to China, which leads to a net export over the years with a huge accumulated export surplus. The reasons are obvious. On the one hand, China's overall technology level was low at the very beginning. Although it has continuously introduced and absorbed excellent foreign technological achievements since the reform and opening up and has kept making innovations on this basis, despite improvement to some extent, the gap between China and foreign countries on the level of technology remains huge, and China's demand for advanced technology is also constantly expanding. On the other hand, the U.S. enjoys leading scientific and technological strength in the world, possesses a large number of advanced and mature technology products, and is also a net supplier of technology around the world. Its share of technology exports accounts for a large proportion of the global total. Second, the U.S. takes the lead among major countries and regions in China's technology imports. The increase in the contract amount of U.S. technology exports is relatively stable, unlike that of other countries and regions, which is subject to large fluctuations. This situation reflects the strong economic and technological power of the U.S. in the first place. Furthermore, the U.S. economy is dominated by its domestic demand, and its dependence on exports is relatively low. Hence, its technology exports have relatively little stimulating effect on its domestic economic development, so the country holds a less active attitude towards promoting technology exports. In contrast, other countries and regions, such as Japan and Germany, are much more active in promoting technology export due to their obvious outward orientation of economies, greater dependence on exports, and greater driving effect of technology export on economies. When they take various measures to expand their technology exports, their shares in technology exports to China will rise sharply for a while. However, due to their relatively weak competitive advantage in technology, when ineffective measures are taken, their shares may experience a sharp drop. Despite intense competition from other countries and regions in terms of technology exports to China, U.S. technology exports to China have always maintained a considerable share, which reflects its strong scientific and technological strength. To be fair, this is the result even under the condition of the U.S. exerting control over technology exports to China; otherwise, its share will be even higher. Third, U.S. technology exports to China account for a small proportion of its total exports to China, which is not commensurate with its status as a technology power. Due to the disparity in scientific and technological capabilities between China and the U.S., the trade between the two countries is mainly inter-departmental trade. The comparative advantage of the U.S. lies in its advanced technology products, so according to the principle of comparative advantage, its technology exports to China should take the leading position in U.S. exports to China. This has to do with the strict controls of the U.S. over technology exports to China. During the Cold War, under the U.S. proposal, in order to prevent the Soviet Union from developing high-end weapons, 17 western countries established the Coordinating Committee for Multilateral Export Controls (CoCom) in Paris in November 1949 to restrict member countries from exporting high-tech and strategic materials to socialist countries. The embargo targets about 30 countries in all, including not only socialist countries but also some nationalist ones. In July 1950, the CoCom trade control was extended to China, and China was forced to embark on the arduous road of independence and self-reliance. In 1972, after U.S. President Nixon visited China, the U.S. relaxed its export control over China. In the same year, the CoCom agreed to loosen the export controls on China and allow China to get equal treatment like the Soviet Union. Since 1981, China has been able to get access to more advanced technologies from the U.S. and other western countries. In December 1985, based on the "green line" policy of the CoCom, China began to develop arms sales with France and other countries. After 1989, the CoCom decided to cancel the previous relaxation of the export controls on China. E.U. countries followed the U.S. to implement military sanctions against China, and the fledgling arms sales between China and Europe ended. After the dissolution of the CoCom, representatives of 33 countries, including the U.S., signed a new agreement—the Wassenaar Arrangement—in Wassenaar, a small town in Dutch, in July 1996, continuing and strengthening the restrictions on the export of so-called sensitive technologies. It is fair to say that from the CoCom during the Cold War to the later Wassenaar Arrangement, the control of high-tech exports by western countries has not been weakened but strengthened. The nature of such control is to safeguard national strategic security and economic interests to the greatest extent. The Wassenaar Arrangement has had a great impact on China. When a member country intended to export a high technology to China, the U.S. would even directly intervene in the trade. For example, when the Czech Republic was planning to export a passive radar system to China in 2004, the U.S. pressured the Czech Republic into ceasing the deal. The Wassenaar Arrangement also prevents China from joining the global production system. For example, China's semiconductor industry is developing rapidly but lacks the core technologies and key equipment. Chinese enterprises have all encountered the restrictions of the Wassenaar Arrangement in purchasing equipment in the international market. Coupled with the industry's own limitations, China's semiconductor equipment manufacturing industry still lags behind the international advanced level by 2 to 3 generations and 5 to 10 years.[①]

Although the technology trade between China and the U.S. has gone through many twists and turns and has suffered constant frictions, it still moves

---

[①] China Fortune Land Development Industry Research Institute, "A Major Obstacle to China-U.S. High-tech Trade—*Wassenaar Arrangement*," Oct. 29, 2018.

forward in the face of adversity. The development of technology trade between China and the U.S. not only conforms to the trend of economic globalization but also plays a positive and beneficial role in the economic and trade development of the two countries. For example, the transfer of technologies in the aviation industry and the computer industry from the U.S. to China has accelerated the industrialization of China's aviation manufacturing industry and computer industry, while the U.S. enterprises have also gained more trade opportunities with China in these two fields. For China, actively expanding China-U.S. technology trade, especially technology imports, can not only save its precious and limited R&D funds but also make up for the deficiencies in its basic research. Through learning, imitation, and innovation, China can further enhance its overall level of technology in a short period of time, and its gap with foreign countries can be further narrowed. It can not only improve the production efficiency and production capacity of China's enterprises and enhance their competitiveness in domestic and international markets but also help China adapt to the requirements of the international trend of industrial structure adjustment and promote the optimization and upgrading of China's industrial structure. In addition, it can also reduce the U.S. trade deficit, the China-U.S. trade frictions, and the protectionist pressure in the U.S. Therefore, China should actively take all possible and feasible measures to promote the development of its bilateral technology trade with the U.S.

First of all, China should continue to communicate with the U.S. through various channels to exert positive influence on the U.S. side as much as possible. In a nutshell, the strategy of "communicating with the government and lobbying through non-governmental organizations" can be adopted: on the one hand, China can try to persuade the U.S. Congress as well as other government departments and agencies involved in developing and implementing export control policies through official channels to enhance the U.S. officials' understanding of and trust in China so as to stimulate U.S. technology exports to China from the top; on the other hand, private channels can be used to push forward U.S. technology exports to China from below. Many enterprises and enterprise associations in the U.S. have close economic and trade relations with China and have lost many trade opportunities with China due to the export control policies. China can rely on them, as well as influential Chinese Americans and Chinese entrepreneurs in the U.S. to lobby the U.S. government and Congress and exert certain influence.

Second, China should continue to deepen domestic system reform, further improve its legal system, vigorously strengthen the protection of intellectual property rights (IPR), and provide the necessary healthy internal institutional environment and relaxed external conditions for continuously promoting the technology trade between the two countries and expanding technology imports. The U.S. has once made a big fuss about the problems in China's intellectual property protection, so China should pay special attention to this. It should not only strengthen the protection of intellectual property rights directly related to technology trade, such as copyright, patents, layout designs of integrated circuits, and unpublished information, but also strengthen the protection of other intellectual property rights not directly related to this field. It should strictly follow the rules of the WTO's Agreement on Trade-Related Aspects of Intellectual Property Rights (TRIPs), not giving the U.S. any excuse for attack. Since the reform and opening up, especially since the 18th CPC National Congress, China has continuously intensified its protection of intellectual property rights, adhering to the equal treatment and protection of intellectual property rights of domestic and foreign enterprises. In June 2018, China's State Council Information Office published a white paper titled "China and the World Trade Organization," emphasizing that China is strengthening IPR protection on its own initiative. Strengthening IPR protection is the centerpiece for improving the property rights protection system, and it would provide the biggest boost to the competitiveness of the Chinese economy. It not only serves China's own development needs, but also helps cultivate a business environment that is law-based, internationalized and business-friendly. The white paper points out that since acceding to the WTO, China has formulated and improved its laws and regulations on IPR protection, set up IPR working mechanisms with many countries, drawn upon advanced international legislative practices, and built an IPR legal system that conforms to WTO rules and suits national conditions of China. The white paper also mentioned that in recent years, the State Intellectual Property Office has been restructured to strengthen law enforcement. China strengthened administrative law enforcement on intellectual property protection and launched special campaigns targeting outstanding problems, such as the "Convoy Campaign" for protecting patent rights, which effectively protected intellectual property rights. Since 2001, intellectual property royalties paid by China to foreign right holders has registered an annual growth of 17 percent, reaching \$ 28.6 billion in 2017. In 2017, China received 1.382 million invention patent applications, ranking the first in the world for the seventh consecutive year. Nearly 10 percent of the applicants were foreign entities and individuals. Invention patent applications filed by foreign entities and individuals in China reached 136,000, growing by threefold compared with 33,000 in 2001. According to the World Intellectual Property Organization, 51,000 patent applications filed from China through the Patent Cooperation Treaty were accepted in 2017, second only to the U.S. In 2018, the total royalties of China's import and export of intellectual property exceeded \$ 35 billion. Meanwhile, the total amount of patent and trademark pledge financing reached 122.4 billion yuan, up by 12.3% year on year.

Third, Chinese enterprises can also expand technology introduction by means of merger and acquisition in the U.S., establishment of strategic alliances with U.S. enterprises and construction of research institutions in the U.S. Through merger and acquisition, Chinese enterprises can absorb the assets and personnel, as well as the technology, of their U.S. counterparts, thus bypassing the constraints of the U.S. export control policy and reducing the impediments to technology introduction. Establishing strategic alliances with U.S. enterprises can give full play to the advantages of both sides in technology R&D. The two sides can exchange technologies for technologies, thus realizing the mutual exchange of needed products and acquiring advanced technologies. Chinese enterprises listed in the U.S. can also employ U.S. technology researchers and directly absorb the advanced technologies and processes by setting up research institutions in technology-intensive areas.

Finally, China can continue taking advantage of the competitive relationship between developed countries in technology export and strive for U.S. technology export to China. Generally, it can adopt the method of international competitive bidding, which is accepted at home and abroad, to open the door to technology introduction and attract enterprises from various countries to bid. Sometimes, when the U.S. notices that other countries also have the intention to export certain technology to China—that is, other countries will still export the technology to China even if the U.S. does not—it may loosen its control and allow U.S. enterprises to export this technology to China.

China should not only vigorously introduce advanced technologies but also continue absorbing and digesting the introduced technologies and actively make innovations on this basis. This way, China can create and improve its science and technology innovation system and develop new technologies and products with independent intellectual property rights so as to enhance China's technology export capacity and expand China's share in technology exports. To some extent, the possibility of technology introduction is directly proportional to the technology export capacity. The stronger China's technology export capacity is, the stronger China's negotiation ability in technology introduction will be, and the more it can weaken the adverse impacts of the U.S. technology export control policy.

Former U.S. President Clinton once pointed out that a strong and stable China is beneficial to U.S. strategic interests as well as safeguarding world peace and stability. More and more Americans have realized that China's prosperity cannot be "contained." If the U.S. continues the policy of "containing" the development of China, it will only benefit others and harm the interests of the U.S. itself. In this respect, the U.S. has had hard-learned lessons. For example, its export control on China over nuclear energy technology, integrated circuit technology, stored program control exchange technology and equipment, and advanced machine tools and equipment alone has deprived its enterprises of trading opportunities totaling tens of billions dollars and made it lose hundreds of thousands of jobs that could have been added. China has an ancient saying that "reviewing the past enables us to learn about the law governing the evolution of history." Obviously, expanding technology trade between China and the U.S. is in the long-term interests of both sides. Discord is inevitable in the process. As long as the U.S. abandons the Cold War mentality and as long as the two sides strengthen dialogues, communication, and mutual trust, misunderstanding can be removed. Whether certain people like it or not, the trend of the times is irreversible. In the same way, we can say that the China-U.S. technology trade should have and will certainly have a bright future.

Chapter VII
Analysis of Common Interests in International Human Capital Flow

Section I Analysis of Interests with Theory of International Human Capital Flow

The contribution of human capital to sustained economic growth has been demonstrated in many areas. Also, only because of the introduction of human capital as a special element can the research on the theory of trade in services be incorporated into the analysis framework of traditional international trade theory. An analysis of the special relationship between human capital and modern international trade in services will help the government to choose the right development path and through education and training policies, influence the accumulation of domestic production factors, drive service growth, and enhance the competitiveness of service trade.

I. Relationship between Human Capital and Trade in Services

Human capital refers to the assets formed by people's investment in school education, trainings, medical care, migration, and information acquisition. Human capital is opposite to physical capital. Physical capital is tangible capital, including plants, machinery, equipment, raw materials, land, currency, and other securities. However, human capital is the asset embodied in human beings—that is, the combination of general education, vocational training, and other expenditures on laborers. It is the stock of all kinds of production knowledge, labor and management skills, and health embodied in human beings.[1] The three factors of tangible goods production are land (natural resources), capital, and labor, While the three factors of service production are capital, labor, and knowledge and technology.[2] Among them, knowledge and technology are the most important. It expresses the core utility of services to consumers, such as medical treatment, education, consultation, etc. Since services differ from tangible commodities, i.e., the unity of production and consumption, the core utility of services must use human beings—the service providers—as the embodiment. As such, the combination of various factors centered on human beings has formed a relatively independent and important factor of production—human capital. In the process of service production, human capital functions as the most core factor of production. At the same time, from the perspective of the demand side, the degree of satisfaction that people can achieve for consumer services also depends on the quality and knowledge level of consumers themselves (i.e., human capital status). It is because of the importance of human capital to service production that human capital plays an extremely important role in promoting the development of international trade in services. ① Human capital has brought about the rapid development of science and technology and improved the tradability of services. For instance, consultation, banking services, and visual and audio entertainment can also be traded through multimedia remote interactive information systems. ② The enhancement of the overall level of human capital improves the efficiency and quality of service output. For example, high-level supply chain management in retail services can improve the quality of overall retail services. As the level of human capital varies among countries, the mutual

---

[1] Tan Yongsheng, *Human Capital and Economic Growth*, Beijing: China Financial & Economic Publishing House, 2007.
[2] Chen Xian and Cheng Dazhong, *International Trade in Services*, Beijing: Higher Education Press, 2003.

demand for trade in services between countries is increasing.

There are two reasons for incorporating human capital to analyze whether the international trade theory is applicable to trade in services. ① The differences between service production and tangible goods production are related to the different applications of human capital in the two. ② Human capital is crucial to both the supply and demand of services, and the comprehensive interpretation of practices by the international trade theory also takes both of the two factors into account. In addition, the theory of comparative advantage based on factor analysis and the theory of competitive advantage based on competitiveness analysis have comprehensively explained the international trade practices. Therefore, this book also attempts to analyze the role of human capital in explaining the application of international trade theory to trade in services from these two angles and on this basis provide some enlightenment on improving the competitiveness of China's trade in services.

II. Comparative Advantages in Trade in Services and Human Capital

The comparative advantage analysis in trade in services is based on the logic trend of the development of the theory of comparative advantage in the international trade theory, which includes the theory of absolute advantage, the theory of comparative advantage, the factor endowment theory (H-O model) and the intra-industry trade theory.

1. Theory of absolute advantage and theory of relative advantage

English Classical economists represented by Adam Smith and David Ricardo successively put forward the theory of absolute advantage and the theory of comparative advantage. On the assumption that the measure of labor is the same across countries, they believed that countries with different labor productivity can develop their absolute and comparative advantages, carry out a completely specialized division of labor, and specialize in producing the products with absolute and comparative advantages. Through international trade, all countries can benefit. In other words, it is the differences in labor productivity that lead to the differences in costs, thus leading to division of labor and exchange. In the production of services, human capital, as a factor of production, can directly change labor productivity. High-level human capital leads to high proficiency in service production and huge capacity in service supply. Therefore, if a country has pooled human capital in a service industry, then the country's labor productivity in this field must boast absolute or relative advantages. For example, RoK exports its beauty and medical services to the world, while the Philippines exports its household services (Filipino domestic workers). Considering that the theory of absolute advantage and the theory of comparative advantage, which assume a completely competitive market structure, constant returns to scale of production, and the inability of resources and factors of production to flow internationally, the conclusion that differences in labor productivity lead to cost differences which in turn lead to division of labor and exchange also functions in trade in services. The advantage in labor productivity here refers to the least labor time and the lowest costs in producing a unit of commodity in commodity trade; while in trade in services, it refers to the most services output and the highest quality produced by a certain amount of human capital.

2. Factor endowment theory (H-O model)

Factor endowment theory chooses the consistency of labor productivity as the starting point for analysis It assumes that when two countries use two kinds of resources to produce two products, each country will be in a better position if it engages in specialized production and international exchange of commodities with its relatively abundant production factors. If the the two countries' ratios of stock of factors of production are different, even if they have exactly the same productivity for the same factors of production, there will be a difference in production costs, hence trade between the two countries. In a word, the H-O model believes that differences in the stock of resources lead to cost differences, which further bring division of labor and exchange. Service production also requires a variety of factors, but the most important of them is the human capital factor which integrates financing, labor, and technology. If two countries produce the same kind of service product but have different stock of human capital at the same technical level, then the price of human capital is relatively low in the country with large stock of human capital, endowing the country with a comparative advantage in producing this kind of service. In other words, the relationship between factor prices and the scarcity of resource endowments in the production of tangible goods also applies to service production. Comparative advantages come from price differences, which in turn come from two sources. The first is differences in labor productivity, as mentioned in the theory of absolute advantage and the theory of comparative advantage, and the second is differences in stock of factors, as mentioned in the H-O model. In the production of services, labor productivity largely depends on the level of technology contained in human capital. Meanwhile, human capital is also the most important factor input in this process. Therefore, in terms of services, human capital is very important to both of the above-mentioned two aspects determining the price differences and comparative advantages. In fact, high-income countries boast abundant human capital with a high level of technology content, so they have comparative advantages in capital-intensive and technology-intensive services such as finance, engineering consulting, and information processing because the prices are relatively low; in contrast, developing countries have a large labor force, but the human capital has a relatively low level of technology content, so they offer relatively low prices and thus enjoy comparative advantages in labor-intensive services such as engineering contracting.

3. Intra-industry trade theory

The theory of absolute advantage, the theory of relative advantage, and the H-O model can explain very well why trade occurs across industries, but what about intra-industry trade? Intra-industry trade includes such trade of homogeneous products and heterogeneous products. Within the framework of traditional international trade theory, we use the existence of economies of scale to explain the intra-industry trade of homogeneous products and use the differences in product brand, specification, and service characteristics to explain the intra-industry trade of heterogeneous products. Trade in services is also divided into inter-industry trade and intra-industry trade. For example, country A exports tourism services to country B and imports education services from country B. Tourism and education belong to completely different service sectors, so such trade is inter-industry trade in services. If country A exports audio-visual services to country B and also imports such services from country B at the same time, then it is intra-industry trade in services.

The realization of economies of scale in the service industry is different from that in the manufacturing industry. Due to the inseparability of production and consumption, it is impossible to achieve concentrated production, as often applied in goods manufacturing, for services. Many services have multiple entry points for consumers over a large area, so the way to realize economies of scale in services is very different from that in tangible goods production. Manufacturing can concentrate the means of production in a certain place for mass production and then transport the products to the ultimate consumers. However, service production, such as banking services and retail services, needs to be as close to consumers as possible. Therefore, in order to realize economies of scale in the service industry, only by using intangible assets and management resources on a large scale can the contradiction between the large scale and the decentralization of the operation and management in the industry be resolved. From this perspective, the level of human capital largely determines the ability to use, allocate, and manage resources on a large scale.

Intra-industry trade of heterogeneous products in the service industry is common. For example, for concerts or acrobatic performances in entertainment services, although each country has its own high-level bands or acrobatic troupes, there is still the need and possibility for countries to communicate with each other. Because each country's bands or acrobatic troupes have their own national characteristics and performance characteristics, consumers can enjoy the exotic customs and be nurtured by multiple cultures without going abroad. This trade in services occurs mainly because the trading countries have some different cultures in human capital.

These trade theories prevalent in different periods all explain the occurrence of service trade relatively well because of the introduction of human capital. It can be seen that the comparative advantages in trade in services are based on human capital.

III. Competitive Advantages in Trade in Services and Human Capital

A trade theory is incomplete without the theory of competitive advantage. The theory of comparative advantage guides a country to produce and export according to its existing conditions, while the theory of competitive advantage guides a country on how to produce to gain a favorable position in international trade. The theory of competitive advantage in international trade theory is represented by the theory of competitive advantage of nations proposed by Professor Michael Porter at Harvard Business School. According to Michael Porter, at the micro level, a nation's competitive advantages lie in the vitality and innovation of enterprises; at the medium level, the high added value brought by innovations in R&D, sales, and service in the process of development is the key for an industry to obtain competitive advantages; on the macro level, it is emphasized that a country should make arrangements from an overall perspective and integrate local advantages into comprehensive competitive advantages based on all the resources that can be allocated within the territory. Like in trade in goods, comparative advantages in trade in services is dynamic as well. Traditional comparative advantages are static advantages determined by factor endowments and trading conditions, but the comparative advantages of a country is not immutable.[1] Over time, old comparative advantages will fade away, and new ones will emerge. Only in the constant dynamic changes can comparative advantages turn into competitive advantages. The comparative advantages in trade in services are based on human capital, so human capital plays an important role in the process of transforming

---

[1] Jiang Yonghong, *Research on Human Capital in the Context of China's Sustainable Development*, Beijing: Economic Science Press, 2007.

comparative advantages into competitive advantages in trade in services. How can a country use human capital to gain competitive advantages in trade in services? One way is through the accumulation of human capital, and the other is to rationally leverage the high flowability of human capital.

1. Competitive advantages in trade in services gained through human capital accumulation

In production, a country can change its factor endowments through the accumulation of human capital. Due to the extremely close relation between the service industry and human capital, when a country's accumulation of human capital is faster than its accumulation of material capital, the service industry among the three industries will develop rapidly, and trade in services will also grow as a result. At the same time, the internal structure of the service industry will also be upgraded due to such accumulation. In other words, due to the increase in human capital, a country's comparative advantages in service production and trade will shift from labor-intensive service sectors or capital-intensive service sectors to human capital-intensive service sectors. Modern service industry will replace traditional service industry as the dominant industry of the country's trade in services, and the original traditional industry will also enhance its competitiveness as a result of the improvement of human capital. In addition, the law of increasing marginal returns of human capital makes the increase in output brought by the increase in human capital far greater than that the increase in output brought by the increase in physical capital. Therefore, the accumulation of a country's human capital will also promote the accumulation of physical capital, thus promoting the balanced development and evolution of the country's industrial structure. The interactive growth of material output and service output driven by the accumulation of human capital in turn improves the overall competitiveness of the service industry and trade in services.[1] From the

---

[1] Shen Pu, *Research on Dynamic Comparative Advantage in Service Trade*, Shanghai: Fudan University Press, 2005.

perspective of demand, accumulation of human capital can improve the structure of domestic service demand and the scale of service market, thus boosting the competitiveness of the service industry and trade in services. Compared with the production of tangible goods, service production places more emphasis on demand-side factors. In countries that focus on the accumulation of human capital, the quality of people, the level of education, and people's income have generally been enhanced. As such, more cooperation from the demand side in service production will lead to higher service production efficiency, and service demand preferences will become diversified and multilayered. Fueled by the demand, the service industry of the whole nation will develop faster. In other words, human capital is highly related to income, and income is closely linked to demand. Therefore, the increase in service demand and the diversification of the demand structure become the driving forces for the expansion of trade in services and the diversification of the trade pattern, and human capital is the catalyst for forming these driving forces.

2. Competitive advantages in trade in services gained by making full use of the flowability of human capital

The occurrence of trade in services usually coincides with the movement of factors. Whether it is cross-border delivery, consumption abroad, commercial presence, or movement of natural persons, it always involves one or more movements of labor force, capital, and information. The factors of production move much more frequently in trade in services than in trade in goods. First, service factors are highly mobile. Second, each factor of service production can flow independently, especially human capital, which must be included in any form of service provision. Therefore, in the process of liberalization of trade in services, participating countries can use the view of competitive advantage and combined with their own national conditions, make full use of the factors of human capital flowing at home and abroad from the perspective of the overall national situation to enhance their competitiveness in trade in services. The above analysis has important implications for the development of China's trade in services. Abundant human resources are China's static comparative advantage in the development of trade in services. In the short term, giving full play to this comparative advantage means to a large extent giving full play to the quantitative advantage of China's labor force and developing a labor-intensive service industry, creating conditions for the dynamic transformation of comparative advantages and the evolution and upgrading of the trade pattern by gradually accumulating capital and increasing the capital-labor ratio. In the long run, avoiding comparative disadvantages and enhancing international competitiveness mean to a great extent overcoming the "low-level trap" of human capital and vigorously developing a "knowledge and technology intensive service industry." From short-term comparative advantages to long-term competitive advantages, the key lies in turning the abundant human capital in its natural state into strong human capital with practical production capacity and knowledge and skills through appropriate ways and mechanisms.

Section Ⅱ Analysis of Common Interests in Practice of International Human Capital Flow

With the inception of the concept of "human capital," the role of human capital has received extensive attention among economists and has become a new and important field for studying economic growth and development. Some scholars believe that the outflow of human capital is an important factor limiting a country's economic development. Some scholars believe that the international flow of human capital will not only bring permanent disparity in income between countries but also bring permanent disparity in economic growth rates between countries. Therefore, the international flow of human capital may become an important explanatory variable for the differences in economic growth rates between countries. The importance of international flow of human capital has drawn more and more attention from scholars.

I. Directions and Causes of International Human Capital Flow

The flow of talents has long been a controversial worldwide problem, whose impacts on the entire world economy and the outflow and inflow countries have not yet been determined. Since the second half of the 20th century, international migration has been characterized by diversity. The most prominent feature is that the proportion of senior talents, who mainly flow from developing countries to developed countries, in international migration has increased. With economic globalization, the proportion of high-quality population migration will continue to expand. Allan M. Williams (2005) classified the international flow of human capital according to the static influence of the international distribution of intelligence, dividing international flow of human capital into brain exchange, brain drain, brain overflow, brain waste, brain circulation, etc. Among them, brain drain is the most controversial focus in international flow of human capital because the permanent flow of human capital from developing countries to developed countries will bring far-reaching and complex impacts on the balanced development of the entire world economy. This is also the focus of this book.

1. Direction and flow rate of human capital flow

Since the 1990s, there is no exact data on the international flow of highly skilled talents, but there is evidence to indicate that more and more talents are flowing from developing countries in Asia, Africa, and South America to the U.S., Canada, Australia, and developed countries in Western Europe. Brain drain has become the main form of international human capital flow. Specifically, it has the following two characteristics.

(1) Developed countries are the major inflow countries of human capital, among which the U.S. is the largest. In addition, Canada, Germany, France, and the U.K., as well as some emerging industrial countries in Asia such as Singapore, are also net inflow countries of human capital. By 2000, highly

skilled foreign immigrants had accounted for a significant proportion of the total number of highly skilled workers in developed countries.

(2) Developing countries are the main outflow countries of human capital. Africa is the region with the most serious brain drain. In 1999, in 40% of African countries, more than 35% of their college graduates settled abroad. Small countries in Central and South America and the Caribbean have lost nearly one-third of their highly skilled talents. Asia is the region with the largest population of brain drain, and India is the main outflow country. Other Asian countries such as Pakistan, China, Thailand, Sri Lanka, and Vietnam also face various problems brought by brain drain.

2. The main reasons for international flow of human capital

The root cause of the emergence and development of the transnational flow of talents is the development of international division of labor and the integration of the world economy, which is the result of the objective laws of economic development. Specifically, the reasons for the transnational flow of talents can be summarized in two aspects: personal motivation, including expectations for good economic returns, personal development prospects, and working environment, etc.; external factors, including the differences in political and economic environments between different countries, the degree of control and policies on the flow of factors of production, and the investment and trade behaviors of multinational corporations in various parts of the world.

(1) Personal motivation for transnational flow of talents.

First, the pursuit of economic benefits. From a microscopic point of view, the decision-making of each flow depends on the measurement of the income and the cost of the flow by the subject of the flow. Economists have long noticed that the financial factor is the most fundamental factor affecting decisions of human capital flow. Schultz's theory of human capital points out that salaries mean prices, and they imply the laws of the market. For special high-tech salaries, the market will expand to the international scope. As a reflection of the salaries in the market, people will move between countries.

Therefore, some human resources are allocated internationally.① That is to say, human resources are highly mobile internationally. If the salaries and remunerations in developing countries fail to catch up with those in developed countries, their talents may migrate to developed countries and regions to get access to better treatment. This reflects the talents' nature as "economic men." Therefore, the pursuit of higher expected returns is a fundamental driving force for the international flow of talents. Of course, the expectation of returns not only takes wages and treatment into account but also comprehensively considers the overall results of migration costs, employment probability, various benefits, costs, and risks of living in the relocation area, including psychological factors, etc. The international flow of talents is actually a "self-choice" process driven by expected returns. When the net returns after deducting various costs is greater than the expected returns at home, people will choose to migrate. A large number of talents from developing countries flow to developed countries precisely because they see that they can obtain more expected returns in developed countries with high national income and good social welfare.

Second, the pursuit of success. Apart from obtaining higher economic returns, pursuing career and academic success is also an important factor for talent flow, especially for scientists, students, and academic researchers. Talents always flow to places that are conducive to their career development and fully reflect their own values. Developed countries such as the U.S. have a strong economy and large investment in science and technology. They possess most of the world's scientific and technological resources and bring together world-class outstanding scientists and prestigious universities. The R&D expenditure in developed countries accounts for more than 2% of their GDP on average, accounting for 84.4% of the world's total R&D expenditure, while the R&D expenditure in developing countries accounts for only 0.6% of their GDP

---

① Theodore W. Schultz, *On Human Capital Investment*, Beijing: Beijing College of Economics Press, 1990, p. 184.

on average, accounting for only 15.6% of the world's total.[1] The huge gap in investment in science and technology education has resulted in an extremely uneven distribution of science and technology resources in the world. It is the rich science, technology and education resources in developed countries that greatly attract scientists, scholars, and overseas students, especially those in developing countries, to work and study in developed countries such as the U.S. These countries have a high overall knowledge level, fast information dissemination, frequent academic exchange and cooperation, and good environments for knowledge production where it is easier to make achievements whether in study or in scientific research. The fact that most Nobel Prize winners are American is a case in point.

Third, the pursuit of working environment. The working environment, especially the entrepreneurial environment, is a direct factor influencing the flow of entrepreneurial talents. Entrepreneurs refer to those who have capital and business ideas for the purpose of establishing a business organization or engaging in certain business activities. They are a group of special talents, with not only higher education but also special talents in business creation and resource utilization. A good investment environment, sufficient venture capital, a perfect capital market, preferential tax policies, and the support of public funds are the greatest attractions for entrepreneurs, the most basic characteristics a good business environment, and the necessary conditions for successes of start-ups. The reason that many excellent entrepreneurs from developing countries and even developed countries in Europe flock into the U.S. is that that the U.S. has advantages in the business environment for start-ups. Silicon Valley is the best example. It is recognized as a model of "entrepreneurship" in the world. Since 1980, Chinese and Indians have established more than 3,000 technology companies in Silicon Valley. Apart from Asians, a large number of European entrepreneurs have also gathered

---

[1] UNESCO website: http://stats.uis.unesco.org/unesco/tableviewer/document·aspx? FileId = 76.

here, which has a lot to do with the lack of venture capital and adventurous spirit in Europe.

(2) External factors for transnational flow of talents.

First, environmental differences between countries. Differences in the political and economic environments across countries in the world are significant macro factors that lead to the cross-border flow of talents. Generally speaking, people tend to work and live in a harmonious and stable social environment. Domestic political turmoil and unstable economic environment are among the reasons that many outstanding talents leave their home countries one after another. When large-scale social unrest or even wars occur in a country, flocks of talents are bound to move abroad. The most typical example is that scientists moved to the U.S. during the Second World War. During that period, many Jewish businessmen and scientists fled the main battlefields in Europe for a less war-torn America due to the war and Nazi Germany's crazy persecution of Jews. Nearly 200 scientists from Germany and Austria alone moved to the U.S., including Einstein, the best scientist in the 20th century. The flood of foreign talents has saved the U.S. a huge investment in intelligence and promoted its domestic social and economic development. After the Second World War, the U.S. became the world's largest economy. Judging from the practices of talent attraction in the U.S. after the Second World War, overseas study, immigration, and work visa are regarded as the three magic weapons for the U.S. to win in the fierce international competition for talents. Its key advantages in attracting foreign talents hinge on a highly developed education and scientific research system, good salary and working and living conditions, a highly open and inclusive social environment, and broad space and opportunities for success.

Second, differences in talent policies between countries. The transnational flow of talents is the reallocation of human capital in the world. Therefore, it is bound to be influenced by countries' degree of control and policies on talents—that is, the scale of transnational flow of talents is bound to be influenced by the policies of countries on the flow of talents. In the global talent competition, both developing and developed countries have developed a series of preferential policies to enhance their attraction to senior talents. On the contrary, some countries have adopted strict policies to restrict the flow of talents, making the international flow of talents quite difficult. For example, Germany and France used to be economically and technologically developed countries. However, due to their strict immigration policies, relatively few high-tech talents have flowed into these two countries. In contrast, the U.S. has adopted various preferential policies to attract foreign high-tech talents and has hence received a flooding of high-tech talents.

Third, the global expansion of multinational corporations. The transnational flow of talents is also closely related to the global expansion of transnational corporations. Since the 1950s, multinationals based in the U.S. have started to expand abroad, while multinationals in Western Europe and Japan have also risen rapidly and expanded overseas through mergers, acquisitions, and new branches or subsidiaries. The booming overseas business of multinational corporations has created a huge demand for new senior managers and key technical personnel. In the early stage of development, in order to meet the overall strategic needs, maintain the consistency of corporate culture, and retain the technological edges and monopoly in the host countries, multinationals usually adopt the method of internal personnel transfer, namely, the method of sending senior managers and key technical personnel from the head office or parent company to local branches or subsidiaries. This thus creates a flow of managers and technicians from one country to another. Such international flow of talents is not the result of personal choices but the result of corporate decision-making. However, with the development of economic globalization, transnational corporations have conducted investment and trade in every corner of the world, almost covering all economic fields and industrial sectors in all countries and regions of the world, thus dominating the global economy. Moreover, the investment of multinational corporations in various parts of the world has driven the cross-border flow of talents, and the internationalization of talents is increasingly becoming a common phenomenon.

II. Impact of International Human Capital Flow on Interests

With regard to the cross-border flow of talents, governments and academia all over the world generally hold two kinds of attitudes: "international mode" and "national mode."①

Those who support the "international mode" believe that international flow of talents is the reallocation of human capital in the world, which is conducive to the effective use of resources and is beneficial to the whole world, without damaging the outflow countries. They think that there is no need to make a big fuss about the "brain drain." Looking at the whole world as a supply and demand market for human resources, the flow of talents is the result of the natural adjustment of supply and demand in the talent market. As long as people can contribute their talents to the whole mankind, it is a good thing no matter which country the talents flow to. To say the least, the cross-border flow of talents is also beneficial even to developing countries where brain drain is more severe, as brain drainers can serve as bridges for economic, cultural, scientific, technological, and educational cooperation between the home country and the rest of the world. If restrictions are imposed on the flow of talents or if overseas talents are forced to return home, then limited by domestic economic development or scientific and technology level, the talents may not be able to give full play to their strengths, leading to a waste of talents instead. Needless to say, scholars who hold this view mostly come from the countries that have a net inflow of talents and have benefited greatly from the transnational flow of talents.

Scholars who support the "national mode" argue that because of the

---

① Chen Shaoguang and Yuan Lunqu, "Analysis of the Effect of International Mobility of Talents," *Management World*, 2004 (10).

incompleteness of the labor market, transnational flow of talents will harm the welfare of developing countries. "Talents" belong to a country's human capital. Brain drain is like capital outflow or plundering of resources. It means a great loss for the country experiencing talents outflow. From a country-to-country perspective, the influx of talents from developing countries into developed countries is like poor countries aiding rich ones with talents, which will result in a serious imbalance in the distribution of human capital in the international community and aggravate the Matthew Effect that the rich get richer and the poor get poorer." People who hold this view are mainly scholars from developing countries who are at a disadvantage in the mechanism of transnational talent flow. They insist on the backflow of talents mainly from the perspective of national interests.

Both views are biased, to some degree. Transnational flow of talents is the reallocation of human capital in the global market. As a free flow of factors of production, it has both advantages and disadvantages for both the inflow countries and the outflow countries of talents. Therefore, when analyzing the effects of transnational flow of talents, a holistic approach should be adopted.

1. Impact of international human capital flow on interests of entire international community

The loss of human capital will lead to a permanent decrease in the growth rate of per capita income in the outflow country while the impact on the economic growth of the inflow country is not clear as it will change along with the two countries' average human capital level. Further research shows that the flow of human capital will cause permanent differences in economic growth rates among countries. Some scholars also proposed to use the S-shaped production function model to analyze the impact of brain drain on the overall international welfare. This model describes the different marginal rates of return of human capital at different levels of development, which can be increasing, decreasing, or negligible. Developing countries are at the bottom of the S-shaped production function model, which means that marginal rate of return will increase when a new senior talent is added. On the contrary, as developed countries may be at the top of the S-shaped production function model, under the premise that they already have a large number of high-quality talents, an additional talent may bring about a diminishing marginal rate of return. In extreme cases, the least developed countries (LDC), at the very beginning of the S-shaped production function, own a tiny number of senior talents and do not meet the minimum threshold for generating the marginal rate of return. In this case, the marginal rate of return of human capital is insignificant. However, adding a certain quantity of senior talents to exceed the "threshold" of human capital can bring about significantly increased rate of return. Therefore, senior talents are more valuable in developing countries than in developed countries. The decrease in the number of talents in developing countries may even cause their production function to regress to the beginning of the S-shaped function, thus making them fall into the trap of scarcity of human capital. Brain drain cannot bring about a "win-win" result, and to a large extent, it is a "lose-win" situation, which means that the improvement of one side's welfare is based on the reduction of the other side's welfare. Developing countries are the victims of brain drain, whose negative impacts are not limited to the economy but also involve all aspects of social life. The widening wealth gap between developing and developed countries and the various serious social problems in developing countries are not good for developed countries themselves as well.

2. Impact of international human capital flow on interests of outflow countries

For developing countries, the benefits of human capital outflow mainly depend on the talents that went broad bringing back the advanced ideas and technologies they have learned in other countries and applying the ideas and technologies to practice in their homeland. However, in fact, the talent flow between developing countries and developed countries is mostly one-way—that is, migrants from developing countries are more inclined to stay in developed countries to work and live. For example, from 1990 to 1991, 79% of the Indian students studying in the United States and 88% of the Chinese students studying in the United States continued to stay in the United States after obtaining their PhD degrees. In contrast, only 11% of the RoK students and 15% of the Japanese students studying in the United States chose to work in the U.S. through 1995 after obtaining their PhD degrees in science and engineering. Therefore, for developing countries, brain drain may bring great negative effects.

(1) Impacts on the fiscal revenue. Brain drain has a relatively great impact on the fiscal revenue of developing countries. On the one hand, brain drain will reduce the tax base of tax revenue; on the other hand, senior talents are often the objects of the highest tax rate. Therefore, the national fiscal revenue will decrease with the loss of senior talents. According to statistics, although Indian Americans make up only 0.1% of India's total population, their income in the United States is equal to 10% of India's national income. Relevant research shows that nearly one-third of India's personal income tax has vanished with the departure of emigrants. Other developing countries are also facing similar problems.

In addition to the direct impact on personal income tax, brain drain also has indirect impacts on other types of taxes. The loss of high-quality talents makes direct taxes more difficult to collect, and the government relies more on indirect taxes. Like many developing countries, India relies on indirect taxes to a greater extent, with about 65.6% of its revenue coming from indirect taxes. Furthermore, brain drain will also distort taxation. In order to retain talents, governments reduce the marginal tax rate of personal income tax, making low-income earners bear heavier burdens accordingly and thus weakening the significance of tax revenue as a social regulator.

(2) Impacts on the education system. In most countries, the state will allocate a large amount of the fiscal revenue to finance part of the education expenses, which comes almost exclusively from taxpayers. Brain drain means

that when talents from developing countries leave their countries after completing their higher education with taxpayers' aid. On the one hand, they have not devoted the knowledge they have accumulated back to their own countries for the benefits of their own people; on the other hand, they have not fulfilled their obligation to pay taxes to their homeland to finance the education of the next generation. As brain drain has taken away a large part of the government's fiscal revenue, the government will have insufficient funds for civic education. What is more serious is that because previous investment in education has vanished with the brain drain, the government and taxpayers will have increasingly fewer incentives to further invest in education, thus increasingly weakening a country's education system. At the same time, due to the lack of favorable educational conditions in their homeland, more students will choose to receive education and live abroad, thus plunging the country's education into a vicious circle: brain drain leads to a lack of incentives for educational investment, which reduces educational investment and deteriorates educational conditions, and this leads to a further outflow of students and brain drain, thus further deteriorating educational conditions.

(3) Impacts on establishment of the talent system. Mihir Desai, a professor at Harvard University, believes that the loss of a large number of the "best and brightest" talents will bring incalculable negative impacts to a country. These losses will hurt the so-called "facilitating factors"—the integration of highly skilled talents, ordinary workers, entrepreneurs, and capital providers. Furthermore, the massive loss of highly educated talents may even result in a country's inability to meet the minimum need to form a "critical pool" of talents, and the country would not be able to form a complete domestic talent system. After studying the theory of "critical pool," economist Thomas Schelling pointed out that brain drain may lead a country into a vicious circle: the loss of high-quality talents will bring about more and more brain drain. This is because talents need the group's assistance and cooperation. First of all, talents themselves need the cooperation of other talents to complete their work,

thus contributing to the society. The characteristics of modern science and technology such as diversification, wide range, comprehensiveness, and marginalization determine that it is difficult for a single person to complete a scientific research project with his or her own limited energy, ability, and knowledge structure. Second, people need a sense of belonging. A highly educated person needs to belong to a group with a higher level of knowledge. He expects that people around him have the same abilities and knowledge structures as him. When these conditions are not met, he needs to leave and go abroad to look for such groups. Therefore, there is a chain reaction of everyone's leaving and staying. The number and scale of such groups become smaller and smaller as individuals leave. Therefore, the loss of human capital will aggravate itself, thus affecting the establishment of a country's complete talent system.

(4) Impacts on reform of the national system. Becker, an economist believes that the loss of human capital in developing countries is not only a "loss of intelligence" but also a "loss of change" as these intellectuals should have helped the country to reform and revitalize. Their departure, to a certain extent, takes away the stable and powerful influence of the middle class on politics. Meanwhile, economic, social, and educational progress depends especially on a sufficient number of high-quality talents to find the most effective use of human capital and a basic outlook on the system applicable to the country in the future. The loss of human capital undoubtedly restrains the pace of national system reform.

3. Impact of international human capital flow on interests of inflow countries

(1) Positive effects on inflow countries. The positive effects on the inflow countries are mainly reflected in three aspects: ① Foreign talents often engage in jobs for which the inflow countries have an insufficient supply of labor. Thus, this is an effective supply of talents for the inflow countries and can alleviate the plight of the shortage of talents in these countries. ② The inflow of talents will increase the total human capital of the inflow countries, saving a lot

of education and training funds for them. Higher returns are achieved without increasing input, which will undoubtedly contribute to the long-term economic development of the inflow countries. As an inflow country, the U.S. has acquired millions of specialized talents from dozens of countries through various ways and means in the past 30 years. It has saved $300 billion in education expenses alone, which is equivalent to an inflow of funds that are worth $300 billion into the U.S. ③ The inflow of foreign talents will drive the rapid economic development and enhance the competitiveness of the inflow countries. Take the U.S. as an example. Its rapid economic development and its status as a world economic power have benefited to a great extent from the high-level talents it attracted from other countries. According to a survey, the U.S. gets a benefit of $6 billion from brain gain every year, while losses from brain drain in developing countries amount to $8 billion every year. From 1949 to 1969, the U.S. obtained 143,000 high-level talents from developing countries, who have created at least $100 billion worth of wealth for the U.S. in the 20 years. Between 1969 and 1979, the U.S. embraced a total of 500,000 professionals of all kinds, 375,000 of whom were from developing countries. In 1987, there were 300,000 foreign students studying in the U.S. universities, 60% of whom studied science and engineering, and 25% of them settled in the U.S. after obtaining positions as scientists or engineers, thus incorporated into the "talent pool" of the U.S.① In 2004, nearly 40% of the world's international students went to study in the U.S. In the 2006 – 2007 academic year, the U.S. accepted 583,000 international students. After graduation, most foreign students have stayed in the U.S. to pursue further study or find jobs. Half of them have settled in the U.S., many of whom have become the backbone in the field of science and technology. Practice has suggested that the open policy and the high standard of education and science in the U.S. have attracted scientists and

---

① Chen Zhaofeng and Huang Weidong, "Research on Ways to Gather Overseas Scientific and Technological Talents for Entrepreneurship," *Science & Technology Progress and Policy*, 2001 (6).

artists from all over the world, and these immigrants have served as a powerful driving force for its economic and cultural development and have made great contributions to the country with fruitful achievements in scientific and technological research and artistic creation. Many immigrants have made significant contributions to scientific research in the U.S., winning the Nobel Prize in physiology or medicine, physics, chemistry, and economics. From 1901 to 2016, a total of 911 individuals and organizations in different countries won the Nobel Prize, with 350 American winners, more than 100 of whom were born outside the U.S. territory. Albert Michelson, winner of the Nobel Prize in physics in 1907, was the first American to win the prize. He was born in Prussia. Bengt Holmstrom, who won the 2016 Nobel Prize in economics, was born in Finland and now teaches at Massachusetts Institute of Technology (MIT). Over the years, there were also a number of British and German winners, many of whom, it should be noted, were working in the U.S. The 9 winners of the 2016 Nobel Prize in science were all teaching in prestigious universities in the U.S. They were not born in the U.S. but came from Britain, Turkey, Finland, and Ireland. The results of various awards in the U.S. also tend to show that there are many outstanding immigrants. Immigrants have accounted for a large proportion of the Pulitzer Prize winners for years. The U.S. National Book Award has also been awarded to a number of Chinese American writers. For the John Bates Clark Medal, which is awarded to outstanding American economists under the age of 40, 35% of the winners were born in countries like India, Turkey, and Ukraine. In his article "Immigrants Have Enriched American Culture and Enhanced Our Influence in the World," Daniel Griswold, Co-Director of the Trade and Immigration Project of George Mason University, wrote the following: "We are a nation of immigrants. Successive waves of immigrants have kept our country demographically young, enriched our culture and added to our productive capacity as a nation, ... enhancing America's ability to trade and invest profitably in the global economy. They keep our economy flexible, allowing U.S. producers to keep prices down and to respond to changing consumer demands. An authoritative 1997 study by the National Academy of Sciences (NAS) concluded that immigration delivered a 'significant positive gain' to the U.S. economy."[1] Farhad Manjoo, illustrated with facts that Silicon Valley wouldn't work without immigrants, in his "Why Silicon Valley Wouldn't Work Without Immigrants" published on *New York Times*,[2] Shaywitz pointed out that 51% of the most valuable start-ups in the U.S. were founded by immigrants.[3] In recent years, the U.S. government has imposed restrictions on people-to-people exchanges between China and the U.S. on the grounds of "national security." In April 2018, at the request of the National Institutes of Health, University of Texas MD Anderson Cancer Center dismissed three senior researchers, accusing the three Chinese researchers of "seriously violations of policies." In May 2019, Emory University expelled two senior ethnically Chinese biologists and closed their laboratories. In this context, far-sighted people are laden with worries. Daniel Griswold wrote, "It would be a national shame if, in the name of security, we closed the door to immigrants who come here to work, save and build a better life for themselves and their families." He also wrote, "Silicon Valley and other high-tech sectors would cease to function if we foolishly were to close our borders to skilled and educated immigrants."[4] President of Yale University Peter Salovey published an open letter, stressing that international students and scholars are welcome and respected and that openness is the key to the excellence of top U.S. research universities and must remain a hallmark of Yale.[5]

(2) Negative effects on inflow countries. The transnational flow of talents

---

[1] Daniel Griswold, "Immigrants Have Enriched American Culture and Enhanced Our Influence in the World," Cato Institute, Feb. 18, 2002.
[2] Farhad Manjoo, "Why Silicon Valley wouldn't work without immigrants," *New York Times*, Feb. 9, 2017.
[3] David A. Shaywitz, "Immigrants Make Silicon Valley Great," *FEE*, Sep. 23, 2016.
[4] Daniel Griswold, "Immigrants Have Enriched American Culture and Enhanced Our Influence in the World," Cato Institute, Feb. 18, 2002.
[5] "The 'China phobic' paranoia harming Sino-U.S. Relations," China Plus, May 26, 2019.

also has certain negative effects on the inflow countries, which are mainly reflected on the level of employment and wages. Since talents are a kind of senior factor of production, the inflow of talents will have an impact on the labor market of the importing country. According to the general theory of economics, if the supply increases while the demand remains unchanged, then the price will drop. This is manifested in the labor market as wages decreasing. In addition, immigrated international talents will have the "crowding out effect" and the "substitution effect" on the employment of domestic workers of the same type, thus affecting the employment of native residents who are related to the affected fields.

Section III Realization of Common Interests of China and Developed Countries in Human Capital Flow

In the past ten years, multinational corporations are changing their previous method of engaging in R&D at home and accelerating the process of transferring their R&D bases overseas. UNCTAD's survey of the multinational corporations that spent the most on R&D in 2004-2005 showed that more than half of the multinationals carried out R&D in China, India, or Singapore. The proportion of multinationals' overseas R&D expenditure in their total R&D expenditure has increased from 22% in 1995 to 43% in 2003 in Sweden and from 11% in 1994 to 13% in 2002 in the U.S. The share of foreign-invested enterprises in R&D spending in developing countries has risen from 2% in 1996 to 18% in 2003. Developing countries such as India and China have been able to generally participate in international R&D.[1] The trend of integration of global

---

[1] Jiang Xiaojuan, "Utilizing Global Science and Technology Resources to Improve Independent Innovation Ability," *Economic Reform and Development*, 2006 (7): 38-40.

scientific and technological innovation is becoming increasingly prominent. The close interaction of scientific and technological resources between multinationals in the process of global integration of innovation will inevitably be accompanied by frequent international human capital flow. Under this background, the international flow of human capital in China presents some new features, which affect the development of China's innovation system.

The relevant theoretical research on international human capital flow mainly focuses on the following three aspects. The first aspect is exploration of the causes of international human capital flow. Factors such as misallocation of personnel, imbalance in interpersonal relationship, achievement motivation, difference in income between two places, changes in job opportunities, and transfer costs lead to international human capital flow, and this flow has accelerated with the globalization of scientific and technological innovation.[1] The second aspect is study of the advantages and disadvantages of international human capital flow. There are two schools of thought. One advocates the "national mode." Scholars such as Bhagwati (1974) and Mcculloch (1975) believe that because of the incompleteness of the labor market, brain drain will harm the welfare of developing countries. For enterprises, it will cause the instability of organizational structure, damage the cohesion of enterprises, reduce work efficiency, and increase the training costs. For the country and the society, serious brain drain will result in a decrease in the supply of key specialists in developing countries, hence leading to higher socio-economic costs for the whole society.[2] The other supports the "international mode." Scholars such as Grubel (1985) and Stark (1998) believe that the international flow of human capital reflects the differences in marginal productivity, contributes to the effective utilization of resources, increases world welfare, and does no harm to

---

[1] David C. Meclelland, "N Achievement and Entrepreneurship: A longitudinal Study," *Journal of Personality and Social Psychology*, 1965(1): 389-392.

[2] Liu Jian, Niu Qiang and Li Guoping, "Studies on the Characteristic of Intelligence Outflow in China in the new Period and Its Countermeasure," *Studies in Science of Science*, 2005 (3), pp. 352-356.

the countries where outflow of human capital occurs. On the contrary, the effect of brain gain brought by the return migration of human capital is conducive to the satisfaction of talents' desire of self-development and the innovation of organizations (enterprises, scientific research institutes, and political organizations), thus making the whole society full of vitality.[1] The third aspect is study of the specific measures for international human capital flow. Measures such as improving the economic and non-economic benefits of human capital, building a community of shared interests, creating a harmonious environment, and promoting the traditional national culture can be implemented to prevent brain drain.[2] The international flow of human capital is becoming a hot research topic at home and abroad. At present, the relevant analysis on this phenomenon lacks a specific contingency environment and a specific target, resulting in a relatively large number of disputes. This book will focus on the impact of the new characteristics of international human capital flow on China's innovation system under the specific background of global integration of scientific and technological innovation and the design of the corresponding guiding mechanism.

I. New Characteristics of International Human Capital Flow in China

With the acceleration of the process of global integration of scientific and technological innovation, scientific and technological resources interact closely through transnational innovation networks, which spurs the frequent flow of human capital globally. Under this background, the international flow of human capital in China has taken on new features. In recent ten years, China has suffered serious loss of high-end human capital. Of the 200,000 engineers and technicians in Silicon Valley, 60,000 are Chinese. In 2001, Chinese

---

[1] Grubel H G, "Economics of the Brain Drain," in *International Encyclopedia of Education*, Oxford, 1985.
[2] Chen Shaoguang and Yuan Lunqu, "Analysis of the Effects of International Flow of Talents," *Management World*, 2004 (10): 147-148.

accounted for 10% of the 11,595 H-1B visa holders that the U.S. introduced from overseas. Recently, the U.S. proposed to attract at least 1 million high-tech talents from abroad in the next 10 years. Britain, Germany, Japan, and other developed countries have all introduced various generous immigration and study-abroad policies to attract high-end human capital from other countries. With the advancement of scientific and technological innovation and global integration, the proportion of migration of high-quality talents will continue to expand. China's international human capital flow has experienced two different ways: the "obvious flow" and the "obscure flow" (which is a relatively new kind of international flow after the "obvious flow"). The "obvious flow" refers to the outflow of China's human capital in large quantities through overseas study, overseas labor service, and skilled migration. Since 1978, less than half of the overseas students sent abroad by the government returned to their motherland after graduation, even less than a third in some years. These are the main manifestations of this "obvious flow." In recent years, with multinational corporations implementing the talent "localization" strategy, the human capital in China is experiencing an "obscure flow"—talents still work in their home country but serve multinational corporations or international groups. Multinationals have shifted their talent strategy from competition in the international market to local plunder. The competition for high-tech talents has become "face-to-face" with "zero distance." First, they establish research institutions to attract a large number of outstanding talents. According to a research report of the former Ministry of Personnel, more than 400 of the Fortune 500 from 14 countries have set up R&D institutions in China, mainly focusing on computer, communication, chemical industry, electronics, automobile, medicine, etc. Second, they set up "management colleges" or "training centers" to speed up the "localization" of talent training. For example, Motorola University provides training for a large number of young students in China every year to inculcate Motorola's corporate culture and business knowledge. Third, they not only discover existing talents but also look for potential ones. For example, Motorola launched the Star of Hope Scholarship in China in 2000, which turned simple financial assistance into talent training.

While China's human capital has experienced a large outflow, it has seen a trend of backflow in recent years. As China's economy is growing, coupled with many preferential policies provided by the Chinese government for returning students, the rate of returning students has increased steadily. From 1978 to 2005, the total number of returning overseas students reached 179,000. Of these, in 2005, a total of 118,500 students studied abroad and a total of 34,900 students returned home, an increase of 41.5% over 2004. This was the first time since the reform and opening up that the annual number of Chinese students returning from abroad exceeded 30,000. On December 23, 2008, the General Office of the CPC Central Committee forwarded the Opinions of the Central Talent Coordination Group on the Implementation of the Overseas High-Level Talent Introduction Plan, organizing the implementation of the Overseas High-Level Talent Introduction Plan and vigorously attracting the overseas high-level talents to return home for innovation and entrepreneurship. By the end of 2016, the total number of Chinese students studying abroad had reached 4.5866 million, and the total number of returning students had reached 2.6511 million. Xinhua News Agency called it "a rare wave of backflow of talents in the national history." Among these returning talents, there are many influential people. In 2017, Andrew Chi-Chih Yao, a world-renowned computer scientist, renounced his U.S. citizenship and became an academician of the Chinese Academy of Sciences. Overall, the proportion of returning students to those studying abroad is rising. In addition, the number of overseas students studying in China has also increased significantly in recent years. Statistics released by China Scholarship Council show that since 1999, the number of overseas students studying in China has basically increased by an average of 20% annually. In 2002, a total of 85,829 overseas students of all kinds from 175 countries were studying in China. Compared with 2001, the number of countries increased by 6, accounting for 38.7%. In 2004, the number of overseas students studying in China exceeded 110,000. Statistics show that in 2017, overseas students from 204 countries and regions studied in 935 universities in 31 provinces, autonomous regions, and municipalities directly under the central government, of which about 75,800 were studying for a master's or doctoral degree, with an increase of 18.62% over 2016. Overseas students studying in China continues to increase, and China has become the largest destination for overseas study in Asia. In 2018, a total of 492,185 overseas students of all kinds from 196 countries and regions studied in 1,004 universities in 31 provinces, autonomous regions, and municipalities, 3,013 more than the number in 2017 with an increase of 0.62% (the above data do not include data of China's Hong Kong, Macao and Taiwan regions).

II. Impact of International Human Capital Flow on China's Innovation System

The international flow of human capital promotes the flow of advanced knowledge and technology into China, greatly driving the development of related domestic industries. At the same time, the international flow of human capital in China has great risks, which brings severe challenges to the development of China's innovation system. Human capital outflow can be divided into two types according to whether it returns or not. One is transitional outflow. It refers to the situations where those who study abroad return to China after obtaining the degree or completing the required education and the situations where those who work abroad return to China after a period of time. Most government-sponsored overseas students belong to this type, as well as those who provide design or consulting services overseas and those dispatched by domestic organizations. The other is permanent outflow, which refers to the situations where students study abroad and settle abroad and where workers work abroad as skilled migrants. This is truly a brain drain. These two types of human capital outflow have completely different impacts on China's innovation system. Transitional outflow of human capital has a driving effect on the development of China's innovation system. As mentioned above, in recent years, there has been a trend of backflow of students studying abroad. A number of those working in overseas research institutions or studying abroad, many of whom are outstanding talents in related fields, have returned to start their own businesses. This trend will continue to intensify for some time to come. These experts and scholars have a clear understanding of the cutting-edge technologies and the development trend in their respective fields. Some of them are even interdisciplinary talents in science and technology and management. Their returns will further drive international R&D personnel to start businesses and work in China. Permanent human capital outflow, however, restricts the development of China's innovation system. At present, most of China's human capital outflow involves high-level and high-quality talents, among whom quite a lot are even elites among the senior talents. The number of Chinese students studying abroad has been on rise in the past ten years. Except for 2007, 2013 and 2016, the number exceeded 30,000 in other years. After hitting a nearly decade-high of 27.53% in 2009, the growth rate declined slightly every year. In 2013, the growth rate fell by a large margin, to 3.6%. In 2018 and 2019, it rose back to above 10%. The year of 2015 saw the largest-ever increase in the number of overseas students, an increase of 63,900 over 2014, up by 13.9%. In 2016, however, the growth rate of the number of students studying abroad dropped back to single digits, shrinking to 3.97%. Since the 1990s, a large number of outstanding graduates from well-known domestic universities have gone abroad, which has had a profound impact on China's future potential in scientific and technological development. In Peking University alone, more than 600 students chose to study abroad at their own expenses in 1998. 50%, 35%, and 32% of its undergraduate students majoring in physics, chemistry, and biology respectively chose to study abroad, and Pecking University was jokingly called "a university set up for foreign countries." 28.2% of the 2017 undergraduate graduates of Tsinghua University chose to go outbound to study further for a master's or PhD degree—that is, on average, one in four students will go outbound. Of the 2,436 master graduates of Tsinghua University in 2017, 8.9% chose to further their studies, of which 6.3% chose to go outbound. There were 1,296 PhD graduates in Tsinghua University in 2017, 33.3% of whom chose to further their study (generally for a postdoctoral degree), with 21.1% staying in China's mainland and 12.1% going outbound. 2,645 undergraduates, 3,604 postgraduates and 1,213 PhD students graduated from Peking University in 2017. Among them, 75.16% of the undergraduates choose to further their study, of whom 816 (30.85%) chose to go outbound. The proportion of postgraduate students who chose to further their study was relatively small (8.97%), of whom 197 (5.47%) chose to go outbound. 31% of the PhD students chose to pursue postdoctoral degrees, of whom 222 (18.3%) chose to go outbound. The growth rate of Chinese students going to the U.S. for study was close to 30% in the 2008/2009 academic year and then slowly decreased to 10.79% in the 2014/2015 academic year. The annual net growth reached 41,568 in the 2012/2013 academic year and then slowly decreased, with the net growth expected to be around 20,000 in recent years. At present, China's top universities and research institutions are unable to retain outstanding young researchers, and there is a serious shortage of outstanding young talents. The loss of high-level scientific and technological talents, even including the academic leaders in some disciplines, inevitably has a huge impact on China's scientific research and technological development and reduces China's scientific and technological competitiveness and international competitiveness. In The World Competitiveness Yearbook 2000 released by the International Institute for Management Development located in Lausanne, Switzerland, China was ranked the last in the list of availability of qualified engineers and was ranked the second to last in terms of availability of qualified technicians, suggesting that China is extremely short of key technical personnel. This is in sharp contrast to the grim reality of a large high-level human capital outflow. At present, it has become a new investment trend for multinational corporations to set up R&D institutions in China. Such R&D mainly focus on high-tech fields such as software, communications, biology, and chemical industry, with the majority of institutions engaged in industries such as computer, software, and communications. These transnational R&D activities include setting up R&D departments within independent business departments or joint ventures, teaming up with Chinese universities and scientific research institutions, and carrying out work as independent R&D institutions. By directly making R&D investment in China, transnational corporations have attracted high-tech human capital from China to joint transnational R&D institutions, which has played an active role in promoting the openness, cooperation, exchange, and diffusion of the world's advanced technologies. This has offered favorable conditions for China's innovation system to integrate into and adapt to the global system as soon as possible and has also provided a guarantee for the "introduction, digestion, absorption, and innovation" of technologies in China. However, multinationals have shifted their talent strategy from competition in the international market to local plunder, which directly hits China's science and technology innovation system. As domestic senior engineers, scientific research leaders, and other high-end talents switch to the R&D institutions set up by multinationals in China, they are bound to take away the R&D capital with the job-hopping. This will lead to vacancies in key research positions in domestic enterprises and research institutions, the loss of core competitiveness, and a sharp increase in talent training costs, hindering the development and improvement of China's science and technology innovation system. Relevant data shows the following: there were about 1.3 million IT vacancies in North America in 2002; different industries have created 1.6 million technical positions in the U.S., but nearly half of them were vacant; Germany needed to recruit 20,000 foreign IT talents; in Europe, there would be a shortage of 1.5 million Internet talents in 2006 alone. To fill the huge gap in IT talents in Europe and the U.S., multinationals are bound to set up R&D institutions in other countries to attract talents locally. However, in 2006, there was a shortage of at least 300,000 IT talents in China. Based on the current training rate of IT talents, there will still be a shortage of at least 200,000 IT talents every year in the future. The global integrated circuit industry is developing rapidly, and the global distribution of integrated circuit talents is also undergoing development and changes. Judging from the quantity and quality of talents, the U.S. is in the first hierarchy and is much superior to other regions in terms of both the knowledge level and the overall quality of its talents. Japan and RoK belong to the second hierarchy. At present, judging from the condition of talent development in China's mainland, it is mainly at the bottom of the second hierarchy. After years of development, it has cultivated a pool of talents. However, the talent pool, in terms of both its quantity and its quality, is not enough to support the rapid development of the current industries. Not only is there a lack of high-end talents, but there is also a lack of basic talents in the field of integrated circuits. According to an industry white paper titled "2016-2017 Professionals for China's Integrated Circuit (IC) Industry" issued in May 2017 by the Software and Integrated Circuit Promotion Center (SICP) under China's Ministry of Industry and Information Technology, the total number of employees in the integrated circuit industry in China was less than 300,000, but 700,000 were needed to meet the production demand, which means that there is a shortage of 400,000 chip talents. The total number of trained talents is seriously insufficient.[①] As a result, high-tech talents will remain in short supply globally for a long time to come. The establishment of European and American R&D institutions in China will lead to an outflow of human capital in China, which will inevitably seriously hit China's scientific and technological innovation system.

III. The Design of Guiding Mechanism for Human Capital Flow in China

As mentioned above, the international flow of human capital has both

---

① "How to Make up for the Shortage of 400,000 IC Talents," Global Times, Apr. 24, 2018.

favorable and harmful impacts on China's innovation. Therefore, it seems especially important to design a scientific and effective guiding mechanism for the human capital flow that can retain the benefits while avoiding the negative effects, thus promoting the overall construction of China's scientific and technological innovation system. For enterprises, the establishment of a scientific and reasonable incentive mechanism human capital is the key to effective employment and retention of talents. In all the institutional arrangements of enterprises, the fundamental core is the system of property rights, which requires enterprises to establish human capital's status in property rights from the perspective of arrangements of property rights and corporate governance, to ensure their rights and interests as the main body, and to design and improve the equity incentive plans such as appraisal of technology as capital stock and democratic control. On this basis, a series of performance evaluation and reward systems and informal institutional arrangements such as corporate culture and team spirit can be established. This way, the subjective initiative, creativity, and sense of belonging of high-tech talents will be stimulated. Judging from the measures taken by countries all over the world to attract and compete for talents, the talent aggregation effect is a prominent feature of human capital flow, and there is a strong attraction and "self-incentive effect" among talents themselves. From this perspective, enterprises should try to retain research leaders and build a "talent magnetic field" to attract like-minded people around the world. In recent years, a new type of high-tech enterprises has emerged in China. Although the capital, technical foundation, human capital and market of the enterprises are highly internationalized, the main body of the enterprises are based in China, and they are not subsidiaries of any foreign multinational tycoon. For example, the president and the group of technical backbones of Vimicro, which developed China's first world-leading mega-CMOS digital image processing chip "Xingguang Smart No. 1" with China's independent intellectual property rights, are all overseas returnees. Among them, more than 20 are senior experts specialized in software and hardware, multimedia, and network technology from world-renowned enterprise giants such as Intel, SUN, IBM, HP, and Kodak. The two founders of Xinwei Group, which established China's own wireless communication standard SCDMA, came from Motorola's semiconductor department and the University of Texas at Austin respectively, and its research team also has many overseas returnees. Likewise, Semiconductor Manufacturing International Corporation (SMIC), which was founded in the Pudong District of Shanghai, also belongs to this type of companies. At present, it takes the lead in China's chip manufacturing industry. The key to realizing the backflow of talents and curbing the outflow trend lies in the improvement of the domestic hardware and software environment. To establish a long-term mechanism for the backflow of overseas human capital, it is necessary to further improve the domestic scientific and technological innovation environment, effectively establish start-up bases for outstanding overseas returnees, and attract talents to return to China through multiple channels. It also calls for the improvement of relevant laws and regulations, the reform of the distribution system, and the implementation of a distribution system based on human capital that truly realizes distribution based on capacity, contribution, and market pricing. Meanwhile, China should further implement preferential policies for talents in salary and allowance, scientific research funds, housing, insurance, employment of family members, and education of children to clear their worries and allow returnees to retain dual nationality, striving for the free flow of talents between home and abroad. In order to effectively attract overseas elites to return to China, China's influential enterprises should actively implement the "go global" strategy and invest abroad to acquire core technologies. From the wave of Chinese and Indian skilled migrants in Silicon Valley, the connections between Silicon Valley and places such as Hsinchu in the Taiwan region of China, Zhongguancun in Beijing, and Bangalore in India can be seen. It is these migrant engineers who have provided the key connections and technologies that have enabled a lot of high-end human capital to return to their motherland.

Domestic enterprises already have the strength to acquire advanced technologies through mergers and acquisitions of foreign enterprises or the establishment of overseas R&D centers. According to the data from China's Ministry of Commerce, cross-border mergers and acquisitions have become an important mode of outbound investment for Chinese enterprises, often targeting foreign enterprises or R&D institutions that have run into trouble but still boast excellent core assets, especially technologies and human capital. Many domestic enterprises have developed their own core technological capabilities and global brand influence through the above-mentioned approaches. Shang Gong Group, specialized in sewing equipment manufacturing, acquired Germany's Dürkopp Adler AG which ranked third globally in the field of industrial sewing machines and which covered almost all fields of high-end sewing machines. As a result, Shang Gong Group's technology level leapt forward to the forefront of the world. Wanxiang Group, based in Zhejiang Province of China, acquired several enterprises with core technologies in the U.S., Britain, Germany, Canada, etc., and obtained their technology patents, customer resources, and global market networks. Among them, there were even some cases of "apprentices" acquiring "masters." For example, Shanghai Mingjing Machine Tool Company acquired Wohlenberg, a renowned German numerically-controlled machine tool maker, and thus obtained multiple patents, advanced technologies, and the brand name. Earlier, Mingjing had manufactured brand-name products for Wohlenberg for more than 20 years.[1]

---

[1] Xu Helian, Wang Yan and Zou Wuying, "Human Capital and International Expansion of Technology: Empirical Studies based on Import Trade," *Journal of Hunan University (Social Sciences)*, 2007(2): 62-66.

Chapter VIII
Analysis of the Common Interests of International Community

Section I Common Interests and State Interests in International Community

In the globalized era where all countries are facing common global crises, state interests and common interests have become a key issue. We should figure out the connotations of state interests and common interests in the globalized era and the significance of safeguarding state interests and global common interests. In the globalized era, global crises call for the joint efforts of the whole human society, the constant development and growth of international mechanisms and relevant international organizations have posed threats to states, and the advance of science and technology and the rapid economic growth have provided the material foundation for the safeguarding of common interests. Because of the above-mentioned three aspects, the existence of common interests features rationality and practical necessity. By the same token, because state interests are still a major force driving the intercourse in the international community, because safeguarding state interests is a basic means of realizing regional and people's interests, and because safeguarding state interests can reinforce the cohesion among a country's people, the existence of state interests also features rationality and practical necessity. Both consistency and differences exist between state interests and common interests.

A state needs to properly coordinate the relationship between the two by actively engaging in international organizations, pushing for the improvement of the global governance mechanism, striking a balance between principles and interests, and giving consideration to both its own security and the world's security.

I. State Interests Remain Most Important Leading Power in International Community

At this point, the international community is dominated by three major forces: states, inter-governmental international organizations, and non-governmental international organizations. With their legal personality as an indisputable fact, international organizations have played an important role in safeguarding world peace and security, promoting the coordinated development of world economy, ensuring basic human rights, and settling international disputes. There are over 3,000 international organizations in today's world. As the third force in international community, non-governmental organizations have played a prominent role in giving play to their social rights and enabling a more democratic international community. To be specific, they have played unique roles in international legislation and compilation, international judiciary, and the supervision and implementation of international law. However, the advantages of a state lie in its four elements: nation (residents), territory, government, and sovereignty, to which other major forces are incomparable. James N. Rosenau believed that although the pillars of Westphalian temple are decaying, the problem is not serious enough to threaten the status of states as the central unites in world politics. Reasons include the following four aspects. ① Governors have the desire to prevent their rights from being violated. ② In terms of people's political loyalty, there is no transnational ideology that can compete with states in a real sense. ③ From historical experience (and/or the visible possibilities), we know that overlapping political authorities and politically competing loyalties will lead to massive violence and chaos. ④ A set of universally agreed values can produce elements that respect other countries and their rulers. ⑤ A state can offer its people important benefits, namely protecting their lives and providing economic welfare.① Therefore, states protecting their own interests from being harmed fits the current logic of the reality in the international community. International organizations also have their own interests, but they are not a leading force. Even when a state is engaging in the process of integration, there are also state interests behind this engagement. A state joins economic blocs to obtain returns as much as possible while giving out as little as possible or to enjoy the most rights as possible while undertaking the fewest obligations as possible.② The U.K. rejected the suggestion of France, Germany, and other four countries in June 1955 to join the Treaty of Rome because it did not want to be restricted by any regional association in Europe, and even less to establish any form of supranational institution. However, the U.K. started to apply to join the European Economic Community (EEC) in 1961 because the benefits brought by the formation and development of EEC have greatly attracted the U.K. At the same time, the U.K.'s understanding of economic integration has undergone significant transformation, and it started to accept the limited sovereignty transfer and supranational regulation in the process of integration. The U.K. came to realize that the special relationship between the U.K. and the U.S. would not help it establish a leading position in Europe; on the contrary, by excluding itself from a higher level of European economic integration, the U.K. faced the danger of losing its leading position. As such, the overall consideration of political interests and economic interests finally forced the U.K. to make the decision to join the EEC. In this sense, international organization is only a tool used by states.

---

① James N. Rosenau, *Governance without Government: Order and Change in World Politics*, Cambridge: Cambridge University Press, 2008.
② Ye Zongkui and Wang Xingfang, *Introduction to International Organizations*, Beijing: China Renmin University Press, 2001, p. 243.

Realist scholars have illustrated the issue of national sovereignty very well. As Hans J. Morgenthau believed, as long as the world is still made up of states politically, the final language in international politics is state interests. Of course, he fundamentally counterposed common interests to state interests, as shown in his opinion that once the spirit of nationalism has been realized within a nation-state, it will be proved to be fully loyal to the state's interests and exclusive, rather than cosmopolitan and humanitarian. He also strongly belittled the role of international law and international organizations. Neo-realist scholar Kenneth Neal Waltz saw anarchy and self-help system, distribution of rights, the self-interest feature of nations, and survival needs as the core concepts in international relations.[1] In his book *War and Change in World Politics*, Robert Gilpin used assumptions in realism to re-explain the western history over the past 2,400 years. Robert Gilpin assumed that states are principal actors in world politics and carry out cost/benefit calculations when choosing courses of action.[2] For instance, a state would seek to change the international system if it finds that such an approach will deliver more expected benefits than costs. Chinese scholars have also pointed out the following: sovereign countries remain the main actors in the international community; as long as nation-states exist, state interests will not disappear; states pursue wealth because wealth is the absolute basic element of power; states pursue strength because strength is the most reliable means of acquiring wealth.[3]

II. Common Interests Are Fusion Agent of International Community

While international cooperation and international law are important forms of the integration of the international community, common interests are the

---

[1] Alexander Wendt, *Social Theory of International Politics*, Cambridge: Cambridge University Press, 2011.
[2] Robert Keohane, *Neorealism and Its Critics*, New York: Columbia University Press, 1986.
[3] Chen Jianfeng and Ni Shixiong, "National Interests and International Integration," *International Review*, 1998 (2): 8-11.

basis for the formation of international cooperation and international law. As the most important means of the governance of the international community, international law is nothing but a balance of the interest relations among members or subjects of the international community and reflect the common interests among subjects of the international community. Countries come together to form a group for their common interests that enable extensive intercourse among them. Differences in culture, economic structure or political system *per se* do not affect the existence of the international community as one of the basic factors of international law.① The preamble of the Draft Declaration on Rights and Duties of States passed by the General Assembly of the United Nations in 1949 confirmed that states have formed a community governed by international law. Regarding issues concerning transnational crimes and international cooperation, some jurists argue the following: the distinctive feature of international law is being the most universal law; international law relies on the common interests among countries; the existence of common values makes it possible for countries to identity with similar problems.② When explaining how international mechanisms are formed after the decline of hegemony, Robert O. Keohane noted that whether hegemony exists or not, the formation of international mechanisms depends on the existence of common or complementary interests. These interests must be realized by the political actors, which makes actions of common production and joint benefits rational.③ Neoliberal institutionalism represented by Robert. O. Keohane places great emphasis on the role of international organizations, international regulations, and international practices. While acknowledging the importance of the logic and architecture of anarchy, neoliberal institutionalism stresses that

---

① Robert Jennings, *Oppenheim's International Law*, Beijing: Encyclopedia of China Publishing House, 1995, pp. 93-95.
② *See* Henkin L, Conceptualizing Violence: Present and Future Developments in International Law, *Albany Law Review*, 1997, 60(3).
③ Robert Keohane, *After Hegemony: Cooperation and Discord in the World Political Economy*, Revised edition, Princeton: Princeton University Press, 2005.

states can take absolute benefits as the basic consideration and that the international system can reduce the negative impacts of anarchy by reducing transaction costs and uncertainties, thus leading to substantive cooperation among states. Chinese scholars also pointed out the following: integration into the international system can not only contribute to the common growth of state interests and the collective settlement of global issues but also promote overall international cooperation and reduce international conflicts by strengthening the contractual external constraints over sovereign states; for specific countries, they can take a 'hitchhiking strategy' to acquire the various public goods offered by the system for free or with low costs (such as the security guarantee in NATO, loans provided by the World Bank in the international currency system, etc.).[1] Even Hans J. Morgenthau, a power politics scientist, agreed when talking about the emergence of international law that the existence and implementation of international law stemmed from two factors: power distribution (balance of power) among countries and their consistent or complementary interests; without balance of power and common interests, international law will not exist; "balance of power" is the essential condition for the existence of international law; international law can only exist when a balance of power exists among members of the international community, and none of the rules of law will have any power if countries cannot restrict each other; common interests are an objective demand and the lifeline of international law.[2] Judging from the general mechanisms of the emergence of international law, only with the existence of common interests can there be common unity and agreements featuring coordinated wills among members, namely the emergence of conventions. International practices have showed that the international community, consisting of equal parties, has formed some basic values or common interests that need to be protected by international law, and

---

[1] Guo Shuyong, "Integration with International System and National Interests," *World Economics and Politics*, 1999 (4).
[2] Hans J. Morgenthau, *Politics among Nations*, New York: McGraw-Hill Education, 1990, p. 347.

these basic values or common interests constitute the foundation for the establishment and existence of international community.[1] It is generally understood that in the international community, common interests include common interests among states and the interests of mankind. The former refer to bilateral or regional interests, which are also short-term and local interests compared with those of mankind, mainly manifested in economic, political and cultural aspects. While the interests of all mankind are global, sustainable, and long-term interests, such as peace and security, human rights, environment, and the protection of the global commons. In a word, common interests play a fundamental role in the formation of international law, which in turn can enhance the degree of integration of the international community.

III. Common Interests are the Spillover of National Interests

Only the convergence of state interests becomes common interests of the international community. Common interests are always generated through the transfer of sovereignty, with specific forms including international agreements, international organizations, international arrangements, etc. For instance, the E.U. has realized the following: common customs, trade, and commercial policies; common policies of labor and employment, personnel mobility, and social welfare; common transport, agriculture, and fishery; common policies of competition, technology development, and environment; common foreign and security policies, mutual legal assistance, and cooperation in internal affairs. The appeal of common interests has enabled the continuous development and growth of the E.U. In terms of E.U. institutions, the first was the European Coal and Steel Community established by six countries in 1951; in 1957, six countries signed the Treaties of Rome (officially Treaty Establishing European Economic Community and Treaty Establishing the European Atomic Energy

---

[1] Ma Chengyuan, *International Crime and Responsibility*, Beijing: China University of Political Science and Law Press, 2001, p. 415.

Community) and established the European Economic Community (EEC) and the European Atomic Energy Community. In 1965, the European Economic Community (EEC), the European Coal and Steel Community, and the European Atomic Energy Community were consolidated into the European Community. In 1993, the European Community was renamed as the European Union (E.U.). Some scholars even predicted that with the birth of the European constitution, a European federation is well-poised to emerge. The E.U. membership has expanded several times. The E.U. originally had only six member states: Belgium, France, the Federal Republic of Germany, Italy, Luxembourg, and Netherlands. In 1973, Denmark, Ireland, and the U.K. joined the E.U.; in 1981, Greece became a member of the E.U.; in 1986, Portugal and Spain got included; in 1995, Austria, Finland and Sweden joined in; in 2004, Cyprus, Czech Republic, Hungary, Latvia, Lithuania, Poland, Malta, Estonia, Slovakia, and Slovenia joined the bloc; in 2007, Bulgaria and Romania became E.U. members; in 2013, Croatia became a member. As of 2018, the E.U. had a total of 28 member states. The WTO has established common principles and standards that member countries must abide by. These principles include the most favored nation treatment principle, the national treatment principle, the reciprocity principle, and the "special and differentiated" treatment principle. Technical standards and measures include product quality inspection standards, origin standards, health quarantine standards, pre-shipment inspection standards, etc. Regarding sovereignties and national interests, there are limitations on member states in the following fields: tariff and non-tariff barriers, agricultural policies and subsidy policies, investment policies, intellectual property rights, competition policies, environmental policies, and even conventional state-owned industries such as finance, insurance, and telecommunications. These standards and principles are the results of compromises made by member states based on common interests.

The formation of common interests and the spillover of national interests are the results of the interaction between the various factors of the theory that "sovereignty is relative, not absolute" against the backdrop of globalization. Network integration, the interdependence in economy, politics, and culture, and the prominence of global problems are all important signs of globalization. Network integration and the long-range missiles have rendered national borders meaningless. Economic interdependence has forced countries to make compromises on certain aspects of sovereignty and state interests to integrate into a free international economic system. Human rights, environment protection, nuclear proliferation, terrorism, and other global public issues have prompted countries to take common actions. The formation of common interests also conforms to the shift from the absolute sovereignty theory to the relative sovereignty theory. Hobbes, Rousseau, and Hegel, among others, held an absolute view of sovereignty. For instance, in his *The Social Contract*, Rousseau argued that sovereignty is inalienable as it is a reflection of the common good and an expression of the general will, thus being an indivisible whole and cannot be represented.[①] Yet there are many other international jurists who hold a relative view of sovereignty, such as Hugo Grotius, Fernando Savater, Cornelius van Bynkershoek, and Lassa Francis Lawrence Oppenheim. *Oppenheim's International Law*, edited by Robert Jennings and Arthur Watts, expresses the viewpoint that sovereignty is divisible. This book offers examples in three aspects: the first is the existence of states with incomplete sovereignty; the second is that the transfer of sovereignty of E.U. member states has not affected their continued existence as states in international law; the third is that the concept of "international law being binding on all countries" has taken roots in the hearts of people. The relative view of sovereignty is more in agreement with the reality. Most Chinese scholars hold the relative view of sovereignty. Wang Tieya holds that sovereignty is relative rather than absolute because the reality is that international law and state sovereignty co-exist in the international community. Zhao Jianwen argues that the exercise of national

---

① Rousseau, *Social Contract Theory*, Xi'an: Shanxi People's Publishing House, 2004, p. 20.

sovereignty must not harm other countries and must not injure the common interests of all countries or the interests of all mankind. Universally recognized international law represents the international order and the general interests of mankind, and national sovereignty cannot be exempted from the restrictions of international law.[1]

IV. Conflicts Exist between Common Interests and State Interests

On the one hand, common interests are sacrificed under the pretext of state interests. The most typical case is the Iraq War. Hit hard by the September 11 terrorist attacks, the U.S. unilaterally exaggerated the threat of terrorism to the U.S. and believed that the threat came from Iraq. According to the U.S.'s "reliable intelligence," Iraq possessed weapons of mass destruction, mainly aimed at the U.S.. Using this as the main reason, the U.S. launched a war against Iraq. According to Article 51 of the Charter of the United Nations, "Nothing in the present Charter shall impair the inherent right of individual or collective self-defense if an armed attack occurs against a Member of the United Nations." It means that such a self-defense has the premise of being attacked by force. However, an imminent military attack is not a future military attack. The threat or potential danger posed only by bellicose remarks, military mobilization, preparation of attack plans, and launching or deploying missiles, etc., may render it reasonable for a country to worry about its security but cannot become the legal basis for self-defense. The deployment of missiles or nuclear capabilities *per se* does not constitute an armed attack.[2] What's more, this kind of war has not been authorized by the U.N. Security Council. In the preamble of the U.N. Charter, it is pointed out that it aims "to ensure, by the acceptance of principles and the institution of methods, that armed force shall not be used, save in the common interests." Article 41 of the U.N. Charter

---

[1] Zhao Jianwen, "Theoretical Evolution of the Nature and Status of State Sovereignty," *Journal of Zhengzhou University (Philosophy and Social Sciences)*, 2000 (6): 113-119.

[2] Yu Mincai, "Legal Determination of Armed Attack," *Law Review*, 2004 (1).

states, "The Security Council may decide what measures not involving the use of armed force are to be employed to give effect to its decisions, and it may call upon the Members of the United Nations to apply such measures." Article 42 of the U.N. Charter states, "Should the Security Council consider that measures provided for in Article 41 would be inadequate or have proved to be inadequate, it may take such action by air, sea, or land forces as may be necessary to maintain or restore international peace and security."[①] These articles show that for the purpose of the "common interests" of safeguarding international peace and security, the U.N. can authorize its member states to take coercive measures such as sanctions or force attacks through resolutions. Back then, the U.K. and the U.S. spared no effort in selling their idea of using military force to the international community and to persuade major powers to support their determination to use force. However, the international community was unmoved. Seeing that there was no hope for the Security Council to pass a resolution, they could not wait to launch a war against Iraq. Apart from bogging the belligerent states down in the war, the Iraq War also broke the existing international legal order, constituting a serious challenge to international peace and security. On the other hand, state interests are injured under the pretext of common interests, like in cases where states interfere with other countries' sovereignty using human rights protection as a pretext. Using human rights to interfere with sovereignty means criticizing the human rights situation in other countries in disregard of the particularity of human rights and even using economic sanctions, military attacks, and other means to interfere with the sovereignty of other countries. "Neo-interventionism" is a representative theory in this aspect. According to this theory, the major problem facing today's international community is not peace and stability or promoting universal economic development, but the serious infringement upon people's rights on the

---

① Zhou Hongjun, *International Conventions and Practices (Public International Law Volume)*, Beijing: Law Press, 1998.

part of some "unruly" countries and some other "autocratic countries." The theory believes that human rights are the starting point and destination of peace and development, that the international community should not sit watching "humanitarian crises," and that responsible democratic states should take the lead in "humanitarian interventions." Based on this theory, a war against Kosovo was launched. Of course, we have to recognize the fact that the internationalization of human rights exists at present. For instance, one of the aims and purposes of the United Nations is to promote and encourage respect for human rights and for fundamental freedoms for all mankind; countries must abide by international *jus cogens* such as the prohibition of genocide, apartheid, and racial discrimination; human rights treaties recognized and acceded to by states must be observed; humanitarian relief provided for victims of war and famine does not constitute interference. However, using human rights to interfere with sovereignty actually refers to cases where a country does not have any norm of international *jus cogens*, international treaty, or customary international law as the basis, unilaterally takes actions against other countries according to its own human rights concepts and relevant systems, and ask other countries to make substantial changes. This constitutes interference in internal affairs of other countries. Such practices violate the particularity of human rights and the phased development feature of human rights.

In today's international community, state interests and common interests are always intertwined, featuring both opposition and unity. States and state interests remain the most important leading forces in the international community, and state interests are still the basic motivation and starting point for state actions, and international organizations are only tools for states to realize their goals. As the spillover of state interests, common interests are relatively active factors in today's world and are of great significance to international integration. However, the two are in constant contradiction. A proper handling of the sensitive opposition between the two requires giving full play to the supervisory role of international public opinion and international organizations.

V. Measures for Properly Coordinating State Interests and Common Interests

While safeguarding state interests, states should give due considerations to common interests, and strike a balance between common interests and state interests. To be specific, the following measures can be taken.

States can balance state interests and common interests by actively engaging in international organizations. In the era of globalization, the increasing complexity of international environment means that many international affairs cannot be accomplished only by a few countries, and the international mechanisms of international organizations and institutions should be relied on. The overall context propels countries to extensively engage in international organizations and institutions and actively participate in global governance. Of course, in today's world, international organizations are mainly dominated by developed countries. However, developing countries should not retreat but should become more active in engaging in international cooperation while resolutely safeguarding international interests. Relevant international organizations such as the International Monetary Fund, the World Trade Organization, and the World Bank have played a key role in boosting communications between developing and developed countries and realizing universal development. As such, developing countries should not resort to seclusion for the sake of avoiding risks. Though to some degree, in international organizations, the right of speech is determined by a country's overall strength, international organizations can still play a role in coordinating state interests and common interests.

States can build an international environment to coordinate state interests and common interests by actively pushing for and improving international mechanisms. International mechanisms are set up for all countries that participate in international relations rather than just a few developed countries.

A fair international environment is crucial for coordinating the interests of each country and their common interests. Of course, such fairness is by no means absolute fairness, which is impossible. Such an international environment is what the world should strive for in nowadays. Therefore, the international community should push for the reform and improvement of international organizations and mechanisms and respect each other's sovereignty based on the principles of fairness and justice. Especially, developed countries should attach importance to the sovereignties of developing countries. In today's world where peace and development are the two underlying themes, active participation in international organizations and mechanisms will facilitate countries in seeking common development and prosperity.

Countries should pay attention to principles and interests and strike a balance between the two. All the foreign strategies of each state should center on safeguarding its own state interests. That being said, not all matters that are in the state interests of a country will be in the common interests of human society. For example, when the U.S. attacked Iraq, most other states opposed it. However, the U.S. bypassed the U.N. and the E.U. to make inroads into Iraq directly, obviously for its interests in the so-called world hegemony. Though the interests seemed to meet the U.S. state interests, such action violated the recognized basic principles in interstate interactions, thus contrary to common interests. That is why the U.S. failed to convince other countries and people despite its victory in the Iraq War. Thus, we can see the importance of the principle-interest balance in coordinating state interests and common interests. While opening itself to the outside world, China should consider how to balance principles and interests—viewpoints on international hot issues, attitude towards the so-called humanitarian intervention, or, as the world's largest developing country, what opinions China should hold when facing conflicts between developing countries and developed ones. Besides maintaining the basic consistency of principles, China should also advance with the times and firmly safeguard state interests and common interests in order to balance the two.

A country should pay special attention to security and balance the security of its own and that of the world as a whole. Here, security is the primary confluence of state interests and common interests. In the globalized era, countries maintain close contacts, leading to the increasing security dependency—namely, a country's security issue is exerting greater impacts on the security of other countries and even the world. Under normal conditions, the overall strength of a country is an important factor when it copes with security threats. Nowadays, the E.U., APEC and other non-state subjects are playing a greater role in international relations. In the increasingly complex international environment, to gain the upper hand in international engagement, a country should be forward-looking and realize that conventional security means are not enough any more to cope with the security threats it faces, and it should use both conventional and non-conventional means, give consideration to both its own security and the world's security, and coordinate the relations between state interests and common interests. After the Cold War and especially the September 11 attacks, the whole world came to realize the importance and necessity of building a safe world. As such, states started to seek common ground while reserving differences and engage in full cooperation to improve international environment and build a safe atmosphere for international relations. In such a context, concepts like cooperative security and common security have been accepted by a growing number of countries and organizations, and giving considerations to both state security and world security has become a major move in coordinating state interests and common interests. In the midst of a key period of reform and opening up, China should mobilize more domestic forces such as enterprises, social organizations, and even individuals to cope with the security issue, while also making use of important international forces. That is how it can balance both state interests and the interests of mankind.

Section II International Common Interests and International Cooperation

In the post-Cold War period, with changes in the international and domestic environment, countries were bound to adjust their ways of pursuing interests accordingly, and their internal and external policies were bound to change. In order to realize their national interests, states have to consider how to make new value judgments on their interests and what approaches should be taken to resolve the new prominent issues in international politics. Hans J. Morgenthau, founder of the realist theory, stressed that as long as the world is still made up of states politically, the final language in international politics can only be state interests.[1] State interests are the prerequisite for a country's survival and development, the starting point and destination for national activities, and also an important content in the research of international politics. It is generally believed that the common problems facing mankind in the new context have offered opportunities for international cooperation and also constitute the foundation of the universal state interests that make international cooperation possible; after the Cold War, countries have duly adjusted their internal and external policies, thus making international cooperation possible. This book will analyze and discuss the inevitable trend of international cooperation from the perspective of the actual existence of universal state interests.

The most profound change in international politics is the collapse of the U.S.-Soviet bipolar pattern. In world economy, a new round of scientific and technological revolution has accelerated economic globalization. Economic

---

[1] Cheng Yi, Xia Anling, *Cross-Century World Pattern and China*, Wuhan: Central China Normal University Press, 1999, p. 19.

globalization has deepened the economic interdependence among countries. During the process, global issues are becoming more prominent, making profound and lasting impacts on the production and life style of the human society and even the international relations. Inevitably, such historic changes have forced countries to make new judgments and choices regarding some factors in traditional state interests. If we review the policy adjustments and diplomatic practices of major countries after the Cold War, we can see common characteristics in the changes in the focus points of state interests. A clear understanding of these characteristics is very important if we are to understand the development and evolution of international relations, which have state interests as the core, and formulate appropriate foreign policies. After the Cold War, peace and development have become the main aspiration of people around the world. While the world is moving towards relaxation, order, and cooperation, it is also confronting new and grave challenges. As Wang Yizhou noted, a major distinction between the age of interdependency and the age of mutual isolation is that domestic politics is also international politics in a sense. Domestic conflicts often become the blasting fuse of international conflicts directly or indirectly. When a government cannot properly handle its internal problems, those problems will not only harm its own people and their descendants but also harm the people of other countries and even the global environment.[①] Despite declining risks of a world war, there are still local and global crises, such as the nonstop regional conflicts, the increasingly worrying nuclear proliferation and spread of weapons technology, the widening wealth gap, food shortage, population explosion, drug abuse, AIDS, international terrorism, environmental pollution, ecological imbalance, and resource depletion. Most of these problems have transcended national boundaries and have become issues of interdependency, closely linked with the interests of each

---

① Wang Yizhou, *An Analysis of Contemporary International Politics*, Shanghai: Shanghai People's Publishing House, 1995, p. 31.

country. Interdependence theorists believe that the trend of interdependence has dissolved state sovereignty and national interests and propelled the formation of interests of all mankind.① As such, the development of the international community has made mankind become a whole. So to speak, it is the omnibearing influences of global issues on mankind that have made it urgent for governments to jointly resolve problems based on their common interests.

Global issues are the common interests of all countries, Global issues have highlighted the survival and interests of the entire human race and make them more acute. No country or nation can escape the influences and restrictions of global issues.② In the long run, such a scenario means "living and dying together" and "sharing weal and woe together" to some degree. What's more, these problems cannot be resolved with the efforts of only a single country, nor can they be resolved at the expense of other countries' interests. Therefore, a narrow view of state interests should be abandoned and a global perspective should be embraced to give consideration to the common interests of all countries. Countries should communicate with each other and join hands to coordinate their own state interests, make decisions on the above-mentioned key problems that can achieve the maximum realization of common interests, and establish regional and even global mechanisms for coordination, cooperation, and control. That is how a tragic ending of mankind can be avoided. In a word, to solve global issues, we have to consider the whole world and the fate of mankind. Only by doing so can human societies survive and develop. In today's world characterized by globalization, the growing global problems will concern not only the fate of a single country and nation but also the future of all mankind, making common interests all the more important. Many scholars believe that the decision-making of nation-states is showing less

---

① Ni Shixiong, *Contemporary Western International Relations Theory*, Shanghai: Fudan University Press, 2001, pp. 320, 338.
② Cai Tuo, *Global Issues and Contemporary International Relations*, Tianjin: Tianjin People's Publishing House, 2002, p. 441.

loyalty to narrow state interests but more to global interests.① In reality, the common interests of mankind are formed because of the interdependence of people all over the world. It is the growing economic globalization that has made global issues more salient. Mankind's common interests or universal state interests have taken shape. Correspondingly, the focus of people's way of thinking should shift from state interests to the overall interests of mankind. With the advancement of science and technology and the development of international economy and politics, countries have more frequent and extensive contacts. At the same time, they are showing greater mutual influence and mutual reliance in terms of security, economy, environment, and the proliferation of weapons technology of mass destruction. The international community is becoming an increasingly indivisible whole where no country can survive and develop independently. As the overall interests of mankind are becoming increasingly important, countries have to consider the world's common interests when they pursue state interests. The author believes that universal state interests relate to four aspects. The first is security. As economic globalization gathers pace, the security interests of countries have changed, and due considerations have been given to the influences of transnational and global factors. These factors include regional conflicts, terrorism, transnational crimes, and other issues. While considering their own security interests, countries have to consider regional and global interests, which affect their own interests. The second is economy. With economic globalization becoming the underlying trend of the times, the development of transnationals, the formation of a world market, and the internationalization of finance, currency, and capital makes the production of any country become part of the world economy. All kinds of economy penetrate and depend on each other, forming a situation featuring strong integration. For example, the Thai financial crisis in 1997 hit not only Thailand and the whole Southeast Asia but also Europe, Latin

---

① Cai Tuo, "Globalism and Nationalism," *Social Sciences in China*, 2000 (3): 18.

America, and other regions, including some developed countries; besides, the September 11 attacks not only cost the U.S. direct economic losses of around $100 billion but also harmed the regional and world economy. In 2008, the U.S.'s subprime mortgage crisis directly dented global economic growth. In 2018, the U.S. launched a trade war against China and other countries, seriously hampering global economic growth. In his report released on June 2, 2019, Chetan Ahya, Morgan Stanley's chief economist and global head of economics, noted that if U.S. president Donald Trump levied a 25% tariff on another $300 billion of Chinese goods and China counterattacked, global economic decline might begin as early as within nine months. Goldman Sachs also warned on the same day that it was predicted that the U.S. would levy a 10% tariff on the rest $300 billion Chinese imports and all Mexican goods. Therefore, the bank lowered its expectation on the U.S.'s economic growth in the second half of this year by about 0.5% to 2% and greatly raised the subjective possibilities of the Federal Reserve's interest rate cuts.[①]

The third is environment. The modern deterioration of the ecological environment is qualitatively different from the deterioration before the Industrial Revolution. Modern environmental pollution is mainly the industrial and agricultural production emitting different kinds of substances to the biosphere. These pollutants are mainly toxic substances that contaminate waters and the atmosphere, change the composition of the biosphere, and break the ecological balance, thus seriously threatening the survival of all mankind and all living things. Cases of pollution include the severe damage on the ozone layer, air pollution and the resulting acid rain, land desertification, water pollution and the resulting drinking water crisis, forest decline, the greenhouse effect, and species extinction.

The fourth is the threat of weapons of mass destruction. Since the

---

[①] Zhou Zhiyu, "Morgan Stanley: If the U.S. continues to levy tariffs, the global economy may enter recession within 9 months," *21st Century Business Herald*, Jun. 3, 2019.

emergence of nuclear weapons, their destruction power has also been constantly increasing. The monopoly of nuclear weapons has long been broken. Apart from the U.S. and Russia, China, France, the U.K., India and Pakistan also own nuclear weapons. In today's world, several thousand of nuclear missiles are still in combat readiness, and nuclear submarines are still shuttling in deep sea. There are also biochemical weapons. Among them, biological warfare agents produced through genetic engineering may induce new harmful species beyond the control of human beings and the nature, which would bring devastating destruction far greater than nuclear weapons to humans and the ecological system. Once a modern nuclear war and a war using biological and chemical weapons erupt, the entire human race will be destroyed. In brief, with the increasing interdependence between the world and states, the state interests of a country overlap to an increasingly greater degree with those of other countries and the world's common interests. Different from the traditional interests of isolated nation-states, in many aspects, state interests have evolved into universal state interests, namely the world's common interests. The formation of universal state interests has changed the traditional "beggar-thy-neighbor" approach of acquiring state interests, and interests previously obtained through wars can be realized through peaceful cooperation.

With the profound changes in international circumstances after the Cold War, there are also corresponding changes in the priorities of state interests, the means of realizing state interests, and the objectives of pursuing state interests. As such, major countries have all made important policy adjustments in diplomatic practices. A prerequisite for countries to realize their state interests is that other countries also have their legitimate state interests and a country should not pursue its own interests at the expense of other countries' interests."[1] Today, the principle of state interests is the prime principle for

---

[1] Yan Xuetong, *Analysis of China's National Interests*, Tianjin: Tianjin People's Publishing House, 1996, p. 266.

sovereign countries in handling domestic and foreign relations. In terms of the fields that state interests involve, there are mainly three aspects: a country's political interests, economic interests, and security interests. Facing the new circumstances after the Cold War, all governments have made corresponding adjustments over the means and methods of pursuing state interests. Compared with traditional means, they emphasize more on a shift towards obtaining state interests through negotiation, dialogues, and cooperation.

First, the realization of a country's political interests is shifting from an ideological contest to a competition in the overall national strength. The approach of establishing regional economic blocs with ideology as the distinguishing criterion during the Cold War period has been discarded completely, and countries are all dedicated to economic development. After the Cold War, the intensifying regional conflicts and turbulence and the contradictions arising from intense economic frictions between developed countries have become more salient and important compared with the ideological strives in the past, requiring more coordination and cooperation to get resolved. The pros and cons of a political system eventually come down to whether the system and ideology can continuously create conditions for economic development and enhancement of the overall national strength.

Second, the means of countries in pursuing interests are shifting from mainly relying on the military power to mainly relying on the economic and technological power. After the Cold War, countries have remodeled their military policies: the task of military forces is more focused on creating a favorable external environment for economic development, and military deployment and arms building focus more on strengthening the rapid response capability in preventing regional conflicts. As a means of realizing state interests, military strength is becoming more indirect. In dealing with international affairs and pursuing national interests, countries are depending more on the economic and technological means.

Third, the priority of state security is shifting from political and military security to economic security. After the Cold War, profound changes have taken place in the world's political and military landscape, and the international political and economic landscape has shown a trend of multipolarization. The attempt to seek state interests with force has been greatly suppressed; economic globalization has rendered greater interdependence among countries, the importance of economic security is becoming more prominent, and countries are obtaining more state interests through mutual cooperation. As such, countries have to give top priority to economic security among different dimensions of state security. Major powers have changed their strategy of pursuing of military superiority as a means to safeguard their own interests in political and military security.

Finally, as the fundamental interest of a country, national sovereignty has also shifted from being indivisible and inalienable to partially reasonably transferable and shared. After the Cold War, for their long-term state interests, many countries have transferred and shared part of their existing national sovereignties in order to accelerate economic development and implement an opening up policy. For instance, the transfer of part of the state-owned land and resources to foreign capital for development and utilization contains the transfer and sharing of sovereignty. Moreover, global economic organizations and regional economic organizations have developed rapidly. In these economic organizations, member states enjoy many rights and undertake many obligations at the same time. These obligations can restrict national sovereignties to some degree and can be seen as a form of sovereignty alienation. It can be said that the sovereignty theory and practice have undergone one of the most profound changes in international cooperation for the sake of state interests.

In today's world, all sovereign states, regardless of the size of their territories, the scale of their population, their social system, and their national strength, have their own state interests, and all governments give top priority to their state interests. The consciousness of "a global village" is being strongly stimulated, prompting "villagers" (sovereign states) to work to eliminate differences or suppress conflicts, discuss ways of overcoming crises, and intensify the role of international organizations or enhance regional and multilateral coordination and cooperation to avoid the consequences of human destruction caused by people's own behaviors.① State leaders and decision-makers, whether they support the idea of state interests or not and no matter what kind of view of state interests they hold, are required objectively to determine and carry out domestic and foreign policies for the sake of state interests; otherwise, their rule will be destabilized.

After the Cold War, the interests of states exhibit more and more common ground. As economic interdependence increases, state interests start to move from the so-called "high politics" to "low politics."② All major countries are seeking to build a new type of cooperative partnership as they realize that to tackle the functional issues such as proliferation of weapons of mass destruction, deterioration of the ecological environment, and the financial crisis, it is important to establish global cooperation based on global stability.③ The author believes that such stability is premised on the common state interests among countries. In recent years, China, the U.S., Russia, Japan, and the E.U. have adjusted their strategies successively, aiming to build bilateral or multilateral cooperation and enhance exchange in politics, economy, security, and other fields based on universal state interests. Despite occasional conflicts among countries, the countries have eventually resorted to dialogues, negotiations, and other cooperative means to resolve various problems based on common interests. In the international community, the E.U.'s common security policy, the Shanghai Cooperation Organization (SCO) summit, and the security cooperation of ASEAN Regional Forum have offered important enlightenment to the concept of inter-state security cooperation in terms of mutual trust,

---

① Wang Yizhou, *An Analysis of Contemporary International Politics*, Shanghai: Shanghai People's Publishing House, 1995, p. 31.
② Yu Zhengliang, "Changing State Interests and View of State Interests," *Fudan Journal (Social Sciences Edition)*, 1994 (1): 41.
③ Wang Jisi, *Too High to Touch*, Beijing: World Affairs Press, 1999, p. 341.

mutual respect, mutual compromise, etc.

The fundamental objective of international cooperation is to realize the state interests of each country. Interdependence is a prerequisite for international cooperation and can also bring cooperation benefits. Countries are the main units in the international community. Under the premise of state interests, states take a rational approach to assess various benefits and losses and choose appropriate state behaviors to meet their own state interests. Resources in the international community are limited, and countries are vying for them. Yet, the international community is in a state of anarchy. Thus, win-win or all-win can be achieved only by enhancing their mutual interests through international cooperation under the guidance of universal state interests. Robert Keohane believed that interests are an important starting point for research on cooperation. Under some circumstances, cooperation can be fostered based on complementary interests. Yet, common interests among countries can only be materialized through cooperation.① Therefore, with the relaxation and development of the international situation, it is inevitable that international cooperation based on interests will gradually surpass international conflicts.

In general, during the post-Cold War period, amid the great changes in domestic and foreign circumstances, many countries have responded to the trend of the times and made proactive efforts to shift their priorities, means, and methods in realizing their state interests, redefine their state strategies, and adjust their diplomatic policies. In this connection, the system of international relations has undergone profound changes and is moving towards a direction of mutual understanding and accommodation, cooperation, and consultation. Yet, we have to admit that there are still inequality and injustice in international relations. Therefore, while pursuing universal state interests, countries should seek international cooperation under rational institutional norms to equalize the

---

① Ni Shixiong, *Contemporary Western International Relations Theory*, Shanghai: Fudan University Press, 2001, pp. 320, 338.

rights and obligations of different countries. If the international system is too unfair, then international cooperation will only harm the interests of small and medium-sized countries.

Section III Common Interests of Mankind and China's Peaceful Development

I. Major Manifestations of Common Interests of All Mankind

The common interests of all mankind are the major prerequisites and basic conditions for mankind's survival and development. Without these prerequisites and basic conditions, mankind cannot live or their survival will be threatened, let alone development. For this reason, common interests of mankind are mainly manifested as survival interests and development interests of mankind. The prerequisites for the maintenance of mankind's survival and development include space, resources, and the environment. The basic conditions for mankind's survival and development include: the space for the survival and development of sovereign states does not disappear or be compressed because of external aggression; there is a balanced distribution and exchange of resources for the survival and development of all mankind; the environment for the survival and development of all mankind is not extensively damaged. The common interests of all mankind features eternity, universality, irreversibility, super-ideology, and correlation among all interest factors.

Under the theme of peace and development, science and technology is advancing by leaps and bounds; information is being transmitted quickly and conveniently; knowledge economy is expanding with great momentum; and the tide of globalization is unstoppable. Thus, the transform of the world's outlook is happening at an accelerating pace. While seeking their state interests, the vast majority of countries are attaching greater importance to the common interests of all mankind and becoming more fully aware of the interconnection between their own state interests and the common interests of mankind. Because of this, they have started to coordinate their state interests with the common interests of all mankind. Such coordination, which is part of the world's trend of development, is in essence coordinating the world's diversity and homogeneity. It shows that safeguarding the common interests of all mankind is the basis of respecting and developing the world's diversity, which will enrich and sublime the common interests of all mankind. To sum up, the common interests of all mankind are mainly manifested in the following aspects.

(1) The vast majority of countries are working to realize the balanced distribution and exchange of resources for the survival and development of all mankind. Only by doing so can they ensure the sustainable existence of mankind and provide the conditions for common development. It is a kind of "consensus of the majority," aiming to promote the establishment of the order and norms of subsistence and finally bind the subsistence behaviors of all states, thus shaping a win-win scenario where all countries can survive. Such a major interest appeal targets at the harsh reality that the subsistence resources worldwide are limited.

(2) The vast majority of countries call for the scientific utilization of the subsistence resources for mankind, such as the efficient cyclic utilization of renewable resources and the economical utilization of non-renewable resources. They hope to engage in global cooperation for these purposes. At the same time, they believe that effective measures should be taken to forestall global population explosion and to to alleviate as much as possible the conflicts between population growth and resource shortage.

(3) The vast majority of countries argue that the resources for mankind's development should be shared, including material and intellectual resources.

(4) All countries are calling for the protection of the global ecological balance and the environment, stopping desertification, increasing forest and vegetation coverage area, eliminating the pollution of the atmosphere, oceans, rivers, and lakes, and ensuring clean drinking water and domestic water

for mankind.

(5) All countries demand global cooperation to prevent the spread of various diseases and to conquer hunger and poverty.

(6) The vast majority of countries oppose international terrorism, transnational crimes, and the spread of drugs and demand that both the symptoms and the root causes be addressed in order to eliminate these social ills.

(7) People all over the world long for peace, oppose war, demand equal rights to survival and development, aspire for better lives and social progress, and envision a new era of international cooperation.

It should be pointed out that the interest appeals of the developing countries, which account for 90% of the world's population, constitute a huge driving force for the demonstration and pursuit of the common interests of all mankind. The U.N. and other relevant international organizations are also constantly making active efforts for those purposes. Since the 1960s, the Group of 77, the Non-Aligned Movement, the Organization of African Unity (the present African Union), and the Arab League have been calling for the establishment of a fair and rational new international economic order, "which in essence asks for control over their own destinies in subsistence. Such legitimate efforts of the numerous developing countries are still going on. In 1974, the 6th Special Session of the U.N. General Assembly approved the Declaration on the Establishment of a New International Economic Order and the Programme of Action on the Establishment of a New International Economic Order. In December of the same year, the 29th Session of the General Assembly approved the Charter of Economic Rights and Duties of States. The essence of these three documents is to strive for mankind's co-existence and promote the gradual realization of equal development among countries. Since the beginning of the 21st century, we have witnessed increasing North-South dialogue and cooperation centering on the realization of mankind's common interests, and the international community is reaching consensus on the common interests of mankind. The Doha Round of WTO negotiations, the contest between the majority of countries and certain individual countries over the Kyoto Protocol, the development and cooperation issues involved in APEC and Asia-Europe Meeting (ASEM) summits, the worldwide fight against terrorism, the international efforts in debt relief and AIDS prevention for African countries, and the summit dialogue between the G8 and major developing countries all show that the common interests of mankind have transcended the social system and ideology boundaries and become the common concern among different states and nations.

II. Common Interests of All Mankind Face Challenges

In today's world, on the one hand, the common interests of mankind have become more prominent; on the other hand, they are also facing harsh challenges, as shown in the following aspects.

(1) The space for mankind's survival and development is threatened. The major deserts and Gobi belts are all continuing to expand, devouring vegetated land year after year. The El Nino phenomenon caused by global warming has led to not only the dissolution of ice sheets at the North Pole and South Pole but also the shrinkage or disappearance of the Quaternary glaciers on the continents of Eurasia, North America, South America, and Africa. Melting ice sheets and glaciers have generally raised sea levels of the Pacific, Indian and Atlantic oceans, shrinking global land area on a macro scale.

(2) The resources for mankind's survival and development are becoming increasingly scarce. This is mainly manifested in the absolute reduction of non-renewable resources, the predatory destruction of renewable resources, and the unfair distribution and exchange of these two types of resources. For instance, the U.S. is home to about 1/30 of the world's population but consumes 1/3 of the world's resource output each year. U.S. companies and multinationals controlled by U.S. funds control 60% of the resource exploitation rights in the world. From another perspective, developed countries, which account for 10% of the world's population, control 80% of the resource exploitation rights in the

world.[1]

(3) The environment for the survival and development of mankind is damaged. As a multitude of factories in many countries discharge toxic substances into land, rivers, lakes, and seas, only 1% of the earth's water resources are available for human use. Global atmospheric monitoring shows that the ozone layers over the Pacific Rim, the Indian Ocean Rim, and Eurasia have been seriously damaged. The low-altitude air quality in the Mediterranean Sea, Central and Eastern Europe, South Asia, the Middle East, East Asia, and Central and South America is worrying, and industrial acid rain is increasing. The world's largest natural grassland across Russia, Central Asian countries, China, and Mongolia is rapidly deteriorating. Satellite remote sensing images show that in the Sahara region, the Middle East, Central Asia, west China, Mongolia, South Asia, Southern Africa, Oceania, the North American Southwest, and Southern Latin America, wind-erosion and wind-accumulated landforms are expanding at a rate of nearly 0.5% per year, generating more sandstorm sources at the same time, lifting up about 700 million tons of sand and dust every year. Apart from the North and South Poles, Northern Europe, northern Russia, Canada, Central Latin America, Central Africa, and Southeast Asia, 70% of the world's land is undermined by sandstorms to varying degrees.

(4) Some unfair or unreasonable rules in the current international economic order undermine the balanced and equal realization of the common interests of all mankind. For example, in the international production system, the industrial division of labor is still unreasonable, and developing countries are still in a dependent position. On the one hand, western multinationals control the exploration, development, and sale of natural resources in most developing countries, thus deforming the economic structure of the latter and making their

---

[1] Refer to the World Resources Report 2000 – 2001 co-written by the United Nations Development Programme, the United Nations Environment Programme, the World Bank, and the World Resources Institute.

production and consumption subject to the needs of developed countries. The previous international division of labor pattern of "industry from Europe and America and raw materials from Asia, Africa, and Latin America" has evolved into a pattern of "Europe and America developing hi-tech and eco-friendly industries and Asia, Africa, and Latin America introducing polluting and sunset industries." The environmental disasters that occurred in western countries during the time when large-scale was prosperous are now basically transferred to developing countries. In the international trade system, developed countries manipulate world markets with their powerful economic strength. They purchase primary products and low-tech products from developing countries at monopoly prices and dump manufactured products to developing countries at monopoly prices at the same time, causing the trade conditions of developing countries to continuously deteriorate. In the international monetary and financial system, the law of the jungle prevails, which means that the weak will stand as an easy prey to the strong that the winner takes all, leaving developing countries to be exploited. For example, most of the voting rights in the International Monetary Fund are controlled by developed countries, and developing countries can hardly influence any major decision of the Fund. Meanwhile, developed countries directly affect the fiscal, monetary, and economic policies of developing countries through the unlimited expansion of their capital around the world.

(5) Power politics and hegemonism still exist in the current international political order, with developing countries' rights to survival and development being trampled on now and again. A review of the evolution of modern international relations shows that some major global and regional powers have pursued power politics and hegemonism, causing serious consequences. After the end of the Cold War, due to the serious imbalance in the global balance of power, some countries have been more unscrupulous in their pursuit of power politics and hegemonism. Prompted by the so-called "Manifest Destiny" and out of ethnic arrogance and a sense of superiority in institutions and values, they

wave the flags of "democracy" and "human rights" to blatantly interfere with the choices of developing countries in their systems and development paths, classify developing countries into "democratic countries" and "authoritarian countries," and label some countries as "rogue states," "outposts of tyranny," "lawless regimes," and "axis of evil"; they frequently impose sanctions, block and crack down on other countries, and even bypass the U.N. and trample on international law; they even "take pre-emptive actions" to start wars and overthrow the legitimate governments of relevant countries, seriously poisoning international relations. Power politics and hegemonism have become the main sources of the aggravation of the primary contradictions in the world, damaging the common interests of all mankind.

(6) Unforeseen factors in traditional and non-traditional fields of security challenge the common interests of all mankind. Because of the difficulties in eliminating certain unfair or unreasonable regulations in the current international economic and political order and because of the economic, political, and social unbalances among countries, unforeseen factors in traditional and non-traditional security fields have been on the rise, posing threats to world stability and human coexistence. For example, terrorism has been flaring up; weapons of mass destruction continue to proliferate; drug abuse and transnational crimes have become international public hazards; financial crises have broken out successively in Asia, Russia, Mexico, Argentina, and other regions or countries; infectious diseases such as AIDS, SARS, bird flu, and mad cow disease have affected or continue to affect the economic development and public health of relevant countries or regions; earthquakes, tsunamis, mudslides, droughts, floods, insect disasters, forest fires, and other disasters have brought losses to people in many countries.

III. Realization of Common Interests of Mankind Needs China's Peaceful Development

China is a key part of the world. Chinese people's survival interests and development interests are closely linked with the common interests of all mankind. China is a country with a population of over 1.3 billion, accounting for about 1/5 of the world's total, and a land territory of 9.6 million square kilometers. If a survival crisis or civil war happens in China and the government does not have the power to control it, then it will be a disaster for the surrounding countries and even the world. In this respect, Deng Xiaoping had insights and made incisive analysis.[1] In this sense, those who dream of starving more than 1.3 billion Chinese people, those who try to persuade the governments of relevant countries to adopt the state policy of obstructing China's development, and those who clamor for the "China threat theory" in fact desire to see the world be plunged into chaos. In the same sense, any attempt trying to obstruct the subsistence and development of the Chinese people is actually obstructing the realization of the common interests of all mankind. It is true that offering food, clothing, housing, and transportation to more than 1.3 billion people requires a lot of resources, but no country can survive and develop without resources. From the perspective of the development of human culture and world civilization, the material and spiritual wealth created by over 1.3 billion people has rendered the world more colorful and splendid; from the perspective of human's subsistence and development, the whole world will benefit.

The world needs China, and China cannot exist without the world—this is the relationship between China and the world. Just like fish cannot live without water, China is sharing weal and woe with the world. Needless to say, the Chinese people need to live in peace and cooperation; the Chinese people need to develop and have chosen the path of peaceful development. The common interests of all mankind is facing ever increasing challenges and difficulties, and it is imperative for countries to engage in longstanding cooperation. Against such a backdrop, the world increasingly needs China's peaceful development to

---

[1] *Selected Works of Deng Xiaoping Vol. III*, pp. 347-348.

face the challenges collectively and safeguard the common interests of all mankind. The reasons are as follows.

(1) China is a staunch force to safeguard world peace. The Chinese people love peace, as shown in its time-honored peace philosophy. While standing for domestic peace, Chinese people also wish to see "all nations live side by side in perfect harmony," namely "safeguarding world peace and building a harmonious world." Since the Spring and Autumn and Warring States Periods, ideas such as "harmony is most precious," "doctrine of the mean," "benevolence," "righteousness," "ceremony," "don't do to others what you don't want others to do to you," "non-offence and peace," and "universal love and mutual benefit" have become China's mainstream values, not only regulating the behaviors of the Chinese people but also guiding the diplomatic behaviors of all dynasties. The People's Republic of China, born in 1949, has inherited this philosophy and culture of peace that lasted for 5,000 years and has pursued an independent foreign policy of peace. Promoting and maintaining peace, seeking cooperation, striving for equal coexistence, and realizing common development have become the essence of China's diplomacy. When peace is facing serious threats, China has always stood up and defended peace. When opportunities arise for peace-building, China have always gone with the historical trend and promoted its realization. From the 1950s to the 1970s, in order to maintain peace on the Korean Peninsula and in Indo-China, China, on the one hand, spared no expense in national sacrifice to fight with the people of DPRK and Vietnam against the war of aggression launched by the superpowers; on the other hand, China actively participated in the Geneva Conference on the peaceful settlement of the issues on the Korean Peninsula and the Paris peace talks on the peaceful settlement of the Vietnam War, making its utmost efforts for peace and promoting political settlements. China opposes wars of aggression anywhere in the world and holds a clear-cut and firm stand. As a permanent member of the U.N. Security Council, China has firmly advocated the peaceful resolution of crises through political and diplomatic means and

opposed the use of force when major international crises have arisen. In recent years, China has actively hosted the Six-Party Talks aiming at the peaceful resolution of the nuclear issue on the Korean Peninsula, supported the E.U.-Iran dialogue on the nuclear issue, supported the Road Map for Peace in the Middle East, and supported the peaceful resolution of hot issues in all regions. China has implemented the U.N. resolutions and sent peacekeeping troops or police to Cambodia, East Timor, Liberia, Congo, Haiti, and other countries successively, faithfully fulfilling its peace mission and thus being widely praised.

(2) China is an important force in driving the world economy and promoting common development. Since the 1980s, China's economy has grown at an average annual rate of 9%, becoming an emerging market economy that gathers worldwide attention. In 2018, China's GDP was 90.03 trillion yuan, ranking second worldwide; its imports and exports of goods totaled 30.505 trillion yuan, which is the world's largest trade volume; its foreign exchange reserves reached $3072.7 billion, ranking first worldwide; it attracted 885.6 billion yuan of foreign direct investment, becoming the second largest recipient of FDI in the world.[1] Considering the world's economic slowdown for several years in a row, the above economic achievements made by China are especially outstanding. China's annual import demand of more than $500 billion has strongly stimulated the exports of neighboring countries and a number of developing countries and has exerted a positive impact on the economic operation of these countries. China's annual export of nearly $6 billion has provided consumers in many countries with goods of good quality and low prices, saving their consumption expenditure, enabling them to spend more money on tourism, entertainment, and other forms of consumption, and also stimulating the economic development of a number of countries. When the

---

[1] Source: National Bureau of Statistics, "Statistical Communiqué of the People's Republic of China on the 2018 National Economic and Social Development in 2018," February 18, 2019.

Asian financial crisis struck, China adopted a responsible attitude and, while providing aid, kept RMB from devaluing, thus enabling relevant Asian countries to tide over the difficulties one after another. Facing the pressure of RMB appreciation, China has also adopted a responsible attitude and allowed a small floating of RMB, bringing benefits to many countries in terms of macroeconomy. From the 1960s to the 90s, China built many infrastructure projects free of charge for some countries in Africa, the Middle East, South Asia, Indochina, and other regions. These projects, which included railways, dams, highways, ports, hospitals, stadiums, schools, and conference centers, have promoted the economic and social development of relevant countries. In recent years, Chinese companies have contracted a number of residential and infrastructure projects overseas. They have honored agreements in good faith and delivered those projects on time with good quality, thus benefiting the local people. As for the key issue of under what conditions human beings should survive and develop, China advocates promoting the reform of the international financial system and creating a fair, stable, and efficient financial environment for world economic growth. Meanwhile, China champions the building of a multilateral trading system in order to build a fair, just, reasonable, and open trading environment for world economic growth and ensure that most countries, especially developing ones, benefit from it. The above facts show that China's peaceful development is by no means dispensable to the subsistence and development of all mankind.

(3) China is a healthy force in promoting human justice and progress. China respects the diversity of the world and believes that diversity is the basic feature of world civilization and that complementation and exchange among civilizations is an important force driving human development. Never drawing lines according to systems and ideologies, China abides by the international law and is willing to enter friendly cooperation of equality and mutual benefit with all countries on the basis of the Five Principles of Peaceful Coexistence. China opposes hegemonism, bullying, the strong oppressing the weak, and the rich

oppressing the poor. It advocates the democratization and the diversification of development patterns in international relations. It calls for multilateralism to promote global governance. On the issue of anti-hegemonism, China is opposed to hegemonic acts, not to a certain country, still less to the people of a certain country. China has no enemy country in the world. However, in the face of major international crises or events and when confronting power politics and hegemonic acts, China unifies the fundamental interests of its own people and those of the people of the world, decides its own position according to the rights and wrongs, and upholds justice by speaking up for justice; China is not afraid of ghosts, does not believe in evil, and does not yield to high pressure; China defends developing countries' rights to survival and development while also respecting the reasonable rights and interests of developed countries. China follows a foreign policy of good-neighborliness and friendship, strengthens friendly cooperation with neighboring countries, and deepens regional cooperation. China actively develops its relations with developed countries, strives to expand the convergence of common interests, and properly handles differences. China actively participates in international multilateral diplomatic activities and maintains and strengthens the authority and leading role of the United Nations and its Security Council. China has acceded to and ratified more than 200 international multilateral treaties, covering fields such as economy, politics, diplomacy, culture, science and technology, military affairs, human rights, and environment. China has conscientiously fulfilled its treaty obligations and made its own contribution to human progress.

(4) China is a positive force in promoting international cooperation, coping with global challenges, and safeguarding the common interests of all mankind. China does not shy away from all the different kinds of challenges facing all mankind but actively participates in international cooperation and plays a positive role. China attaches great importance to the problems of the living space, living resources, and living environment of all mankind and calls for giving full play to the guiding role of the United Nations Framework

Convention on Climate Change, the United Nations Convention on the Law of the Sea and the Kyoto Protocol. China urges developed countries to take the lead in ensuring compliance and calls for developing countries to fulfill their obligations in protecting the survival interests of all mankind. In order to safeguard the survival and development interests of all mankind, China has engaged in large-scale afforestation, soil and water conservation, ecological protection, and desertification prevention for decades and has restricted greenhouse gas emissions from enterprises at the legal and industrial policy levels, thus alleviating the climate change and maintaining the ecological balance in Eastern Eurasia and Western Pacific from a macro perspective. By spreading eugenics knowledge among the people, China has enabled people to voluntarily adopt birth control measures, resulting in China having hundreds of millions fewer births over the past 30 years. As such, China has made outstanding contributions to the mankind's response to the grim issue of population explosion. China believes that maintaining the stable growth of the world economy serves as the most effective way to promote the well-being of people around the world and also contributes to world peace and stability. It is necessary to solve not only the problem of survival but also the problem of sustainable development, especially the survival and development of developing countries. Otherwise, developed countries will also have a hard time. China has played an active role in the international cooperation against drugs, terrorism, and transnational crimes. It cooperates not only with the member states of the Shanghai Cooperation Organization in the fight against the "three forces" (of separatism, extremism and terrorism) but also with the U.S., the E.U., ASEAN, INTERPOL, and other parties in the above-mentioned cooperation. China has taken an active part in international disaster prevention and mitigation and international philanthropy. In the earthquake-stricken areas in Iran, Algeria, and other countries, as well as in the countries hit by the Indian Ocean tsunami, China's rescue teams have shown selfless dedication to helping the victims regardless of their own safety. Chinese medical teams have performed their duty in Africa and selflessly helped the African people to fight against various diseases. Some medical personnel even gave their lives. All unbiased people in the world admit that China is a responsible country in dealing with global challenges and safeguarding the common interests of all mankind.

Ⅳ. China Will Realize Peaceful Development by Mainly Relying on Its Own Subsistence Resources

In recent years, the development of China's economy and the improvement of its overall national strength have gathered worldwide attention. There are both positive and negative comments. On the one hand, positive comments regard China's peaceful development as an opportunity for its neighbors, the Asia-Pacific region, and the whole world. Farsighted politicians such as French President Chirac, German Chancellor Schröder, European Commission President Barroso, Pakistani President Musharraf, Thai Prime Minister Thaksin Shinawatra, Egyptian President Mubarak, South African President Mbeki, and Brazilian President Lula all believe that China's peaceful development is in the interests of the world. Their views have influenced the attitude of most countries towards China's peaceful development and have given rise to an objective and fair international consensus. On the other hand, negative comments are mainly manifested as the "China threat theory." In recent years, the "China economic threat theory," "China military threat theory," and "new 'yellow peril' theory" have derived from the "China threat theory." According to the "China economic threat theory," China's extensive production with low technology, high resource consumption, and high pollution has accumulated a rapidly expanding economic aggregate and overall national strength, making it a colossus and causing a "power gap" between China and a large number of small and weak countries; meanwhile, China's "dumping spurt" of labor-intensive products overseas with prices below costs has not only impacted the employment opportunities in developed countries but also crushed a large number of national industries in developing countries, thus threatening their economic viability. At the same time, China has imported a large amount of energy and industrial raw materials, leading to a shortage in global resources and a sharp rise in raw material prices, damaging the interests of a large number of raw material importing countries. That is how China has posed "economic threats" to the world. According to the "China military threat theory," China has accelerated military expansion and preparedness, together with frequent military exercises; its nuclear submarines haunt the territorial waters of neighboring countries from time to time; there are many doubts about the announced military expenditure; the tendency of militarism is obvious in the trend of nationalism in China; although no one believes that China will launch a war against the U.S., this does not mean that it will not use force against its neighbors. Among the small group of people spreading the "China military threat theory," there are both senior officials in the U.S. government and hack writers in the Japanese government. In particular, a very small number of Japanese people have gone against the wishes of the majority for Japan-China friendship and against the historical trend, who not only spread the "China threat theory" but also overturn aggression history, stand for war criminals, and pave the way for the revival of militarism theoretically. This trend deserves the vigilance of the Japanese people, the Asian people, and people of the world. According to the "new 'yellow peril' theory," tens of millions of Chinese are rooted in the 100-plus countries around the world and have a strong ability of multiplying and thriving. Thus, after several generations, they may reach hundreds of millions, which will change the ethnic and demographic structure of some countries. At present, Chinese capital have basically controlled the key economic branches of some countries. A few countries even have Chinese people in power or participating in politics. If allowed to develop, this could become a potential disaster. These various versions of the "China threat theory" mentioned above are either derived from the Cold War mindset or from narrow national self-interests. They are not only alarmist talks but have also confused the public and deceived many people.

However, facts speak louder than words. The development of People's Republic of China for more than 70 years proves that China mainly relies on its own resources and the extraordinary creations of its own people to survive and embark on the road of peaceful development. From the early 1950s to the early 1970s, first the Western World headed by the U.S. and then the two superpowers and many of their followers imposed a comprehensive embargo and blockade and a strategic siege on China in an attempt to strangle the newly-born China in its cradle. At that time, even if China wanted to open up to the outside world, it did not have the conditions. It could only rely on its own resources and the hard work of its people to ensure the subsistence of the country and its people and lay the foundation for future peaceful development. From the mid-1970s, the blockade and siege against China began to crumble. A growing number of countries began to realize that no power in the world can starve the Chinese nation to death or hinder China's development and progress and that it is in their interests to develop mutually beneficial cooperation with China. Since the 1980s, China has been open to the whole world and joined hands with more and more countries to collectively meet the challenges for the common interests of all mankind. China's development path is one featuring peaceful development. It is a road with no end because the Chinese nation will live and develop forever. This is nothing unusual, just as all countries in the world are seeking subsistence and development. China's peaceful development is an integral part of the current era of world peace and development. It has the following five distinctive features.

(1) Peaceful subsistence will be the basic content of China's peaceful development for a long time to come. Meeting the food, clothing, housing, and transportation needs of more than 1.3 billion people in China is an arduous task, which is essence an issue of subsistence. The continuous improvement of people's material and cultural lives on this basis essentially belongs to the category of development and is a higher goal pursued by China. However, from the perspective of the Chinese nation's sustainable subsistence and development,

peaceful development is an eternal strategic choice because whether to maintain basic subsistence or to improve the quality of people's lives, it always ultimately depends on whether China can achieve peaceful development.

(2) China's peaceful development, accompanied by the peaceful development of many other countries, is a symbiotic phenomenon in the trend of world progress. From this perspective, peaceful development has become the pursuit of all mankind and constitutes the basis for realizing the common interests of all mankind.

(3) China's peaceful development is the peaceful development of developing countries. If developing countries face obstructions everywhere in their subsistence and development, it will be difficult for the world to see a bright future and the hope of human progress.

(4) China's peaceful development does not constitute a confrontation to the mainstream of the contemporary world system and international order, let alone a threat to the common interests of all mankind. China is part of the developing world. There is nothing excessive for China to call for changes in the unreasonable components of the international economic and political order because such a demand is not only the voice of developing countries but also understood and supported by most developed countries.

(5) China's peaceful development is the realization of development through peaceful means, and China relies on development to maintain peace, including peace in its surrounding countries, regional peace, and even world peace. A peaceful environment is essential to development. That is why China works to promote the peaceful settlement of various conflicts and confrontations. While considering its own peaceful development, China also believes that the common development of all countries is conducive to China's peaceful development. China needs to cooperate with other countries in its pursuit of peaceful development. Such cooperation should be based on equality and mutual benefits; otherwise, it will lose its foundation. This kind of cooperation will definitely lead to the dependency of interests; otherwise, the cooperation will not last

long. China's cooperation with other countries is actually a relationship where parties try to provide what each other lacks and features mutual benefits. Globalization promotes the opening up of all countries, and China is no exception. However, China always follows such a principle: China will forever rely on its own people's creations and mainly rely on its own resources to realize peaceful development. Such an approach allows China to be more responsible for the common interests of all mankind, more capable of pursuing an independent foreign policy of peace, more firm in advocating democracy, progress, and justice, better positioned to strengthen solidarity and cooperation with other developing countries, and better poised to develop an all-round relationship of equality and mutual benefits with developed countries. In a word, such an approach will help build confidence and national cohesion. China is blessed with the natural resources, human resources, and scientific and technological resources needed for peaceful development. In terms of natural resources alone, China is listed as the world's resource powers together with Russia, the U.S., Canada, Australia, Brazil, South Africa, etc. With the rapid advancement of science and technology, especially in the field of resource exploration, China will see continued increase in the prospective reserves of oil, natural gas, iron ore, aluminum, copper and other resources. At this point, China still needs to import oil and some other raw materials, but the proportion is not large compared with developed countries such as the U.S. Many politicians and entrepreneurs in the world who hold an objective and fair attitude believe that the world will not face a crisis in subsistence and resources just because China imports some raw materials. Meanwhile, China is also offering a great deal of subsistence and development resources to the rest of the world. In a word, China's peaceful development does not go against the common interests of all mankind. Just as China's former President Hu Jintao noted in 2005, "China's development has not only benefited Chinese people, but also brought development opportunities to other countries. As China's economy develops, China will contribute more to the growth of world economy."[1] In the 21st century, China will follow the trend of the times and the wishes of the people to cooperate with the whole world for win-win results. Based on its own peaceful development, China will partner with the international community to safeguard the common interests of all mankind.

---

[1] Refer to the written speech of President Hu Jintao at the dialogue meeting with leaders of five countries at G8 on July 7, 2005.

Chapter IX
Countermeasures and Suggestions for Realizing Common Interests

Section I Principle of Common Interests in International Trade Policy

From the 1947 Geneva Round to the ongoing Doha Round, the international community has formulated a series of international trade policies that have functioned importantly in regulating international trade activities. However, while maintaining a normal international trade order, these international trade policies have also exerted different influences on different stakeholders, which means the non-neutrality of international trade policies. From the perspective of economics, international trade policies are a kind of public good with common interests as its value orientation. Only international trade policies formulated by following the principle of common interests will be conducive to the improvement of global or state interests.

I. Common Interests Safeguarded by International Trade Policies

An analysis of the connotations of common interests shows that scholars have mostly emphasized understanding common interests from the unity of opposites between individual interests and common interests. Then what are the common interests safeguarded by international trade policies as a kind of public good? Generally speaking, the formulation and improvement of international trade policies will be conducive to the effective, smooth operation of international trade activities. However, the implementation of international trade policy may exert different influences on different kinds of interests, such as local interests and global interests, common interests and individual interests, the interests of different groups, economic interests and non-economic interests, etc. With a "cooperation method that only requires a consensus in terms of means rather than objectives," we will analyze the common interests safeguarded by international trade policies according to the principle of fair compensation, with tariffs (subsidies) as an example.

International trade policies have impacts on a country's common interests. Though some international trade policies also improve private welfare while enhancing public welfare, in most cases, private welfare and public welfare may conflict with each other, and some international trade policies harm the welfare of the general public for the sake of some industries' interests. International trade policies affect not only social and economic welfare but also social stability and development, such as the protection of infant industries in developing countries and the protection of stagnant industries in developed countries. The protection of infant industries contributes to the growth of national industries. While stagnant industries belong to industries that should be eliminated, if they are allowed to be closed down, it may trigger a string of social problems, such as unemployment of workers, closure of enterprises, loss of capital, and social unrest. So, neither blind protection nor a laissez-faire approach towards the above-mentioned industries will be conducive to social development. The government can levy common interest compensation fund (or auction the protection rights) over protected industries, as a way to balance social and economic welfare on the one hand and social stability and development on the other.

II. Mechanism for Realizing Principle of Common Interests

In order to establish a fair and reasonable international economic order and maximize the common interests, the international community can adopt the following mechanisms.

1. Monitoring mechanism

Total social welfare is divided into indemnity fund and public welfare under the current trade policies. Under such circumstances, the realization of common interests depends on the substitution rate of the two and the utilization efficiency of indemnity fund. If the government spends the indemnity fund on infrastructure, basic research, social relief, and other aspects, it means that the losses brought by the protected industries are made up to the society in another way. At the same time, the development of infant industries and the protection of stagnant industries in developed countries will boost the development of national industries, increasing employment and maintaining social stability; however, if the government does not spend this part of indemnity fund on the expenditure of public welfare, the society's common interests will be harmed even more. Generally speaking, the utilization efficiency of the indemnity fund is related to the government's decision-making and the democratic supervision mechanism. Therefore, it is necessary to design reasonable mechanisms to supervise the collection and the use of the indemnity fund (or the auction of protection rights).

2. Competition mechanism

Whether a country's international trade policies can be recognized by the international community depends on whether these policies conform to the principle of common interests. If some international trade policies are obviously unfair, they will be revised or discarded during the competition among countries. Under normal circumstances, countries consider not only how to benefit directly from international trade policies but also various factors such as their own reputation and their positions in the international order so as to reach international cooperation and collectively sign international trade policies that reflect the principle of common interests. Even if a hegemonic country has formulated an international trade policy favorable to itself within a certain period of time, the cost of this international trade policy as a public good is borne by the hegemonic country while the benefits are shared by different countries. Therefore, other countries may acquire more benefits than the hegemonic country does by "free ride" and gradually surpass the hegemonic country. During the competition among countries, international trade policies will eventually converge towards common interests. Besides, after long-term games, countries may cooperate to formulate international trade policies that reflect common interests and collectively bear the formulation costs of international trade policies and share the benefits from those policies.

3. Game mechanism and incentive mechanism

In a sense, the process of international economic organizations formulating trade policies is a process of mutual game playing. The "prisoner's dilemma" often appears in international trade activities: as stakeholders seek their own interests, the losses of common interests occur, which leads to a negative result for all. A more effective way to resolve the "prisoner's dilemma" is to use the hearing system and establish corresponding incentive mechanisms to prompt all parties to adopt a cooperative strategy. If the interests of all parties are expressed effectively at hearings, the government will be well-poised to set up a reasonable substitution rate and enhance the utilization efficiency of the indemnity fund. For a certain issue in international economic activities, the World Trade Organization would announce a proposal first and then host a public hearing where technical experts, consumers, industry representatives, government officials, and other stakeholders present their views. The statements of points of view by all parties not only reflect their interests but also offer the necessary information for the formulation of international trade policies, thus providing a platform for formulating international trade policies that reflect common interests. For instance, before deciding whether to launch anti-dumping policies and collect anti-dumping duties, a country should hold a confrontational hearing with complainants, importers and their representative groups, representative users, and representative consumer groups. Relevant authorities will make a decision after considering the interests of all parties.

4. Regional economic cooperation mechanism

From the above analysis, we can see that when national and foreign governments offer the same tariff protection for the same industries, the effects of such protection would offset each other, and the public interests here equal to the common interests in free trade. Under such circumstances, the losses in the public interests of this country and its trading partner countries will be minimized. Therefore, if two sides cooperate in the selection of protected industries and the degree of protection, unnecessary losses will be reduced. Besides, such a method can also be used in the reduction of non-tariff barriers. As tariff rates drop, countries formulate different standards and create technical barriers in trade so as to protect their own industries and markets. Differences in standards have obstructed the development of international trade and the realization of common interests. To resolve the disputes caused by the differences in standard requires regular communication and a high degree of trust between trading partners. In this respect, regional trade agreements have promoted dialogues and communication, and it is easier to reach agreements on certain standards within a region. Therefore, countries can first reach consensuses on certain standards and consistency assessments in regional trade agreements and then coordinate among different regions to realize the unification of standards and consistency assessments at the global level. Such an approach will help safeguarding regional interests or global common interests.

Section II Common Interests in Economic Globalization and Countermeasures

I. Economic Globalization and Trend of International Interest Relations

Judging from the inherent requirements of productivity development, the essence of economic globalization reflects the needs of socialization and internationalization of production with highly concentrated productivity. Judging from the internal requirements of production relations, the essence of economic globalization is a trend of international interest relations formed by countries that expand their interests in pursuit of greater self-interests. Marxist economics holds that "everything for which man struggles is a matter of his interest"① and that "[t] he economic relations of a given society present themselves in the first place as interests."② Western economics also regards maximizing benefits as the essence of "an economic man" and the basic logic of human economic behavior. Therefore, all countries, developed or developing, socialist or capitalist, will not violate this axiom of economics in the process of economic development. However, the nature of interest subjects in pursuing interests determines that they will not be bound by national boundaries. When they cannot achieve the goal of maximizing their interests domestically, they will naturally eliminate the barriers between countries and pursue the larger global economic interests. As such, a pattern of increasingly close economic interest relations is bound to form among countries.

Undoubtedly, while driven by international productivity, the current economic globalization has also been boosted by western developed countries subjectively and objectively as they maximize global economic interests. Meanwhile, relying on their economic strength and political influence, these western developed countries have gained greater global economic benefits. As for this rule in world economy, Lenin pointed out that they divide the world according to capital and according to strength and that there is no other means of dividing under the commodity production and capitalist system. For example, developed countries control the information technology foundation and the global economic network for the development of economic globalization, and world financial centers and networks are concentrated in developed countries.

① *Marx & Engels Collected Works Vol. 01*, p. 171.
② *Marx & Engels Collected Works Vol. 23*, p. 379.

The currencies of developed countries are used in global economic activities. The "rules of the game" of economic globalization are mainly formulated by developed countries. Thus, developed countries have naturally gained the greatest benefits in economic globalization. According to the statistics of the annual Human Development Report released by the U.N. on July 12, 1999, under the current development of global integration, seven western countries monopolize the power of economic development; the fifth of the world's people living in the highest-income countries control 86% of world GDP; the U.S. is the country that has gained the most from economic globalization. Data shows that since 1991, the U.S. had maintained a sound trend of economic growth with the co-existence of low inflation and low unemployment for 10 years; during the same period, its capital outflow was $478 billion, its capital input was $733 billion, and the net flow of foreign capital was $255 billion; its two giants, General Motors and Coca-Cola, have risen to the 1st and 2nd among the top 1,000 global multinationals in terms of performance within the 10 years. In 1997, the Asian financial crisis triggered global economic crisis, and countries around the world suffered to varying degrees. Only the U.S. made quite a profit: within less than one year after the Southeast Asian financial crisis broke out, $700 billion flowed to the U.S. from Asia alone. The U.S. took the advantage of the crisis to purchase at a low price the national assets of the countries suffering from the financial crisis, which had greater potential value. Similarly, the E.U. and Japan also gained their own economic benefits through economic globalization to varying degrees. In the process of economic globalization, developing countries can also gain some benefits through "economic globalization." Against the backdrop of economic globalization, many developing countries in Asia have vigorously promoted export-oriented economy to varying degrees and worked to introduce direct investment and other types of foreign capital since the 1980s. Through foreign trade and foreign capital introduction, these countries have accumulated more capital and gained various advanced technologies needed for industrialization, thus narrowing the gap with developed countries in terms of technology. That is why they can leverage the advantages as "latecomers," shift from exporters of primary products to exporters of manufactured goods in a short period of time, and become emerging industrialized countries. What's more, during a timeframe of some 10 years, they have maintained fast economic growth. A typical case is China, which has gained huge benefits by engaging in economic globalization through reform and opening up.

However, it is obvious that compared with developed countries, developing countries have gained very few economic benefits in the process of economic globalization. As shown in the United Nation Development Programme (UNDP)'s Human Development Report released in 1999, less than 20 developing countries have benefited from economic globalization, and in 80 developing countries, the personal income level is lower than the level 10 years ago.

Both developed and developing countries have obtained corresponding benefits through economic globalization to varying degrees. In the process of economic globalization, this distribution of benefits is uneven. Developed countries are at an advantageous position and benefit more, while developing countries are often at a disadvantageous position and benefit relatively less.

II. An Institutional Interpretation of Benefit Distribution

1. Market structure of incomplete competition

The so-called complete competition is only a special case of "incomplete competition." The market structure in today's international community basically features monopolistic competition or oligopoly. The law of economies of scale has greatly reduced production costs and enhanced economic benefits. Because of this, together with the government's protectionist policies, in reality, most market shares are monopolized by a small number of enterprises. For example, the world's automobile market is controlled by several multinationals such as Toyota, GM, and Mercedes-Benz. In foreign investment, multinationals are the main investors, accounting for some 80% of the world's total foreign investment; in world trade, the trade volume of 100 super-large multinationals accounts for about 1/3 of the world total; in international technical payments, 70% are carried out within multinationals. Since multinationals control the world's economic lifeline, in setting the prices of goods and labor, their prices are always higher than marginal costs. That is how they gain excess profits. Under the reality that developed countries have the vast majority of large multinational corporations, such a pattern of production, trade, investment, and technology transfer naturally enables developed countries to obtain more economic benefits than developing countries.

2. Unbalanced distribution of political and economic power in international economic and political system

The varied political and economic strength of countries leads to their different positions in the international economic and political system. The U.S., Japan, and the E.U. have cultural and scientific dominance, technological advantages, military hegemony, economic welfare, and the ability to transform the world economy and society. They occupy the dominant positions in the international economic and political system, enjoy greater power, and control world organizations such as the WTO, the World Monetary Fund, the World Bank, and the United Nations. Just as the U.K. professor Susan Spann analyzed, in the basic power structures and the hierarchical power structures of the international economy, be they the safety, production, finance, and knowledge structures that belong to the former or the transportation, trade, energy and welfare structures that belong to the latter, developed countries always hold the controlling positions. They decide the formulation of rules and supervise their implementation; they also determine the organizational goals as vehicles of rules. After the Second World War, the U.S. grew into a super power and led the establishment of the International Monetary Fund and the World Bank according to its own interests. With the largest share of contribution, the U.S. has held a dominating position. Now, the two organizations have spread the neo-liberalism of the U.S. to all parts of the world. They connect "assistance" to developing countries with new-liberal policies, reduce tariffs, privatize state-owned enterprises (SOEs), implement strict financial budgets, and stabilize exchange rates, making international financial organizations serve as its tools of resolving the world's economic problems.

3. States intervene in international economic activities

Since Adam Smith, western capitalist countries have implemented policies of economic liberalism where states do not interfere in economic activities. After the Second World War, Keynesianism prevailed, and states intervened in the economy, implemented new forms of trade protectionism and strategic trade policies, created tariff and non-tariff barriers, and restricted the flow of technology and knowledge. The reasons for such intervention are as follows: the first is the internal motivation of maximizing state interests; the second is the pressure from domestic interest groups. In fact, state interests are consistent with the interests of multinationals. The interests of states and multinationals are intertwined, resulting in a trend of confrontation with the market mechanism, and new alliances between companies and states have been formed. The core of these alliances is that corporations demand their states make timely response to economic globalization for the sake of the globalization of themselves, while state governments offer various conditions for the globalization of the corporations for the sake of their own legitimacy and authority. Some scholars have argued that economic globalization weakens the power of governments. Such an argument lacks scientific basis. In today's world, governments formulate rules and create the environment for economic operations on the one hand and serve the public on the other hand. Huge changes in the public expenditures of developed countries reflect a stronger role of the governments. Data shows that the proportion of government expenditures in GDP in developed countries rose from 10% in 1913 to 45% in 1996, which shows that economic globalization has strengthened government power, and as a result, developed countries' intervention in economic activities has become more obvious and powerful. In the process of China's accession to the WTO, what the U.S. and E.U. did was a typical example. During the 14 years, they spared no effort in raising the threshold for China's accession to the WTO, aiming to create favorable competition conditions for their enterprises in the future economic globalization so as to obtain more state benefits. Polarization continues to intensify around the world. French scholar Jacques Ada calculated the international differences in per capita income worldwide and figured out the per capita GDP of all countries and regions in 1996: the U.S., 100; Japan, 86; Europe, 71; the Four Asian Tigers, 67; China, 13; South Africa, 4. How to explain the facts? Obviously they reflect the reality of today's international politics and economy, involving not only economic issues but also institutional factors, making some countries gain more and others less.

III. Vigilant of Deglobalization's Harms to Common Interests

At present, the tide of deglobalization is eroding the concept of coexistence. Going against globalization, deglobalization obstructs the global flow of production factors, not only estranging global cultures but also triggering international conflicts. Brexit and other events are prominent examples of deglobalization. Advocating "America First," U.S. President Donald Trump has exited several international multilateral organizations and agreements such as the Trans-Pacific Strategic Economic Partnership, the Paris climate agreement, UNESCO, and the Global Compact for Safe, Orderly and Regular Migration, pushing deglobalization to a climax. Deglobalization has greatly obstructed global governance and harmed the basis of common interests.

Although the U.S. talks a lot about "rules" and "order," it has adopted unilateralism, protectionism, and hegemonism in its actions. Only two years in office, Trump has already quitted several U.N. organizations and international agreements, including the Trans-Pacific Partnership, the Paris climate agreement, UNESCO, and the Global Compact for Safe, Orderly and Regular Migration (see Table 9-1). In 2018, he successively withdrew from 10 organizations or treaties including the Iran nuclear deal, the United Nations

Human Rights Council, and the Intermediate-Range Nuclear Forces Treaty. More than 190 countries have signed the Paris Agreement, and the U.S. withdrew from it. The Iran nuclear deal (formally the Joint Comprehensive Plan of Action) was approved by the U.N. Security Council, and the U.S. withdrew from it. The U.S. has also withdrawn from other international organizations such as UNESCO and the United Nations Human Rights Council. The U.S. is an important member of the WTO, but it openly violates multilateral trade rules and frequently uses and brandishes "tariff sticks." At the Munk Debates held in Toronto on May 9, 2019, Kishore Mahbubani, former president of the U.N. Security Council, publicly criticized that the greatest threat in the world came from the U.S.[①]

Table 9-1　Organizations and Agreements that Trump Administration Has Exited or Threatened to Exit

Name	Member(s)	Time of Exit	Reason for Exit
U.N. Industrial Development Organization (UNIDO)		December 4, 1995	Domestic budget difficulties
U.N. World Conference against Racism		September 3, 2001	Opposition to Israel emerged at the meeting
Rome Statute of the International Criminal Court		August 10, 2002	The U.S. tried to reach immunity deals with the U.K. and dozens of other countries to protect its citizens from prosecution
Trans-Pacific Partnership (TPP)	12 countries including the U.S.	January 23, 2017	America's manufacturing industry was hit
Paris climate agreement	Signed by more than 190 contracting parties around the world and ratified by more than 180 contracting parties	June 1, 2017	Other countries benefited and the U.S. suffered

(To be continued)

---

① "Kishore Mahbubani: The greatest threat in the world comes from the United States, not China," *Reference News*, May 21, 2019.

(Continued)

Name	Member(s)	Time of Exit	Reason for Exit
UNESCO	193 global members	October 12, 2017	Arrears; the organization has "prejudice" against Israel
Global Compact for Safe, Orderly and Regular Migration	193 U.N. members	December 2, 2017	The agreement runs counter to U.S. domestic policies
Iran nuclear deal	Iran, the U.S., Russia, China, the U.K., France, Germany	May 8, 2018	The agreement cannot prevent Iran from continuing its ballistic missile program and supporting terrorism
U.N. Human Rights Council	47 members	June 19, 2018	The organization has "prejudice" against Israel and cannot effectively protect human rights
Vienna Convention on Diplomatic Relations	192 parties	October 3, 2018	Response to Palestine filing a complaint against the U.S. with the International Court of Justice
Treaty of Amity, Economic Relations, and Consular Rights (also known as U.S. Friendship Treaty with Iran)		October 2018	Iran filed a "groundless" complaint with the International Court of Justice, challenging U.S. sanctions
Universal Postal Union	192 members	October 17, 2018	The organization's international postal tariff rules hurt American businesses
Intermediate-Range Nuclear Forces Treaty	U.S., Russia	February 2, 2019	Russia violated the treaty, undermining the possibility of improving relations between Washington and Moscow
Arms Trade Treaty (ATT)	130 signatories	April 26, 2019	The treaty gives foreign agencies the right to restrict U.S. citizens from possessing rifles.
U.S.- Korea Free Trade Agreement	The U.S. and Korea		The agreement has caused a trade deficit between the U.S. and Korea
North American Free Trade Agreement (NAFTA)	The U.S., Canada, Mexico		The agreement causes U.S. trade deficit
World Trade Organization (WTO)	164 members		Unfair to the U.S.

Source: news reports.

IV. China's Strategy in Participating in Economic Globalization

Economic globalization is a vehicle for the common interests of all countries. Both developed countries and developing countries engage in economic globalization and leverage their comparative advantages to gain corresponding benefits. Because of the intervention of institutional factors, institution internalizes benefits and externalizes costs, making the benefits of economic globalization relate to the international political and economic systems. Thus, we can formulate the strategy in the process of economic globalization.

First, an institutional framework that adapts to economic globalization should be built to ensure that domestic subjects of interests can participate in economic globalization and strive to gain benefits. We should encourage enterprises and other subjects of interests in the whole society to participate in economic globalization and maintain people's participation in economic globalization through a series of specific institutional arrangements; while introducing foreign capital, China should also encourage enterprises to make investment overseas, aiming to gain investment benefits in the global economic space; China should renew its efforts in opening up to create conditions for further participation in economic globalization.

Second, China should work to form its own advantages in export products and participate in the process of economic globalization. China should export more labor-intensive products. China's textile and clothing industry has export advantages, which should be harnessed to boost the export of relevant products. The government should fully deploy the facilitation and coordination role of industrial associations, coordinating home enterprises while also intensifying the combination and merger with multinationals, to promote the formation of oligarchic enterprises and enhance their competitiveness. China should foster high-tech enterprises as soon as possible, enabling them to own original achievements with intellectual property rights, get industrialized gradually, and establish overseas presence. Too much focus on the development of labor-intensive industries will not be conducive to the development of major industrial sectors at home. If that happens, China will always be a second-rate industrial country in economic globalization and cannot occupy a place in the high-tech field, and the goal of catching up with and surpassing developed countries will just be empty talk. The state should help enterprises that have advantages in the high-tech field to establish a system of venture capital in science and technology as soon as possible so that they can have original intellectual property rights and quickly become a new force in overseas investment.

Third, China should actively engage in multilateral cooperation organizations and international organizations to increase China's voice and influence in economic globalization. At present, developed countries have manipulated and controlled the formulation of international systems and rules, while developing countries are excluded. As a result, the formulation of the systems and rules lacks equality, democracy, fairness, and transparency, making the formulation of international economic systems and rules to the detriment of developing countries. The more a country breaks away from the development trend of world economy, the more it lacks a say in the formulation of international economic systems and rules. Therefore, we should try every means to join the existing international organizations and strive to become the initiators of the international organizations to be established soon or in the future. We cannot be held hostage to the promise of "non-alliance" and must form economic alliances.

V. China's Policy Choice to Deal with Cross-Border Flow of Global Talents

Generally speaking, developing countries, including China, are countries with talent outflow, while developed countries, led by the U.S., are countries with talent inflow. For countries with talent outflow, on the one hand, they bear huge losses of human capital and other related economic losses because of the outflow; on the other hand, talent outflow facilitates economic exchange among countries, and the backflow of talents will boost economic development in the outflow countries. Therefore, China and other developing countries should realize the importance of talents, introduce targeted measures to reduce talent outflow and bring in various kinds of talents urgently needed for economic development, work to facilitate the backflow of talents, and draw on its advantages and avoid its disadvantages to accelerate national economic development and enhance the technology level at home, thus narrowing the gap with developed countries in terms of economy and technology.

Judging from the reality of China's economic development, currently, China has emerged as the world's second largest economy. However, both China's economy and trade are "huge in size but weak in strength." That is to say, China's economic size and trade volume are huge, but the quality should be further improved. The key problem is that China lags far behind developed countries in terms of production technology, product brands, enterprise competitiveness, industrial competitiveness, education level, etc. To solve these problems, the key lies in talents. With the ever deepening economic globalization, the easier flow of international production factors, and China's further opening up, China will face fiercer international economic competition, and talents will be a core element for the transformation and development of China's economy. Thus, reducing talent outflow, introducing foreign talents, and bringing back Chinese talents will be some harsh challenges that Chinese government need to tackle with.

(1) The state and local governments should give top priority to the issue of talents, and governments at all levels should formulate talent strategies as soon as possible that are in line with local economic development and the development trend of the world talent market. A key aspect of the ever fiercer international competition is competition in science and technology, which is determined by top-notch talents. The competition in science and technology is ultimately competition in top-class talents. The factor of talents and the

corresponding technology factors are becoming decisive factors in economic development. Thus, all countries are sparing no effort in attracting talents. At this point, global competition for talents has risen from the enterprise level to the state level. The quantity and quality of talents a country possesses are important factors affecting its economic development and directly affect its international status. As China is at the crucial stage of economic transition and development, talents and technology are the key factors for China's successful economic transition and development.[①] Therefore, the central and local governments must attach great importance to the issue of talents, and governments at all levels should formulate talent strategies as soon as possible to meet the needs of local economic development and the development trend of the world talent market. They should work to retain domestic talents and reduce talent outflow, introduce as many foreign talents as possible, and facilitate the backflow of Chinese talents.

(2) To reduce talent outflow, it is important to offer higher salaries and better work environment for Chinese talents, especially high-end talents, invest more in education, and enhance the quality of China's higher education. There are two major reasons for China's talent outflow: the first is the relatively low salaries and poor work environment; the second is the relatively low level of education at home. Among all talents, the most mobile are technical experts with certain academic qualifications and professional skills. Such talents include scientists, engineers, and R&D personnel. Possessing expertise and mastering the advanced technologies in the industry, they have a wider range of choices and broader development space, thus more employment choices. The demand for such talents in foreign countries is also the biggest, and all countries have offered preferential policies for these talents in terms of migration and visa to facilitate their outflow. The outflow of these talents is mainly caused by low

---

[①] Shen Kunrong and Sun Wenjie, "Factor Analysis of Economic Growth: Based on China's Experience," *The Journal of Jiangsu Administration Institute*, 2009 (2): 52-56.

salaries and poor work environment. As such, China can explore methods of distribution by factors of production such as technology and management and gradually form distinctive distribution and incentive mechanisms for various industries that focus on performance and contributions and value outstanding talents and key positions so as to enhance the salaries and work environment for such talents. It is worth mentioning that this kind of talent outflow is only a small part of China's overall talent outflow. Overseas students are a major part of China's talent outflow, for which the relatively low quality of China's higher education should be blamed. Therefore, the Chinese government should invest more in education and improve the performance of its higher education as a way to reduce talent outflow.

(3) To bring in foreign talents and accelerate the backflow of talents, it is important to improve the relevant policies to attract overseas talents and build an enterprise-oriented talent system. Enterprises are the most direct force in national economic construction and also the largest place to accommodate talents. Thus, the Chinese government should build a talent-attracting system that is talent-featured, enterprise-centric, and market-oriented with industry-university-research combination. Such a system enables enterprises to become the major body of R&D investment, technical innovation, and the application of innovation achievements and comprehensively enhances the ability of enterprises and talents to innovate independently. In the past, the majority of China's students who had studied abroad chose to work in institutions of higher education and research institutes after returning home. However, these institutions' ability of accommodating talents is limited. With the advent of the knowledge economy and the adjustment of China's industrial structure, it is necessary for enterprises to become the major body of R&D. Therefore, guiding domestic enterprises to develop and utilize overseas talents and making them the new players is the development trend in China's developing and utilizing overseas talents. Chinese enterprises are still weak in terms of R&D and need a large number of technology talents. Under such circumstances, China's relevant departments

should actively help overseas talents in building entrepreneurship platforms at home, offer more subsidy to returned overseas students, and formulate policies to guide and help enterprises in bringing in overseas talents. For instance, enterprises that bring in overseas talents can enjoy tax relief and access R&D funds. Such an approach can help bringing in foreign talents and bringing back Chinese overseas students. It can also enable enterprises to grow both in size and in strength and enhance their production technology, which is in line with the direction of China's economic transition and development.

Ⅵ. Strategies for China's Engagement in International Technology Transfer

1. Expanding international channels of technology transfer

In the analysis of technology transfer, there are disputes among many economists regarding the methods of technology transfer and whether technical innovation and economic development of developing countries and their home enterprises bear great importance.

Some people argue that the technology transfer channels have great significance. In the 1960s-1970s, it was generally believed that some technology transfer channels were superior to others in terms of emulating. The main rationale was that the more ownership foreign enterprises hold, the more its social costs will be greater than its social benefits. The selection of technology transfer channels is based on the inversely proportional relationship between costs and ownership. According to the amount of benefits brought to the technology recipient, the choices can be divided into direct purchases, licenses, turn-key factories, imports of capital goods, venture syndication, and international direct investment in sequence. With such a sequence, the suitability of the transferred technology is gradually increasing, but some informal transfer channels and alliances are neglected. When costs are seen as the most important factor in technology transfer, the learning potential of the technology transfer channel should also be considered because the transfer mechanism used for the transferred technology has important influences on the extent to which the technology can be absorbed. Parker and Kamu suggested that a set of analysis rules should be developed from the perspective of developing countries to assess the various technology transfer channels. Such assessment should contain a balance between the ability of introducing technologies and that of absorbing the latest technological knowledge. Regardless, the objective of empirical analysis is to prove the importance of technology transfer channels.

Some other people believe that the selection of technology transfer channels is of secondary importance. They support such a view with facts from two aspects: from the micro level, research shows that the implementation ability in the process of technology transfer is more important. That is because gaining technological benefits from foreign technologies relies more on the implementation of the selected channels rather than the selection of channels; from the macro perspective, it is difficult to judge the success or failure of the technology transfer in a host country only from the perspective of the transfer channel. The secondary importance of technology transfer channels is especially obvious from the macro level. Particularly in fast growing economies, with the enhancement of the absorbing capacity of the economies, many factors that are very important in a still framework will become less important. In such economies, enterprises and policy-makers are more concerned with the dynamic development potential of certain technologies rather than the short-term costs.

The middle ground is that technology transfer channels are exclusively owned by enterprises to a large extent. It is difficult to sum up the general rules applicable to technology transfer, and the space for policy continuity applicable to certain technology transfer is also limited. The selection of technology transfer channels should be determined according to the features (mature or complex) and the accessibility of the technology. The combination of the special factors of companies, industries, and states matters greatly to the selection of technology transfer channels, a conclusion that has been verified by many empirical research projects. Some scholars believe that the following factors have an important impact on the selection of technology transfer channels: the competition that the supply manufacturer faces, the age of the transferred technology, the nature of the transferred technology, and the importance of technologies to the supply manufacturer.

Research on technology transfer channels shows that the environment and the model of transnational technology transfer are still at the stage of exploration. Yet from the practical perspective, it is of practical significance in terms of spreading risks for developing countries to utilize multiple channels in the process of international technology transfer. With the passage of time, the roles of various transfer channels are also constantly changing in different countries and industries. Furthermore, non-leading technology transfer channels such as exports, imports of capital goods, subcontracting, and alliances cannot be ignored either in the technology transfer in developing countries. Therefore, as the largest developing country, China should attach great importance to expanding the channels of international technology transfer.

2. Valuing the position of organizational changes in international technology transfer

Along with the increase in the knowledge content of new technologies and the complexity of technological changes, the main difficulty in implementing new technologies is not technical but organizational. Following such a view, Kaplinsky believed that technological changes mainly happen in organizational fields. Kaplinsky also believed that the introduction of new technologies must coordinate with organizational changes and that otherwise, important learning opportunities would be lost.

Huge potential exists behind technological changes, which do not entail too much capital. Normally, what limit changes is not the ability to access the technology but how to effectively use it. Whatever the nature of organizational changes is, they are less accessible in comparison with material technologies.

The enhancement of efficiency in each link is related to organizational changes. For example, if there is no suitable organizational structure for the introduced technology in the process of application, it is difficult to avoid the inefficiency of idle technology in production. From the perspective of technology transfer policies, organizational changes reflect the limitations of focusing on material technology policies and the importance of using organizational changes to facilitate the technology transfer mechanism. As such, in order to narrow the gap with developed countries, developing countries should not only engage in international technology transfer but also promote relevant organizational transfer.

3. Reducing transaction costs of participating in international technology transfer

Since the concept "transaction cost" was proposed by Ronald H. Coase, there appears a large amount of literature that expands the contents of transaction costs to explain many problems in the reality. Generally speaking, transaction costs consist of coordination costs, information costs, and strategy costs. Coordination costs are the sum of time capital and personnel costs in aspects such as investment negotiation, supervision, and agreement implementation. Information costs are the costs of information gathering and organization and the error costs caused by the lack of knowledge or the ineffective mix of general scientific principles. Strategy costs are the increased costs caused by situations where individuals take the advantage of the asymmetric distribution of information, power, and other resources and gain benefits at the expense of others' interests, such as free-riding, rent-seeking, and corruption.

The establishment of the concept of transaction cost is of special importance to the understanding of the relation between costs and behaviors in international technology transfer. Transaction costs vary under different system structures of international technical transfer. If we cannot reduce transaction costs by selecting behaviors and systems, it will be impossible to realize Pareto optimality and effectively regulate the behaviors of "an economic man."

Therefore, developing countries intervene in technology transfer policies and policy implementation, and the effect of policy implementation highly relies on the transaction costs of the governments' implementation of the policies. For policies with the same contents, there should be no difference in their impacts on final results. Yet for policies with the same standard, because of differences in the transaction costs of implementation, the final results will be sharply different. Policies with the same standard will lead to different results because of different transaction costs of the implementation of state policies and different national backgrounds.

At present, the majority of developing countries are faced with technology scarcity, and their economic development requires a large input of technological factors. Therefore, it would be necessary to introduce advanced foreign technologies for a long period. That is the same with China. It is also necessary for a country to consider the fields of strategic importance to national development when determining their foreign capital policies. Before capital accounts are fully open to the outside world, it is also necessary to review foreign-related projects. However, in this respect, developing countries have also learned painful lessons. Over the past 20 years, capital flight in Asia and some South American countries has taken a heavy toll on the local economies. However, excessively strict and tedious reviews will only drive the rise of transaction costs, making small and middle-sized multinationals lose out many business opportunities and obstructing developing countries' technology introduction. Therefore, efforts should be made to streamline the review and approval system and enhance the transparency of the system. Furthermore, the review and approval of technology introduction should be different in the procedures and conditions from the review and approval of ordinary projects. Meanwhile, foreign exchange control, taxation on investors, and other aspects should be institutionalized and be made transparent. These measures will reduce the transaction costs for China to engage in international technology transfer and finally increase the benefits from participating in international technology transfer.

Section Ⅲ International Economic Order and the Realizing of Common Interests

As economic globalization accelerates and its connotations extend, both its positive and negative influences are becoming more salient, especially widening the wealth gap, which has drawn serious attention of the international community and developing countries. Former U.N. Secretary General Kofi Annan noted, "in an age when globalization and new technology are bringing hitherto unimaginable benefits to one part of humankind, it is shameful and unacceptable that another part—and by most reckonings the larger part—remains excluded from those benefits, subjected to a life of grinding poverty often accompanied by malnutrition and disease."① A growing number of countries are urging for the reform of current international agencies and rules and the gradual establishment of a new international political and economic order that is fair and reasonable so as to make economic globalization conducive to the world's economic and social development and the realization of common prosperity around the world.

Ⅰ. Consensus and Differences

Before the First World War erupted in 1914, there were no "international rules" in economic globalization. In this context, western powers arbitrarily plundered the human and natural resources of Asian, African, and Latin American countries and regions. In 1945, after the Second World War, the World Bank, the International Monetary Fund, the General Agreement on Tariffs and Trade, the World Trade Organization, and relevant international

---

① "'Shameful' to Exclude Part of Humanity from Globalization's Benefits, Says Secretary-General in Address to Headquaters Meeting," SG/SM/7363, April 18, 2000.

rules were established successively. However, those international institutions and rules were established and formulated with western countries playing the dominating role and thus were favorable to those western countries. The international political and economic order was still unfair and unreasonable.

With the efforts of developing countries, on May 1, 1974, the Sixth Special Session of the U. N. General Assembly passed the Declaration on the Establishment of a New International Economic Order. According to the Declaration, the international community shall "work urgently for the establishment of a new international economic order based on equity, sovereign equality, interdependence, common interest and cooperation among all states, irrespective of their economic and social systems which shall correct inequalities and redress existing injustices, make it possible to eliminate the widening gap between the developed and the developing countries and ensure steadily accelerating economic and social development and peace and justice for present and future generations." On December 12 of the same year, the U.N. General Assembly passed the Charter of Economic Rights and Duties of States, which stressed "the need for strengthening international cooperation for development."

When Chinese leader Deng Xiaoping met with Sri Lankan President Ranasinghe Premadasa on September 21, 1988, he noted that a new international economic and political order should be established. When he met with the delegation of the Japanese Association for the Promotion of International Trade on December 2, 1988, Deng Xiaoping said that new situations had appeared in international politics, with a shift from confrontations to dialogues and from tension to relaxation, and that it was time to propose a new political order. The new order should follow the Five Principles of Peaceful Coexistence, which can be furthered enriched and developed. When he met with Rajiv Gandhi, Prime Minister of India, in late December of 1988, Deng Xiaoping further pointed out, "The general world situation is changing, and every country is thinking about appropriate new policies to establish a new international order. Hegemonism, bloc politics and treaty organizations no longer work."① During the drastic changes in Eastern Europe and the disintegration of the Soviet Union, U.S. President Bush proposed the establishment of a "new world order" led by the U.S. On September 11, 1990, Bush addressed a joint session of the United States Congress, "The crisis in the Persian Gulf, as grave as it is, also offers a rare opportunity to move toward an historic period of cooperation. Out of these troubled times, our fifth objective—a new world order—can emerge: a new era—freer from the threat of terror, stronger in the pursuit of justice, and more secure in the quest for peace. An era in which the nations of the world, East and West, North and South, can prosper and live in harmony." In August 1991, in the preface "A New World Order" that he wrote for the National Security Strategy of the United States, Bush announced that the opportunities displayed by the world enable the U.S. "to build a new international system in accordance with our own values and ideals." "And in doing this, American leadership is indispensable." "We must ... help create a new world in which our fundamental values not only survive but flourish."②

As for what kind of new world order should be established, great differences exist not only between developing countries and developed ones but also among developed countries. In the 1990s, the international community mainly discussed the issue of economic and social development. In June 1992, the United Nations Conference on Environment and Development was held in Rio de Janeiro, Brazil. Delegations from 183 countries and representatives from 70 international organizations attended the conference. 102 heads of state or government addressed the conference. The Rio Declaration on Environment and Development, Agenda 21, and other documents were passed and signed at the

---

① *Selected Works of Deng Xiaoping Vol. III*, p. 275.
② George W. Bush, "Address Before a Joint Session of the Congress on the Persian Gulf Crisis and the Federal Budget Deficit," The American Prsidency Project, September 11, 1990; The White House, *National Security Strategy of the United States*, August 1, 1991.

conference. The consensus reached at the conference marked the re-understanding of environmental and development issues by the international community and countries around the world. It is a milestone for mankind in changing its traditional development mode and mode of production and take a path of sustainable development.

From March 6 to March 12, 1995, the United Nations World Summit for Social Development was held in Copenhagen, capital of Denmark, which was attended by representatives of 180-plus countries, including 118 heads of state or government and over 10,000 representatives of international organizations, government agencies, and non-governmental organizations. The meeting identified three core issues: coordinated development and reduction of unemployment, international cooperation and poverty eradication, and social integration and coordinated social development. The meeting adopted the Copenhagen Declaration on Social Development and the Programme of Action of the World Summit for Social Development. The 118 participating countries and another 65 countries made 10 commitments in the Copenhagen Declaration: ① creating an economic, political, social, cultural and legal environment that will enable people to achieve social development; ②eradicating poverty in the world, through decisive national actions and international cooperation; ③ promoting the goal of full employment as a basic priority of our economic and social policies; ④ promoting social integration by fostering societies that are stable, safe and just; ⑤ promoting full respect for human dignity and achieving equality and equity between women and men; ⑥ promoting and attaining the goals of universal and equitable access to quality education, the highest attainable standard of physical and mental health, and the access of all to primary health care; ⑦ accelerating the economic, social and human resource development of Africa and the least developed countries; ⑧ ensuring that when structural adjustment programs are agreed to they include social development goals, in particular eradicating poverty, promoting full and productive employment, and enhancing social integration; ⑨ increasing significantly and/

or utilizing more efficiently the resources allocated to social development; ⑩ an improved and strengthened framework for international, regional and subregional cooperation for social development, in a spirit of partnership, through the United Nations and other multilateral institutions. This meeting reflected that the pursuit of development and social stability has become the common aspiration of the international community and countries around the world.

From June 26 to June 30, 2000, a U.N. special session on the implementation of the outcome of the 1995 World Summit for Social Development was held in Geneva, which was attended by about 2,000 people, including representatives from the 188 member states of the United Nations, observers, and non-governmental organizations. Based on the United Nations World Summit for Social Development held in Copenhagen in 1995, the meeting aimed to further materialize the objectives set forth by the Copenhagen meeting and promote social development. The General Assembly adopted an outcome document entitled "Further initiatives for social development," which stressed the importance of debt reduction, open markets, and more assistance, called on the United Nations to launch a global campaign to eradicate poverty, and set a target of reducing the proportion of people living in extreme poverty by one half by the year 2015.

II. Promises and Fulfillment

For over half a century, the United Nations and other international agencies have made important contributions in eliminating and ending colonial rule, safeguarding world peace, and promoting economic and social development. However, overall, in important fields such as improving North-South relations, helping developing countries, and eradicating poverty, there are still more promises than fulfillment, and the global wealth gap is widening.

In 1960, the U.N. passed two important resolutions: U.N. General Assembly Resolution 1515 reiterates that a prime duty of the U.N. is to accelerate the economic and social advancement of the less developed countries of the world; U.N. General Assembly Resolution 1522 expresses the hope that the flow of international assistance and capital should be increased substantially so as to reach as soon as possible approximately 1 percent of the combined national incomes of the economically advanced countries. To this end, the U.N. began to implement the international development strategy. By 1990, the U.N. had put forward four U.N. development decades. On May 25, 1994, U.N. Secretary-General Boutros Boutros-Ghali put forward a report titled "An Agenda for Development," and the Agenda for Development was adopted at the 51st session of the United Nations General Assembly on June 21, 1997. The Agenda for Development elaborated on development issues from three aspects: setting and objectives, policy framework including means of implementation, and institutional issues and follow-up. The main objectives of the Agenda for Development were strengthening international cooperation for development, enhancing the role, capacity, effectiveness, and efficiency of the U.N. system in development, and promoting development based on an integrated approach. However, due to the reduction of assistance from developed countries and other reasons, the international development strategy and the Agenda for Development proposed by the U.N. have achieved limited results so far.

Developed countries have promised to allocate 0.7% of their GNP as official development assistance to developing countries. However, statistics show that the proportion of official development assistance provided by developed countries in their GNP has dropped from 0.35% in 1982 and 0.33% in 1992 to 0.25% in 1996 and 0.22% in 1997. On June 29, 2000, French President Jacques Chirac called on economically advanced countries to increase their development assistance at the special session of the General Assembly in Geneva. At present, only Denmark, Norway, the Netherlands, and Sweden provide more than 0.7% of their GNP as assistance, with France providing 0.4% and the U.S. providing 0.1%. Chirac proposed that they should restore the ambition they had 15 or 20 years ago and set foreign development assistance to at least 0.7% of their GNP.

Almost every annual meeting of the World Bank and the International Monetary Fund has the topic of reducing the debts of developing countries and eradicating poverty. In late September 1997, at the 52nd annual meeting of the World Bank held in Hong Kong, China, World Bank President Paul Wolfowitz called the widening wealth gap a "time bomb" in his speech, urging the international community to "take action now" and launch a new battle against global poverty. He said, "without economic hope we will not have peace. Without equity we will not have global stability. Without a better sense of social justice our cities will not be safe and our societies will not be stable." He said that the World Bank has made assistance to poor countries one of its priorities, aiming to help recipient countries to formulate comprehensive economic, social, and environmental development strategies. However, every meeting was full of talks but with little action, and the external debts of developing countries have increased sharply. From the 1960s to the 1970s, developing countries borrowed heavily to speed up their economic development. Developed countries raising interest rates and the deteriorating trade conditions have greatly increased the debt burden of developing countries. According to World Bank statistics, by 1980, the total foreign debt of 109 developing countries was $430 million. By 1986, these countries had paid $652 million in debt service, including $320 million as interests, while the total foreign debt was still $882 million. At present, the total foreign debt of developing countries has reached $2.5 trillion. As of 1999, the total foreign debt of African countries was equivalent to 80% of their GNP. Many countries rely on new debt to repay old debt or fall into the plight of being unable to repay debt.

From the General Agreement on Tariffs and Trade to the World Trade Organization, the development of world trade has been greatly promoted by global trade negotiations, tariff reduction, and dispute settlement. However, the "price scissors" between prices of manufactured goods and primary products, the export subsidies of developed countries, and various non-tariff barriers have seriously harmed the economic interests of developing countries, especially the least developed countries. UNCTAD statistics show that the population of the 48 least developed countries accounts for 13% of the world's total population, while their exports only account for 0.4% of the world's total. The foreign direct investment in these countries only accounts for 0.4% of the total transnational direct investment. In the process of the acceleration of the economic globalization, these countries are in danger of being "marginalized." On May 6, 1998, Bangladeshi Prime Minister Sheikh Hasina, on behalf of the 48 least developed countries, requested developed countries to import their goods duty-free and increase investment in these countries. She pointed out that accelerated economic globalization may further widen the wealth gap.

The history of world economic development shows that the reasons that the economic gap between many developing countries and developed ones is widening involve not only the historical long-term colonial invasion and plunder but also the current unjust and unreasonable international rules and political and economic order. One of the key reasons is that international institutions and especially developed countries have made many promises of assistance but failed to deliver them. Professor Madison, a famous Dutch economic history expert, conducted calculations and statistical analysis according to the U.S. dollar exchange rate in 1990. In 1000, the world's GDP per capita was $420. Specifically, the per capita GDP of western countries was $406, and that of Asia, Africa, and Latin America was $424, slightly higher than that of western countries. In 1500, the world's GDP per capita was $545, with the GDP per capita of western countries being $624, slightly higher than the $532 of Asia, Africa, and Latin America. In 1820, the world's GDP per capita was $675, with the GDP per capita of western countries being $1,149, significantly higher than the $594 of Asia, Africa, Latin America, and other regions.[①] After the Second World War, with accelerated economic globalization

---

① *Wall Street Journal*, Jan. 11, 1999.

and the rapid development of science and technology, social wealth has increased dramatically, but the wealth gap is also widening. According to the calculations and statistics by the World Bank based on exchange rates, the world GNP increased from $5 trillion in 1950 to $29.9257 trillion in 1997. Specifically, the GNP of high-income countries, whose population only accounted for 15.9% of the world's total population, accounted for 79.5% of the world total. The GNP of low-income countries, whose population accounted for 35% of the world's total population, only accounted for 2.4% of the world total. The ratio of rich countries' per capita income to that of poor countries has expanded from 30∶1 in 1960 and 60∶1 in 1990 to 74∶1 in 1997. The world's richest 225 people, including 60 Americans, had assets of $1 trillion, equivalent to the total income of the 2.5 billion poor people in the world.①

The growing poverty in many countries has severely restricted their economic development. First, the limited funds are mainly used to provide food, clothing, housing, and transportation, and those countries are unable to increase investment in R&D and carry out economic restructuring. A report issued by the United Nations Development Programme on September 9, 1998 pointed out that the rich, who accounted for 20% of the world's population, consumed 86% of the world's goods and services, 58% of the world's energy, 84% of the world's paper, and 87% of the world's automobiles, while the poorest 20% of the world's population consumed only 1.3% of the world's goods and services and 5% of the world's meat and fish. While per capita GDP in rich countries had reached $20,000, $30,000 or even $40,000, by then there were still 1.5 billion people living on less than $1 a day. Residents in Europe and the U.S. spent $17 billion each year to buy food for pets, while about 1.1 billion residents in developing countries still lacked housing.② In 2000, 33 countries were suffering from extreme food shortages, and some 790 million

---

① *The Christian Science Monitor*, Nov. 6, 1999.
② Ibid.

people in the world were starving.① 1.2 billion people have no access to clean water and 3 billion people lack adequate sanitation. The Millennium Forum, attended by representatives of 1000-plus non-governmental organizations, pointed out in its Declaration and Agenda of Action issued on May 26, 2000 after its closing at U.N. Headquarters in New York that this was the most widespread violation of human rights in the world.

Another great impact of poverty is education backwardness and brain drain. According to UNESCO statistics, in 1995, the average number of students enrolled in institutions of higher learning per 100,000 people in developed countries was 4,110; the number in less developed countries was 824, one-fifth of that in developed countries; the number in least developed countries was 296, only one-fourteenth of that in developed countries. The world average of the gross enrollment rate of young people of the same age (i.e., after graduating from high school) in institutions of higher learning is 16.2%; the average of this number is 59.6% in developed countries, 8.8% in less developed countries, and 3.2% in least developed countries. There are still 260 million children who cannot attend school. However, developing countries are facing increasingly serious brain drain. According to statistics of the American International Education Society, during the 1998–1999 academic year, 491,000 foreign students studied in American universities, accounting for about one-third of the world's total overseas students, more than half of which are Asian students. Most foreign students stay in the U.S. to engage in R&D and innovation after graduation. During the World Economic Forum annual meeting in Davos in 1999, Bill Gates pointed out that the "talent war" had just begun. Thomas A. Stewart, a member of the Board of Editors of *Fortune* magazine, told delegates attending the World Economic Forum annual meeting in Davos in 2000 that finding, training, and retaining talents was the biggest challenge facing companies. Intel Vice President Paul Stevens Otellini said that they had a five-

---

① A report released by the Food and Agriculture Organization (FAO) on February 16, 2000.

point plan for recruitment, retaining talents, compensation, work-life balance, and corporate culture.① Developing countries, especially least developed countries, will face more severe brain drain.

Due to the lack of R&D investment, lagging education, and brain drain, there is a huge gap in technology innovation and dissemination between poor and rich countries. Professor Jeffrey Sachs, director of the Center for International Development at Harvard University, pointed out in an article entitled "A New Map of the World" the following facts: "A small part of the globe, accounting for some 15% of the earth's population, provides nearly all of the world's technology innovations. A second part, involving perhaps half of the world's population, is able to adopt these technologies in production and consumption. The remaining part, covering around a third of the world's population, is technologically disconnected, neither innovating at home nor adopting foreign technologies."② If this situation does not change, the global wealth gap will continue to widen.

III. Starting from Reform

Economic globalization and political multipolarization are the defining trend and are irresistible. It is necessary to establish a just and reasonable new international political and economic order to safeguard peace, strengthen cooperation, seek benefits and avoid disadvantages, and realize universal development and prosperity. However, history has shown that we should start from reforming the existing international agencies and rules to gradually realize the common goals of mankind.

1. International financial institutions and rules need to be reformed

Since the early 1990s, a series of financial crises have shown that the international financial institutions and rules are in urgent need of reform.

---

① *Financial Times*, Feb. 1, 2000.
② *The Economist*, Jun. 22, 2000.

French Prime Minister Lionel Jospin has proposed a series of reforms of the World Trade Organization and the International Monetary Fund.

The World Bank, the International Monetary Fund, and the World Trade Organization are called the three pillars of world economy and the "economic United Nations." After the Asian and Russian financial crises in 1997 and 1998, international financial institutions such as the World Bank and the International Monetary Fund took some measures, but they were not carried out in time and were inflexible and ineffective. In his speech delivered at the New York Stock Exchange on September 21, 1998, British Prime Minister Tony Blair pointed out that the weakness of the World Bank and the International Monetary Fund set up in 1944 at a conference in Bretton Woods, New Hampshire, have been illustrated in the current financial crisis and that there had got to be reform. He noted that the Bretton Woods system was no longer suitable for the modern rules of international capital operation, and called for a new Bretton Woods for the new millennium.

The reform of international financial institutions and rules must start with a shift from "unilateralism" to genuine "multilateralism." The International Monetary Fund's regulations stipulate that its major contributors have the final say. For example, the U.S., which provides 18% of the funds in the International Monetary Fund, has about one-fifth of the veto power. For every important measure the organization takes, the U.S. has almost the complete veto power. In addition, with the support of other western powers, the U.S. can also get the support of a truly natural majority. As a leader of RoK's Samsung C & T said, in the International Monetary Fund, whoever gives money has the right to decide the rules of the game.① French Prime Minister Lionel Jospin recently condemned the U.S. "unilateralism." Any reform of international financial institutions must be based on the principle of genuine

---

① *Young Africa Magazine*.

multilateralism and must not be heavily biased in favor of the U.S.[①]

The World Bank and the International Monetary Fund should proceed from reality and "suit the remedy to the case" for the problems in different countries. Assistance should be provided without political conditions or interference in internal affairs. For a long period of time, we should give priority to the following three aspects: first, we should establish and improve early warning and supervision mechanism to prevent the outbreak of global financial crises. Second, we should make coordinated efforts to offer more loans and assistance to developing countries for their scientific and technological development. The loans and grants offered by the World Bank each year for scientific and technological development are less than 1/10 of the R&D budget of a pharmaceutical company in the U.S.[②] The World Bank should increase its assistance to developing countries to enhance their scientific and technological capabilities. Third, practical measures should be taken to reduce the debt burden of developing countries.

Finance ministers and central bank governors of the G20, including the G7, E.U., Argentina, Australia, Brazil, China, India, Indonesia, Mexico, Russia, Saudi Arabia, South Africa, Korea, and Turkey, had a meeting in Berlin, Germany, on December 16, 1999. The meeting stressed that the G20 was a new mechanism for informal dialogues within the framework of the Bretton Woods system, aiming at promoting the international financial system reform and laying a broad foundation for discussion and consultation on substantive issues in order to seek cooperation and promote the stable and sustained growth of the world economy. At a press conference held after the meeting, Canadian Minister of Finance Paul Martin, chairman of the meeting, pointed out that economic globalization entails the formulation of global rules of the economic game. He believed that the first meeting of the G20 marked the

---

① *International Herald Tribune*, April 18, 2000.
② *The Economist*, Jun. 24-30, 2000.

first step in the reform of the international financial system. The GNP of these countries accounts for 85% of the world total, and their population accounts for two-thirds of the world total. Countries around the world hope that these countries will contribute to the reform of the current international financial institutions and rules.

2. Reforming and strengthening WTO

The WTO is the only international organization in the world that formulates and implements international trade codes and standards. While formulating and regulating international multilateral trade rules and organizing global trade negotiations to promote the reduction of tariff and non-tariff barriers, the WTO also presides over the settlement of disputes among its members. However, the WTO still has some limitations, such as unfairness and unreasonableness, making reform necessary.

The number of WTO members has increased from 23 when GATT entered into force to 135, more than three-fourths being developing countries. According to the principle that major decisions get adopted with the support of a three-fourths majority, developing members should be playing an important role. However, with the insistence of developed countries such as the U.S. and Europe on the principle of "consensus," the major decisions of the WTO are still dominated by a few large western countries. At the WTO Ministerial Conference of 1999 held in Seattle, developed countries still focused on their own economic and trade interests and related issues, ignoring the legitimate demands of developing countries and even excluding developing members to engage in separate consultations, thus causing dissatisfaction among the great many developing members. Latin American countries issued a joint statement saying that they would refuse to sign any agreement reached without their engagement. In April 1999, Renato Ruggiero, Director-General of the WTO, whose term of office had expired, proposed based on his experience and the encountered problems that in the decision-making process regarding world economy at the highest level, it was necessary to change from unilateral leadership to collective leadership so that developing countries and countries with economies in transition could participate in a more open decision-making mechanism rather than a mechanism dominated by a few developed countries.

In promoting the liberalization of trade, investment, and financial services, the WTO should give full consideration to the affordability and economic security of developing countries and urge developed countries to lift trade barriers, expand imports from developing countries, and ensure fair trade. In February 2000, during the United Nations Conference on Trade and Development held in Bangkok, Thailand, WTO Director General Mike Moore said that he was drafting a series of agreements to make it easier for poor countries to enter profitable markets. The vast majority of developing countries, especially the least developed ones, hope that his promise can be fulfilled gradually.

Looking back on the past century, we can see that the 20th century was not only a century full of hardships and sufferings in the process of world civilization but also a century in which incomparable material and spiritual wealth was created and coexisted with the widening wealth gap. People hope that war, hunger, and poverty will become history, and peace, progress, universal development, and prosperity will become the main theme of the 21st century. As long as countries deepen their reform and expand opening up, respect each other and treat each other equally, and seek common grounds while preserving minor differences in the process of reforming the existing international institutions and rules, we will gradually establish a just and reasonable new international political and economic order and will be able to turn the beautiful vision of mankind into reality.

Section IV　Actively Participating in Global Governance to Realize Common Interests

The rise and development of global governance, the Commission on Global

Governance composed of 28 international celebrities was established in 1992. After more than two years of deliberation, the Commission defined global governance as "the sum of many ways individuals and institutions, public and private, manage their common affairs. It is a continuing process through which conflicting or diverse interests may be accommodated and cooperative action taken."① The Commission also pointed out four characteristics of global governance: governance is not a set of rules or an activity, but a process; the basis of the governance process is not control but coordination; governance involves both public and private sectors; governance is not a formal system but a process of continuous interactive decision-making. We can see that this concept contains more extensive contents. It not only defines governance as a continuous interactive process but also provides a further and more comprehensive definition in terms of the subjects and modes of governance.②

Global governance is to solve global problems such as the ecology, drugs, human rights, immigration, and infectious diseases through state actors and non-state actors, without strong central authority intervention and using widely recognized laws, norms, and systems, so as to promote the common development of world politics and economy and safeguard common interests. "Global values must be the cornerstone of global governance."③

I. Reasons for China's Participation in Global Governance

After the victory of the anti-fascist war, China actively participated in the building and maintenance of a new world order. Although blocked by the western world for a period of time after the founding of the People's Republic of China, China has been actively exploring and eager to communicate with the

---

① Pang Zhongying, "The Transformation of Global Governance: From World Governance to China Governance," *Foreign Theoretical Trends*, 2012(10): 13-16.
② The Commission on Global Governance, *Our Global Neighborhood: The Report of the Commission on Global Governance*, Oxford: Oxford University Press, 1995.
③ Ibid.

outside world. With the development of reform and opening up, China's economy and overall comprehensive strength have increased significantly. China has always been a maintainer and constructor of the existing international order, making increasingly important positive contributions to global governance and playing an increasingly prominent role as a leading power in global governance. At specific regional levels such as the Asia-Pacific region and other regional mechanisms, China has also actively provided public goods and played a more constructive role.

As an emerging power, China does not seek to challenge the dominating position of the U.S. in global governance, nor does it seek to establish confrontational or alternative international mechanisms outside the existing global governance system. Instead, China abides by the existing global rules and is willing to assume corresponding responsibilities in the existing system according to its own capabilities. On the one hand, China actively renews the concept of global governance, advocates the construction of a community with a shared future for mankind, and clearly leads the shaping of a new type of international relations with win-win cooperation as its core. These ideas and proposals have been warmly echoed and widely recognized by the political circles, academic circles, and press circles and have produced strong international appeal and influence. On the other hand, China is actively leading the world economy and global governance towards the right direction. China has hosted a successful G20 Hangzhou Summit, which put forward the Chinese Approach for the fundamental problems facing the world economy and pointed out the direction for global economic governance. At the 2016 APEC Ministerial Meeting in Lima, Peru, President Xi Jinping directly addressed major issues such as deglobalization, protectionism, and scattered regional cooperation, making a strong voice of China and leading economic globalization towards a more inclusive path. These propositions have played a positive role in boosting world confidence and building global consensus. The forthcoming 5~10 years will be a period of strategic opportunities for China to engage in the reform of the global governance mechanism. Active participation in global governance is of great significance and necessity to China.

1. China still needs to participate in global governance to maintain international environment of peace and development

In general, emerging powers including China are beneficiaries of the current international governance mechanism and the peaceful international environment. Since the end of the Second World War, East Asian countries such as Japan, Singapore, and Korea, as well as the Gulf countries, Brazil, Russia, Mexico, Turkey, and other countries have made great strides in economic development and have witnessed sustained enhancement of their economic strength. At present, although the existing international rules are confronted with many challenges, the basic framework and structure have not been fundamentally subverted. What has changed is only the lineup or ranking of the main regulators. As such, China has the opportunity to play a more important role in the existing international governance system and thus continue to share the "peace dividend" with the world.

2. Inadequate supply of international public goods will affect China's own interests

For a long time, China has always supported the smooth functioning of the existing international regulatory system and has invested huge resources in this regard. In terms of political security, China has always abided by the purposes and principles of the U.N. Charter and firmly upheld the international law and international norms governing international relations. When it comes to international trade regulations, China has achieved common development and prosperity with other countries and actively participated in the formulation and improvement of multilateral trade rules over the 10-plus years since it joined the WTO. In the field of international monetary and financial affairs, China is an important member of the International Monetary Fund (IMF). Its economic development is drawing increasing attention from the IMF. In terms of funds, China has transformed from a debtor to a creditor and has continuously provided loans and assistance to IMF. If China does not actively participate in the maintenance of the international order and thus affects the operation of the international mechanism and the efficiency of the supply of international public goods at this time, it will not only directly reduce the level of China's benefits gained from international public goods but also cause great waste in terms of the resources that China has already invested and cannot be withdrawn.

3. Active participation in global governance also gives China opportunity to improve its soft power

The international community needs a new concept of growth and a concept of competition restricted by fairness and justice, with inclusive development as the core value. To realize inclusive development, all countries should assume international responsibilities that match their own capabilities and historical circumstances so that emerging economies will not be imposed excessive responsibilities and burdens by developed countries in the name of freedom and equality. Meanwhile, inclusive development also requires developed countries to shoulder their responsibilities, earnestly fulfill their commitments, and give priority to the reasonable appeals of less developed countries for subsistence and development.

In recent years, the rise of emerging markets has come with new contents beyond the traditional South-South cooperation. Emerging cooperation represented by the BRICS mechanism has given developing countries an unprecedented voice. In this context, China's idea of inclusive development is well-poised to generate a global impact and even become a policy framework and institutional arrangement at regional and global levels. This will not only significantly enhance China's soft power but also serve the common interests of emerging countries.

II. Challenges Confronting China's Participation in Global Governance

Although China faces unprecedented opportunities, it also faces many difficulties and challenges. Amid the ever-changing international landscape, the intertwinement of unresolved old problems and emerging problems has generated more complicated dilemmas.

1. Being subject to international political games

At present, a sense of responsibility for global governance is absent. In the international political game, some big powers not only embrace power politics but also follow "unilateralism," thus causing the existence of "hegemony." A typical case is the U.S.-led western developed countries forcibly interfering in internal affairs of other countries under the guise of "world police" and "humanitarianism." They even launch wars for their own interests, ignoring the hard-won peace of the world today. In the absence of a world government, there is a serious problem of responsibility deficit in global governance. That is to say, when major powers realize that global governance will harm their own interests, they will take the initiative to break the rules and abandon their international responsibilities, thus leading to a series of chaos. Although an emerging power, China is still a developing country. Its participation in global governance is bound to be restricted by international political games, thus limiting its role.

2. Weak awareness of cooperation among emerging powers

Global governance has exceeded the governance capacity of a certain region or a certain country, so global cooperation is necessary. If the existing global governance system is not adaptable, it will lead to crises, which will change the world power structure and accelerate the transfer of global power. The transformation of the power structure is actually a game between countries. While China and other emerging countries are becoming more powerful, established powers are unwilling to abandon their own vested interests. Therefore, they do not actively cooperate with the transformation of the power structure, thus affecting the settlement of global governance problems. In addition, emerging forces and established ones have not reached to a consensus, making it difficult for all countries to form genuine cooperation and leaving them acting in their own ways. As a result, the progress of global governance is slow and chaotic.

3. Serious obstacles posed by deglobalization

At present, the tide of deglobalization is eroding the concept of coexistence. Going against globalization, deglobalization obstructs the global flow of production factors, not only estranging global cultures but also triggering international conflicts. Brexit and other events are prominent examples of deglobalization. Advocating "America First," U.S. President Donald Trump has exited several international multilateral organizations. deglobalization has greatly obstructed global governance.

4. International organizations do not have a strong global awareness

The effective development of global governance depends on the establishment of globalism, which requires international organizations to strengthen communication and exchange, cooperate with each other, and further solve global problems. However, different countries have their own considerations regarding the perception of interests. Some countries place one-sided emphasis on nationalism and isolationism, which is in unignorable contradiction with globalism. Globalism emphasizes international law and world alliance but requires all countries to give up certain sovereignty. In order to safeguard their state interests, countries are playing games. Some countries purely pursue nationalism and ignore the interests of other countries, making the global alliance essentially become empty talk. Under such circumstances, countries are caught in the stag hunt game, naturally making it difficult for them to cooperate with each other. As a result, global governance is hindered and difficult to progress.

III. Strategies for China's Participation in Global Governance

To deal with the current predicament in global governance, China shoulders heavy responsibilities and has much to do. A set of Chinese Approach featuring China's wisdom are vigorously pushing the global governance system out of the predicament and towards just, orderly, balanced, and inclusive development. The new ideas, new paths, and new propositions contained in the new strategy are leading global governance into a new era.

The "Two Insistences" have resolved the problem of the absence of a sense of responsibility in global governance and demonstrated China's commitment.

Chapter IX Countermeasures and Suggestions for Realizing Common Interests

China insists on focusing its efforts on economic development, works to run its own affairs well, and continuously strengthens its ability to speak out and act in the international arena. China actively participates in global governance and takes the initiative to assume international responsibilities while "doing its best and doing what it can"; China insists on the principle of "consultation, contribution and shared benefits" because the promotion of global governance is a common cause of the international community, and the idea of global governance development should be translated into consensus and concerted action. We must persist in speaking up for developing countries and strengthen the solidarity and cooperation with them.

"Win-win Cooperation" has resolved the problem of the weak awareness of cooperation in global governance and demonstrated China's manner. China is the representative of emerging powers, and the U.S. is the largest economy in today's world. Cooperation between the two is of great importance to the development of global governance. With cooperation, both China and the U.S. will gain benefits; without cooperation, both will be harmed. China and the U.S. have different history and culture, are in different stages of development, and have different views on the future international order, but they have common interests and broad cooperation space in developing global governance. China and the U.S. should transcend their differences, give full play to their respective advantages, and explore new ways to jointly promote global governance. The concept of "a community with a shared future for mankind" has resolved the problem of the weak awareness of coexistence in global governance and demonstrated China's aspiration. The international community is increasingly becoming a "community of common destiny" where state interests are closely intertwined. In the face of global problems, no country can only care for itself. The so-called "community with a shared future for mankind" is to break through the barriers of nationalism, place China within the large world, promote an inclusive, open, and shared globalization process, carry out economic, conceptual, and cultural exchange with other countries, and follow the path of development and mutual benefits. On February 10, 2017, the concept of "a community of shared future for mankind" was first written into a U.N. resolution. This concept has been widely recognized by the international community and represents China's contribution to the cause of world peace and development.

China's support for "multilateralism" has resolved the problem of the weak global awareness in global governance and demonstrated China's broad mind. China adheres to a win-win strategy of opening up and actively advocates and practices international cooperation and multilateralism. China pursues global governance within the framework of international organizations and multilateral mechanisms such as the U.N., APEC, G20, and the Group of 77 to safeguard international fairness and justice, promote international cooperation, and strive to contribute more to the cause of human peace and development.

Generally speaking, China in the new era contributes the Chinese wisdom and the Chinese Approach through active participation in global governance. This set of plans are not only the accumulated result of practice but also effective solutions to the current predicaments in global governance, laying a new path for further development of global governance. This path is wide enough to accommodate different international players to move forward together; this path is long enough to accompany mankind into a new era of common destiny; this path is bright enough for the "Chinese dream" and the "world dream" to reflect each other and make the ideal a reality.

Section V   Actively Promoting Belt and Road Initiative to Realize Common Interests

Ⅰ. Belt and Road Initiative: Best Solution to Realizing Common Interests

The implementation of the Belt and Road Initiative is conducive to strengthening cooperation among the countries along the Belt and Road, promoting regional prosperity, and safeguarding world peace and stability. It is a great cause benefiting all mankind and is of great significance to the world, B&R countries, and China.

1. To the world: promoting balanced global development as new economic driver

Since the outbreak of the international financial crisis in 2008, the global economy has suffered from lingering sluggishness and slow recovery, regional economies have faced serious polarization, and countries still face a severe economic picture. China has maintained an average economic growth rate of over 8% for more than 30 consecutive years. According to IMF statistics, China contributed an unprecedented 27.8% to the global economic growth in 2014. China has become an engine for global economic growth in a real sense. As a responsible world power, China put forward the B&R Initiative when deep-seated impacts of the international financial crisis continued to manifest. China is committed to exploring new impetus for global economic growth and laying a solid foundation for the sound, stable, and sustainable development of the global economy. The emergence and rise of traditional globalization was based on oceans, making coastal countries the leaders and the biggest beneficiaries of globalization. They can maximize their own interests by formulating globalization regulations and maintaining the globalization order. At the same time, traditional globalization has also created a huge gap in economic development between coastal and inland countries, a huge gap between the East and the West, and a series of unequal international rules. The proposal of the B&R Initiative is an active exploration in global governance models and international cooperation. It provides a broad platform for economic exchanges and cooperation among the large number of inland countries. It is also a new regional cooperation order established and led by developing countries, fully reflecting the international interests of developing countries which are in the "marsh land" of development. It is conducive to the establishment of a more equal global partnership for development and more balanced globalization.

2. To countries along B&R: identifying new regional cooperation model for regional integration

Worldwide, economic globalization and regional economic integration coexist and promote each other. China has proposed the B&R Initiative innovatively from the perspective of coordinated economic development and mutual benefits among all countries in a region. This strategy is a great innovation in regional cooperation and opening up in the new era. It integrates the economic corridor theory, the economic belt theory, the industrial transfer theory, the regional cooperation theory, the theory of international division of labor, and the globalization theory. Specifically, China will share its dividends, experiences, and lessons from the 40 years of reform and opening up with B&R countries, make up for the shortcomings in the industrial development of B&R countries with its own production capacity advantages, fill the gaps in infrastructure construction in those countries with its financial advantages, comprehensively boost the industrial upgrading of those countries with its technological advantages, and push for the production development of those countries with its market advantages, injecting vitality into regional development and promoting regional integration.

3. To China: necessary requirement for transformation from a large country to a world power

(1) It can help China cope with the external pressure brought by the trade friction with the U.S. and the building of the Transatlantic Trade and Investment Partnership (TTIP). On the one hand, China, as the largest developing country, the world's second largest economy, and an open economy, has similar trade conditions with the great many developing countries; on the other hand, the huge spillover effects released by the new round of reform and opening up will bring new development opportunities to trading partners. Therefore, China has the conditions to deal with the external challenges brought by the trade friction with the U.S. and the TTIP strategy through new regional cooperation models. The B&R Initiative involves not only developed

countries such as countries in Western Europe, Japan, and Korea but also former Soviet and Eastern European countries in Central Asia and Eastern Europe and third world countries in South Asia, West Asia, and Africa. With the B&R Initiative, China seeks to build a new pattern of all-round opening up and a new framework for international cooperation. Through the implementation of a more proactive opening up policy, China can meet the challenges brought about by the trade friction with the U.S. and the TTIP.

The B&R Initiative is conducive to expanding the space for China-E.U. cooperation. During his visit to Europe in March 2014, President Xi Jinping noted that China and Germany are located at the two ends of the Silk Road Economic Belt and are the growth poles of the two major economies of Asia and Europe. The two countries should strengthen cooperation and promote the building of the Silk Road Economic Belt. Subsequently, China and the E.U. issued a Joint Statement Deepening the China-E.U. Comprehensive Strategic Partnership for mutual benefit. It pointed out that negotiating and concluding such a comprehensive China-E.U. Investment Agreement, covering investment protection and market access, will convey both sides' willingness, once the conditions are right, towards a deep and comprehensive free-trade agreement. The consolidation of China-E.U. economic cooperation is conducive to enhancing China's position in the European market, coping with the challenges brought by TTIP to China's economic and trade cooperation with Europe, and deepening cooperation with neighboring countries in Central Asia, Southeast Asia, and South Asia. It will give full play to China's advantages in capital, technology, talents, and industries, promote cooperation with neighboring countries in infrastructure construction, energy, and real economy, and enhance the influence of China's economy on its neighbors. It is conducive to deepening economic and trade cooperation between China and Arab countries. At the China-Arab States Cooperation Forum in June 2014, President Xi Jinping called on the two sides to carry forward the Silk Road spirit, deepen China-Arab cooperation, and deepen their cooperation in energy exploitation and transportation through basic economic, trade, and investment measures.

Relying on the B&R Initiative, China and Europe can effectively enhance the interaction between China and countries and regions in Europe, Asia, and Africa in terms of human capital flow, logistics, capital flow, cultural flow, and commodity flow and promote the formation of communities of shared interests among countries and regions along the Silk Road by implementing more proactive opening-up policies and creating new mechanisms for the economic integrated development of Asia and Europe, with China actively playing its role in regional economic and trade cooperation.

(2) China can play an active role in international and regional cooperation. First of all, the investment opportunities and projects along the Belt and Road are numerous and have great potential, which provide a broad space for China's foreign investment. At the same time, they are also conducive to the rational use of China's huge foreign exchange reserves and the promotion of RMB internationalization. Second, they provide a new path for China to optimize its industrial structure under the new economic normal. China and B&R countries are at different stages of economic development and thus have complementary advantages. Strengthening cooperation in the industrial chain is conducive to resolving the problem of excess manufacturing capacity in China's manufacturing industry and establishing reasonable industrial division of labor. Finally, they provide new opportunities for China to promote balanced regional development.

(3) It can improve the quality of China's open economy. Since the reform and opening up was initiated, China has formed a foreign fund-centered processing trade model. Multinationals invest in China mainly through the combination of capital and labor, transferring their home country's sunset industries and obsolete technologies to China through the inter-generational or gradient transfer of industries. In recent years, although multinationals have also established regional headquarters and R&D centers in many regions of China, they only cooperate with the headquarters in their home countries or

carry out supporting R&D. Thus, China has not really become the operational and strategic center of multinationals. In terms of the export structure in trade, China mainly exports labor-intensive and resource-intensive products, with a large proportion of the products featuring "high pollution, high energy consumption, and resource consumption," and the products have low technological contents. Being at a low end of the value chain, these products have low added value. At the same time, from the perspective of China's regional opening-up pattern, China's foreign trade, foreign capital, and foreign investment are mainly concentrated in the eastern coastal areas due to factors such as the order of opening up, policies, and geography. In 2012, the 12 provinces, cities, and districts in the west accounted for only 5.96% of the total import and export volume of China. The number of registered foreign-funded enterprises and the total investment volume in the west accounted for 8.33% and 8.17% of the national total respectively. The non-financial foreign investment volume of the 12 provinces, cities, and districts in the west accounted for 12.76% of the national total. The non-financial foreign investment volume of the eastern coastal areas, in contrast, accounted for 75% of the national total. Their total import and export volume accounted for 86.41% of the national total, and the number of registered foreign-funded enterprises and the total investment volume in the east accounted for 66.17% and 80.8% of the national total respectively.

In the implementation of the B&R Initiative, the first task is to optimize the regional opening-up layout. China should take advantage of the new opportunities provided by the new round of international industrial transfer to create new external conditions for its inland and border areas to enhance the scale and quality of foreign capital utilization and expand opening up. The second task is to coordinate with the B&R and neighboring countries in terms of policies, infrastructure, laws and regulations, and culture, which can provide excellent basic conditions for Chinese enterprises and individuals to expand their foreign investment, promote the outward transfer of surplus industries and labor-intensive industries, and allocate and utilize resources globally. The third task is to sign bilateral or regional trade and investment agreements with B&R countries and regions. On the one hand, it will help China avoid trade frictions with other countries. On the other hand, it will establish a cooperation mechanism in security through bilateral or regional agreements to ensure the security and stability of China's foreign trade and economic cooperation on land and sea, enhancing China's political and economic influence.

II. Problems in Current B & R Building

1. Prominent competition among big countries in regional economic cooperation

Major countries along the Belt and Road whose interests are involved mainly include the U.S. and Japan, which are outside the region, and India, which is within the region. After the Obama administration came to power, the U.S. launched the "rebalance to Asia and the Pacific" strategy and the Indio-Pacific geopolitical strategy. The U.S. intensified its involvement in Southeast Asia, joined the Treaty of Amity and Cooperation in Southeast Asia, held the U.S.-ASEAN Summit and the Lower Mekong Initiative (LMI) Ministerial Meeting, and launched the Mekong River Initiative. The U.S. has courted the Philippines, Vietnam, Myanmar, India, and other countries, created tensions over the South China Sea and the competitive atmosphere between China and India, incited tensions between Southeast Asian countries and India on the one hand and China on the other, and displayed its determination to defend its leadership in the region in a high profile. Since the Trump administration came to power, it has frequently initiated trade wars between China and the U.S. The Abe administration of Japan has actively cooperated with the U.S. strategy of "rebalance to Asia and the Pacific," encouraged the Philippines and Vietnam to compete with China for sovereignty over the South China Sea, and roped India in to participate in the plan to create a "democratic security diamond" in Asia. India regards South Asia and the Indian Ocean as its sphere of influence and has doubts about the B&R Initiative. India believes that the Bangladesh-China-India-Myanmar Economic Corridor and the B&R Initiative are unilateral initiatives put forward by China to solve its own problems and suspects that deeper strategic intentions lie behind them. Therefore, even as a regional economic cooperation initiative, the Bangladesh-China-India-Myanmar Economic Corridor has shown only modest performance among the six major economic corridors.

2. Trade barriers of different levels among countries along the Belt and Road

Most of the 64 countries along the Belt and Road are developing countries. Amid the global economic downturn, some countries have taken protective measures to protect the development of their own industries. For example, there are trade barriers in customs clearance and technical barriers in Central Asian countries, making trade frictions between China and B&R countries occur from time to time. Some countries, especially those in Southeast Asia and South Asia, have similar trade structure and export products with China and have launched many anti-dumping, anti-subsidy, and safeguard investigations against China. For example, Malaysia and India have launched many anti-dumping investigations against Chinese steel products, while India has launched anti-dumping investigations against Chinese chemical products.

3. Different development levels, social instability, and complex domestic problems in countries along the Belt and Road

Some countries have relatively low levels of economic and social development, backward infrastructure, unsound systems, different standards, and lack of funds, seriously affecting the process of interconnection. For example, countries such as Vietnam, Laos, Cambodia, and Myanmar have relatively low levels of development, single economic structure, backward hardware and software facilities, and fledgling related systems. In particular, the northern regions of these countries are poorer and more inaccessible, all affecting the process of infrastructure interconnection. Some countries are undergoing political and social transformation and are vulnerable to the influence of western political trends and non-governmental organizations, adding to the difficulties faced by Chinese investment. For example, the current Myanmar government has weak governance capacity and is easily manipulated by the public opinion which is greatly influenced by western-dominated non-governmental organizations and media. The Myanmar people have a bad opinion of China and its enterprises. The Myanmar government is greatly influenced by the public opinion in decision-making. In Myanmar, many large-scale projects invested by China, such as the Myitsone Dam project, were suddenly halted. Some countries are facing political turmoil, rampant terrorism, serious separatism, and salient security problems. These problems are especially serious in Pakistan and Afghanistan. The security issue has become the primary obstacle to economic development in Pakistan and Afghanistan. The government of Pakistan has become fully aware of this problem and has solemnly stated on many occasions to effectively protect the safety of Chinese personnel in Pakistan. It has also set up a special security force to protect Chinese engineers. Because security issues such as terrorism are closely related to development, if the China-Pakistan Economic Corridor is completed, it may help improve the local security situation.

4. China's own problems in B&R building

(1) Weak engagement ability of Chinese enterprises.

The major players in B&R building should always be enterprises. The government should only play a facilitating role, and enterprises should be the major actors. Currently, Chinese enterprises face many obstacles in overseas development, which cannot be overcome in a short time. For instance, many enterprises are accustomed to the relatively loose regulatory environment in China and do not have a deep and accurate understanding of international free trade rules. As such, they are prone to violate rules, cause disputes, and face problems in the process of operation and management. Besides, in terms of environmental protection and social responsibility, Chinese companies are different from the enterprises in some B&R countries in corporate governance. This is also an important reason that Chinese enterprises are boycotted or even expelled in the process of "going global." The lack of corporate management systems that are in accordance with international standards is a major shortcoming in China's corporate development. Many home enterprises have chosen to participate in the B&R Initiative without first understanding international rules. As a result, it is easy for them to obtain orders, but it is difficult for them to operate and gain profits. Furthermore, the way to safeguard their rights is unclear. It is difficult to protect their rights when they are faced with problems such as litigations, and it is also difficult for them to withdraw funds quickly when major risks occur. Therefore, we should rectify the situation by improving the corporate management of Chinese enterprises, strengthening the construction of corporate culture, and facilitating enterprises to go global in a better way and make full use of the opportunities provided by the B&R Initiative.

(2) Capital shortage and poor cooperation.

In the B&R Initiative, the government is responsible for the construction and operation of infrastructure. However, there are still many potential problems on this issue. We have to admit that large-scale investment in infrastructure construction is the first step in implementing the B&R Initiative. With reasonable planning and proper construction of the infrastructure, the pressure on investment funds in the later stage will be smaller, trade will be much smoother, and the resource or labor force advantages of the regions along the Belt and Road will soon be highlighted. However, without proper infrastructure design or sufficient funds, projects will be halted, which will directly lead to the waste of the large amount of previously invested capital resources and labor and even directly drag down the local economic development under the most serious situations. Investment in infrastructure is different from the purchase of several sets of machinery and equipment by enterprises. It generally has the characteristics of large investment scale, long investment cycle, and low rate of return. Therefore, ordinary enterprises often lack the ability to withstand these pressures and do not have the motivation to invest in infrastructure. Thus, even if private funds are to be introduced, the government needs to provide sufficient subsidies.

In addition, the governments of relevant countries and partners may hold different ideas about the B&R Initiative, resulting in ineffective governmental policies, insufficient cooperation in various aspects, and refusal to provide guarantee for the financing of projects. For example, Russia and Kazakhstan engage in high levels of strategic cooperation with China, but they do not provide guarantee for financing and do not effectively cooperate with China or provide special policy support in terms of the B&R Initiative.

(3) Economic risks and security problems.

Besides the above problems, there are also certain economic risks and security problems in many countries along the Belt and Road. For example, some North African countries face frequent terrorist attacks and poor social security. Such problems also exist in Venezuela, the Philippines, Vietnam, Afghanistan, Algeria, and other countries. Terrorism, national turmoil, and war threaten these countries along the Belt and Road from time to time and also affect the transaction security and mutual cooperation among those countries, causing serious impacts on participating enterprises and citizens. A stable society and a sound economic and social order underpin the implementation of the B&R Initiative. If these problems cannot be effectively solved, the B&R Initiative may face problems such as the failure in implementing some plans and materializing some projects.

III. Future Priorities in Implementation of B & R Initiative

1. Accelerating five-pronged construction with neighboring countries and regions

According to the Five-Pronged Approach of "policy coordination, transport connectivity, unimpeded trade, currency convertibility, and closer people-to-people ties" in building the Silk Road Economic Belt, China should work with countries and regions along the Belt and Road to promote the construction of channels in various aspects.

First, China should actively sign relevant bilateral or regional trade agreements with countries and regions along the Belt and Road in Central Asia, South Asia, and the E.U. Negotiations on trade agreements should be carried out to realize policy coordination in terms of international trade, culture, and politics, as a way to create a sound policy environment for the implementation of the B&R Initiative.

Second, connectivity of the infrastructure should be enhanced. China should firmly seize the opportunities provided by the arising third industrial revolution, such as the new generation of information technology, high-speed rail, and new energy. Making use of and improving the existing local transportation infrastructure, China should enhance or expand the carrying capacity, speed, efficiency, and content of the B&R corridor and improve the interconnection and interoperability of the infrastructure.

Third, relying on the large corridor construction, China should further relax foreign investment access for countries and regions along the Belt and Road. China should expand the foreign investment of domestic enterprises and individuals in countries along the Belt and Road, build cross-border investment, production, and trade networks and cross-border industrial chains between the two sides, and improve the efficiency of intra-industry and inter-industry economic and trade integration within and outside the countries along the Silk Road in terms of production, supply, and marketing, upstream and downstream industries, and domestic and foreign trade.

Fourth, China should give further play to the role of RMB internationalization in promoting trade and investment facilitation. China should expand cross-border RMB business in key domestic cities along the Belt and Road, expand RMB capital settlement and clearing channels in the existing pilot provinces and make them more convenient and smooth, and further meet the actual demand of enterprises for RMB settlement in cross-border trade. Meanwhile, China should actively promote financial cooperation with countries along the Belt and Road, expand the service scope and fields of Chinese financial institutions in such products as asset custody, asset management, overseas syndicated loans, export seller's credit, trade financing, international settlement, and overseas RMB wealth management, and set up a financial supply chain to serve Chinese enterprises and economic development along the Silk Road.

2. Building high-standard free trade zone network with B & R countries and regions

In order to respond to the new trend of world trade and investment liberalization, the rapid growth of regional agreements, and the gradual enhancement of international trade standards, with a view to giving full play to China's leading role in solving the next generation of trade and investment problems, the Third Plenary Session of the 18th Central Committee of the Communist Party of China proposed to reform the administration systems such as market access, customs supervision, and inspection and quarantine, speed up negotiations on new issues such as environmental protection, investment protection, government procurement, and e-commerce, and form a global network of high-standard free trade zones. In recent years, China has successively signed free trade zone agreements with nine countries and regions such as ASEAN and Pakistan. Free trade zone agreements with the Gulf Cooperation Council, Australia, Norway, Korea, and Japan and the Regional Comprehensive Economic Partnership (RCEP) with ASEAN are under negotiation. Compared with the E.U., Japan, Korea, and other countries and regions, China has signed relatively few FTAs, covering relatively low levels of countries, trade fields, and standards.

The Belt and Road Initiative has brought new opportunities for China and countries along the Belt and Road to make better use of the new external environment, participate in the formulation of new rules for international trade and investment, and promote regional cooperation. To this end, new free trade agreements should include the following two aspects. The first is the implementation of a high-standard opening-up policy. We will promote the mutual opening up of China and other countries along the Silk Road and their neighboring countries in the fields of finance, education, culture, medical care, and other service industries and the full opening up of the manufacturing industry. We will greatly relax the restrictions on foreign investment in green space investment, mergers and acquisitions investment, securities investment, and joint investment. The second is a comprehensive institutional arrangement. In areas such as trade in goods, investment protection, rules of origin, customs procedures, trade relief, sanitary and phytosanitary measures, technical barriers to trade, competition policy, intellectual property rights, government procurement, labor and environment, temporary entry, transparency, dispute settlement, partnership, administrative systems and clauses, and general and exceptional clauses, China should establish institutional arrangements that not only conform to the high-end development of world trade standards but also reflect the specific national conditions and development needs of the Belt and Road related countries and neighboring countries. By signing high-standard free trade zone agreements, China should work to conform to international high-standard rules.

3. Expanding regional international cooperation based on priority areas

Over the past five years, the B&R Initiative has been at a stage of advertisement, expanding the "friend circle," which fit the actual needs in the initial period of the implementation of the B&R Initiative. In the coming five years, China should focus on priority partner countries along the Belt and Road and work to establish models. China should identify the priority fields and partners, and priority should be given to quality partners with reliable bilateral political relations, stable and secure domestic situations, and integrity. At the same time, China should also carefully select B&R projects and work to shift from an extensive path of quantity increase to a path featuring an increase in flagship projects.

The construction of the Maritime Silk Road is beneficial in many aspects.

First, in Southeast Asian regional cooperation, Japan and Korea are important trade partners of China. China, Japan, and Korea are mainly import-export oriented, with large trade flows of intermediate products and certain convergence and complementarity in trade structure. Promoting the construction of a free trade zone between China, Japan, and Korea can further enhance the level and efficiency of competition, enhance the level of vertical and horizontal division of labor in trade, and accelerate the adjustment of the industrial structure of the three countries.

Second, in terms of ASEAN, the trade spillover effects of Chinese economy on Southeast Asian countries should be tapped to accelerate RCEP negotiations, enhance the level of mutual investment management and the market access of service industry in the existing China-ASEAN free trade zones, and deepen China-ASEAN economic cooperation. By pushing forward RCEP negotiations, China should work to take strategic initiative in the Asia-Pacific regional cooperation pattern.

Third, in terms of Oceania, efforts should be made to expand the cooperation space of the China-New Zealand free trade zone in fields such as trade in goods, trade in services, investment, and market openness and accelerate the negotiation on free trade zone with Australia so as to increase China's economic influence on Oceania. In a word, based on the B&R Initiative, China should play a greater role in linking and leading the China-Japan-Korea free trade zone, China-ASEAN free trade zone, China-New Zealand free trade zone, and China-Australia free trade area in the future so as to solidify the foundation of the existing Asia-Pacific cooperation and push forward the integration of the Asia-Pacific region.

4. Improve quantity and quality of trade investment in domestic regions along the Belt and Road; as for investment layout, the suggestion is to shift from "heavy asset-oriented" to "light asset-oriented" economic cooperation to reduce risks

For a long time, infrastructure construction has been the top priority of the implementation of the B&R Initiative, with great achievements having been made in infrastructure connectivity. That being said, infrastructure investment features long construction periods, huge capital input, and slow returns. In the coming five years, China should accelerate the expansion of cooperation in innovative areas such as IT and digital economy, incorporate emerging technologies such as e-commerce, big data, cloud computing, and AI into the implementation of the B&R Initiative, make high-tech and innovation-based enterprises the major forces and pioneers in going global, and build digital corridors and information corridors to share the dividends of technology innovation.

References

[1] Marx & Engels Collected Works [M]. London: Lawrence & Wishart.

[2] Lenin Collected Works [M]. Moscow: Progress Publishers.

[3] Collected Works of Stalin [M]. Beijing: People's Publishing House.

[4] Selected Works of Mao Zedong [M]. Beijing: Foreign Language Press.

[5] Selected Works of Deng Xiaoping [M]. Beijing: Foreign Language Press.

[6] Selected Works of Jiang Zemin [M]. Beijing: Foreign Languages Press.

[7] Xi Jinping: The Governance of China [M]. Beijing: Foreign Languages Press.

[8] Adam Smith. An Inquiry into the Nature and Causes of the Wealth of Nations [M]. Beijing: Commercial Press, 2002.

[9] Alfred Marshall. Principles of Economics [M]. Beijing: Commercial Press, 1964.

[10] Avinash K. Dixit, Robert S. Pindyck. Investment under Uncertainty [M]. Beijing: China Renmin University Press, 2002.

[11] Bin Xu. Multinational Enterprises, Technology Diffusion, and Host Country Productivity Growth [J]. Journal of Development Economics. 2000, 62 (2).

[12] Borensztein Eduardo, J. D. Gregorio, Jong Wha Lee. How Does Foreign Direct Investment Affect Economic Growth [J]. Journal of International Economics, 1998, 45 (1).

[13] Branko Milanovic, Shlomo Yitzhaki. Decomposing World Income Distribution: Does the World Have a Middle Class [A]. World Bank Working Papers, 2001.

[14] Branko Milanovic. True World Income Distribution, 1998 and 1993 First Calculations Based on Household Surveys Alone [A]. World Bank Working Papers, 1999.

[15] Chen Daisun, Li Yining. History of International Finance Theory [M]. Beijing: China Financial Publishing House, 1991.

[16] Chen Feixiang. On Open Interests [M]. Shanghai: Fudan University Press, 2004.

References

[17] Chen Fengying. Focuses in the Development of China-U.S. Business Relations [J]. China Development Observation, 2007 (1).

[18] Chen Jianjun. An Empirical Study on Regional Industrial Transfer in China at Present—Analysis Based on Questionnaire Survey Reports of 105 Enterprises in Zhejiang Province" [J]. Management World, 2002 (6).

[19] Chen Tingting, Wang Shan. The Influence of International Flow of Human Capital and Countermeasures [J]. Popular Science & Technology, 2006 (8).

[20] Chen Tingting, Wang Shan. The Influence of International Flow of Human Capital and Countermeasures [J]. Popular Science & Technology, 2006 (8).

[21] Chen Ying. The Thought of Common Prosperity of the Three Generations of Leaders of the Communist Party of China and Its Spatial Layout Strategy of Common Prosperity [J]. Research on Mao Zedong Thought, 2002 (5).

[22] Chen Zhiang. Economic Globalization and "New Triffin Paradox" [J]. Economic Theory and Business Management, 2005 (1).

[23] David Ricardo. On the Principles of Political Economy and Taxation [M]. Beijing: Huaxia Publishing House, 2005.

[24] David T. Coe, Elhanan Helpman. International R&D spillover [J]. European Economic Review, 1995, 39 (5).

[25] Eduardo Borensztein, Jose De Gregorio. How Does Foreign Direct Investment Affect Economic Growth [J]. Journal of International Economics, 1998, 45(1).

[26] Enric Detragiache. Technology Diffusion and International Income Convergence [J]. Journal of Development Ecnomics, 1998, 56 (2).

[27] Fan Jiazhou. International Trade Theory [M]. Beijing: People's Publishing House, 1985.

[28] Fan Yongming. Western International Political Economics [M]. Shanghai: Shanghai People's Publishing House, 2001.

[29] Fan Zengqiang. Analysis on Technology Diffusion and Spillover Effect of Transnational Corporations [J]. Science of Science and Management of S. & T., 2003 (4).

[30] Fan Zengqiang. Analysis on Technology Diffusion and Spillover Effect of Transnational Corporations [J]. Science of Science and Management of S. & T., 2003 (4).

[31] Francois Bourguignon, Christian Morrisson. Inequality among World Citizens: 1820-1992 [J]. The American Economic Review, 2002, 92(4).

[32] Francois Chesnais. Capital Globalization [M]. Beijing: Central Compilation & Translation Press, 2001.

[33] Friedrich List. The National System of Political Economy [M]. Beijing: Commercial Press, 1997.

[34] Fu Zhengping. Comparative Analysis of Comparative Advantage and Competitive Advantage [J]. Journal of International Trade, 1999 (8).

[35] Gao Jian. The Economic Foundation of a Harmonious Society—A Community of Interests [J]. Productivity Research, 2006 (6).

[36] George Crane, Abla Amawieds. The Theoretical Evolution of International Political Economy [M]. Oxford: Oxford University Press, 1991.

[37] Guo Jianzhong. On the Location Choice of China's Foreign Direct Investment [J]. Journal of Beijing Technology and Business University, 2002 (4).

[38] He Jian, Yu Jiuhong. Theoretical Research on Foreign Direct Investment of Transnationals [J]. Productivity Research, 2004 (12).

[39] He Xiaomin. Expanding Common Interests and Building a Harmonious Society [J]. Zhejiang Social Sciences, 2007 (9).

[40] Henry Kissinger. Diplomacy [M]. Haikou: Hainan Publishing House, 1997.

[41] Hong Yinxing. From Comparative Advantage to Competitive Advantage [J]. Economic Research Journal, 1997 (6).

[42] Hong Yuanpeng. General Theory on Economic Interest Relations [M]. Shanghai: Fudan University Press, 2004.

[43] Hong Yuanpeng. On Sharing Interests [M]. Shanghai: Shanghai People's Publishing House, 2001.

[44] Hong Yuanpeng. The Trajectory of Economic Theory [M]. Shenyang: Liaoning People's Publishing House, 1992.

[45] Hu Chengjun. The International Community: Between Community Interests and National Interests [J]. Journal of Chifeng University (Philosophy and Social Science Chinese Edition), 2009 (7).

[46] Hu Yangling. Western Human Capital Theory—A Literature Review [J]. Journal of Guangdong College of Finance and Economics, 2005 (6).

[47] Huang Yi, Xu Wei. The Application of Human Capital in the Theory of International Trade in Services [J]. Journal of Hefei Normal University, 2008 (4).

[48] Hui Xiliang. An Introduction to Economic Interests [M]. Chengdu: Sichuan People's Publishing House, 1991.

[49] Huo Yunfu, Chen Xinyue, Yang Deli, Dong Yizhe. Research on Enterprise Innovation

Network [J]. Science of Science and Management of S. & T., 2002 (10).

[50] Jagdish Bhagwat, T. N. Srinivasan. Revenue Seeking A Generalization of the Theory of Tariffs [J]. Journal of Political Economy. 1980, 88 (6).

[51] Jagdish Bhagwat, V. K. Ramaswam, T. N. Srinivasan. Domestic Distortions, Tariffs and the Theory of Optimum Subsidy [J]. Journal of Political Economy. 1963 (71).

[52] Jagdish N. Bhagwati. Lobbying and Welfare[J]. Journal of Public Economics, 1980, 14 (3).

[53] Jay Mazur. Labor's New Internationalism [J]. Foreign Affairs, 2000, 79 (1).

[54] Jeffry A. Frieden, David A. Lake. International Political Economy, Perspectives on Globa Power and Wealth [M]. Bedford: St. Martins Press, 1991.

[55] Ji Fenhua. A Brief Analysis on Western International Direct Investment Theory—From the Perspective of Industry and Location Choice [J]. Social Research, 2003 (9).

[56] Jia Genliang, Liu Huifeng. Self-Organizing Innovation Network and Transformation of Science and Technology Management [J]. Tianjin Social Sciences, 2003 (1).

[57] Jia Genliang, Xu Shang. Comparison of Technology Networks between Korean and Taiwanese Enterprises [J]. Comparative Economic & Social Systems, 2002 (1).

[58] Jia Genliang. Network Organization: Beyond the Dichotomy of Market and Enterprise [J]. Comparative Economic & Social Systems, 1998 (4).

[59] Jia Kang, Yan Kun. China's Finance [M]. Shanghai: Shanghai Far East Publishers, 2000.

[60] Jia Qingwen. China-U.S. Relations in 2007: Increasing Challenges [J]. China International Studies, 2007 (2).

[61] Joan Sperol. The Politics of International Economic Relations [M]. London: Hallman Press, 1990.

[62] Joseph E. Stiglitz. Dealing With Debt: How to Reform the Global Financial System [J]. Harvard International Review, 2003, 25 (1).

[63] Joseph Nye. Understanding International Conflicts: An Introduction to Theory and History [M]. New York: HarperCollins College Press, 1993.

[64] Ken Binmore, Ariel Rubinstein, Asher Wolinsky. The Nash Bargaining Solution in Economic Modelling [J]. Rand Journal of Economics, 1986, 17 (2).

[65] Kiyoshi Kojima. On Foreign Trade [M]. Tianjin: Nankai University Press, 1987.

[66] Klein M. G. Olivei. Capital Account Liberalization, Financial Depth and Economic Growth [D]. Tufts University, 2000.

[67] Li Changjiu. China-U.S. Economic Prospects and Bilateral Business Relations [J]. Pacific

Journal, 2004 (9).

[68] Li Chong. On Interest Distribution in the Process of Financial Globalization [J]. World Economics and Politics, 2001 (2).

[69] Li Dongyang. International Direct Investment and Economic Development [M]. Beijing: Economic Science Press, 2002.

[70] Li Guoxue. On the Principle of Public Interest in International Trade Policy Making [J]. Research on Financial and Economic Issues, 2006 (6).

[71] Li Ling. Human Capital Movement and China's Economic Growth [M]. Beijing: China Planning Press, 2003.

[72] Li Ping. Theoretical and Empirical Research on Technology Diffusion [M]. Taiyuan: Shanxi Finance and Economics Publishing House, 2004.

[73] Li Ping. Theoretical and Empirical Research on Technology Diffusion [M]. Taiyuan: Shanxi Finance and Economics Publishing House, 2004.

[74] Li Zhenfeng, Jing Chunyao. The Formation and Development of Human Capital Theory [J]. Taxation and Economy, 2004 (6).

[75] Liu Chunyang. Development of Western Human Capital Theory, Journal of Shandong Agricultural University (Social Science Edition), 2004 (6).

[76] Liu Hongzhong. Empirical Study and International Comparison of China's Foreign Direct Investment [M]. Shanghai: Fudan University Press, 2001.

[77] Louis Wells. Third World Multinations [M]. Shanghai: Shanghai Translation Publishing Company, 1986.

[78] Lu Xinde. Features of Economic Globalization and China's Countermeasures [J]. Journal of Contemporary Asia-Pacific Studies, 2003 (5).

[79] Ma Xianxian. Location Choice of Chinese Enterprises' Foreign Direct Investment [J]. Journal of University of International Business and Economics, 2006 (1).

[80] Magnus Blomstrom, Fredrik Sjoholm. Technology Transfer and Spillovers: Does Local Participation with Multinationals Matter [J]. European Economic Review, 1999, 43 (4).

[81] Margaret E. Grosh, E. Wayne Nafziger. The Computation of World Income Distribution [J]. Economic Development and Cultural Change, 1986, 34(2).

[82] Masahi ko Aoki. The Role of Government in East Asian Economic Development [M]. Beijing: China Economic Publishing House, 1998.

[83] Maurice Obstfeld. Risk-taking, Global Diversification, and Growth [J]. American Economic Review, 1992, 84 (5)

[84] Michael Porter. The Competitive Advantage of Nations [M]. Beijing: Huaxia Publishing House, 2002.

[85] Mu Liuwei, Zeng Zhigeng, Xie Heng. International Investment and Financing Theory and Practice [M]. Chengdu: Southwest University of Finance and Economics Press, 2004.

[86] Mundell. International Trade with Factor Mobility [J]. American Economic Review, 1957 (47).

[87] Paul Krugman. A Model of Innovation, Technology Transfer, and the World Distribution of Income [J]. The Journal of Political Economy, 1979, 87 (2).

[88] Paul Krugman. New Trade Theory: International Trade Theory [M]. Beijing: China Social Sciences Press, 2001.

[89] Paul R. Krugman. Does New Trade Theory Call for New Trade Policy? [J]. Economic Outlook, 1992, summer issue.

[90] Peng Juan. The Current International Investment Order and the Principle of Common Interests of Mankind [J]. Contemporary Manager, 2006 (21).

[91] Peter J. Buckley, Mark Casson. The Future of the Multinational Enterprise [M]. New York: Holmes and Meiers. 1976.

[92] Peter Martin. The Global Trap: Globalization and the Assault on Prosperity and Democracy [M]. Beijing: Central Compilation & Translation Press, 2001.

[93] Raymond Vernon. International Investment and International Trade in the Product Cycle [J]. Quarterly Journal of Economics, 1966, 80 (2).

[94] Robert C. Feenstra, Jagdish N. Bhagwati. Tariff Seeking and the Efficient Tariff [M]. Chicago: University of chicago Press, 1982.

[95] Robert Cox. Civil Society at the Turn of the Millennium Prospects for an After Native World Order [J]. Review of International Studies, 1999 (1).

[96] Robert Gilpin. The Challenge of Global Capitalism: The World Economy in the 21st Century [M]. Shanghai: Shanghai Century Publishing (Group), 2001.

[97] Robert Gilpin. The Political Economy of International Relations [M]. Beijing: Beijing: Economic Science Press, 1989.

[98] Robert J. Barro, Xavier Sala-i-Martin. Technological Diffusion, Convergence, and Growth [J]. Journal of Economic growth, 1997, 2 (1).

[99] Robert Keohane. Neorealism and Its Critics [M]. Beijing: Peking University Press, 2002.

[100] Robin Lynton. Introducing Political Science: Themes and Concepts in studying Politics [M]. New York: Longman Publishing, 1985.

[101] Ronald Findlay, Stanislaw Wellisz. Endogenous Tariffs, the Political Economy of Trade Restrictions and Welfare[M]. Chicago: University of Chicago Press, 1982.

[102] Ruan Xiang. Research on Location Choice of Chinese Enterprises' Foreign Direct Investment [D]. Master thesis at Zhejiang University of Technology, 2004.

[103] Samir Amin. The Challenge of Globalization [M]. Review of International Political Economy, 1996, 3(2).

[104] Samuel Huntington. The Clash of Civilizations and the Remaking of World Order [M]. Beijing: Xinhua Publishing House, 1999.

[105] Shen Jiahua. On China's Industry Choice and Location Strategy in Foreign Direct Investment [D]. Master thesis of Zhejiang University, 2001.

[106] Sheng Xiaobai. A Brief Comment on the Theory of Competitive Advantage [J]. Journal of International Trade, 1998 (9).

[107] Shu Peng. Analysis of Foreign Direct Investment of Contemporary Developing Countries [J]. Journal of International Trade, 2004 (8).

[108] Song Xinning, Chen Yue. An Introduction to International Political Economics [M]. Beijing: China Renmin University Press, 1999.

[109] Stephen H. Hymer. The International Operations of National Firms: A Study of Direct Foreign Investment [M]. Cambridge: Cambridge University Press, 1976.

[110] Susan Strange. States and Markets: An Introduction to International Political Economy [M]. Beijing: Economic Science Press, 1990.

[111] Tan Peiwen. Marxist Theory of Interests [M]. Beijing: People's Publishing House, 2002.

[112] Tang Yuexuan. On the Conflicts and Common Interests in China-U.S. Business Relations [J]. Science & Technology Information, 2008 (36).

[113] Theodore Schultz. Investment in Human Capital: The Role of Education and of Research [M]. Beijing: Commercial Press, 1990.

[114] V. N. Balasubramanyam, Mohammed A. Salisu, David Sapsford. Foreign Direct Investment and Growth in EP and IS Countries [J]. Economic Journal, 1996, 106 (434).

[115] Victor D. Norman, Anthony J. Venables. International Trade, Factor Mobility and Trade Costs [J]. The Economic Journal, 1995, 105 (433).

[116] Wang Dazhou. Evolution and Governance of Enterprise Innovation Networks: A Literature Review" [J]. Science Research Management, 2001 (5).

[117] Wang Dong. Game between National Interests and Common Interests of Countries around the World amid Financial Crisis [J]. Contemporary Economics, 2009 (9).

[118] Wang Dong. Strategic Economic Dialogue and Thoughts on China-U.S. Business Relations [J]. Hongqi Wengao, 2008 (8).

[119] Wang Guanghui, Wang Yi. Current Situation, Problems and Suggestions of Technology Transfer in China [J]. Taiyuan Science & Technology, 2009 (11).

[120] Wang Lina. The Deep Cause of China-U.S. Trade Friction and Its Alleviation Measures [J]. Practice in Foreign Economic Relations and Trade, 2008 (2).

[121] Wang Minqin. Location Choice of Chinese Enterprises' Foreign Direct Investment [D]. Master thesis at Lanzhou University, 2003.

[122] Wang Wei. Reflections on the Participation of Developing Countries in International Technology Transfer [J]. Social Sciences Journal of Universities in Shanxi, 2004 (3).

[123] Wang Weiguang, Guo Baoping. On Social Interests [M]. Beijing: People's Publishing House, 1998.

[124] Wang Xiaojuan, Yang Shengming, Feng Lei. The Frontier of China's Foreign Trade Theory [M]. Beijing: Social Sciences Academic Press, 2005.

[125] Wang Xiaojuan, Yang Shengming, Feng Lei. The Frontier of China's Foreign Trade Theory [M]. Beijing: Social Sciences Academic Press, 2005.

[126] Wang Xiaolu, Fan Gang. Changing Trend and Influencing Factors of Regional Disparity in China [J]. Economic Research Journal, 2004 (1).

[127] Wang Xuehong. Theoretical Analysis on Transnationals and International Technology Transfer [J]. Journal of Ningde Normal University (Philosophy and Social Sciences), 2000 (3).

[128] Wang Yaozhong, Zhang Yabin. International Trade Theory and Practice [M]. Changsha: Central South University Press, 2003.

[129] Wang Yong. New Progress of IPE [J]. World Economics and Politics, 2003 (5).

[130] Wang Zhen. "The Application of Prime Location in Multinationals' Foreign Direct Investment" [J]. Journal of Nanchang College, 2005 (3).

[131] Wei Houkai. From Repeated Construction to Orderly Competition [M]. Beijing: People's Publishing House, 2001.

[132] Wu Xinbo. The New Pattern of China-U.S. Business Relations and Its Impact on Bilateral Relations [J]. Fudan Journal (Social Sciences Edition), 2007 (1).

[133] Xiang Weixing, Yang Hong. A Summary of Research Progress on International Capital Flow Benefits and Distribution [J]. Review of Economic Research, 2007 (46).

[134] Xiao Xinhua. Research on Location Choice of Chinese Enterprises' Foreign Direct

Investment [D]. Master thesis at Guangxi Normal University, 2005.

[135] Xie Hao. The Unequal Distribution of Benefits in Economic Globalization and Its Institutional Economics Research [J]. Asia-Pacific Economic Review, 2004 (5).

[136] Xu Mei. Theory of Entrepreneurial Interests [M]. Shanghai: Fudan University Press, 2004.

[137] Xue Yongying. An Introduction to Socialist Economic Interests [M]. Beijing: People's Publishing House, 1985.

[138] Yan Xuetong. Analysis of China's National Interests [M]. Tianjin: Tianjin People's Publishing House, 1997.

[139] Yang Xiaokai, Zhang Yongsheng. Emerging Classical Economics and Hypermarginal Analysis [M]. Beijing: Social Sciences Academic Press, 2003.

[140] Yao Xianhao, Qi Changhua. International Trade Theory [M]. Beijing: China Foreign Economic and Trade Publishing House, 1990.

[141] Yu Chuangui. Analysis on Western Human Capital Theory [J]. The Theory and Practice of Finance and Economics, 2001 (5).

[142] Yu Keping. Globalization: Global Governance [M]. Beijing: Social Sciences Academic Press, 2003.

[143] Yuan Kuisun. State Behavior and International Trade [J]. Economist, 1991 (4).

[144] Yuan Yi. Looking at the Theory of Competitive Advantage from the Course of Exploring the Causes of International Trade [J]. International Economics and Trade Research, 2002 (5).

[145] Zhang Erzhen. Research and Comparison of International Trade Policy [M]. Nanjing: Nanjing University Press, 1993.

[146] Zhang Erzhen. Review on the Evolution and Development of International Trade Division Theory [J]. Journal of Nanjing University, 2003 (1).

[147] Zhang Lu, Liu Zengtao. Analysis of China-U.S. Trade Friction and Countermeasures [J]. Economic Research Guide, 2007 (7).

[148] Zhang Weifu. Location Choice and Path Arrangement of Chinese Enterprises' Foreign Direct Investment [J]. Journal of International Trade, 2006 (7).

[149] Zhang Youwen. Common Interests Are the Foundation of China-U.S. Strategic Economic Dialogue [J]. International Economic Review, 2007 (11).

[150] Zhang Youwen. Factor Distribution and Income Distribution of Globalized Economy [J]. World Economics and Politics, 2002 (10).

[151] Zhao Baohua, Qi Jianhong. Analysis on Industrial Organization of Multinationals Entering Chinese Market [J]. Modern Economic Science, 2001 (5).

[152] Zhao Chunming, He Yan. A View of China's Foreign Direct Investment from the Perspective of International Experience [J]. Journal of Beijing Technology and Business University, 2002.

[153] Zhou Shijian. Interdependence in China-U.S. Business Relations [J]. China International Studies, 2007 (2).

图书在版编目(CIP)数据

共同利益论 = Common Interest Theory:英文/池勇海著. —上海:复旦大学出版社,2020.10
(共享经济丛书)
ISBN 978-7-309-14934-0

Ⅰ.①共… Ⅱ.①池… Ⅲ.①国际经济-研究-英文 Ⅳ.①F113

中国版本图书馆 CIP 数据核字(2020)第 185976 号

共同利益论 = Common Interest Theory:英文
池勇海　著
责任编辑/谢同君

复旦大学出版社有限公司出版发行
上海市国权路 579 号　邮编:200433
网址:fupnet@fudanpress.com　http://www.fudanpress.com
门市零售:86-21-65102580　团体订购:86-21-65104505
外埠邮购:86-21-65642846　出版部电话:86-21-65642845
上海四维数字图文有限公司

开本 787×960　1/16　印张 27.5　字数 462 千
2020 年 10 月第 1 版第 1 次印刷

ISBN 978-7-309-14934-0/F·2748
定价:69.00 元

如有印装质量问题,请向复旦大学出版社有限公司出版部调换。
版权所有　侵权必究